Management Accounting for Strategic and Operational Control

Management Accounting for Strategic and Operational Control

Jeff Coates
Colin Rickwood
Ray Stacey

BUTTERWORTH
HEINEMANN

Butterworth-Heinemann
Linacre House, Jordan Hill, Oxford OX2 8DP
A division of Reed Educational and Professional Publishing Ltd

ℛ A member of the Reed Elsevier plc group

OXFORD   BOSTON   JOHANNESBURG
MELBOURNE   NEW DELHI   SINGAPORE

First published 1996
Reprinted 1997

British Library Cataloguing in Publication Data
Coates, Jeff
    Management accounting for strategic and operational control
    1   Managerial accounting   2   Accounting
    I   Title   II   Rickwood, Colin   III   Stacey, Ray
    658.1'511

ISBN 0 7506 2452 3

Typeset by Datix International Limited, Bungay, Suffolk
Printed and bound in Great Britain

Contents

Preface

There are no regulations creating formal boundaries on the scope of management accounting. In meeting the information needs of management, it is extended in form, diversity and function according to the requirements of the organization in which it operates. Within this wide-ranging field, this text particularly emphasizes strategy, control and performance appraisal.

A basic knowledge of management accounting is assumed in the areas of cost classification and behaviour, costing methods, budgeting, standard costing and elementary capital investment appraisal.

While the book takes into account modern concepts, it nevertheless deals with them in a manner which can be readily related to current practice. Applications of management accounting are extended to manufacturing and service industries and the public sector.

In preparing the text, the authors wish to acknowledge the great help of:

Dr Sheila Ellwood, BSc(Econ), MSc, AIPFA, who contributed to Chapter 11. Sheila was formerly Deputy Treasurer to the Worcester and District Health Authority before entering teaching. She joined Aston University in 1989 as a lecturer in Finance and Accounting.

Mr John Williams, BSc(Econ), MSc, ACMA, consultant and associate lecturer at the Liverpool Business School, Liverpool John Moores University, who contributed to earlier drafts of Chapters 2 and 15.

We also wish to thank Mrs Jean Thompson for the considerable help which she gave in preparing the manuscript.

Jeff Coates
Colin Rickwood
Ray Stacey

1

Introduction

What is management accounting?

Many authors distinguish between financial accounting and management accounting in that the former relates to the stewardship function and external reporting, while the latter relates to the provision of information to the managers of the organization for purposes of planning, controlling and decision-making. Thus, for example, Horngren and Foster,[1] state that 'The accounting system . . . should provide information for three broad purposes:

1 Internal reporting to managers, for use in planning and controlling routine operations.
2 Internal reporting to managers, for use in making non-routine decisions and in formulating major plans and policies.
3 External reporting to stockholders, government, and other outside parties, for use in investor decisions, income tax collections, and a variety of other purposes.'

The third purpose, commonly referred to as 'financial accounting' is heavily prescribed by legislation (both British and European) and accepted accounting practices (SSAPs, FRSs etc.). While ostensibly providing a true and fair view aimed at the needs of one particular user group – the shareholders – it is commonly used by a wide variety of interested parties as one means of understanding and interpreting the performance and status of the organization; not least among these interested parties will be the managers of the organization itself.

However, it is to be hoped that the information available to the managers of most organizations will not be restricted to this limited financial view; that additional, purpose-specific information will be made available via the internal accounting system to enable managers to manage – to plan, control and make decisions. For such information, usually termed 'management accounting', there are no prescriptions: managers need not be constrained in any way by legislative requirements or by any generally accepted accounting principles (SSAPs) unless they want to. It is up to management to decide what assumptions, concepts, techniques, presentation etc. are appropriate for a particular purpose and/or personnel at a particular point in time.

The Chartered Institute of Management Accountants, however, has defined management accounting as:[2]

The provision of information required by management for such purposes as:

1   formulation of policies,
2   planning and controlling the activities of the enterprise,
3   decision taking on alternative courses of action?
4   disclosure to those external to the entity (shareholders and others),
5   disclosure to employees,
6   safeguarding assets.

The above requires the management accountant to participate in management to ensure efficiency and effectiveness in:

(a)   formulation of plans to meet objectives (long term planning),
(b)   formulation of short term operation plans (budgeting/profit planning),
(c)   recording of actual transactions (financial accounting and cost accounting),
(d)   corrective action to bring future actual transactions into line (financial control),
(e)   obtaining and controlling finance (treasurership),
(f)   reviewing and reporting on systems and operations (internal audit, management audit).

Figure 1.1 illustrates these aspects.

The reader will note that this definition is considerably wider than that propounded earlier. It may be seen by some as a continuation of the evolution of management accounting from CIMA's[3] earlier and more specific definition of management accounting as 'The application of professional knowledge and skill in the preparation and presentation of accounting information in such a way as to assist management in the formulation of policies and in the planning and control of the operations of the undertaking'.

In this text attention is directed towards those aspects of management accounting which provide management with information for control: to assess and report on management performance; monitor efficiency, effectiveness and value for money; and evaluate the efficiency and effectiveness of information systems. This therefore encompasses the complete control mechanism:

(i)   the setting of appropriate, relevant plans;
(ii)   the establishment and operation of information systems to provide meaningful, understandable and timely feedback;
(iii) the presentation of feedback;
(iv)   the monitoring of events;
(v)   the making of resultant decisions; and
(vi)   the review and audit of plans, controls and decisions.

This is not a process to which a single framework can be applied; simple ready-made formulae will not provide ready-made solutions. Rather it requires the application of appropriate and relevant systems, processes and techniques, adapted as necessary to the specifics of the particular, i.e. the uniqueness of the circumstances – the organization, its industry, its management, its problems and resources, its *needs*. It is the multi-variety of uses and applications of management accounting to planning and control which makes it so complex, stimulating and challenging. It can be applied to any organization, whether public or private sector, whatever its size, nature, objectives, resources or location. It is universally applicable but should be uniquely applied.

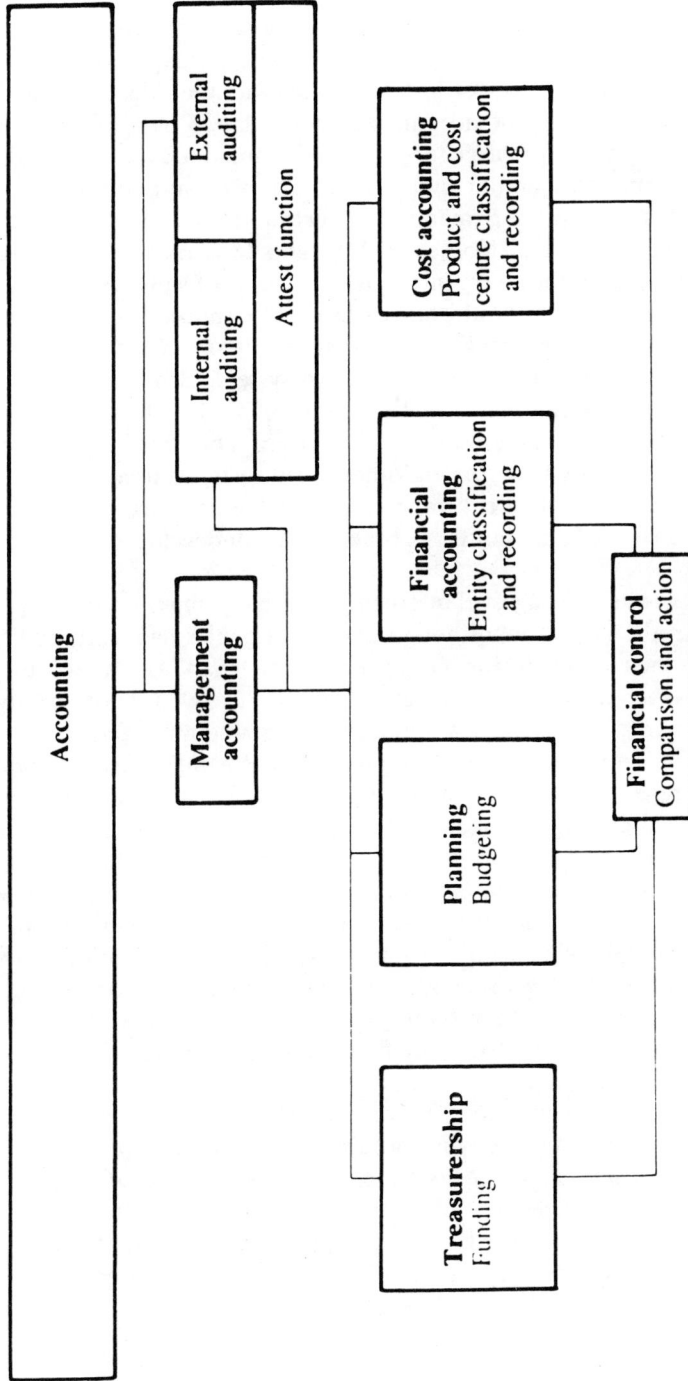

Figure 1.1 Accounting – functional relationships

Origins and development of management accounting

The analysis of management accounting, in its most basic form at least, can be traced back to at least the eighteenth century,[4] and perhaps even as far as the sixteenth century.[5] However, most historians attribute the origins of the development of modern management accounting to the latter half of the nineteenth century and the growth of large organizations and industries – textile mills, railways, coalmining and similar industries.[6,7] The size and complexity of these organizations resulted in a demand for cost and financial information for internal planning and control. These developments tended to be ad hoc reactions by the management of these organizations to the problems they perceived, as little written literature on the subject was available. Indeed much of that which was published related the practices of those businesses which had developed some form of cost or management information system. However, in the US and Europe, particularly during the last two decades of the nineteenth century, a number of writers on management accounting, and costing in particular, explained their new ideas, or, as Solomons[8] suggests, rediscovered ideas that were becoming of great practical importance for the first time but which could certainly have been found, though perhaps in an undeveloped state, in earlier works'.

It would be wrong to suggest that costing or management accounting systems were other than the exception, although many companies had some rudimentary knowledge of their costs if for no other reason than as an aid to pricing decisions. However, it was in this period and the early part of the twentieth century that the foundation of most modern costing and management accounting techniques were laid – cost analysis, marginal costing, absorption costing, machine hour rates, integrated cost accounts, cost allocation, departmental cost analyses, standard costing, management by exception, uniform costing, budgets. 'Virtually all of the practices employed by firms today and explicated in leading cost accounting textbooks had been developed by 1925. These practices were devised by engineers and industrialists, working in actual organizations, rather than by academic researchers. This probably explains the rapid adoption of these innovative practices by other organizations'.[9] Developments since then have been more that of refinements rather than of any new major innovation, with the exception perhaps of discounted cash flow, residual income, risk analysis and inflation accounting techniques.

Little is (apparently) new under the management accounting sun. The skill of the management accountant today is perhaps not in finding new solutions to new problems but in *adapting* old ideas to new situations:[10] perceiving and being prepared to accept the need for different measurement, planning and control systems; and designing adapted or new approaches, selling them to fellow managers and ensuring that they are understood and used appropriately.

Planning and control

The three levels of planning

It is helpful to distinguish between the three levels of planning and control – strategic, management and operational planning.

Strategic planning

This is the process of setting/updating/revising organizational objectives; conducting a SWOT (strengths, weaknesses, opportunities and threats) analysis; and identifying alternative strategies which are capable of achieving objectives by using resources within the anticipated environmental circumstances, evaluating these alternatives and deciding upon one set of strategies to be followed over the next few years by the organization. The emphasis is on long-term planning by the senior management of an organization (or some sub-part of it). Information used is likely to be uncertain, a best guess, but, as errors in strategic planning can be expensive, even disastrous, information should be as considered as possible. There is rarely the need for haste.

Budgetary or management planning

The responsibility of top and line managers, budgetary planning converts necessarily broad-brush strategies into more specific action plans. It puts the flesh on the bones of the framework provided by the long-term plans in order to ensure their achievement. It is more than just a read-off of the first year of the long-term plan. It should ensure that detailed plans are created, responsibilities and resources allocated, and actions are taken not only to achieve the shorter term annual objectives but also subsequent years' objectives. In contrast to strategic planning, as it has to some extent shorter horizons, information used may be more detailed and certain, and there are some time pressures. It is perhaps both less difficult and less critical than strategic planning, but vital and important all the same – after all, it is through management planning that long-term plans are implemented.

Operational planning

This is the means by which management plans are implemented. Operational planning produces nitty-gritty, short-term plans – monthly, weekly, daily or, as one practising manager put it, 'every time the phone rings'. They usually require relatively quick decisions, made by operational and line managers on the basis of relatively firm information, on matters which, if errors are made, are rarely that costly or important in the long term.

Strategic and management planning inevitably compete for the time and attention of senior managers in the same way as management and operational planning compete for the time and attention of middle and line managers. As shorter-term plans often appear the most urgent and addressable, there is always the danger that organizations will be managed by a series of such plans and the achievement of any specified long-term objectives may fail to occur. There is a need for managers to find an appropriate balance in their planning horizons: appropriate attention should be given to both longer- and shorter-term plans, so that neither dominates at the expense of the other and that short-term decisions with long-term implications receive the care and attention they deserve.

The recognition by managers of the types of planning they are responsible for and, in particular, have at present under consideration, can be of vital importance to the organization; the refusal to make a quick decision when it is needed can be as damaging as making a critical but non-urgent decision too quickly and with too little forethought. Further, operational decisions can sometimes have long-term implications, e.g. the decision by a production foreman not to stop a long run of one product to accommodate the short-term demands of a customer for another, might lead to the loss of goodwill and the customer finding alternative suppliers. Decisions with strategic or long-term implications should not be made by junior/operational managers. On the other hand, decisions of long-term strategic importance must sometimes be taken quickly, e.g. when a customer, supplier or competitor becomes available for acquisition or is the subject of a takeover bid by another organization; a bad decision here may be very damaging to the organization, but only a quick decision can be made, perhaps on relatively sketchy and superficial information.

Plans and controls

The attentive reader will have noticed that the foregoing quickly moved from a planning to a decision-making mode. After all, decisions are simply the practical implementation of the planning process. The sequence Planning – Plans – Decisions is, or ought to be, behind all decision making.

A distinction, however, should be made between plans and controls; they are in fact very different processes, though they should be directed towards the same end. Plans should be the result of considering alternative means of achieving objectives in the light of uncertainty: controls should identify when these plans are failing to achieve those objectives set or are deviating in detail in their achievement. What was a good plan at the time it was set may not be so good in the circumstances of its execution, and controls should recognize this. Some plans simply do not permit control to be exercised over them in any detailed manner; outcomes may simply be unmeasurable in cost or benefit terms or too costly to supervise specifically. Besides, while plans should desirably consider all relevant facets, whether quantifiable or unquantifiable, measurable or unmeasurable, objective or subjective, controls can usually only measure the quantifiable, measurable and objective aspects. They are different aspects of management – important, interrelated, but not always completely compatible. Indeed in some situations the existence of one vitiates the other. For example, the expectation that control will be exercised in relation to a plan may encourage the planner to reduce the level of planned expectations lest they be seen to fail, the application of control by stick or carrot can inhibit planners in the same way, the limited ability of control systems to measure only part of the outcomes of a plan can encourage planners to concentrate on only that facet to the exclusion of perhaps equally important but unmeasurable aspects, and the desire not to exceed budgets may dissuade a manager from making desirable expenditures or to manipulate expenditures from one budget heading to another.

Cost concepts for planning and control

A vital objective of controls is to promote and monitor the implementations of plans and policies. When successful, the controls should discourage the manipulation of expenditures and be consistent with encouraging managers to take decisions which are consistent with plans and with the objectives of the organization as a whole. The extent to which this may be achieved in a flexible manner and the scope for individuals within an organization to take actions using delegated authority varies between organizations. In the design of control systems, which is the subject of Chapter 2, consideration of the factors relevant to this flexibility and delegation and the resulting control systems are introduced. It is relevant to give initial consideration here to a pervasive element of the information which the accounting control mechanism utilizes – cost. Cost data has a dominant place in most of the management accounting reports used for control purposes. It is, therefore, important to recognize that there are many concepts of cost and many ways in which cost can be measured, particularly since different measures may provide different incentives. Just as it was suggested at the start of the chapter that management accounting should not be constrained by the regulations which govern financial accounting, concepts of cost used in management accounting are also not bound by such restrictions.

The critical guide in evaluating cost is relevance. Concepts of cost and measurement approaches must be chosen which are fit for the purpose for which they are intended. This may be identified most readily in relation to decisions. Since decisions only have significance if they result in a change of outcome, costs relevant to a decision are just those which will change as the result of the choice of different decision alternatives. The close relationship between planning and decision making means that this view can be readily extended to planning. In connection with control, the relevant costs are those which will change actions of decision makers in relation to plans and objectives.

In financial accounting, considerable effort and attention is given to the apportionment of absorption of cost in the determination of 'full-cost' for inventory and product costing purposes. Methods of ensuring that all production overheads are included in product costs vary from relatively simple to very elaborate schemes. These are likely to be irrelevant to management accounting in many cases. Many readers will be aware of a number of cost concepts employed in management accounting. However it may be useful to review some of the more important types of cost at this early stage.

A common situation to which the concept of cost must be directed is where the critical feature of change is that relevant to changes in volume of activity. Here measurement will need to focus on the response of cost levels to volume. This is reflected by the notion of marginal costs[11] which identifies the ratio of cost change to volume change on a cost per unit basis. Often, this is utilized in the form of incremental cost, i.e. the cost change related to a change in activity from one level to another. In the face of the difficulties of measuring marginal costs when, given a non-linear relationship between cost and volume, these vary continuously, a linear relationship between cost and volume is often assumed. The relationship of total costs (T) and the level of activity (q) are considered to be of the form:

$$T = F + Vq$$

i.e. cost is taken to comprise a constant element, F (fixed cost) and variable cost, an element that varies directly in proportion to the activity (the constant additional cost per unit being V).

An alternative consideration particularly relevant to management control, is to identify the costs which change as a result of the exercise of the discretion delegated to a particular manager. This has obvious links with ideas of responsibility accounting taken up specifically in Chapters 3, 4 and 5. Especially relevant here is the concept of managed costs which are those expended within the scope of the discretion of management and these are discussed in Chapter 8.

Cost is such a familiar word and this familiarity may create the impression that it represents a simple, well understood concept with a single interpretation. For the management accountant, this is far from the case. Great care must be exercised in ensuring that the concept of cost is appropriate for the purpose. The above points to the apportionment of fixed costs, or other costs not associated with the volume but which are being changed or managed, as a particular source of error. Apportionment may be regarded as arbitrary and the possibility of a distortion of outcomes needs to be guarded against.

The control mechanism

In a management context, control is the whole process by which management attempts to direct the efforts of the organization in a complementary manner towards the achievement of common goals. It may operate to ensure that actual outcomes match or even improve upon planned objectives or outcomes. Control cannot be exercised without (i) feedback of information concerning actual events, and (ii) a plan or desired state with which to compare it. The former requires an information system, which will be discussed more fully in the next chapter, although it will be assumed that readers already have some reasonably detailed knowledge of this subject. Similarly, planning has been discussed in the preceding paragraphs and will be expanded upon in Chapter 3.

Control typically takes the form of the process of

1 Comparing feedback with prior expectations.
2 Identifying divergences from the plan (particularly those which are 'undesirable').
3 Identifying means of bringing outcomes back to or nearer those planned.
4 Establishing which actions are to be implemented.
5 Making and communicating the decision.
6 Ensuring its implementation.

The essence of control is the willingness and ability to act. Identifying divergences from expectations and deciding on possible means of correction are simply necessary precursors for control. Similarly action by itself, without prior feedback and an evaluation of the possible effects of decisions/actions, is not control.

Control and human behaviour

The process of management control has much in common with mechanical control devices such as a thermostat, i.e. feedback (by measuring actual temperatures), comparison with the preset requirements, the decision alternatives (turn off or turn on), and action (turning on or off). In management control there is, however, an extra dimension – human behaviour. Thus the potentially irrational behaviour of the decision maker, of those implementing actions and of those affected by them must necessarily be considered as part of the managerial control mechanism. For this reason therefore the following chapters will include consideration of relevant behavioural implications.

Management accounting as a behavioural science

While the uninformed often view accounting in general as akin to mathematics or science, in some respect it is more like an art form, say Picasso style modern art. In the same way that art experts can understand Picasso's paintings because they understand the 'rules' under which they are produced, so accounting is only comprehensible by those who have an understanding of financial rules.

In fact, these analogies can be misleading. Accounting, and particularly management accounting, is in reality a behavioural science. The whole point of producing information is to influence behaviour. The underlying essence of the earlier definition of management accounting is that the role of management accountants is to collect information, retain it, or distribute it, when and to whom, prepared and presented in such style, as they feel fit.

When you read the following chapters, bear this in mind: management accounting is designed to influence behaviour. How might it do so? In which ways might managers react to this information? In which respect might those reactions be good/desired or bad/unwanted?

References

1. Horngren, C.T. and Foster, G., *Cost Accounting*, (6th ed.), Prentice-Hall International, 1987.
2. CIMA, *Management Accounting: Official Terminology*, CIMA, 1991.
3. CIMA, *Terminology of Management and Financial Accountancy*, CIMA, 1974.
4. Solomons, D., The Historical Development of Costing. In Solomons, D. (ed.), *Studies in Cost Analysis*, Sweet & Maxwell, 1952.
5. De Roover, F. Edler, Cost Accounting in the Sixteenth Century. In Solomons, D. (ed.), *Studies in Cost Analysis*, Sweet & Maxwell, 1978.
6. Johnson, H.T., Towards a New Understanding of Nineteenth Century Cost Accounting, *The Accounting Review*, July 1981: and Early Cost Accounting for Internal Management Control: Lyman Mills in the 1850s, *Business History Review*, Winter 1972.
7. Chandler, A.D., *Strategy and Structure: Chapters on the History of the Industrial Enterprise*, MIT Press, 1962.
8. Solomons, *op. cit.*
9. Kaplan, R.S., The Evolution of Management Accounting. *The Accounting Review*, July 1984.
10. Coates, J.B., Rickwood, C.P. and Stacey, R.J., Managed Costs and the Capture of Information. *Accounting and Business Research*, No. 68, Autumn 1987.
11. Rickwood, C.P. and Piper, A.G., *Marginal Costing*, CIMA, 1980.

2

Accounting control systems

Introduction

The previous chapter has drawn attention to the scope of this book, and the principal areas of planning and control have been identified. The range of the application of these functions to organizations is considerable, taking in businesses in which the structure is relatively centralized to those having highly dispersed forms. Financial planning and control is not restricted to the business sector but extends to public sector and not-for-profit organizations. Attention in this book is given to these areas and to the special situations of service activities. Most readers will be familiar with the basic techniques of management accounting, which are designed to carry out the planning and control functions. In this book there is recognition of the factors which impact on their application.

In the context of management accounting systems, information technology has had a significant impact on the development of planning and control activities. This is an example of the impact of environment on management accounting and, more particularly, changes in the environment. This chapter addresses the operation of control, introduced in the first chapter, from a systems point of view giving attention to the key environmental factors, organizational structure, behavioural considerations and change. While reference was made to human behaviour in the previous chapter, further attention is given to each of these three factors.

For many years there have been wide ranging active academic debates concerning the adequacy of the conventional teaching on organizational behaviour as a basis for understanding the choice, design and functioning of control systems. Issues in this debate have included the difficulties of replicating field studies in establishing a scientific basis for early theories, the question of the relevance of the theories to the wide range of organizations, and the development of other theories which have become more generally accepted in psychological and sociological disciplines. This debate has not produced new clear unequivocal answers to old problems. It has not suggested that the old teaching is totally wrong, though it has often discussed its limitations. It has produced new insights into the workings of organizations. It has now reached the stage of not being purely an interesting academic debate, but a framework for considering the application of management accounting to its practical context. Within the scope of this text, a detailed knowledge of the debate may not be required, but an outline knowledge of the more important theories, particularly theories of organizational culture and contingency theory, and their relevance to management accounting is pertinent. Attention is returned to these areas once the general aspects of control systems have been considered.

In relation to the last of the environmental features identified above, it must be recognized that it is not change alone which must be addressed by management controls. The impact of the uncertainty of change has very special significance and merits further attention later in the following section.

The systems view

A common and often successful approach to problem-solving is to carry out an analysis, breaking down the problem into manageable parts. Complementary to this is to consider how the parts relate to each other. It is this concern which lies behind a systems approach. Russell Ackoff[1] has defined a system as 'a set of interrelated elements', and the interrelationship between the elements is one of interdependence. The position of the elements relative to others is important, so that the system view directs attention to their arrangement and not simply their aggregation. Although this may appear complex, it can be illustrated simply in a very familiar way. For example, Stafford Beer[2] introduces a pair of scissors as an interesting illustration of a system. A pair of scissors comprises three elements – two blades and a rivet. However, its performance, although dependent on the properties of those elements, can only be properly understood in the way the elements relate to each other; unless the rivet holds the blades in such a way that they can be readily squeezed together to cut, the scissors do not function.

The systems view will have substantial interest only in those systems which persist, since only then would there be any recognizable structure to be identified. The maintenance of this stability is achieved through some form of control. Control here is not seen merely in its negative sense; too often control is regarded as being a subset of authority, whereas in the systems context the reverse is true – authority is just one means of effecting control. A system's existence is dependent upon control in a much broader sense. It is the co-ordinating mechanism which links the elements which make up the system and it is successful to the extent that it maintains the system's existence.

Management is concerned with control of this nature too. The control objective of management should not be seen within the narrow limits of preventing actions or activities and of reactive response. Far from this, the manager as an entrepreneur has responsibility to create, develop and advance. The role is proactive, and this is entirely compatible with his or her need to provide control. Business organizations can be viewed as systems and since they are human systems they are typically regarded as purposive. The nature of organizational goals is discussed later in the chapter. For present purposes, it is useful to recognize that they are typically formed to achieve objectives over long periods of time by bringing together support from a range of individual sources who are prepared to collaborate in pursuit of these objectives. Their ability to continue to maintain this collaboration in such pursuit, particularly in the face of change and uncertainty, is indicative of the effectiveness of their control systems.

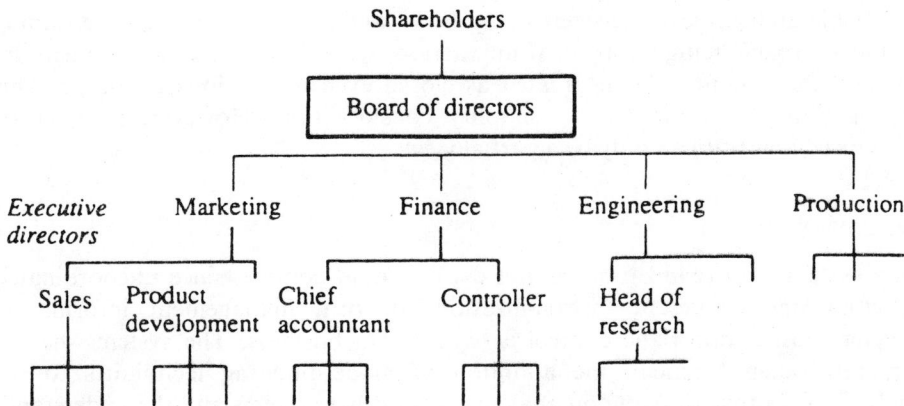

Figure 2.1   *Organization chart*

Features of systems

Some insight into the systems approach is provided by the descriptions and classifications which are used. Attention is often given in the literature to defining the existence of a system by separating it from the environment in which it exists. The systems boundary must be identified and expressed in terms of the limits which delineate it and the field in which it exists. The boundaries may be natural or constructed for convenience or other reasons. Having identified the boundaries, the internal composition can be considered. Within each system there are elements, each of which can be viewed as a *subsystem* distinguishable from, but an element of, the system. Study of the system will include examination of the part to part and part to whole interrelationships of subsystems. In turn each subsystem may be analysed so that it can be viewed in terms of sub-subsystems forming a *hierarchy* of systems. This approach to describing an organization is readily illustrated by the traditional organization chart (see Figure 2.1).

Open and closed systems

An important basis for classifying systems is provided by the distinction between closed and open systems. A *closed system* is one with no environment or one so isolated from its environment that it has no exchange with it. There is neither impact by the system on the environment nor by the environment on the system. An *open system* by contrast is one which exchanges matter, energy or information with the environment. It is interesting to note the inclusion of information as an important form of exchange, since this represents a major feature of many business systems. Observation of supply and customer markets would be just one of the informational exchanges a business is likely to depend upon.

The concept of an open system recognizes transfers across the boundaries between the environment and the system. In this way each system can be seen as just one part of the total hierarchy, the environment comprising supersystems at higher hierarchical levels. Systems may be viewed as closed or open, depending on the approach being adopted. If interactions with an external environment are ignored, the system is being treated as closed even if reactions do occur. This approach may be adopted to simplify consideration. However, it must be recognized that this can only be a partial view.

Systems of control

As a system, an organization cannot exist without control, since uncoordinated activities only represent disorganization. In turn management information systems must support the control activities of a business. The systems view is generally taken to mean the adoption of model-building techniques to the analysis of control, drawing on analogies with other systems and the understanding of the interrelationships between the component subsystems. A general model of control can be described in terms of the following major stages:

1 Identification of objectives.
2 Measurement of achievement.
3 Comparison of achievement with objectives.
4 Identification of corrective action to bring achievement into line with objectives.
5 Implementation of corrective action.

The process of control is carried out by successive repetitions of these five major stages. A thermostatic control system provides a simple illustration of the process (see Figure 2.2).

The objectives are set in terms of the desired range of room temperatures and the thermostat's response to temperature requires measurement of achieved room temperatures. The control follows through the selection of switches to turn on or off heating or air-conditioning systems which act to bring room conditions in line with the chosen settings. The thermostatic control is shown as a closed system, the feedback loop operating only within its own internal boundaries. Business control may be represented by a system in which budgets or plans are set as objectives. Management accounting may then be seen to perform its part by measuring results and presenting an exception report identifying significant variances from the budget. Management would be required to complete the process by selecting and implementing appropriate corrective policies and actions.

If control is to operate in this manner, a number of conditions must be met, related to each of the major stages. These are:

1 Objectives can be defined.
2 Output can be measured.
3 Reasons for failure to achieve objectives can be identified.
4 Predictions of the impact on achievement of possible strategies can be made.
5 A strategy which permits achievement of objective can be determined and implemented.

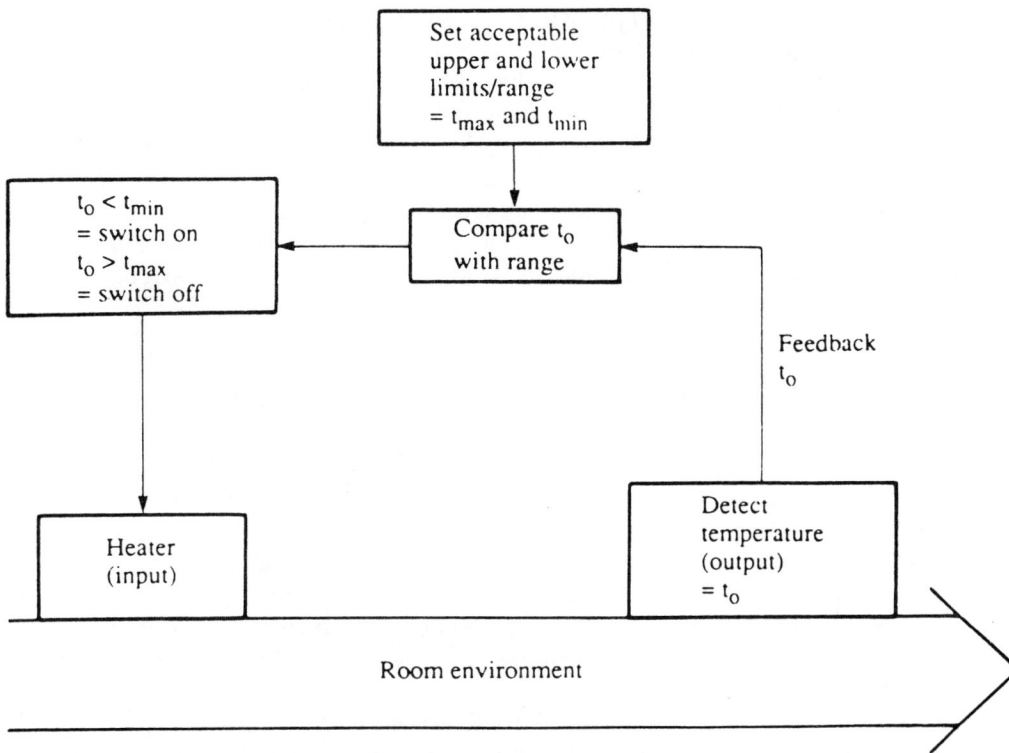

Figure 2.2 *Thermostatic control system as a general model*

A range of circumstances are necessary in order to meet these conditions. Instability in the external environment of the firm, in the form of change and uncertainty, will have a significant impact on objectives. Business budgets, appropriate at the time of planning, can become inappropriate if economic, legal or social conditions change. Internal change may not only affect desired outputs but also the outcomes of corrective strategies. Predictability is vital, not only in identifying the results of possible corrective actions but also in attempting to identify why outcomes fail to match up with plans.

In assessing the potential performance of a business control system, one can identify the important elements by considering again the analogy of the thermostatic control (Figure 2.2). That system was made up from an arrangement of the following: a setting giving the required objective in terms of the acceptable range; a temperature detector or sensor; a comparator capable of identifying if the measured state (t_0) is within the acceptable range ($t_{min} < t_0 < t_{max}$) or is out of control – in this case identifying the direction of unacceptability (too high or too low); a decision process selecting the appropriate action (switch on or off), and the capacity to perform the resulting action (the heater and switch).

In an organization, attention must be given to the same elements. Objectives are set in the form of targets or budgets. The sensors are used internally to assess results and identify needs and problems, e.g. output measurement, cost collection, reporting of stock levels, machine utilization, order levels, etc. External sensors detect market changes, new technologies, etc. Comparisons are facilitated by management reports, exception reporting concentrating on cases where differences from targets are significant and likely to indicate an out of control situation. Critical in restoring control is the ability to select and implement decisions which provide the direction consistent with the objectives.

Two other important factors give the control system form. These are the structure of the control system and the feedback which links the various active elements. CIMA[3] defines feedback as:

> A component of a control system which measures differences between planned and actual results and modifies subsequent actions to achieve the desired results.

Feedback is an element in a feedback system and forms the link between planning and control. The word feedback indicates that it operates by returning information relating to the output of a system to the control mechanism to produce corrective action on subsequent inputs. Of course the cause of the deviation can change, owing to external influences. If the control system takes too long to react or feed back, the reaction may have become inappropriate. The error will also continue, possibly leading to further costs. Control delay detracts from control effectiveness.

In a feedback loop the system reacts to deviations in the measured output from the planned level. In the case of the thermostat the direction of the response generated is opposite to that of the deviation. If the room is too cold, it reacts to provide heat; if too hot, heating ceases. The system is designed to direct output back towards the plan. This is known as negative feedback. In business a production stock system may be used to illustrate a negative feedback loop. Upper and lower control levels can be set. When stock levels are below the control level, the deviation is negative and a positive response is generated by starting or increasing production. Stock is added until the upper limit is reached, when production will be stopped or reduced. The system aims to produce stability.

By contrast a positive feedback loop is designed to maintain or increase deviations. In many cases this would not produce control but would amplify any deviation, leading to instability. It is not usually appropriate in encouraging a steady state but may be useful in promoting growth. If sales of product X exceed budget, this may be taken as a sign of a growing market. In taking advantage of the opportunity this may present, the response would be to increase production and marketing effort on this product. The result should be larger deviations but possibly more profit.

A key determinant of the structure of a control system is its interrelationship with other systems. The stock control system which increased deliveries to stock when levels fell might sound suitable for stability but could lead to violent fluctuations in business activity. If customer orders for company J are very sensitive to delivery time in an industry with a small number of competitors, increases in orders may begin to stretch production capacity. Stock will fall, generating the response to increase deliveries to stock, which can only be achieved by diverting production from delivery to customers. The delivery time lengthens, and orders decline. Stocks can then build up. Customers may begin to observe that delivery times shorten and increasingly direct their custom to company J. The cycle recommences. The larger the response to stock reductions, the more violent the fluctuations. The reaction between the company's own activity and that of its customers should be considered when designing the system.

One way in which control system design may be made more manageable is to produce structures that minimize interdependence. The process is known as decoupling. Buffer stocks usually exist as a decoupling device, permitting decisions to use a stock component to be made without having to co-ordinate it fully with the rate of successful production. However, the production unit's ability to detect or sense an increase in demand will permit the smooth running of both producer and user with limited stocks.

If the demands could be fully anticipated in advance, even smoother relationships would be possible. It is here that feedforward offers an opportunity. In a feedforward system, response to past deviations is replaced by a process of anticipation. Forecasting becomes the source of information, and the quality of forecasts will be a major determinant of the system's performance. The move to a feedforward system of control can have significant benefits for the business organization. Management is no longer confined to a reactive role. Instead proactive, entrepreneurial action is possible through which profit can be made by anticipation of change – buying just before prices rise, selling before they fall, aligning output to the level of demand, etc. Indeed, ability to act in this manner is commonly regarded as a major attribute of a successful manager. An important role of the manager is an understanding of the business and the markets the company operates in. The needs of feedforward control impose demands on the control systems but the extent to which these needs are met will have a significant impact on an organization's management of the uncertainty it faces. Although the approaches to budgetary control in use often have strong resemblance to the feedback approach of the thermostat, attention is given in this book to how management accounting can incorporate feedforward features.

Already, the systems approach has indicated that each application of control will need to be considered in the light of the specific environment in which it is to operate. Interactions with other systems, uncertainty and the impact of change in a dynamic environment will combine with the difficulties of managing a system operated by people of different behavioural types to make system design a matter of skill as well as technique.

A traditional interpretation of control might imply that all control decisions must be regarded in terms of predetermined responses to anticipated changes in order to restore progress to a plan. While this may not fully embody the goals of achieving feedforward and proactive management, control in this form has a role in organizations. Decisions of this nature are classed as programmed decisions. The programmed approach is of value in increasing managerial capacity through delegation. Managers can then leave subordinates to make decisions which carry out management policy in a predictable manner by following prescribed procedures. While it may be useful to set up systems that adopt a programmed approach, in many situations the nature of change and the appropriate response cannot be anticipated; there may be no reliable relation between response and outcome. There is no choice in these non-programmable situations but to make decisions on the basis of judgement, giving the decision maker flexibility. Most situations for which management control systems are to be provided are not clearly programmable or non-programmable. It is necessary to assess whether the losses or benefits of predictability outweigh the advantages and risks of delegated authority for on-the-spot judgement to dictate policy in a potentially unpredictable but proactive manner. Account of the cost of operating either system would also need to be taken.

Organizational theory and structure

It has been made clear that, if the environment has a material impact on a system, then system design must recognize this. It follows that if the management accountant is to make use of an understanding of systems theory in the procedures set down and operated in the management of organizations, this requires due note of the context of the organization. Management accounting systems cannot ignore the organization which forms their environment. Organizations are viewed by many authors as systems themselves. Barnard[4] described an organization as a 'system of consciously coordinated personal activities or forces'. Presthus's definition is 'a system of structural interpersonal relations'.[5] Given that both definitions emphasize people, motivation becomes a relevant consideration and this is given attention later in the chapter. Other aspects given specific attention are organizational goals and structure and administration.

The need for structure and co-ordination may be largely attributed to size. Usually organizations are considered to be of such size that relations and co-ordination cannot be readily maintained through casual contact between people but require some structure. The persistence of structure is a prerequisite for the organization's existence, even though the form of structure may change. Organizations do not need to hold rigidly to one form to retain integrity and continuity. A rock maintains its integrity in the face of a stream's current with a rigid structure, but a river weed's bending response is not terminal. By contrast, a pile of sand lacks the interconnections which would permit it to exist in the face of a hostile current.

The limitations of systems theory

Systems theory has provided a way of thinking about organizations and their structure and functioning, and has been a useful way of explaining organizations. However, it has had significant limitations. Amey[6] explains the problem:

... principles formulated for certain kinds of systems (e.g. physical, chemical, biological) are freely extended by many writers to other kinds of system (social systems, for example) without making the modifications or reinterpretations which are inevitably necessary.

Simple explanations of organizations based on mechanical systems have the same advantages of clarity and ease of understanding as simple economic or cost-volume-profit models. However, human beings are not neatly and easily fitted into such schemes.

While much of the development in organization theory could be categorized as an open systems approach, it is notable that systems thinking has only made limited contributions to the study of management control systems. This is discussed at length by Otley,[7] but is beyond the scope of this book. The development of a soft systems approach in recent years, for details of which Checkland[8] or Checkland and Scholes[9] could be studied, may lead to a greater usefulness of systems theory in developing and applying ideas in management control.

Organizational goals

A further attribute associated with organizations is purpose. Parsons[10] amplifies structure to indicate that organizations are structured so as to attain 'a particular type of goal'. Scott[11] considers the organization to have three objectives – growth, stability and interaction. The last can refer to interaction with the environment or among individuals within the organization. Scott's view may be consistent with no more than survival but, although a more positive view may be taken, this is not universally accepted. Cyert and March[12] state: 'Individuals have objectives; collectivities of individuals do not'. In a free society organizations receive voluntary support from individuals as a means of satisfying their own desires. Business organizations' central purpose is identified in economic terms, which may be seen as a collective transformation of individual economic objectives. Even charities and other not-for-profit organizations have objectives, and their achievement is at least in part dependent upon economic performance.

From an economic perspective, the success of organization is a function of its relative advantage. Alchian and Demsetz[13] make a valuable contribution to this approach, identifying the advantages of teamwork. Teams permit groups of people to achieve more than the sum of achievements the individuals in the team could produce. By way of example, one man might struggle all day to carry a heavy item (say a piano) upstairs. A team of four, taking a corner each, may need to put in much less than a quarter of the exertion of one man to complete the task. The relative advantage can be shared among team members. The teamwork advantages result from co-ordinated effort. Although such co-operation is beneficial, if individuals pull in different directions, the result is counter-productive. As team size grows, the co-ordination problems increase, and Alchian and Demsetz highlight the role of the manager in this task. A major element of their contribution to the organization is through the control of its members. He/she needs to compensate in some way for the possible impact of a 'free-rider' effect, in which an individual can shirk but benefit from the productivity of the team. In addition co-ordination and structure must be provided.

A further problem which the management function must fulfil is heightened by aspects of another feature of organizations – specialization. This refers to the grouping of activities assigned to a particular person based on capacity of workload and expertise or skill. The limited scope of activity of any one specialist makes them dependent upon another specialist. There is a demand for internal communication. Co-ordination and communication are particularly difficult for those operating automated machinery, as the continuous nature of such operations prevent such operators from leaving the machinery to communicate with others.

Management's role can be seen as generating the performance of the organization. In turn this requires management to assess the contribution to performance made by other individuals, this being an element in overcoming the free-rider effect. Performance measurement is important in managing an organization and accounting must carry this out. Although output measures, showing what is achieved, are preferable, the team effect may make it difficult to identify whose effort produced what and input measures (e.g. hours worked) may have to be used.

Theories of organization

The importance taken on by structure as organizations increase in size has already been mentioned. The management and administration of organizational structure have been the subjects of considerable attention by theorists. The insights they provide are of value to the management accountant. Theoretical approaches can be classified in a number of ways[14] largely dependent on the emphasis given to each of three views: prescriptive structure, systems analysis and behavioural approaches based on empirical observation. The analysis of theories does not produce clear distinctions, but Otley[15] has suggested that a distinction into two types can be made, one type of theory viewing organizations as a designed artefact, the other as a natural phenomenon. The former attempts to put forward views of how an organization should be designed to give best performance in achieving its goals; the latter sets out to explain observed organizational behaviour, treating managers as one of many influential elements.

The approach here will be to begin with the designed artefact view bringing in the alternative as a part of a consideration of motivational aspects. Although writers throughout history have given attention to the subject of organizational structure, an early milestone in this as a distinct subject was made by F.W. Taylor[16] in 1913. He suggested all labour's tasks should be analysed and, on the basis of work measurement, payment schemes should be constructed to reward output and provide incentive. It treats people as machines employed to complete specified tasks.

Taylor's approach led to the development of an essentially normative set of ideas about budgeting and the control process – what the well run firm ought to do and how to do it. There was remarkably little discussion of its basis in motivational and organizational theory. Equally when behavioural scientists later studied the budgeting process and the way people reacted to it there was no explicit theoretical basis.

The studies of the human relations school from Mayo[17] to Argyris[18] were generally accepted, but became to most accountants ideas about things that could be done if there were problems with budgeting. They did not disturb the basic implicit ideas about right ways to control firms prevalent in most texts, and originating in Taylor[19] and ideas of scientific management and Fayol[20] and administrative theory.

Later views suggest that while one may wish to 'hire a hand' to do a job, an employee must be considered as the whole person. However, much management accounting practice is based on the assumption that budgets and standards for human organizational performance can be set in a more or less objective and scientifically verifiable manner. To some extent this may be true for well understood tasks. The non-programmable tasks of senior management may be inappropriate for this approach.

Administrative theories of organization concentrate on three aspects: division of labour, structure and span of control. Division of labour takes up the theme of specialization and designing jobs to fit the capacity of one person. Structure considers the line and staff responsibilities linkages; the hierarchical arrangements set out in the traditional organization chart embody the 'one man – one boss' and 'responsibility must equal authority' principles. Span of control questions follow from the formal hierarchical structure. The theories suggest that the solutions in particular cases depend upon the means of communication available, the nature of the tasks and managerial styles. More recent work acknowledges the existence of an informal structure having its own processes for recognition of status, appointment of leaders and communication.

Contingency theory

Reference has been made to the significance of the specific environment in which a control system operates. This implies that different systems should be adopted in response to different environmental conditions (i.e. they are contingent upon those conditions). Identification of the links between conditions and management processes adopted is the concern of contingency theory. A very simplified outline of contingency theory could state:

- Organizations are influenced by their environment and their history; by such factors as the technology employed, the size of firm, the competitiveness of the market, the stability of the environment, and the people involved and the ownership of the firm.
- Hence organizations are unique.
- Structure and control systems in each firm will be influenced by the environment of the firm, and will be different.
- There is no one best system for all firms.

Contingency theory was developed in reaction to the administrative theories described above (Fayol[21] and Weber[22]) and initially stressed causes of differences between firms that would be matters of industrial structure. There was an emphasis on technologies and industrial processes, and later an emphasis on economies of scale and size of firms. The development from administrative theory to a systems approach to organizations in the period 1950–1970 influenced the development of contingency theory. Its main features were:

1 Defining the scope of a system, explicitly not limiting the system to the employees of the firm. Precisely what the system boundary should be has caused problems which would be familiar to those accustomed to the discussion of the definition of stakeholders in a company (i.e. is it just the shareholders? does it extend as far as employees, debtholders, suppliers etc.?). However, the emphasis was clear – an open system, with interactions with the world outside the organization, not a closed self-contained system.

2 Organizational purpose was expressed as successful adaptation to changing circumstances to be able to continue to transform inputs into outputs – possibly summarized as survival. Input–output analysis attracted accountants as a research framework as it has continued to attract economists. This statement of purpose said nothing about individual goals, or the multiple objectives and political processes involved in policy making.

3 Neither environment nor organization remained static; there was a process of adaptive response. Effectiveness was revealed by the success of this adaptation.

4 The normal form of adaptation and improvement was by specialization. This echo of Adam Smith (division of labour limited by the extent of the market) would not necessarily be the sort of conclusion reached today by a business strategist.

Generally this approach produced very limited results – but laid the foundations of contingency theory by breaking away from previous universalistic approaches (one best solution for all organizations) and by emphasizing those specific organization forms/systems best suited to particular environmental considerations. A contingency approach was adopted by many academic writers on management accounting. This came about for a variety of reasons:

• Dissatisfaction with the simple descriptions of the budgeting process in many textbooks when practice was clearly variable between firms.
• Difficulty with proliferation of behavioural studies, which individually seemed sensible, but often came to contradictory conclusions. The lack of a theoretical foundation for these studies meant that they were not testable or validly applicable beyond the particular case studies on which they were based.
• Awareness of developments in psychology and organization theory – and a willingness to adapt and import from these disciplines in the same way as

techniques had been imported into accounting from economics and management science.

- A belief that accounting should not be considered purely a technical exercise, but that it was part of a social science, the study of organizations.

The use of a contingency framework has many advantages in the study of management accounting. Advocates of the use of a contingency framework have tended to claim the following benefits:

- It provides a statement of formal links in testable form between the environment, the organization and the accounting information system.
- The conceptual approach employed in management accounting is related to the mainstream approaches in all other management and social sciences. Benefits arise from common approaches to management and organizational problems.
- Behavioural studies of budgeting and organizational behaviour may be explained by attempting to fit them into a consistent framework. This may offer some form of comparability of behavioural studies as a first step towards being able to synthesize and generalize.
- Very much more contentiously, it could be argued that a possible long-term aim for the development of contingency theory could be to be able to generalize which sort of structure may be best suited to any particular set of contingent circumstances.

Reference should be made to Emmanuel, Otley and Merchant[23] for a summary of contingency theory and a discussion of its limitations, or to Otley[24] or Otley and Wilkinson[25] for fuller critical evaluations, and the achievements from the use of the theory as a framework for research. Features that are common to most studies include:

1 Awareness of change in organizations and the environment, of an increasing rate of change. The traditional budget model is regarded very much as the 'static state' of administrative theory.

2 Awareness of environmental complexity which cannot be captured and modelled with a few simple variables. Note that organizations' adaptive responses can differ, even when the environmental factors appear to be the same.

3 Concern with overall organization structure as well as particular aspects of management such as management accounting. General awareness that the structure is itself a control device.

4 Recognition that control aspects of management accounting (budgeting, divisional performance evaluation) are quite different from short-term decision making. However this distinction becomes blurred when the use of aids to short-term decision making gets built in to a formal decision support system which managers must use.

5   Attempts to identify and study the impact of key environmental factors. The earlier studies stressed much the same factors as Burns and Stalker[26] and Woodward,[27] who were primarily organizational theorists, factors such as:

- Size,
- Technology,
- Product variety, task complexity.

Later studies tended to highlight factors such as environmental uncertainty. Internal factors, organization structure and management style were considered but not emphasized – there was a search for a direct link between external factors and the accounting information system.

Nevertheless, contingency theory is subject to a number of criticisms which include the following:

1   Most studies lack clear definitions of the key contingent variables. Hence the propositions are not easily testable and studies are rarely comparable.

2   Studies are imprecise about the nature of the expected response to environmental factors. There is much difficulty on the issue of whether direct or indirect responses, or a combination of both, should be predicted. Is it possible to delineate cause and effect? The possible responses may be: a direct response by management accounting to the environment; a response by management accounting to management information systems in general, which in turn responds to the environment; the response of management accounting to the organization structure, which in turn responds to the environment. In view of more recent developments of organizational culture approaches it is surprising that there is little if any discussion of management choice or strategy.

3   Issues of power/authority are not discussed. The organization adapts as if guided by the invisible hand. There is no discussion of the control process.

4   There is little discussion of organizational effectiveness or efficiency. However it has to be said that valid measures of either could be extremely difficult.

5   There are obvious limits to the validity of the research methodology, and the extent to which it is possible to generalize from case studies.

6   Perhaps the most effective criticism is Otley's[28] difficulty in seeing a future direction in contingency research, despite the volume of work to date. His suggestions include:

- Better choice of research areas/organizations.
- Better establishment of validity qualitative research (problem of lack of agreed research methodology).
- More interpretative research – why, not just how.
- Action research – is the purpose of research to improve real situations?
- More use of case study method, properly documented.

- Interdisciplinary approaches.
- Closer link of theory to empirical research: (i) Theory developed from empirical studies. (ii) Empirical studies designed to test theory.

Recent developments

While the contingency theory framework continues to be extensively and usefully applied by writers such as Jones[29] it would be unwise to assume that the development of thinking about organizations and accounting has in any sense reached a conclusion. Roslender[30] distinguishes four perspectives which are being actively used by current researchers:

1 Interactionism is an attempt to understand order from the interactions of social actors. It emphasizes people, the compromises they negotiate between each other, the instability and changeability of all structures. It has produced fascinating studies of complex situations, rich in detail, bringing alive the complexities of management accounting in practice, but perhaps a little bland in terms of theoretical analysis, and certainly emphasizing situational uniqueness. An example of such a study is the Berry *et al.*[31] study of the Coal Board and its control procedures.

2 Labour process theory obviously has a Marxist basis but was mainly developed by Braverman.[32] An interesting application that may be cited is that of Hopper *et al.*[33] reinterpreting the previous study of the Coal Board and looking at the management accounting as a system of controlling the work force and the unit managers, and putting this in the context of the development of capitalism and of large scale enterprises.

3 Critical theory again has Marxist origins but was developed by Marcuse and especially Habermas. It emphasizes sectional rather than individual interests, and hence in a capitalist society the interests of the capitalist class. An example of the application of these ideas to help understand accounting in its organizational context is Laughlin.[34]

4 The last set of ideas summarized by Roslender is that of Foucault.[35] Foucault could be described as a critical theorist or possibly as a radical historian. His ideas emphasize the discontinuities, contingencies and continual power struggles that influence history, and continually focus on the relationship between power and knowledge, and the progressive development from historical emphasis on the exercise of sovereign power to the move in a more complex society towards knowledge based disciplinary power. A study based on these ideas is the analysis by Ezzamel *et al.*[36] of the ideas in Johnson and Kaplan's *Relevance Lost.*[37]

An interesting facet of structure is provided by considering decentralization. In the traditional hierarchical structure tasks are delegated on the basis of one person capacity. The extent to which subordinates have autonomy to make decisions without getting specific authority is a measure of the degree of decentralization, which will depend upon the relative advantages of co-ordination offered by centralization and the advantages of local knowledge and local response achieved with decentralization.

A particular type of decentralization which has become widespread is divisionalization. In this structure the organization is divided into quasi-independent units which usually contain a full range of functions, e.g. purchasing, production, administration, sales. It is most effective when, on the basis of product range or other factor, the division is able to operate with a minimum of dependence on the rest of the organization. It aims to take full advantage of decentralization and advantages from any incentives arising from the setting up of local groups and local autonomous positions. Chapter 8 specifically considers performance measures in divisions.

Behavioural considerations and motivation

For the purposes of this text only a limited treatment can be given to what is a subject of considerable size and complexity. The basic approaches that will be given attention had all been articulated by 1960, but they are chosen for good reason. They have provided the main foundations for later work, are more specific in setting out the external factors which lead to motivation, and have clearer relationships with management accounting areas discussed in later chapters.

The first work to be addressed is that of Maslow.[38] In Maslow's triangle of needs he sets out a hierarchy of motivating desires (see Figure 2.3). At the bottom of the hierarchy come the basic needs of food, water and warmth; towards the top come esteem and self-actualization, familiarly referred to as 'doing your own thing'. Maslow's view is that lower needs must be satisfied before higher needs motivate, but that once a need is substantially met, it no longer motivates, i.e. food and drink may be the only incentive for a starving man, but once these needs are met, attention is turned to safety and security. In Figure 2.3 the inner triangle is used to represent fulfilled needs. It shows physiological needs almost fully met and safety and security largely provided. The most effective motivator, according to this theory, would be at the top of this triangle – the need to belong and be accepted by one's social group.

The motivation–hygiene theory put forward by Herzberg[39] is a development of Maslow's theory. His research indicated that the factors or absence of them which made employees dissatisfied were not the same as those producing satisfaction. He labelled the first group, which included money, working conditions and the people they worked for, hygiene factors. They would be the sources of complaints. The group leading to satisfaction was associated with achievement and its recognition, responsibility and trust, plus promotion or other moves to face new and interesting challenges.

A similar perspective is adopted by McGregor.[40] He also produced a two-part framework, distinguishing between Theory X and Theory Y firms. In Theory X

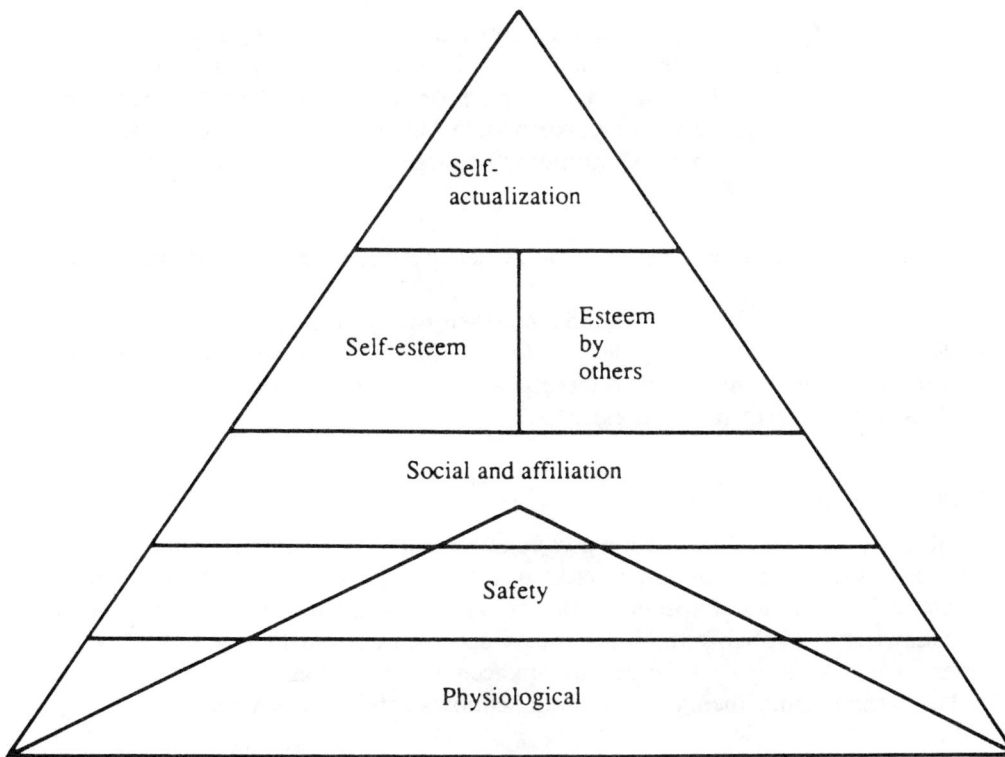

Figure 2.3   *Maslow's hierarchy of needs*

firms managers sought to motivate subordinates assumed to be basically lazy, lacking ambition and wishing to avoid responsibility by providing monetary rewards and paternalistic leadership. Theory Y firms attempted to make use of individuals' enthusiasm for self-achievement. Divisionalization may be one vehicle for this.

Mention should be made of work on the relation between behaviour and targets, particularly budgets. Stedry[41] reported the conclusions resulting from his clinical experiments at about the time McGregor published his Theory X and Theory Y view. Stedry's experimental methods have been the subject of criticism but it may be valuable to consider a summary of the results.

- Repeated failure to achieve targets lowers expectations and performance.
- Success increases expectations and motivates.
- Constant achievement of too easily attained goals adversely affects performance.
- Individuals work harder to achieve those expectations they have helped to set and to which they are personally committed.

The last of these introduces the idea of aspiration levels – the target which the individual sets and strives to achieve. Participation in budget setting is considered to bring aspiration levels closer to targets than externally imposing budgets.

Becker and Green[42] take up the theme of participation, giving some emphasis to the importance of feedback of results. They consider it imperative that a participant knows whether to feel a failure or a success. Only then can the participant know if their efforts are worthwhile. Herzberg's recognition of achievement is clearly relevant here. Conditions for targets to act as motivators can be set out as follows:

- Targets are recognized as legitimately set, by understanding the method of setting.
- Individuals must feel they can influence their own goals.
- Standards should convey the 'freedom to fail' (occasional failure does not produce severe punishment so targets can remain a challenge).
- Feedback of performance is essential.

Expectancy theory

While early theories of motivation give valuable insights and are easily understandable, they suffer from the same defect of a lack of general applicability as early organization theories. Expectancy theory, as developed by Vroom[43] and Porter and Lawler[44] is probably the most widely accepted current theory and has been often used as a framework for research in accounting settings.

Under expectancy theory an individual chooses actions or behaviour:

- On the basis of probabilities perceived, i.e. *expectancies* that the behaviour will lead to certain outcomes.
- On the benefits, personal utilities or satisfactions, in the jargon of the theory *valences*, that can be derived from the outcomes.

Certain formulations of the theory distinguish between valences associated with the action, intrinsic to the behaviour (e.g. feelings of competence, achievement) and valences that are the extrinsic consequences, such as a bonus, or promotion. Ronen and Livingstone[45] argued that this theory is consistent with the conclusions of earlier behavioural studies of the budgeting process:

- Budgets are set at attainable levels.
- Managers should participate in the budgeting process.
- Management by exception principles should be applied.
- Managers should only be held responsible for controllable items.
- Budgets should only control matters that can be measured in financial terms.

Later studies have not always reached the same consistent conclusions. Thus Brownell and McInnes[46] use expectancy theory to explore in an empirical study the relationship between participation and performance, and find a significant positive relationship. However, the expected link of a positive relationship with motivation did not appear. This could be explained by participation leading to improved decision making and performance, or (in reverse) by successful managers being allowed to participate in budgeting. Certainly there remains scope for further research.

Organizational culture

An academic would approach studies of organizational culture by looking at the deficiencies of contingency theory in that it has tended to look most closely at factors external to the firm and their effect on the firm, and insufficiently at the internal factors of the people involved and the organizational history. A manager may well be uninterested in external factors that are beyond control, but much more interested in the factors that can possibly be controlled, or at least influenced, even if only over an uncertain period. Culture is seen to be changeable, if not totally controllable.

Management interest in organizational culture

'The way we do things around here'
It is remarkably difficult to define culture – the mixture of beliefs, attitudes, assumptions, behaviour patterns that determine the way an organization works. It is quite visibly different in various firms:

- ICI – cautious, bureaucratic.
- Sony – innovative.

Management interest is that certain cultures seem to lead to different decision making and behaviour. Certain firms seem to perform better than others – and the difference is ascribed to a different culture. These ideas were originally popularized by the influential book by Peters and Waterman,[47] *In Search of Excellence*, though they can be traced back to Barnard.[48] Peters and Waterman looked at what they saw to be successful firms, and at the factors and practices they saw contributing to that success. They emphasized shared values, mission and strong inspirational leadership – heroes. This approach has since been criticized, on pragmatic grounds, by those who observe that today one would select a quite different list of excellent firms, and probably not include Peters and Waterman's choice of, for example, IBM. It has also been criticized on academic grounds by Hofstede[49] who regarded the emphasis on heroes and rituals as misplaced compared with the alternative approach of measuring values and the extent to which values are shared.

Further examples can be adduced of problems leading to management interest in organizational culture. Mergers can run into major problems when acquiring and acquired firms think in different ways, as well as having different procedures and control systems. Changing systems does not automatically and instantaneously change attitudes. Multinational firms have to cope with different attitudes and cultures operating in different countries, with managers of a variety of nationalities. Japanese firms are clearly managed differently and have a distinctive culture, and Japanese operations outside Japan seem to have been able to create remarkably good labour relations leading to high productivity and negligible absenteeism.

The real interest in culture is that it is internal to the firm and in principle can be changed by management, even if slowly. External factors, as in contingency theory, cannot be changed and are hence of less interest. Typical examples of this approach are:

- Changing the way large firms think to try to make them less cautious and more innovative, trying to make space in their systems for entrepreneurs. Very many large firms have realized that inventions tend to come from small firms because their originators left large firms which stifled initiative.
- Trying to adopt Japanese approaches to quality and productivity and stock control (JIT).
- Trying to adopt Japanese approaches to labour relations – removing job demarcation, status lines, stressing team approaches.
- Changing approaches in nationalized industries prior to privatization.

Different approaches to control (after Ouchi[50])

The sort of framework shown in Figure 2.4 has been used by a number of researchers who regard organizations as a network of transactions which should be conducted or regulated in the most efficient manner – reducing transaction costs to a minimum. Pure markets are defined such that price provides a precise measure which can reconcile widely differing objectives through the price mechanism.

Degree of goal incongruence

		Low	Medium	High
Degree of ambiguity in performance measurement	Low			Markets
	Medium		Hierarchies	
	High	Clans		

Figure 2.4

If goal incongruence and performance ambiguity are both moderately high, markets do not provide control at reasonable levels of transaction costs – hierarchies (bureaucracies) outperform markets. This is because hierarchies can replace individual labour contracts for each task with employment relations and by supervision, because there is acceptance of the system and some degree of common purpose.

When performance ambiguity is very high and goal incongruence low, clans –

'intimate associations of people engaged in economic activity but tied together through a variety of bonds' – perform best. Writing procedures (in hierarchies) or contracts (in markets) become too expensive. The self discipline of the culture controls performance and objectives.

This framework places organizational culture in relation to other forms of control but has not proved very useful for exploring culture:

- It does not explain how culture works as a control. It is highly deterministic. It assumes one best approach in given circumstances, when more than one may be used.
- Concentrating on the economic efficiency aspects of culture may miss the most important parts of the argument, e.g. the objectives of a university.
- It assumes a single organization culture.
- It does not consider changing culture.

Two quite different approaches to research into organizational culture are possible.

The first concentrates on testing the attitudes of members of an organization and comparing the attitudes with those of members of other organizations. This method is reassuring in its use of standard well-proven tests and normal statistical analysis of variance packages. It gives a good snapshot of the configuration of a culture, without saying how it works, how it evolved, and how it might change. An example of this approach is Hofstede's[51] study of the multinational operations of IBM showing the differences in national attitudes despite a very strong organization culture.

The second makes use of case studies of firms and their cultures. These studies have all the predictable advantages and disadvantages of the method:

- Dependency on personal observation with obvious risks of bias and misunderstanding – cases chosen for accessibility/interest – quite often very far from typical organizations, if such exist.
- But they can be illuminating because they can deal with history as well as with the present and can deal with the process of change.

Examples include:

- A large range of studies of budgeting in public sector organizations (more accessible to researchers) ranging from universities to local authorities showing how the negotiation of the annual budget reflects and reinforces organizational values.
- Studies of organizations under forced change, e.g. Dent's[52] study of changes in a nationalized railway, first moving to product managers with profit but not operational responsibility, later moving closer to full divisionalization – all clearly designed to change attitudes from a belief that the business is running a railway to an understanding of the need to be cost effective, and eventually to be profitable.

- Studies of the National Health Service (NHS). Clearly this is an organization which has been run by senior doctors (consultants) who obviously share many attitudes from common training and work experience. This way of running the NHS, caricatured by words about clinical freedom, is under pressure with attempts by a succession of governments to limit indefinite growth in expenditure by introducing new management structures, new budgeting procedures (e.g. clinical budgeting). It can be argued that much of the pressure by governments on the introduction of budgeting systems is at least as much an attempt to change attitudes as to budget effectively.
- Studies of changing attitudes in firms attempting to implement new approaches to production management in response to global competition. Firms found that it was not possible to implement total quality without changes in management style (e.g. quality circles) and that JIT and automated manufacture also demanded team approaches.

It is fairly easy to see why management are often extremely interested in the possibilities of changing organizational culture, quite possibly as part of a process of determining strategy. Different strategies can involve different cultures, as discussed by Simon.[53] Viable strategies are a mixture of what is possible in the market and what it is possible for the organization to do. It is easy, too, to recognize that different cultures exist, and that at times organizational culture has changed, quite often rapidly under acute pressure – competition or takeover.

However, cultures can be persistent: ICL had many problems as an independent firm, not least of which was the way that even 20 years after Hollerith and Powers Samas had merged to form ICL, executives still identified themselves with Hollerith or Powers Samas.

Summary

By bringing together teams of individuals, organizations enable people with limited capacity to achieve monumental tasks. Those familiar with strategic management will be aware of the view that the success of organizations will be dependent on their ability to respond in a co-ordinated and controlled manner to opportunities and threats. Management accounting provides specific tools for managing the implementation of the strategic plans of the organization. Structure and control systems will provide the framework for the management of organizations. Information can be seen as the vital nourishment of these systems. It is here that the management accountant can make a special contribution making particular use of strategic and budgetary planning. These topics are the particular focus of the next chapter. In performing this function he/she must recognize that what is being sought is appropriate response from the organization's members, managed with the aid of suitable control systems which recognize the relevant aspects of human behaviour.

References

1. Ackoff, R.L., Towards a system of systems concepts, *Management Science*, **17**, 662, 1971.
2. Beer, S., *Cybernetics and Management*, EUP (2nd ed.), 1971.
3. CIMA, *Management Accounting: Official Terminology*, CIMA, 1991.
4. Barnard, C.I., *The Functions of the Executive*, Harvard, 1938.
5. Presthus, R.V., Toward a Theory of Organizational Behaviour, *Administrative Science Quarterly*, June 1988.
6. Amey, L.R., *Budget Planning and Control Systems*, Pitman, 1979.
7. Otley, D.T., Concepts of Control: the contribution of cybernetics and systems theory to management control. In Lowe, T. and Machin, J.L.J. (eds), *New Perspectives in Management Control*, Macmillan, 1983.
8. Checkland, P., *Systems Thinking, Systems Practice*, Wiley, 1981.
9. Checkland, P. and Scholes, J., *Soft Systems Methodology in Action*, Wiley, 1990.
10. Parsons, T., A Sociological Approach to the Theory of Organizations, in Parsons, T., *Structure and Process in Modern Societies*, Free Press, Illinois, 1964.
11. Scott, W.G., Organization Theory: An Overview and an Appraisal, *Academy of Management Journal*, April 1961.
12. Cyert, R.M. and March, J.G., *A Behavioural Theory of the Firm*, Prentice Hall, 1963.
13. Alchian, A.A. and Demsetz, H., Production, Information Costs and Economic Organization, *American Economic Review*, 1972.
14. Scott, *op. cit.*; and Otley, D., Management Accounting and organization theory: a review of their interrelationship. In Scapens, R., Otley, D.T. and Lister, R. (eds), *Management Accounting, Organizational Theory and Capital Budgeting*, Macmillan, 1984.
15. Otley, *ibid.*
16. Taylor, F.W., *The Principles of Scientific Management*, Harper & Row, 1947. First published 1913.
17. Mayo, E., *The Human Problems of an Industrial Civilization*, Macmillan, 1933.
18. Argyris, C., *The Impact of Budgets on People*, The Controllership Foundation, New York, 1952.
19. Taylor, *op. cit.*
20. Fayol, H., *General and Industrial Management*, Pitman, 1947.
21. Fayol, *op. cit.*
22. Weber, M., *The Theory of Social and Economic Organization*, Free Press, 1947.
23. Emmanuel, C., Otley, D.T. and Merchant, K., *Accounting for Management Control*, Chapman & Hall (2nd ed.), 1990.
24. Otley, D.T., The Contingency Theory of Management Accounting, *Accounting, Organizations and Society*, 1980.
25. Otley, D.T. and Wilkinson, C., Organizational behaviour: strategy,

structure, environment and technology. In Ferris, K.R. (ed.) *Behavioural Accounting Research: A Critical Analysis*, Century VII Publishing Co., 1988.

26. Burns, T. and Stalker, G.M., *The Management of Innovation*, Tavistock, 1961.

27. Woodward, J., *Industrial Organization: Theory and Practice*, Oxford, OUP, 1965.

28. Otley, 1980, *op. cit.*

29. Jones, C.S., The attitudes of owner-managers towards accounting control systems following management buyout. In *Accounting, Organizations and Society*, 1992 and Jones, C.S., *The Control of Acquired Companies*, CIMA, 1983.

30. Roslender, R., *Sociological Perspectives on Modern Accountancy*, Routledge, 1992.

31. Berry, A.J., Capps, T., Cooper, D. *et al.*, Management control in an area of the NCB: rationales of accounting practice in enterprise, *Accounting, Organizations and Society*, 1985.

32. Braverman, H., Labour and Monopoly Capital, *Monthly Review Press*, New York, 1974.

33. Hopper, T., Cooper, D., Lowe, T. *et al.*, Management control and worker resistance in the National Coal Board: financial controls in the labour process. In Knights, D. and Willmott, H.C. (eds), *Managing the Labour Process*, Gower, 1986.

34. Laughlin, R.C., Accounting systems in organizational contexts: a case for critical theory, *Accounting, Organizations and Society*, 1987.

35. Foucault, M., *Discipline and Punish*, Allen Lane, 1977.

36. Ezzamel, M., Hoskin, K. and Macve, R., Managing it all by numbers: a review of Johnson and Kaplan's 'Relevance Lost', *Accounting and Business Research*, 1990.

37. Johnson, H.T. and Kaplan, R.S., *Relevance Lost: The Rise and Fall of Management Accounting*, Harvard, 1987.

38. Maslow, A.H., *Motivation and Personality*, Harper & Row, 1954.

39. Herzberg, F., Mausner, B. and Synderman, B.B., *The Motivation to Work*, Wiley, 1959.

40. McGregor, D., *The Human Side of Enterprise*, McGraw-Hill, 1960.

41. Stedry, A.C., *Budget Control and Cost Behaviour*, Prentice Hall, 1960.

42. Becker, S.W. and Green, D. Jr., Budgeting and Employee Behaviour, *The Journal of Business*, 1962.

43. Vroom, V.R., *Work and Motivation*, Wiley, 1964.

44. Porter, L. and Lawler, E.E., *Managerial Attitudes and Performance*, Irwin-Dorsey, 1967.

45. Ronen, J. and Livingstone, J.L., An expectancy theory approach to the motivational impacts of budgets, *Accounting Review*, 1975.

46. Brownell, P. and McInnes, M., Budgetary participation, motivation, and managerial performance, *Accounting Review*, 1986.

47. Peters, T.J., and Waterman, R.H., *In Search of Excellence: Lessons from America's Best Run Companies*, Harper & Row, 1982.

48. Barnard, *op. cit.*
49. Hofstede, G., Neuijen, B., Ohayv, D.D. *et al.*, Measuring organizational cultures: a qualitative and quantitative study across twenty cases, *Administrative Science Quarterly*, 1990.
50. Ouchi, W.G., Markets, bureaucracies and clans, *Administrative Science Quarterly*, 1980.
51. Hofstede, G., *Culture's Consequences*, Sage, 1980.
52. Dent, J.F., Accounting and organizational cultures: a field study of the emergence of a new organizational reality, *Accounting, Organization and Society*, 1991.
53. Simon, R., The role of management control systems in creating competitive advantage: new perspectives, *Accounting, Organizations and Society*, 1990.

Further reading

Hopwood, A.G., *Accounting and Human Behaviour*, Prentice Hall, 1974.
Lowe, T. and Machin, J.L.J. (eds) *New Perspectives in Management Control*, Macmillan, 1983.
Roslender, R., *Sociological Perspectives on Modern Accountancy*, Routledge, 1992.
Emmanuel, C., Otley, D. and Merchant, K., *Accounting for Management Control*, Chapman & Hall (2nd ed.), 1990.
Ezzamel, M. and Hart, H., *Advanced Management Accounting: An Organizational Emphasis*, Cassell, 1987.

Questions

1   Examine the view that the cybernetic control model can provide valuable insights into the design and operation of management accounting information systems, but only under circumstances where an organization's environment is stable and predictable and outcomes are clearly measurable.

2   'It seems likely that what constitutes an appropriate budget system is influenced by the characteristics of individual managers, by the type of organization in which it is implemented and by the environment in which the organization operates'. Explain and discuss.

3   (a)   Examine the theories relating to the influence of participation on performance.
    (b)   Evaluate the empirical evidence concerning the relationship between participation and performance.

4   According to Hopwood (1974), 'the control of complex and uncertain enterprises can never be achieved by the use of administrative controls alone. . . . Ultimately they must work as individual and social controls'.

(a) Examine the nature of these three types of control and their relevance in the design of control systems.

(b) Discuss some of the possible implications of the above quotation for the design of management accounting systems.

5   'Participative methods are best used selectively in situations where there is evidence that they will be effective, rather than as a universal philosophy. It is incorrect to assume that participative styles of management are always more effective than other styles' (Otley, 1977). Examine the justification for this statement and describe the circumstances which may influence whether participation affects performance.

6   'The level of costs for which a person will strive (aspired costs) will be conceived by the individual in relation to past experience, confidence in his potential skills, expectation of future difficulties and his feelings about the budget costs. Aspired and budget costs do not necessarily coincide' (Irvine, 1970). Discuss the relevance of this statement for budgeting activities, introducing any empirical work supporting the views expressed.

7   'To manage is to forecast and plan, to organize, to command, to co-ordinate and to control' (Henri Fayol, *General and Industrial Management*). Discuss the above view.

3

Strategic and budgetary planning

Strategic planning

Strategic planning is the process through which an organization derives the strategies it intends to follow to achieve its objectives. As such, planning tends to be longer rather than shorter term orientated, although, as will be discussed, shorter term actions are typically necessary in order to implement the strategic plans agreed for the company. Similarly, shorter term objectives are likely to be important in their own right as a stepping stone to the achievement of longer term objectives.

Planning term and frequency

Strategic, long term planning, in the UK and USA, is typically for three or five years, though some organizations plan for longer periods. Evidence suggests that German companies tend to plan for a longer period of five to ten years,[1] with a few organizations having a 40-year planning horizon. These periods may, however, reflect industry factors, i.e. industries requiring large capital investments, say in plant with long operational lives, products having longer term life cycles and longer term customer contracts are more likely to plan for longer time horizons than those industries with, say, shorter product life cycles and low capital investment. The authors perceive a trend towards longer strategic planning horizons, in spite of, or because of perhaps, the increasing complexities of markets, domestic and worldwide.

What appears to be common to most larger organizations at least, is that while longer term strategic planning may be institutionalized into an annual cycle, typically preceding budgetary planning, it is recognized that strategic planning is a matter of which senior management need to be constantly aware and willing to respond. Coates *et al.*[1] found, for example, that German companies in particular, would use the monthly financial statement revenues as the springboard to discuss potential long term/strategic implications. Senior management, through scanning of the environment, (see later), feel it desirable at any time, to consider changes to an existing plan, if it appears that this is no longer appropriate to the environment.

While strategic planning can therefore be said to be a continuous process, it is to be expected that the essence of corporate strategies will not need to change significantly, even year to year, even though alternatives may be regularly identified and evaluated: frequent changes of strategies would tend to imply either poor planning or an environment too complex to relate to. However volatile the environment, the latter may well be used as an excuse to disguise the reality of the former. In principle, it should be at least as desirable to go through the strategic planning process in a volatile, hostile environment as in one in a relatively steady state. To suggest that the environment is too unpredictable to develop valuable plans and scenarios effectively suggests that there is absolutely nothing that can be done to steer the corporate ship through stormy waters.

The strategic planning process

The strategic planning process is outlined in Figure 3.1. It is essentially a creative, reiterative, attempt to bring together as much knowledge as possible about the organization's resource and ability base, in relation to the environment in which it will be operating, in order to determine the most appropriate strategies the company can adopt to give it the best chance of meeting its mission and objectives over the duration of the plan.

Mission statements

Mission statements are essentially a statement of purpose which will both motivate staff, and give them and other stakeholders the essence of the philosophy, ethos and purpose of the company. Steiner[2] described mission statements as 'not designed to express concrete ends, but rather to provide motivation, general direction on image, a tone and a philosophy to guide the enterprise'.

Mission statements are very popular in the USA and are becoming increasingly popular in the UK, but infrequently used by the Japanese and continental European organizations. One German manager described them disparagingly as being 'merely motherhood statements, that may give you a warm glow but little else'.[1] Readers can decide for themselves their perceptions of the value and desirabilities of mission statements. Their attractiveness may well be a personal and cultural matter; like incentives, they work or not depending on the circumstances, culture and individual reactions.

Objectives

Objectives should be firm statements, quantifying a level of performance in a particular area and the timescale for its achievement. As far as possible, woolly statements should be avoided. One corporation has as its objectives 'To generate sufficient profit to finance continued improvement and growth of the business whilst providing our shareholders with a excellent return on their investment'. Another states it as being 'The maximization of shareholder wealth'. As objectives these are of little value. How will either organization know when it has reached its objective? There is no quantification of achievement level nor time scale stated. Better would be, for example, 'To achieve a real return on net assets employed of 20 per cent per annum by 19XX increasing thereafter at 5 per cent

Mission

Objectives   Social and ethical constraints

External analysis

Economics
Markets
Competitors
Technology
Political and legal changes
Social changes

Opportunities
and threats

Internal analysis

Management
People
Know-how
Market position
Reputation
Brands
Technology
Finance
Tangible assets

Strengths and
weaknesses

Alternative strategic
directions

Evaluate and select

Implement

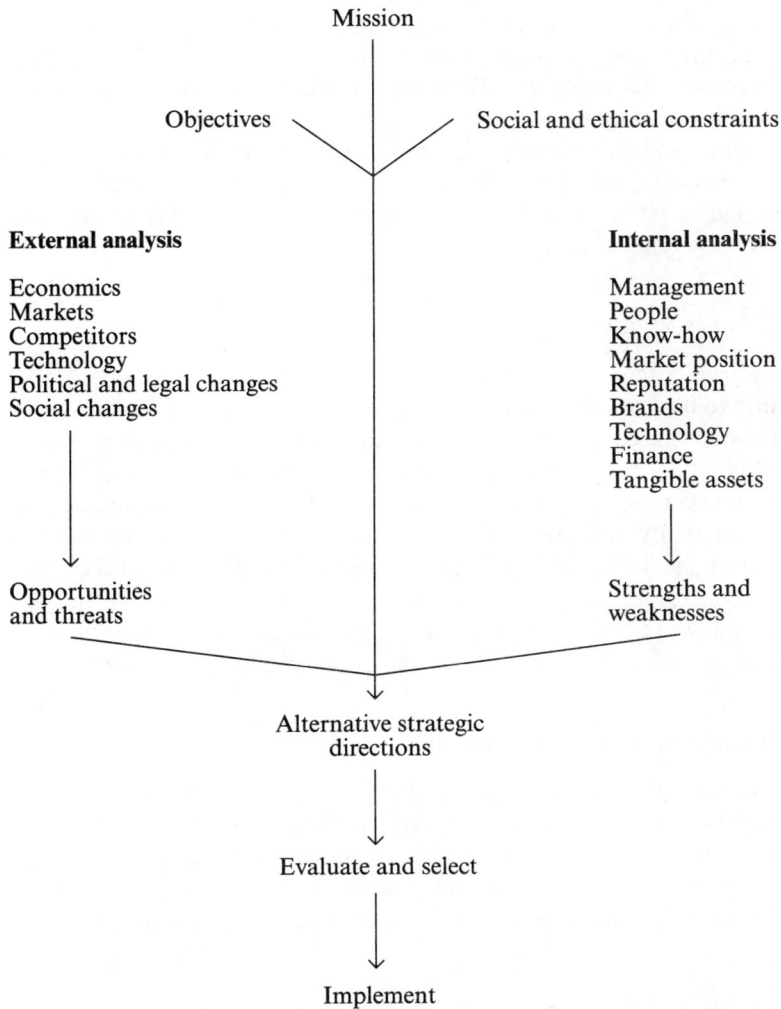

Figure 3.1   *The strategic planning process*

in real terms' or, perhaps, 'To increase EPS by 10 per cent per annum in real terms in each of the next eight years'.

In practice, it is often difficult to frame objectives precisely and unambiguously; imprecise statements are of little value, however.

Of course, objectives are not always going to be profit orientated. Even profit seeking organizations will have objectives in other areas; marketing, production, quality, people, ethics, etc. and these too should be quantified as far as possible with a time scale attached.

Non profit seeking organizations are likely to have objectives framed in terms of service provided, but not profitability. Even so, these service objectives should be quantified as far as possible as otherwise they become little more than general statements of intent or interest.

The internal resource analysis

This appraisal attempts to identify over the term of the planning period, the availability to it of resources and capabilities. In particular, it attempts to elucidate the areas where the company has *strengths and weaknesses* in respect of the quantity and quality of its resources and capabilities in relation to its competitors and potential market needs. This analysis is, in fact, far from simple – does an organization really recognize well its own strengths, let alone its weaknesses. Further, over the life of the plan, the levels and qualities of resources are likely to change; some resources may be effectively exchanged for others; in a business context, money can buy almost everything, given a time span. At extremes, parts of an organization may be sold to provide the resources to expand and develop another.

The external/environmental analysis

This appraisal attempts to identify the future economic and product market environments of each of the countries in which the organization will be working; customers, competitors, technical, social, political and legal trends and changes. In doing so, it is looking for *opportunities* in the environment it can exploit to achieve its objectives and *threats* to survival and objective achievement.

The SWOT analysis

The strengths, weaknesses, opportunities, threats analysis needs to be interrelated as these are areas of relative judgement, i.e. relative to the market and/or the competition. Equally, an opportunity may also be or become a threat and vice versa. Strength, relative to competitors may well turn a market threat into an opportunity to gain market share or drive out a competitor, for example.

Strategy development

Strategy is not simply a matter of doing things better than last year or even better than the competition. It is a matter of exploring the environment for opportunities that the organization has the resources and capabilities to be successful in, while organizing to meet possible environment, market or competitive threats. Through good analysis and interpretation of the SWOT analysis can enable innovative managers to identify which *alternative* strategies could be adapted in respect of opportunities, threats, surpluses or shortages of resources or capabilities to achieve objectives.

There are many potential strategies, for example:

1 Do nothing, i.e. the same as at present, but perhaps better. This is rarely practicable for long.

2 Seek growth, e.g. by exploring possibilities as in the Product/Market matrix, to stimulate thought about growth strategies:

		Markets	
		Existing	New
Products	Existing	Market penetration	Market development
	New	Product development	Diversification

It is often argued that there is synergy, or at least economy, in market penetration or development and product development. Diversification, however, is a higher risk strategy than the others in that management will be going into areas with little prior experience. It may gain management synergy if the previous management was poor, and such could spread the business portfolio risk.

3 Consolidate, i.e. reduce size, specializing in core business areas and selling off those parts of the business that the organization does not see as being profitable in the longer term, within their expertise or capabilities or as distractions from core activities.

4 Close down, divert or liquidate – a necessary strategy for ailing activities in hostile environments. It needs courage, perhaps, but the failure to adapt in appropriate circumstances is likely to lead to serious outcomes and perhaps corporate failure.

Once identified, each strategy needs to be *evaluated* in terms of (1) the extent to which each achieves objectives, consumes resources and (2) the risk that the strategy will succeed or fail in respect of corporate survival and objectives. Management has to balance the risk/return of alternative strategies and decide on those it thinks best in terms of that balance.

Implementation

Once evaluated, the decision as to which strategies are to be followed needs to be communicated to those who will implement them. Typically, plans resulting in actions for implementation will be through capital investment decisions and budgetary planning.

Budgetary planning

Budgets are the shorter term plans of the organization, normally the first year or two of the strategic long-term plan, which have been detailed, quantified and formalized. Effectively, they are management's strategic plan for the coming period, allocating appropriate resources to each part of the business, but expressed in more detail. They are the action plans expressed in terms of numbers and monetary values, brought together in a balanced, co-ordinated manner to guide managers as to their responsibilities, expected resource consumption, and the output and expectations of them. Budgetary planning is a system which uses budgets as a means of planning, and then controlling, all aspects of a company's operations.

The benefits of budgets are briefly that:

1   Management is forced to think ahead, to plan and to formalize these intentions.
2   Standards are set against which performance can be measured.
3   Strengths and weaknesses may be better recognized at the planning or measurement stage and improvements made or remedies found.
4   Business functions may be co-ordinated towards the achievement of agreed plans and targets and such plans and performances are communicated to those functions and the individuals within them.
5   Delegation is encouraged.
6   Managers may be motivated by well conducted budget preparation processes.

Care however has to be taken as:

1   unviable, unrealistic budgets may be de-motivating
2   individual or departmental responsibilities may overlap
3   inflexible controls may act against the company's best interests
4   the costs of administration may be heavy
5   budgetary planning does not replace good management, it only assists it.

Preparation of budgets

Budgeting involves the co-ordination of all aspect of the company's resources and activities into one overall plan. In brief, the preparation of budgets involves the stages as in Figure 3.2.

Although the budgeting process may seem straightforward, in practice significant problems are encountered. The most fundamental of these are shown above as 'limiting factors' – the forecasting of sales and of scarce resource limitations. The significance here is that mis-forecasts of these limitations and

→	Basic assumptions:	The budgetary planning process

The budgetary planning process
Establishment of corporate goals and objectives for
the coming period (a year? two?)

- estimation of industry and national economic forcasts
- strategic SWOT analysis
- corporate straegies

→ Limiting factors: Identifying scarce resources

- facilities
- material
- equipment

Sales forecasts

→ Detailed budgets: Sales forecasts
Production forcasts
Other expense forecasts
Capital and liquidity forecasts

Master budgets   Compilation of summary budgets
(P&L/BS/cash flow statements)
Board consideration
Board acceptance

Disaggregation: Breakdown of master budget to
responsibility area, cost centres, etc.

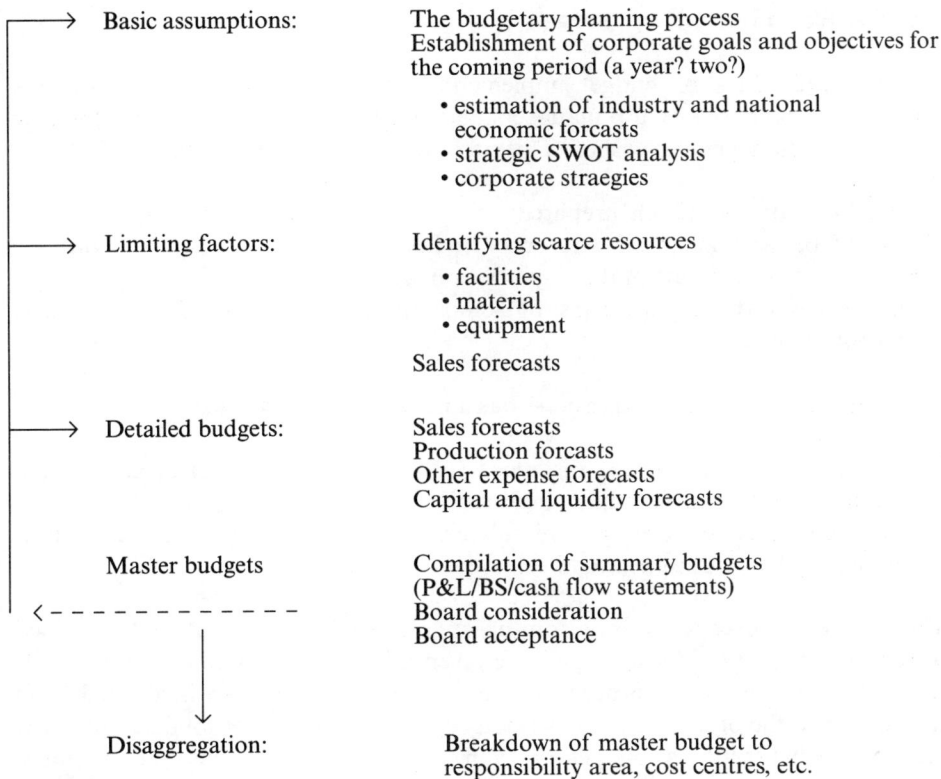

Figure 3.2   *The budgetary planning process*

sales potentials can severely harm the company and render the budgets almost valueless.

The detailed budgetary process ideally stems from strategic planning awareness, leading to the *matching* of limiting factors and especially the balance of what products or services can be sold, and when, in relation to the organization's ability to provide them. It is essentially a resource allocation process to ensure that scarce resources are provided in appropriate priorities to allow market demand to be met as far as possible while achieving profitability and other objectives.

The final plan may not be adequate; budgetary planning is therefore an iterative process, i.e. if at first you don't succeed, try again. In doing so, it must be remembered that time is of the essence – a plan is needed *before* the budget period starts, if actions are to be taken – and reiterative planning can be costly. Further, it may have to be recognized that shorter or longer term objectives may prove to be unachieveable once the more superficial overview of the longer term plan has been looked at in more detail through the budgeting process.

Top-down and bottom-up budgets

In the earlier days of budget implementation within organizations, budgets tended to be prepared by top managers and delegated down the organizations as far as senior management wished. This process has the advantage that budgets:

- may be relatively quickly prepared:
- should be well balanced and co-ordinated in respect of the contributions needed from each part of the organization; and
- are, *per se*, the expectations of senior management in order to achieve corporate objectives.

However, such a formulation process has a number of drawbacks:

- top managers may be too distanced from the realities of each part of the organization to produce viable budgets;
- managers delegated a budget are unlikely to be motivated by it, to accept it as something they can and should achieve.

Thus, in recent decades, the bottom-up style of budget preparation has gained increasing popularity. All managers are given the opportunity to contribute their thoughts to the planning process, i.e. information and opinion is gleaned from the bottom of the organizational hierarchy and collated and consolidated together into the organization's budgetary plan. Such a process has the potential advantages that:

- the plan should be more realistic, reflecting detailed, lower level, local knowledge;
- managers will be motivated by being consulted and will 'buy into' their budgets, i.e. will be committed to achieving them.

However, the reality is typically that:

- such plans tend to be uncoordinated, i.e. the various elements are not well balanced;
- the net effect may well not achieve corporate objectives;
- the process is time and resource consuming;
- managers are likely to add 'slack', i.e. a cushion, into their budget proposals, so that should they fail to achieve what they believe they could, they will not appear to do so. Most of us do not like to be seen to fail, especially when this might lower our esteem, chances of promotion or salary increases.

Budget co-ordination

Most organizations today operate a bottom-up approach, initiated by top-down direction in respect of corporate objectives and SWOT analysis/environmental information. The disadvantages of the bottom-up process are typically ameliorated by a budget officer or budget committee whose role is to collect data, co-ordinate/balance budget holders' assumptions and aspirations and negotiate aspiration and resource consumption levels with as little slack as possible.

Budget officers are frequently accountants, partly at least because they are keepers of financial information, partly because they need to use budget data for the production of budgetary control information (see Chapter 5) and partly (perhaps) because other functional managers show insufficient interest in doing so. In fact, budget officers have significant power and influence through their role; their task ideally requires a balance of skills: entrepreneurial, strategic and technical thinking, data manipulation, behavioural and motivational understanding, negotiation communication, diplomatic. Have accountants the skills needed to conduct such a role? As indicated in Chapter 1, management accounting is a behavioural science. Budgetary planning is perhaps the single most important application of that behavioural science from a management accounting perspective.

Excerpt from the Goon Show:

Moriarty: Neddy, I'm putting you in charge of the bank. Here are the keys.
Neddy: I'm rich, I'm rich, I'm rich.
Moriarty: I wonder if he's the right man for the job?

The role of the budget co-ordinator will be discussed later in this chapter.

Budget centre selection

The term 'budget centre' is defined by the CIMA[3] as 'a section of an organization for which separate budgets can be prepared and control exercised'. In selecting budget centres the following factors need to be considered:

- What are management's objectives in treating a particular part of the organization as a budget centre? These may be to measure the performance of a part of the organization or the management of it, or to motivate its management.
- Are the information systems able to distinguish the separable, controllable and attributable performance of this centre and what would be the (perhaps additional) costs of doing so?
- Is management prepared to recognize such a section as a responsibility centre, nominate an individual to be directly responsible for its performance and delegate the necessary authority for its management?
- What bases will be used to measure the performance of the centre, e.g. as a cost, profit, investment or performance centre.

In most organizations the selection of budget centres is likely to reflect the formal or informal organizational structure. How far down the structure the budget centres are carried is likely to depend upon a variety of factors – the number of management levels, complexity of the organization structure, the degree of participation in budget setting, and the factors considered above. Hofstede[4] advises top and middle management: 'If possible, see to it that budgets and standards are set separately for the responsibility area of each of your foremen, but at least for each line manager'.

The advantages of creating budget and responsibility centres as far down the organization structure as possible are likely to be the following:

1   It encourages and motivates more staff and improves goal congruence.
2   Responsibility and authority areas/levels and the organizational structure itself are reinforced by the delegation of authority and the negotiation of budget responsibilities.
3   More realistic budgets can result because of the detailed knowledge of lower levels of management.

The disadvantages, however, may be that:

1   There would be an increase in the opportunities for building in slack, the fear of budgets and their implied threats, and the possible demotivational effects of any eventual budget imposition.
2   The greater the number of budget and responsibility centres, the longer the budget preparation and disaggregation process, and the higher the costs of budgeting and subsequent monitoring feedback and control are likely to be.

There must obviously be a trade-off between the desirability of consulting managers at all levels, the advantages this might bring and the negative motivational, practicality and cost aspects.

The bases for the measurement of budget centres may be any of the following:

• Cost centres, where the budgeted (and actual) costs are identified, compared with a suitable measure of output and unit cost rates derived.
• Profit centres, where the attributable revenues and costs of budget centres are identified and the resultant profit calculated.
• Investment centres, where the profit achieved is compared to the capital invested.
• Performance centres, where the budget is expressed in quantified but not necessarily monetary terms, e.g. standard hours, units of output, scrap and yield percentages, etc.

A budget centre may incorporate any or all of these approaches, i.e. budgeted cost, profit, investment or performance centres. Indeed each base may be viewed as measuring a different aspect of a responsibility centre's performance or for different purposes. It would be desirable however, to establish which measures are to predominate, as circumstances may well arise where a particular action would improve one measure at the expense of another.

Profit centres appear to be very much more popular with senior management than cost or expense centre approaches, even when the latter are accepted by many managers within the same organization as being more logical.[5] Simon *et al.*[6] and Hofstede[7] concluded that both profit and cost/expense centres work and that there is usually no reason to go over to the often more complicated investment centre system. These topics will be discussed further in Chapters 7 to 11.

Participation and negotiation in budget preparation

In recent years the weight of research and practice has been towards a more participative approach to budgeting. The reality is of course that, even in the most participative of planning processes, senior management must have a very significant input and impact upon proceedings. It is the senior managers' prerogative and duty to establish the corporate objectives and long-term strategies, and authorize the final plan and master budget, even if they play no part in its detailed preparation. Most organizations, however, are likely to adopt a mixed approach, where budgets are negotiated between managers at different levels in the hierarchy, thereby allowing management at all levels to participate in the budget process, and have their particular role in the budget plan.

Why participation?

Chapter 2 introduced research ideas of Stedry,[8] McClelland,[9] Maslow,[10] Herzberg,[11] Becker and Green,[12] Schiff and Lewin[13] and Argyris,[14] amongst others, related to the behaviour of individuals. Their work suggests that allowing individual managers to participate in the creation of that part of the budget which relates to their personal responsibilities is likely to bring significant advantages:

- Their self-esteem and the esteem of their peer group and subordinates are likely to be enhanced.
- They are more likely to internalize corporate objectives and the achievement of them as their own and feel committed towards achieving them.

It is argued that the resultant added motivation and positive attitudes towards the company and its senior management will more than offset the potential disadvantages of:

- The inclusion of slack in the budget by managers to reduce the chances of their failing to meet it.
- The cost of the management time in a process allowing participation and negotiation.

Argyris[14] and others have indicated that if the participation is not genuine (pseudo-participation), individuals will not accept budgets (even if they say they will), with negative motivational results. In such a situation the practice of requiring responsibility centre managers to sign to indicate that they accept their budget is unlikely to have any favourable results from a corporate viewpoint.

The evidence indicates that for participation to have positive results it must be real, in that participators can and do affect the ultimately agreed plans and budgets. The implications for management are reaching farther than might appear at first reading. If participation and budget negotiation are to be adopted, management would need to begin the planning process early enough to allow the negotiation to be completed before the start of the period to which the budget relates. The authors are aware of a number of large organizations where, because the negotiation process is not complete before the next financial year is due to commence, budgets are imposed upon the individual managers of the company. This surely is the worst of all worlds. Not only is it pure pseudo-participation, but, worse, individuals are likely to feel more demotivated than if they had not taken part in the process at all.

Personal aspiration levels

Although the research of Stedry[8] is considered to be flawed methodologically, it is taken to indicate quite strongly that (i) managers who set their own targets are likely to achieve higher performances than those who do not, and (ii) budgets with low aspiration levels are likely to yield poorer results than those with medium to high aspiration levels. It would seem therefore that senior management would be well advised to push negotiated budget aspiration levels as high as is reasonable, as long as (a) pseudo-participation is avoided and (b) it is recognized that too tight budgets are likely to be counter-productive. On the basis of this evidence there appears to be no point in setting loose budgets containing substantial elements of slack.

The aspiration levels of individuals, however, are likely to be very different in any given situation. Some individuals may be optimistic by nature, pleased at having and being seen to have high budget aspiration levels, and will not be too crestfallen if they fail (providing the margin of failure is not too large). Others may be more sensitive and pessimistic, being demotivated by any budget they consider at all difficult to attain and fearing to be seen to fail. Ideally these personal characteristics should be catered for in the budget negotiation process, the agreed aspiration/budget levels being tailor-made to the managers concerned. Management might facilitate this by easing the negotiation pressure exerted or by 'averaging' the optimistic and pessimistic budgets of different managers in relation to total expected outcomes.

Of course management must always remember that it may not be possible to optimize planning on the one hand and performance on the other.

Budget aspiration levels

It is pertinent to ask the following question. Is a budget intended to be (a) what is expected will happen, or (b) a target that is achievable but set at higher aspiration levels than (a)?

Ask a group of managers within an organization and the responses are likely to be quite diverse. Some will argue that a budget is a target, a motivational technique to encourage managers to improve their performances year on year. Others will argue that a budget is management's attempt to anticipate the actual events, resource needs and results of the coming year. Perhaps, too, some will argue that it is somewhere in between – a bit of both.

The potential adverse consequences for an organization where such a dichotomy of views is held are potentially very damaging. Consider this scenario.

The sales director believes a budget is a motivational target. He believes in pushing his sales team and himself harder each year, to improve sales penetration and market share. He therefore targets his budget at a volume 10 per cent above what he might reasonably expect his sales team to achieve and asks for marketing expenditure to support it. The production director, something of a realist, believes that a budget is what he is meant to achieve. He has been asked to obtain the output budgeted by the sales director, so his budget includes capital expenditure for machinery to manufacture the sales increase, expenditures to recruit and train operatives, etc. The net effect of this is that expenditure is generally budgeted at a level 10 per cent higher than it need be, much of which might well be committed in anticipation of increased sales. Of course it would be nice to think that in practice these mismatches do not occur, that a budget co-ordinator would remove these anomalies, but the potential for mismatch is rife. Accountants and managers should ask themselves: 'Is the budget aspiration level in the organization made clear to all participants and is my view the same as that of my colleagues?' Add the problems of managing personal aspiration levels and a significant problem for the budget co-ordinator exists.

Planning and control budgets

Budgets are usually assumed by writers and organizations to be for planning purposes, i.e. to enable management to anticipate and prepare for the period ahead, to make resources available, co-ordinate activities, take opportunities, and avoid pitfalls. For this purpose an expected actual aspiration level would be required.

Usually, however, these same budgets are used as the basis for control, for which purpose a budget comprising some element of target might have more positive motivational benefits for the organization.

The duality of purposes for which budgets are used needs to be addressed by organizations. These conflicts might be resolved by:

1 Basing budgets on an expected actual basis for planning purposes, but using alternative means for control, e.g. MBO to provide the target/motivation element.
2 Budgeting on a target basis for purposes of control, but introducing budgeted adverse planning variances to convert the target into an expected actual.
3 Budgeting on a target/control basis but, in the expectation that not all targets

will be met, keeping a very close rein on resource and expenditure levels in anticipation of, but as yet unachieved, income targets.

4   Preparing separate planning and control budgets, using the control budget for operational control, and planning budgets for top management reporting.

As will be apparent, options 2, 3 and 4 are probably riskier approaches than option 1, as there is always a danger that resources and expenditures will be committed at the target level before target level incomes are known to be achieved or being achieved. Additionally there is the possibility that:

1   Budget-holders will soon realize that they are not really expected to achieve their targets and so will reduce their efforts, motivations and aspiration levels.
2   Management, budget and accounting information may be brought into disrepute if it is seen/believed that two sets of books are being maintained.

However, a control budget is surely the one most likely to achieve the full benefits of participation and the motivation of individuals. The offset of the potential gains against the potential losses must be considered carefully.

Role of budget co-ordinator

The need for a budget co-ordinator has already been mentioned. Some organizations employ a budget officer and others appoint a budget committee, but in many organizations this role is automatically assumed to be that of the accountant.

The work of Argyris[14] and others indicates that budget co-ordinators have a poor reputation within their organizations. It is alleged that they:

• Think of themselves as watchdogs.
• Think budgets are a legitimate means of applying pressure.
• Are inflexible and never satisfied, always trying to increase budget levels.
• Force budgets to an unrealistically high level, leaving little chance for management to succeed.
• Do not see the other person's point of view.
• Believe other managers and workers are lazy and that pressure is needed to obtain/raise production.
• Believe they are superior to others.

With this heritage, it places a considerable burden upon the budget co-ordinator. whatever their background, to fulfil his role.

Argyris recommended that finance staff should have training to equip them for their role as budget co-ordinator. This training should:

1   Help co-ordinators perceive the human implications of the budget system.
2   Demonstrate the effects of pressure on people and understand the advantages and disadvantages of applying such pressure.

3 Include discussions concerning the effects of success and failure.
4 Help co-ordinators perceive their difficult position, namely that of placing others in a position to fail.
5 Include practical techniques which can be used to get along better with managers and employees in difficult functions and at varying levels of the organization.
6 Help them to understand parochial departmental attitudes and the possible lack of group/organizational objectives.
7 Include knowledge of human relations studies.

The basic role of the co-ordinator is routine and administrative. He/she has to advise senior management; recommend and implement planning procedures, timetables, forms and schedules; provide past performance data; translate corporate goals and aims to managers at all levels; collect and collate data; prepare final summaries; and disseminate approved budgets to budget-holders.

To be effective, however, the co-ordinator needs more than simply routine capabilities. It is necessary to sell corporate goals to managers in the hope that such goals will either be adopted or internalized by them or that the goals they do adopt are not discordant with those of the organization as a whole. In addition, the co-ordinator must obtain true participation and encourage high aspiration levels, and ensure that budget aspiration levels are consistent across budget centres.

Constraints on resources

An essential element of strategic and budgetary planning is the identification of and planning within the limited resources available to the organization. A number of important resource related aspects will be considered.

Identifying resource constraints

Many explanations and schematics representing the budgetary process give little attention to resource availability. The strengths and weaknesses analysis of long-term planning should provide this vital information for the preparation of budgetary plans. Its importance lies in the recognition of those resources which are likely to constrain the organization's shorter and longer-term tactics and strategies. It would probably be wasteful, for example, for the sales forecast to be predicated upon higher finished goods stock levels if a likely constraint in, say, finance had been recognized. Some would disagree of course, and argue that it is management's task to remove constraints or find alternative ways of obtaining the same end result – the servicing of such sales volumes as can be reasonably achieved by the sales/marketing function. This sounds very neat, but a few moments' thought will indicate to the reader the likely impracticality of such an approach.

Whichever approach is adopted, there is, as mentioned earlier, a need to *match* sales forecasts with resources, particularly those of operations/manufacturing, before embarking on detailed budget preparation, in which, in turn, detailed resource implications will be identified, probably the last of these being finance availability.

Time-scale of constraints

Limiting factors are not necessarily permanent features. Some constraints may be relatively short-lived, while others may be a long-term feature of operations. A shortage of labour skills may be removed by training or recruitment, whereas a shortage of research and development know-how or a bad reputation may take years to remedy. The likely period and degree to which a resource will be constrained is a vital element in planning decisions. Plans predicated upon a particular limiting factor are necessarily lower achieving as compared to a situation where that resource is not limited or has lower limitations. It should be expected that any plan will attempt, as far as possible and within the long-term plan, to minimize the impact of limitations. In addition, plans will or should have been instituted to improve the supply of that resource and/or find alternatives.

Energies needlessly focused on these aspects will obviously be wasteful and are likely to reduce resultant performances.

Resource interchangeability

One of the main reasons for the relatively short period for which some limiting factors are relevant is the interchangeability of resources. This can take on a wide variety of forms: the use of capital resources to acquire plant and machinery; the conversion of one type of equipment to perform a different task; the sale of surplus machinery to provide finance to buy other assets, e.g. stocks; stock-reducing programmes, such as the sale of slow moving and surplus stocks to provide the finance to buy new machinery; or the sale of a subsidiary or operating unit to permit the expansion of another.

To repeat the point made earlier, resource constraints are not necessarily long-term features. Most limitations can be removed or reduced, given time and relevant actions.

Balance of resources

An almost inevitable corollary of the existence of limiting factors is a surplus of some (other) resources. Decisions regarding the use or disposal of such spare resources should be made. Strategically, decisions are likely to be centred around the anticipated long-term need for these resources, the alternative uses they may be put to and their realizable value. Tactics should obviously be dictated by the strategic view, but assuming the surplus is short-lived, the choice is likely to be between alternative uses/opportunities available in that short term.

Modern budgeting approaches

In recent years, different approaches to budgetary planning have been identified in response to the managerial dissatisfaction with the incremental, i.e. last year plus inflation approach to budgeting so commonly operating in business in relation to overhead budgets in particular. These approaches ask the basic questions of each part of an organization:

1 Justify your existence, i.e. why your service/department should be retained at all, and
2 Give management the option to take your department's/sector's product or services at different levels of quantity and quality.

Thus, catering may be asked 'Why should we require any catering service at all?' and then 'What would be the cost of increasing levels of service, e.g. coffee machines, snack bars, self-service bars and waitress service?' These approaches, exemplified by ZBB (zero based budgeting) and PPBS (planning, programming and budgetary systems) will be discussed in Chapter 9.

References

1. Coates, J.B., Davis, E.W., Longden, S.G., Stacey, R.J. and Emmanuel, C., *Corporate Performance Evaluation in Multinationals*, CIMA, 1993.
2. Steiner, G.A., *Strategic Planning*, Free Press, 1979.
3. CIMA, *Management Accounting: Official Terminology*, 1986.
4. Hofstede, G.H., *The Game of Budget Control*, Tavistock, 1968.
5. Coates, J.B., Rickwood, C.P. and Stacey, R.J., Examination of the Differences Between Academic Concepts and Actual Management Accounting Practices, Report to ESRC, British Library Document Supply Centre, August 1987 and Hofstede, G.H. The Game of Budget Control, Tavistock, 1968,
6. Simon, H.A., Guetzkown, H., Kozmetsky, G. and Tyndall, G., Centralisation vs. Decentralisation in Organising the Controller's Dept., New York Controllership Foundation, 1954.
7. Hofstede, *op. cit.*
8. Stedry, A.C., *Budget Control and Cost Behaviour*, Prentice Hall, 1960.
9. McClelland, D.C., Atkinson, J.W., Clark, R.A. and Lowell, E.L., *The Achievement Motive*, Appleton-Century-Crofts, Inc., New York, 1953.
10. Maslow, A.H., *Motivation and Personality*, Harper & Row, New York, 1954.
11. Herzberg, F., Mausner, B. and Synderman, B.B., *The Motivation to Work*, Wiley, New York, 1959.
12. Becker, S.W. and Green, D., Jr, Budgeting and Employee Behaviour, *The Journal of Business*, Vol. XXXV, October 1962.
13. Schiff, M. and Lewin, A.Y., The Impact of People on Budgets, *The Accounting Review*, Vol. XLV, No. 2, April 1970.

14. Argyris, C., *The Impact of Budgets on People*, Controllership Foundation, New York, 1952.

Questions

1 (a) In high technology small batch manufacture accountants sometimes take the view that standard costing cannot be applied. The move into high technology is generally accompanied by a shift away from labour-dominated to capital-intensive processes. You are required to appraise the application of standard costing in the circumstances described above.

   (b) In order to secure and direct employee motivation towards the achievements of a firm's goals, it may be considered that budget centres should be created at the lowest defined management level. You are required to discuss the advantages and disadvantages of creating budget centres at such a level.

2 Magna plc has a practical operating capacity of 100 Magna-widgets. Historical trends show increasing demand and output which has reached 90 Magna-widgets this year.

   A young and enthusiastic marketing/sales director, recently appointed, is optimistic about future prospects of the company's products. While he estimates that sales of 100 units are likely to be achieved in the coming year, he believes in setting himself and his staff hard though achievable targets, to encourage and extend performance achievement. His budget for the coming year is therefore based on 110 units.

   The production director is a hard-bitten man with long experience in the organization, having started as an apprentice in 1950 and become production director three years ago. In recent years he has experienced an increasing demand on his production capacity which, while resulting in high plant utilization and overtime/shiftworking, has strained resources from time to time, for which his department has been criticized. He dislikes the pressures placed upon him and resents the high regard in which the new sales director is held. He has been told that the sales budget is for 110 units. With the increasing trend in output demands over the past few years, the criticism of actual output in the past, and recognizing that his current practical capacity is only 100 units, he decides to organize his department with resources (machinery, staff, etc.) for a production output of 120 units.

   Examine and comment fully on this situation.

3 'Participatory budgets are a waste of time when eventually the plans of senior management will be those which are to be implemented.' Discuss.

4 What do you consider as being the prerequisite for the successful implementation of a participatory budgetary approach?

4

Standard costing and budget updates

Standard product costs are predetermined costs, analogous to a budget for a product or service. However, they are set assuming prescribed conditions and assumptions that need not be identical to those in the budget – although they usually are.

A standard is defined by CIMA[1] as 'a predetermined measurable quantity set in defined conditions against which actual performance can be compared, usually for an element of work, operation or activity'. The Institute then goes on to add that 'while standards may be based on unquestioned and immutable natural laws or facts, they are finally set by human judgement and consequently are subject to the same fallibility which attends all human activity. Thus a standard for 100 per cent machine output can be fixed by its geared input/output speeds, but the effective realizable output standard is one of judgement'.

Establishing cost standards

A standard, while typically being expressed in financial terms, usually relies on physical standards of performance and utilization having been set. To establish standard costs for a product it is necessary to determine the costs which will be incurred for labour, materials, perhaps direct expenses and (usually) overheads. Thus, ideally, a detailed study of the operations involved in the manufacture of each product or service needs to be undertaken. This will originate with a precise product specification; the physical quantities and qualities of every material and labour input needed to produce the product to specification needs identification, as will the best methods of doing so – machines, tools, etc. Quantities of inputs will then be multiplied by the their specific cost, usually either latest cost (derived from purchasing records) or future, anticipated costs: average costs for the budget year ahead is usual, but by cross referencing computer databases, an up-to-date, most recent cost can be derived. The standard costs for each element of materials and labour are then added, together usually with attributed overhead, to derive the product standard cost.

Methods of standard setting

Standards may be set using different levels of sophistication. At one extreme, engineered standards will be based upon techniques such as methods and time study. Records of past experiences may be a reasonable alternative basis, especially if recorded in detail. At worst, managerial experience may be the best available data – and if that experience is used to price or quote for work, it may be the most appropriate.

Historical standards

One approach to the preparation of management's view of expected future performance can be through the consideration of past actual performances. At its simplest past performances could be averaged. The main shortcoming of this approach is obviously that historical performance will necessarily include all its efficiencies and inefficiencies and the circumstances pertaining when those performances occurred. Additionally, if the standard performance is expressed in monetary rather than physical form, an allowance must be made for future costs being higher or lower than in the past.

This is obviously a 'minimum' approach, available to any organization which cannot afford or believe it would not be worthwhile to adopt more sophisticated techniques, or is in a situation where such techniques would not be feasible. It is of course possible to 'sophisticate' this minimum approach: management may use its subjective opinion and knowledge to adapt the historical performance to reflect those conditions and efficiencies anticipated. This approach is very common in, for example, smaller jobbing/manufacturing organizations.

Engineered standards

The inadequacies of historic standards as comparators, in situations of the sometimes high volumes of similar operations or units of output in many manufacturing industries, have led to the popularity of engineered standards, standard costs and standard costing. The term 'engineered standards' implies a scientific approach to the estimation of the necessary physical resource inputs to produce a detailed product/service specification. Such a standard would comprise the examination of alternative material, labour and other inputs with which the product could be made and the specification of the most suitable materials, grades of labour etc., bearing in mind product operation, methods of manufacture and cost, the application of ergonomics, method, work, and time and motion study to manual and mechanized operations, including the identification of required machinery and tooling.

Material standards

Material standards are best based on product specifications established after an intensive study has been made of the inputs necessary for each unit of output, i.e.

exact descriptions of quantities and qualities of inputs required, after taking into account the normal losses of the production process. The standard material cost is then found by multiplying the standard quantities by the appropriate standard prices. As noted above, these are usually the buyer's forecast of average purchasing prices in the coming year, allowing for planned ordering volumes, frequency, etc. Year averages are useful in order to derive cost information for budgetary purposes.

Labour standards

Labour standards are set in a similar way. Operations required to achieve the desired output are identified, method study determines the most appropriate sequences and efficient means of working, and the skills required to carry out each task. Time studies/measurements are made to determine the number of standard hours which are required for a worker to complete the task, allowing for reasonable and foreseeable delays. Standard rates of pay for each grade of labour are determined. As with materials, this will typically be an expected average pay rate for the year ahead, influenced naturally by budgetary assumptions. The agreed labour rates are multiplied by the standard times to determine the standard labour cost for each operation and hence the total for each product.

Overhead standards

If desired, (budgeted) overheads may be attributed to the products by traditional absorption costing techniques, which with modern computers, can be based on the physical and/or monetary elements of the standard cost. Alternatively, ABC, direct product costing or marginal/variable costing techniques may be applied. It will usually be valuable to identify separately, the fixed and variable components of overheads for a variety of purposes such as pricing, planning and control.

The fact is, however, that even engineered standards require a significant input of managerial estimation. In time study, for example, a number of technical/managerial estimates are needed: the time-study engineer will watch and time an operative performing the actions necessary for a particular task and then consider whether or not the operative is typical, or working faster or slower than an average operative, bearing in mind that the times are recorded on a Friday afternoon when the operative is tired and looking forward to the weekend activities, etc. Then further allowances might need to be made, for example, to allow for legitimate employee down-time and for learning curve related effects.

Managerial estimates

In situations where engineered standards would be unwarranted or unsuitable and yet a comparison with historic standards would be considered inadequate, some form of technical or managerial estimate is often possible. It is frequently suggested, for example, that standard costing is not suitable for service industries, jobbing and contract-based organizations or situations where there is relatively little repetition in operations. The likelihood is, however, that these organizations will have prepared, for each and every job they have, some form of cost estimate in order to assist sales management in quoting for the business. These estimates could be used as a quasi-standard, however rough and ready they might be. At the very least a comparison with such an estimate would give some feedback as to the adequacy or otherwise of the estimation/quotation approach they have adopted. In many jobbing and contracting organizations there is likely to be some reasonable data available, perhaps an estimate of the quantities of various materials and components required, or of labour or machine hours, or analysis of cost between labour, materials, expenses, overhead recovery and profit. Whatever their origin, they are vital information sources from the viewpoint of the organization's profitability.

In any event a wide range of methods and estimating procedures adopted within organizations may not fulfil the full 'sophistication' of engineered standards. Nevertheless they can be usefully applied as a basis for comparison of organizational and product/service performance.

Standard expectations

The levels of performance built into standards is perhaps the most critical element to their acceptance and use. The choice of ideal, normal, or currently attainable levels of performance and efficiency has potentially significant effects both upon those to whom those standards are applied and on those who use those standards for decision making.

Normal standards

Standards of this type represent the normal, i.e. usual standards that are achieved. These enable physical standards to be left unchanged over several years. The main advantage of normal standards is that a base is provided for a comparison of performance over several years. However, if changes occur in methods of production, or other relevant factors, normal standards tend to lose their value.

Ideal standards

These standards represent perfect performance. Ideal standard costs will therefore represent the minimum costs which are possible under the most efficient operating conditions. In practice, although ideal standards are unlikely to be achieved they do identify how far operations are from 100 per cent efficiency. However, as managers and labour will recognize that these standards are impossible to achieve, they are unlikely to treat any variances seriously and may become demotivated.

Currently attainable standards

These standards represent those costs which should be incurred under those levels of efficiency attainable within the period to which the standards apply –

typically the budget year. They are standards which are difficult, but within the competence of managers to achieve within the timescale involved. Allowance is made for reasonable wastage, machine breakdowns and lost time. In practice, currently attainable standards are the most frequently used standard, as they provide a fair base from which to measure variations. As such, they should provide a good motivational target for managers and labour and represent cost data consistent with the expectation levels of the budget.

Management might prefer an expected actual level if standards are to be easily incorporated into the budgetary process, but perhaps a target if used as the basis for employee incentive payment. In the latter case, of course, it is quite common for standards used as a basis for incentives to be 'negotiated' between management and employee representatives, in which case the resultant standard may bear little resemblance to any 'choice' of performance level. Miles and Vergin[2] suggest that the standards for management control systems could reflect just such a process, i.e. 'be established in such a way that they are recognized as legitimate ... that the method of deriving standards must be understood by those affected ... that "employees" should feel that (they have) some voice or influence in the establishment of (their) own performance goals'. However, Lupton[3] implies that if standards are used as the basis for payment systems, such are likely to degenerate and be distorted fairly rapidly.

Indeed while it may be tempting to establish a standard of physical performance which can remain unchanged over time (even if the monetary standard inflates), in practice standards can be expected to change. Standards after all are based upon assumptions of conditions and circumstances prevailing in a future period which may never result or may not persist for more than short periods of time. Thus such standards might need to be updated to reflect, for example, the learning curve phenomenon, operations outside the previously assumed relevant range, changes in operational methods and experience of actual performances.

Thus standards cannot be considered as being fixed for all time. Management must weigh up the desirability and cost of updating standards in the light of the purposes to which the standards are put.

Appropriateness of a standard costing system

Standard costing is most suited to organizations whose operations are of a common or repetitive nature, such as manufacturing industries. However, the approach can be applied in most business situations, whether service or manufacturing organizations, dealing in large or small volumes. It can be applied to any situation where tasks of similar nature are repeated.

Standard hours as a measure

It is frequently impracticable to measure *output* in terms of units produced as each product or service has required different amounts of inputs or operations from each part of the organization. This problem can be overcome by comparing units of output in respect of the standard hours of input required for each, i.e.

standard hours acts as the common denominator for adding together the production of dissimilar items.

Variance analysis

Material variances

The cost of the materials used in a manufactured product can be determined from two basic factors: the prices paid for the materials and the quantities of materials used. Actual prices and usage and therefore total cost may well differ from the standard cost giving rise to a material price and/or usage variance.

Material price variances

The difference between the standard material price (SMP) and the actual material price (AMP) per unit purchased, multiplied by the quantity of materials actually used is the material price variance. In practice, most businesses calculate material price variances when the purchase invoice is received or order placed, as that is the point in time at which the variance is actually incurred. Thus materials are costed in stocks at standard and not actual price.

Material usage variances

The material usage variance is the difference between the standard and actual amounts used of each material, multiplied by the standard price of each material. This variance is usually identified when additional material is required to complete the required quantities and/or when a component or product is scrapped on inspection.

Material yield variances

The material yield variance results from the actual output from a process being higher or lower than that of the standard. It is calculated as being the difference between the quantities of input that should have been used to obtain the actual output and the actual input quantity, multiplied by the standard cost per unit of output. This variance is principally used in process industries and may need careful differentiation from the mix variance.

Material mix variances

This variance results from the *mix* of materials input to a process being different from standard. It is calculated by comparing the standard cost of the actual total quantity of material used *assuming* a standard mix with the standard cost of the actual mix used for the same actual quantity of input.

Labour variance

The labour variance is calculated in a similar way to that for material variances, except that it is usually identified at a different point in time, i.e. at the completion of each operation. In total, it is the difference between the standard and actual labour cost for the products produced.

Wage rate variance

The wage rate variance is the difference between the standard and actual hourly rates of pay of labour multiplied by the actual hours worked. It is usually identified each day or week as standard and actual hours of work and time-cards are processed. Such variances can be analysed by cause – if managers attribute all non-standard hours to non-productive account codes.

Labour efficiency variance

The labour efficiency variance is the usage variance for direct labour. The standard and actual number of hours of labour required to produce the actual output is compared and the difference multiplied by the standard hourly wage rate. These variances are usually identified as each operation, batch, process, job, etc. is completed.

Production overhead variances

Overhead variances explain the difference between actual production overhead and the overhead absorbed as a result of applying the company's absorption rates to production volumes. This variance may result because overhead spending is different from that budgeted, i.e. an overhead spend variance, and/or because production volumes are different, i.e. a production volume variance. Further analysis is sometimes made producing, for example, variable overhead variances and capacity variances.

Sales variance

If management so desire, this approach can be used in respect of sales. Thus if the budget specifies standard (expected?) volumes and prices for each product (phased monthly preferably), sales price and volume variances can be calculated. Thus, for example, standard less average actual sales prices can be multiplied by actual sales volumes to derive the price variance; standard/actual sales volumes can be multiplied by the standard price to derive the sales volume variance.

Variance reporting

Accountants will typically prepare monthly, or perhaps weekly, statements of operational, production and sales activity. Where standard costing information is available, these statements are likely to summarize the variances as outlined. A simple example of this is shown in Tables 4.1 (question) and 4.2 (answer). The reader will note that the answer incorporates a flexible budget explained a little later in this chapter.

The answer summarizes the total impact on the company, by variance type, of a month's operations. Readers of such statements should bear the following fundamental points in mind.

1   The totals are summaries of variances over the period. Each variance consists perhaps of many events. One of the big advantages of control through standards over budgetary controls, is that total variance can be analysed in full detail if required.
    Thus, as examples, the following:

    • Each purchase invoice passed in that period can be examined to explain the total materials price variance. Thus the total favourable variance of £8,400 in Table 4.2 can be explained and understood.
    • Each operation in the factory can be examined: how long did it take, how long should it have taken.
    • Each material issue beyond the quantity required for the standard can be identified.

    By so doing events, positive and negative, may be identified. A small total variance which may appear to indicate no problems may hide a large number of positive and negative variances. A sophisticated system may enable all positive and negative variances to be totalled separately on management by exception allowing longer variance to be flagged at appropriate parts in the information processing system.

2   If the standards are the average for a year, one might expect earlier months to show favourable price/rate variances, the latter months negative. In Tables 4.1 and 4.2, therefore, bearing in mind it is month one, a question to be asked is whether or not the favourable price variances are as big as might be expected at that stage of the year.

3   Care has to be taken in the use of variance analysis. Even assuming calculations are error free, variances should raise the question 'Why?' in the minds of managers. Explanations should be sought and thence understanding and, perhaps, decisions and actions, should and will result. A variance in one area may appear to be the responsibility of one manager but may in fact result from actions elsewhere. Thus, as examples, the following:

    • An adverse labour efficiency variance may result from the purchase of poor quality material, of later delivery of materials or of sub-standard operations in earlier process.
    • A material price variance may result from later changes in production scheduling.
    • Production variances may result from helping sales with last minute orders or short production runs.

Table 4.1   A simple standard costing question

The Glob Ball Co. makes glass paperweights which are sold through wholesalers and small retail outlets. The operating statement for the first month of 1996 was as follows:

	Budget	Actual	Variance
Sales			
Units	240,000	280,000	40,000
£	192,000	218,000	26,400
Costs:			
Materials	48,000	58,800	(10,800)
Labour	72,000	98,000	(26,000)
Fixed overheads	60,000	56,000	4,000
	180,000	212,800	(6,400)

Operating statistics for the same period were as follows:

	Standard (Budget)	Actual
Units produced	240,000	280,000
Materials: lbs per unit	0.5	0.6
Labour: Time per unit	10 mins	12 mins
Average wage rate per hour	£1.80	£1.75

(a) Prepare a statement for management using variance analysis to show management the real causes, good and bad, of the reduction in profit.
(b) Comment briefly on possible reasons for each variance.

- Sales volume variances may result from failures in production or distribution departments or sales price variances from the need to sell sub-standard output.

In this connection one event may result in a chain of variance. Thus, hypothesizing, in the case of Glob Ball; sales accepted a large order at a discounted price of a slight adaption of the normal product, promising the customer a quality level higher than that normally produced by the company. As a result, production deliberately slowed down the production process to obtain the quality desired and rejected all products not of the desired standard. As a result, perhaps, the following variances resulted:

	£
Sales volume variance	12,000
Sales price variance	(5,600)
Material usage variance	(11,200)
Labour efficiency variance	(16,800)
Fixedoverhead(specialdelivery)	(4,000)
Net effect	(£25,000)

Table 4.2   A suggested answer to Glob Ball Co. (Table 4.1)

	Budget	Actual	Flexed Variance	Budget	Variance
Sales					
Units	240,000	280,000	40,000	280,000	—
£	192,000	218,400	25,400	224,000	(5,600)
Costs:					
Materials	48,000	58,800	(10,800)	56,000	(2,800)
Labour	72,000	98,000	(26,000)	84,000	(14,000)
	120,000	156,800	(36,800)	140,000	(16,800)
Contribution	72,000	61,600	(10,400)	84,000	(22,400)
Fixed costs	60,000	56,000	4,000	60,000	4,000
Profit/(Loss)	£12,000	£5,600	£(6,400)	£24,000	£(18,400)

Analysis of variance

	Total (£)	Variances Favourable (£)	Unfavourable (£)
Volume variance			
40,000 units × 30p	12,000	12,000	
contribution/unit			
(or Fixed budget – Master			
budget)			
Sales price variance			
280,000 units (80p – 78p)	(5,600)		5,600*
Production variances			
Material price:			
(40–35)p × 0.6 × 280,000		8,400	
	(2,800)		
Material usage			
(0.5 – 0.6)lbs × 40p × 280,000			11,200
Labour price/rate			
(1.80 – 1.75)p × 12 mins ×		2,800	
280,000	(14,000)		
Labour efficiency			16,800
(10–12)mins × 1.8 × 280,000			
Fixed overhead spend	4,000	4,000	
Total variance =	£(6,400)	£27,000	£33,600

A disaster? Well at least now the company knows the total impact of the decision, whereas otherwise they might not have done. In practice, of course, for smaller orders, similar variances may be hidden within the totals, but can be traced should management believe it worthwhile. There is a cost of costing!

Performance reports

Performance showing sales and production variances can be presented in a variety of ways according to corporate culture, managerial responsibility and the problems management wish to address. For operational level reports for example, it may be desirable to have more frequent reports, concentrating on the larger instances of variance and showing both physical and quantitative information. Sales reports may concentrate on sales variances but are likely to need at least a summary of operating variances – after all, their actions may have caused these variances. This raises the crucial point of variance analysis: the objective should be to learn from the knowledge of the cause and effect of variances and not be used as a means of attributing blame. Variance reports should lead management to answers to the question 'Why?'.

Revision of budgets and standards

Budgets are considered by many organizations to be unchangeable and inviolate. The reasons for this are probably twofold. Firstly, there must be a danger that budgets will fall into disrepute if management is prepared to alter them. How seriously would managers take the budget preparation process if they realized that senior management accepted that budgets would need to be changed before the end of the budget period? Secondly, the comparison of the original master budget with actual revenues and costs is a valuable one, even if the latter operated under very different conditions from that originally anticipated: the resultant variances should be examined to establish (i) how far actual results diverged from those budgeted, which after all represented (or ought to have) the first stage of the organization's long-term plan, and (ii) why the organization's management failed to anticipate the actual situation and identify how such failures might be reduced in future planning, plans and budgets.

However, there are situations where management may consider that the original master budget is insufficient as a prediction of future outcomes and/or as a control yardstick, and where alternative measures may be desirable.

Flexible budgets

The term flexible budgets has a very specific meaning in accounting usages, even though some managers and accountants attribute other interpretations to it. CIMA[4] defines a flexible budget as 'A budget which, by the difference in behaviour between fixed and variable costs in relation to fluctuations in output, turnover, or other variable factors such as numbers of employees is designed to change appropriately with such fluctuations'.

Essentially, flexible budgets are adaptations of the original master budget which reflect a change in the level of activity from that planned, all other assumptions being considered constant. The value of such flexed budgets is that (i) in the budget preparation phase management can identify likely outcomes should their output be higher or lower than that planned, i.e. sensitivity analysis,

(ii) as a control mechanism managers can be made aware of what their revenue, expenditure and efficiencies should be if activity levels are proving to be different from that planned, and (iii) management can exercise control by comparing actual performance against the flexed budget, which variance will not be clouded by any differences caused by the differences between actual and budgeted activity levels. In principle the flexing of budgets relies upon two factors, (i) knowledge of cost behaviour (the fixity and variability of costs with changes in activity levels), and (ii) identification of a suitable activity measure.

While a knowledge of an organization's cost behaviour might be considered a desirable prerequisite to good managerial decision making, many managements have not obtained such information, and even if they have, the problem of the relevant range over which each cost is fixed or variable may be very different one from another. These factors need not, however, eliminate the possibility of applying flexed budgets within an organization. If, when managers are preparing the budgets for their responsibilities, they were required to state and justify at what levels of activity they would expect to need, say, extra supervisory assistance, or to reduce the same, these could be used as a surrogate for a full cost behaviour analysis, and to reflect the variability of semi-variable costs, and to approximate the relevant ranges of fixed costs. While this approach would not be so practicable as using a top-down budgetary approach, and might be considered too time-consuming, it is applied successfully in many organizations.

The identification of a suitable activity measure is very difficult in many organizations, as units of output is unlikely to be adequate in a multi-product/service organization. Standard hours is perhaps the most likely activity measure, but that presupposes that this information is available within an organization. Tons of output, for example, is apparently popular as a measure of output within the foundry industry, but has inherent anomalies regarding product mix, i.e. the work done and time consumed on a small complicated item may be larger than that on a large, heavy but simple item. It is right that different industries and businesses adopt those activity measures which they feel most suitable to their circumstances.

Rolling or continuous budgets

Some organizations adopt what are usually termed rolling or continuous budgets. CIMA[4], for example, defines these as 'The continuous updating of a short term budget by adding, say, a further month or quarter and deducting the earliest month or quarter so that the budget can reflect current conditions.'

It is argued that 'Such procedures are beneficial where future costs and/or activities cannot be forecast with any degree of accuracy,' in CIMA[1] official terminology. However, this argument is surely illogical. If it is difficult to forecast ahead accurately when, once a year perhaps, management devotes considerable time and attention to it, how likely is it that managers can do the same forecast more accurately every month or quarter? The danger is that the rolling budget will become the last period plus or minus a bit, and be representative of absolutely nothing by way of policy, and meaningless for prediction or control purposes.

If, however, management expects the rolling forecast to be updated both by adding another period and by updating the intermediate periods to changed circumstances, it could be argued that management should obtain a more realistic forecast of the coming months than it would if no updating or rolling of budgets was required. In such circumstances management must necessarily ask how valuable such revised forecasts are likely to be in relation to the cost of the time spent by managers updating their forecasts.

Forecast revisions

If management wishes to identify what the budget period's actual results are likely to be, an alternative to rolling budgets is to require managers to re-forecast each period/month/quarter the expected actual figures at the end of the total budget period/year. This would enable management to identify the extent to which their managers' anticipated outcomes will vary from their last forecast and thus to keep in touch with and understand the problems being encountered by managers, month by month and quarter by quarter.

Actuals could then be compared with both the original budget and the revised forecast of, say, the last quarter. While this should create a better managerial awareness of current and future operating conditions and expectations, the benefits from a control viewpoint are less easily identifiable.

Revision variances

An alternative approach to updating which has the virtue (if that it be) of retaining awareness of the original budget is the adoption of revision variances. Under this approach updating of the original budget to revised circumstances and expectations is achieved by adding an allowance for expected variances (plus or minus) to the original budget to reflect the deviation expected from it. Control may then be maintained by analysing the total actual variance from the original budget and comparing this with the revision variance, this difference reflecting changes from that more recently anticipated.

External economic change

The environmental assumptions upon which strategic and budgetary planning are based may well prove to be very different from those conditions encountered during the budgetary period. In these circumstances the master budget may be considered less than ideal, even inappropriate for either planning/resource allocation or control purposes.

The alternatives available to the organization are:

1   to continue with the original budget, making allowances as necessary,
2   to adapt the original budget to reflect the changed circumstances,
3   to adopt a rolling budget or forecast revision approach, or
4   to rebudget.

The decision is likely to depend partly upon the degree of variation from the budgeted assumptions and partly upon the uses management makes of the budget, e.g. as authority to spend or limits on spending.

If environmental conditions are not significantly different from those budgeted for, it may be sensible to retain the original budget and expect middle and junior managers to adapt to the changed circumstances within the framework of the original budget. This would retain the integrity of the budgetary planning procedures and probably be a practicable and economic approach.

If the different conditions revolve around only one or two assumptions made, it *might* be sensible and practicable to adapt the master budget to the new situation, particularly if the budgetary data is held in a sophisticated computer financial model. However, this presupposes that the changed circumstances do not require a complete rethink of the budgetary plan and that information is held in a suitable fashion for it to be updated. As the revised budget would be based on the original budget, it is more likely to be accepted by managers, who would appreciate the need to reflect the new conditions. Additionally, such changes are unlikely to be expensive.

Rolling budgets and forecast revisions are more likely to be practised as a matter of routine managerial philosophy rather than as a response to a particular or unexpected situation. Such an experience, however, may well be the trigger for the routine adoption of such information processes.

The larger the divergence of actual conditions from those budgeted, the more logical would be the decision to recognize the inappropriateness of the original budget and the need to rebudget. Failure to do so might permit managers to waste limited resources or use them inappropriately to the new circumstances either because they are unaware of the changes, or because they believe they are still expected to try to attain the original budget despite the changes in circumstances. Thus, for example, operational management might continue to recruit and train new employees for the budgeted expansion which senior marketing personnel now realize is unlikely to occur; or middle and junior selling and marketing managers might pursue a price increase oriented campaign in spite of increased competition and price cutting by competitors, because they believed such was still senior management's strategy or tactics, or because their own performance measures required it.

The cost of rebudgeting must be recognized and offset against the advantages of doing so. If circumstances are significantly different, the continued use of a budget that managers perceive as being inappropriate may not only lead to bad decisions but create low morale. Even in this situation, management would do well to remind managers at all levels that the original budget is not totally forgotten, and be prepared at some stage to ensure that all managers remember the 'lessons' from the failure to anticipate actual conditions and apply them to future planning situations.

It is essential that managers at all levels adapt to new environmental circumstances, and that strategies and tactics are changed if necessary. The failure to do so could be catastrophic. If that means sacrificing the sacred cow of the master budget, then so be it.

Internal changes

In contrast, a reluctance to change shorter-term budgets and standards because of internal changes may well be justified. Such budgets are less likely to impact seriously upon the organization's survival, market position and long-term prosperity.

However, the impact of internal changes upon an organization can be very significant, even within a budgetary period of, say, a year, and may make the agreed budget, certainly in its detailed form, completely inappropriate to the situation. Consider, for example, such changes as:

1 An organizational restructuring, say, from a functional to a divisional structure.
2 A modification of objectives, financial or otherwise, particularly if this causes changes in the product/market portfolio of the business.
3 The merging of acquired businesses within the existing organizational framework.
4 Mechanization/automation resulting perhaps in significant learning curve effects.
5 The earlier than expected completion of R&D, resulting in either new production technology or new product/markets.

The state of flux in such situations may of course be such that it would be impracticable to budget for it, and would in any event waste managerial time and energies better spent ensuring the changes are made efficiently and effectively. The danger, however, must be that, where no budgetary control exists, cost control is neglected in the drive for completion of change, and that effectiveness is achieved at the expense of efficiency. Obviously in managerial situations much must depend upon the specific case in point, the degree of change, the quality of the managers and the availability of control measures other than that of the budget.

Impact of inflation

The impact of inflation upon revenues and costs has been incorporated into the budgetary planning of most organizations for many years. This did not derive from a sudden rise in inflation or the inflation/current cost accounting/SSAP 21 debate of the 1970s but from an earlier, perhaps instinctive, recognition of the need to reflect estimated actual revenues and costs in planning data if realistic budgetary plans and controls were to be obtained.

Although the high levels of inflation in the UK of the 1970s will, it is to be hoped, not be repeated, inflation is an inevitability, and one certainly difficult to forecast. Management may reflect inflation in its budgets by:

1 requiring managers to budget today's levels of costs and revenues, and incorporating inflation as a separate element,

2   budgeting under inflation rates assumed by senior management, or
3   budgeting under inflation rates assumed by local/middle management.

The advantage of the former two approaches is that, as the budget for inflation is known or easily calculable:

1   plans can be revised to reflect different levels of inflation, and
2   control by means of variance analysis can differentiate between the effects of inflation and those of other causes.

The other side of the coin is that individual budget-holders may have a much better appreciation of the likely effects of inflation in their industry, types of cost and locality than would more senior management. However, there must always be the danger that the delegation of the decision on inflation levels to each budget-holder encourages pessimism, the building in of 'slack' and the creation of unrepresentative budgets.

With the advent of computer modelling in budgetary and indeed strategic planning, the desirability of the separate identification of inflationary effects would appear to be overwhelming. The 'revision' of budgets to reflect inflation should perhaps be seen in a very different light to the revisions due to external and internal changes discussed above. Such adaptations can surely be viewed similarly to flexible budgeting, i.e. as part of variance analysis. In the same manner that flexible budgets reflect variations of the original master budget due to changes in volume of activity, so inflationary budgets reflect changes in levels of revenues, costs and profits due to changes in inflation from that anticipated. Flexed inflationary budgets can then be seen to reflect variances caused by factors other than volume or inflation, removing an excuse for managers to hide behind, and concentrating attention upon the real cause of any variances.

The exception to these considerations, however, may be when the impact of inflation upon a business is significantly different between revenues and costs, one type of cost and another or one unit or another. Consider, for example, a situation where costs are increasing faster than sales price for some products or services. In such circumstances management may need to rethink its whole product/market strategy/tactics. Thus, if labour costs are increasing at a faster rate than, say, capital equipment, it may be best to switch to labour-saving manufacturing/operational processes. In larger companies, with operating units in different countries, relative changes in the rates of inflation on operating costs may result in the switching of work from one unit to another, perhaps necessitating a significant revision of short- and long-term plans.

References

1.   CIMA, Management Accounting: Official Terminology, 1986.
2.   Miles, R.E. and Vergin, R.C., Behavioural Properties of Variance Controls, *California Management Review*, Vol. VIII, No. 3, Spring 1966.

3. Lupton, T., *Payment Systems*, Penguin 1972.
4. CIMA, *op. cit.*

Questions

1 The fuels department of Bionic Engineering Inc. is a semi-autonomous unit manufacturing and selling a product known as Krypton. The management of the department is responsible for purchasing raw materials, setting production levels and selecting the method of production to be used. Bionic Engineering also run an independent Department of Economic Forecasting, which supplies information to central and departmental management.

Two formulae are available to the fuels department, producing Krypton X and Krypton Y respectively. Each method of production requires all the inputs for a particular batch to be introduced into huge chemical vats at the start of the process; processing takes one month to complete. However, before the processing of each batch, it is necessary to carry out extensive cleaning and calibration. Once started, it is impossible to change the calibration, and calibration settings must be adapted specifically to the batch volume and formula to be used.

Planning in the fuels department is made easier by the existence of a contract with Titanic Distributors requiring all output to be sold to them at a price given by the following:

Price in pence per 100 litres $= 4,400 - 0.04q$
where q is the quantity sold in units of 100 litres.

Titanic makes payments for the output immediately processing is completed. The following production data is available:

Materials	Krypton X *(per 100 litres)*	Krypton Y *(per 100 litres)*
DNX	50 litres	—
DNY	—	8 kg
Biobase	12 kg	12 kg

Conversion costs
Variable cost (in pence) $900 + .1q$ $900 + .1q$
where q is the quantity of Krypton produced (in 100 litres).

Fixed costs are £8,000 per month during processing and £6,000 per month during cleaning and calibrating. Under a long-term contract, Biobase is bought at £0.50 per kg. All materials are ordered one month before processing begins and paid for two months later, at which time conversion costs are met. DNX and DNY are received two days before processing begins; any of these materials left unused must be discarded.

Central management uses a system of budgetary control to assess the performance of departments. On 1 March 2001, based on the forecasted prices for DNX of £0.28 per litre and of DNY of £1.70 per kg, central management budget for fuels to produce a profit of £22,350 in the quarter ended 30 June 2001.

On 31 March the forecasts predict prices for DNX of £0.34 per litre and DNY of £2.05 per kg. On this basis fuels management calculates the optimal quantity of output and formula. By 1 May the prices to be paid are known, DNX being £0.30 per litre and DNY £2.00 per kg, and a profit of £10,150 is forecast, given that the departmental plan must now be carried out. This latest forecast is duly achieved.

Central management is concerned that the profit achieved is less than half the budgeted figure and a variance analysis is carried out as follows:

	£	£	£
Actual profit			10,150
Selling price variance		1,800 F	
Cost variances			
DNY		10.800 U	
Conversion		4,500 F	
Rate variances		4,500 U	
Volume variances		7,700 U	
Total variances			12,200 U
Budgeted profit			22,350

A meeting is called to review the results. It is suggested on behalf of the department that their action was entirely caused by the revision of forecasts and the economic forecasting department is to blame for the volume variance. The forecasting department considers its forecasts to have helped and argues that, if the original plan had been adopted, things might have been worse. The head of chemical research offers another point of view: 'I have carried out a few calculations and consider the most serious mistake was making Krypton Y in the first place. It would have been cheaper to have made Krypton X this month. A profit of £15,000 could have been achieved.'

(a)   Present statements showing the budget, departmental plan, actual results and the suggestion of the head of chemical research.
(b)   Critically compare all three approaches to variance analysis, using the calculations carried out above.

2   In what circumstances might it be appropriate to change the annual budgets before the end of the accounting year and what might be the repercussions of doing so?
3   'Rolling budgets are essential if an organization is undergoing rapid change.' Is this really true and what are the arguments for and against such a budgetary approach?

4   Bob Lord, the new managing director of the Abco Group, has engaged Ray
    Consultants to advise him on the operation of the group's budgetary planning
    and control. Bob Lord's previous experience has been within companies
    where there has been little or no participation in the budget preparation
    process other than that of senior management.

    The Abco Group has a highly participative budgetary process. All managers
    with budget responsibilities play a part in the preparation of their contribu-
    tions to the overall budget and these are used as a significant part of the
    annual performance appraisal and thereby can lead to financial and other
    rewards.

    Bob Lord has asked Ray Consultants to write a report for him, explaining
    and summarizing as clearly as possible the believed *practical* and *theoretical*
    pros and cons of a participative budget approach, the problems such an
    approach is likely to encounter and how these can be best ameliorated, in
    order to obtain as balanced a view as possible to aid him in his consideration
    of the existing system within Abco.

    What should such a report contain?

5   In what circumstances would standard cost not based on engineered standards
    be appropriate for an organization?

5
Budgets and control

Introduction

In this chapter aspects of the collection and presentation of budget information for control purposes are considered, followed by a discussion of the ways variance investigations may be triggered.

Control of an enterprise is the principal responsibility of management, and this responsibility includes all aspects of budgetary planning and control: strategic and tactical, long-term and short-term. These activities are a part of management's objective to develop a successful business. The focus of this chapter, however, is on control in the narrower but perhaps more usually understood meaning of exercising regular control over current budget plans by comparing planned with actual results. The emphasis of such comparisons is corrective in the short term, though the process of establishing how and why differences have arisen contributes not only to bringing activities back into line immediately, but also to the identification of fundamental changes in the conditions on which plans have been founded and hence to amendments and revisions of longer term plans.

It is conventional to regard these comparisons as being a part of the scheme of management by exception in which, if there are no significant departures from plans, then all is deemed to be under control and proceeding as anticipated. Managerial time, effort and cost are only to be expended where the differences according to certain criteria are judged to warrant it. It would be overly simplistic to proceed this way at all times though: for example, plans which are regularly fully realized may themselves need investigation on the grounds they are too unambitious.

The fundamentals of budgetary planning and control and standard costing systems have long been established and there is a substantial history surrounding their usage. Solomons[1] traces the development of cost ascertainment methods, including standard costing, budgets and budgetary control, and variance analysis back to significant periods in their emergence as separate entities, finally coming together in the early part of this century in systems which would be readily recognized today. Towards the end of his paper he remarks:

'If there is one conclusion to be drawn from the foregoing study, it is that there is remarkably little in modern costing which our fathers did not know about. What can be fairly claimed for the period 1910–1950 however, is that great strides were made in converting ideas into widely adopted practices.'

Since then there have of course been many notable further advances in the practice of budgetary planning and control. Important among them has been the recognition of the cost of information, a subject which has received much attention from the late 1960s onwards. Previously, by implication, information was treated as costless, being available as and when required.[2,3] One of the principal points which emerges from the debate on information economics is the pervasive presence of uncertainty as the background to all management decision problems. This in turn affects both the cost of acquiring information and the benefits expected from it. A satisfactory balance in the cost-benefit trade-off needs to be achieved, if possible.

Additional significant issues which have been debated over a roughly similar period and up to the present deal with the need for an understanding of the part played by managers in the creation and capture of information and the way information is presented to them and subsequently handled. Recognition, and proper appreciation of behavioural influences are as important, from an organization's point of view, in the successful pursuance of control as are the accounting numbers which provide the immediate basis of analysis and for investigation.[4] A stereotyped picture of the way management accountants may be thought to (or actually) behave with respect to the application of these systems is described by Tait.[5]

Collection and presentation of budget information for control purposes

Many books and articles[6] discuss this activity of collection and presentation. Key among them are the definition of the sphere of managerial responsibility, the controllability (by a manager) of the variables to which budget data relate and the main purposes of the control activity. These purposes may be briefly summarized as:

- Notification of the extent of departure of actual from budget.
- Analysis and presentation of information explaining the nature and causes of such departures, to be used as a basis for pursuing corrective action, which could include major revisions to budgets.
- Provision of information for use in the assessment of the performance of sections of the business: achievement of targets, improvements in productivity and efficiency.

Interest in outcomes is obviously not confined to subordinate managers and their immediate superiors but goes right through to top management, subject to filtering and amalgamation of data. It is also increasingly becoming a province of interest to internal audit departments in their role as independent observers and reporters on departmental target-setting and performance achievement.

Using actual company cases,[7,8] we now introduce three examples which serve to illustrate how certain organizations have addressed a number of the technical

Table 5.1   Report format

	Operating company	Business centre	Individual product lines
Sales	x	x	x
Prime costs	x	x	x
Sales gross margin	x	x	x
Direct marketing	*x*	*x*	*x*
Net product margin	x	x	x
Product attributable			
Indirect costs	*x*	*x*	*x*
Production contribution	x	x	x
Business centre			
Attributable indirect costs	*x*	*x*	
Business centre			
Contribution	x	x	
Factory general overheads	x		
General selling expenses	x		
Company administration	x		
Company marketing	*x*		
Operating company contribution	x		
Apportioned services	*x*		
Gross trading profit	*x*		

and behavioural issues in the creation and transmission of information for budget-control purposes.

Case 1

The report format in use by company management accountants is given in Table 5.1. It was devised following an organizational restructuring which decentralized its operations. The main purpose of the scheme was to secure as accurate an attribution as possible of direct costs to various levels of the company, from product lines to the company as a whole. This helps to ensure that both responsibility and controllability are properly matched, with apportionments of cost kept to a minimum.

Direct marketing costs are predominantly packaging, but for the remainder the stratification of information clearly recognizes controllability and responsibility, since managers are assigned to product lines. Prime costs and direct marketing are regarded as variable, though the company is fortunate here to be able to use temporary labour to achieve variability in direct labour costs. Probably the most difficult category to define and assign is that of indirect cost into the 'product' and 'business' attributable categories. The condition used as the criteria for the division is that it must be possible to 'manage' the costs in line with changes in the level of business generated within some specified time limit. Managers' agreement is needed to an item being classified one way or the other or being split. Costs which would come in for examination would be, for example, indirect labour and supervision, power, depreciation, heat, light, maintenance, shift premiums and insurances.

The level of costs in the managed category is set by decisions preceding actual activity and hence the costs are budget totals, but not now automatically carrying labels of 'fixed' or 'variable'. Once there is a commitment to the acquisition or disposal of certain resources, it may indeed result in an essentially fixed level of expense for a certain period. Even then, if there are marked variations in activity from planned, managers are expected to avoid entering into commitment as to resources which will create difficulties in the future. Overall line managers are accepting the need to manage their resources to no more than that which the general level of business can support.

A similar set of appraisals takes place at the level of the business centre, where managers accept certain amounts of administrative and selling expense as being necessary to run their part of the business. This is not the result of a simple apportionment process, but of realistic identification of what would be needed if the business were on a stand-alone basis, though it must be tempered to some extent where appropriate by the benefits of economies of scale, e.g. in the provision of such services as accounting. The aim is to minimize the extent of arbitrary apportionment so far as possible, important in costs which account for 58 per cent of total value added in the operating company. One management accountant's view of apportionments carried out the traditional way was, 'they generate a lot of heat and not much light'.

Case 2

In this case also the emphasis is on how production and other managers are encouraged to manage costs, though here the labels of variable and fixed were being applied. Lack of precision in defining cost variability outside the ambit of a few items such as direct materials is recognized but the aim is to obtain the 'right response' from managers having expenditure responsibility. This is considered best attained by labelling expenses 'variable' wherever there is reasonable doubt whether or to what degree a cost really is variable. The psychology of the case for approaching the problem this way is that to call a cost 'fixed' invites the response that there is little that can be done to control it in the short run.

Approaching the problem along these lines is thought to help put pressure on managers to improve efficiency in adverse conditions, though the twin dangers of finally causing managers to reach the conclusion that the variability is spurious and efficiency therefore unattainable and what to do if conditions finally improve, have to be carefully monitored. The company in question has been in a period of long-term contraction, so the latter problem has not really emerged. Little hostile reaction is reported from managers whose spending budgets have been controlled in part at least this way. The application of the idea is to most cost elements except the very evidently fixed ones such as depreciation and rates.

Table 5.2   Multinational's report format

	Product (budget)	Actual	Proportion of total business (%)
1 Sales (including inter-company transfers)	x	x	
2 Cost of sales	x	x	
(*Prime costs*)	—	—	
3 Sales gross margin	x	x	
4 *Direct overhead*	*x*	*x*	
5 Contribution	x	x	
6 Indirect (apportioned) costs	x	x	
(including interest charged on assets)	x	x	
7 *Operating profit*	*x*	*x*	
8 *Assets managed*	*x*	*x*	
% return on assets managed (7 ÷ 8)			

Case 3

Set out in Table 5.2 is the report format in use by the internal audit department of a large multinational company. The report itself is used to provide the department with all that it regards as being the necessary salient information in monitoring division and product line performance. It is not dissimilar to the Case 1 example, but each comes from a totally different industrial sector.

As in the earlier case, considerable effort is made to ensure costs are directly attributed and, as before, the main problem area lies in the division of the indirect costs. An interesting feature of this case was that the manager responsible for the product group was also primarily responsible for determining the extent to which the overhead costs – in the main, production and marketing – were to be divided between directly attributable and apportioned non-attributable. This does not have any effect on the overall return on assets managed measure, but it does affect the contribution figure, which is a key element in monitoring the profitability of the product group within the business as a whole.

A manager would on the face of it seem to have carte blanche to adjust the overheads figure in his favour, even to the extent of recording no controllable direct overhead. However, the internal audit department, while accepting that absolute precision cannot be achieved in valuing each category of expenditure, looks for a reasonable attitude in the acceptance of some responsibility for this type of spending by the product group manager: the actual existence of the group must mean it causes a certain proportion of the overheads to be incurred. Where a manager is trying to improve his performance by too obvious an attempt at minimizing these costs, he provokes a visit from the internal audit staff.

The Budget and Actual columns also record the standard profit and the variances of individual items of sales and costs as a percentage of that figure, showing the significance of each element in turn in the way it affects the

Table 5.3 Staff task plan

Objective	Control area	Project completion date	Staff assigned	Risk factor
1 Develop and publish for approval a work in progress valuation	Inventory	10/93	J. Smith	M
2 Develop and implement a bill of material audit analysis, etc.	Manufacturing	10/93		L

achievement or otherwise of the standard profit. This provides managers and auditors alike with the initial information on where significant departures from plan appear to arise. Internal audit operations also have the further guide of the proportion of business accounted for by the product group. In a business with some 15 main divisions and a very large number of product groups, this document serves as the key to highlight what are regarded as all the significant areas for the exercise of control, while leaving operational managers within a substantially decentralized environment.

Measurement and control of staff performance

Department or section output, ratio analysis of resource usage and variance analysis all contribute as measures of performance for the group of individuals working within a department. Individual contributions themselves are frequently less easy to measure, especially in service departments, where, for example, a person is producing advice based on expertise. Often much reliance is placed on the 'professionalism' of the person for assurance that his/her activities are both effective and economic. Management by Objectives (MBO) is a tool which has been in use for some time, though not apparently uniformly or with total success[9] across companies. It aims to put some substance, particularly in staff situations, into the assessment of the level and content of work which it is expected staff will perform. The programme of work is agreed with individuals concerned as to content, time allowed and scheduling, and is subsequently audited by managers.

An appropriate example is taken a company's accounting department, which is divided into six main functional areas. One of these deals solely with accounting for inventory. In the first place the objective of the function is stated, followed by a listing of the activities which come within its purview, such as control and reporting of stock positions, product cost development, finished goods administration and so on. These are the objectives the unit as a whole is expected to aim at. To do so will frequently require completion of specific tasks, to which individuals can be assigned. In this section, a plan (Table 5.3) is drawn up.

It is the section manager's job, carried out with the function head's approval, to establish this plan and assign persons to projects. The risk factor covers the competence of the person given a project to complete the task without assistance and within the period allotted. The more assistance needed from outside the function, the greater the perceived risk level. In turn this forms part of the background to the final project appraisal, where reasons for over- or under-achievement are required in exactly the same way as explaining a standard cost variance. The degree to which such projects can be accurately measured depends on the section manager's own experience and knowledge of the staff's abilities. Such project assessments are common of course where the service is or contributes directly to a saleable product, e.g. in the development of computer programmes in software houses, or aerospace engineering projects, but is a less common planning and control feature of routine service and administration.

Variance analysis

The purpose of calculating a variance is to show departures from standard or budget, which may be either favourable or unfavourable. The systems which incorporate the forecasts and budget plans and capture the actual data for comparison with them are often detailed and complex, requiring budget manuals in order to see they are properly executed. In contrast, there is much less formality and guidance available as to how to use the variance information thrown up by the comparisons, yet the choice to investigate a variance or not is central if not crucial to the achievement of operating control.

Some of the important elements of the problem may be considered as follows:

- The fact that a variance has been recorded (favourable or adverse) does not automatically mean anything is wrong or doing particularly well. The result may be one that has occurred simply by chance.
- To investigate a variance will cost money – the time of persons assigned to the task, those who have to be interviewed, maybe material and equipment costs in test work.
- Benefits may be even more difficult to discern and evaluate than costs: improved competitiveness and better customer goodwill may well be, for example, among the eventual outcomes of an investigation which leads to improved quality and service, but they will not be easy to quantify. On the other hand, as part of the same investigation, scrap and rework cost reduction is much more readily quantifiable. The problem with benefits is compounded by the possibility that nothing is out of control, in which event no benefits arise from a study, but there will be costs.

Experience is certainly a valuable asset in the circumstances, since it contributes insights and knowledge not apparent in the figures: for example, is the recurrent nature of a result new or has it occurred in the past; if so how was it dealt with and with what effect? Experience will also help to spot cause and effect and interlinked outcomes, again contributing to better decision making on the choice of whether to investigate a variance or not.

Thus many factors and unknowns enter this particular decision area, to the extent that it is not possible to be prescriptive as to how to proceed. A number of choices are offered, some quite formal and systematic, others, such as experience, far more intuitive. Again they need not be regarded as exclusive alternatives to each other. The most widely discussed approaches are outlined below.

Reliance on experience

A partial or complete reliance on experience is likely to be widely adopted in practice. Even if more formal analysis is applied to earmark apparently important variances, it is still probable that a judgement based on experience will be the deciding factor as to whether an investigation should proceed.

Ad hoc rules

The development of ad hoc rules are used to highlight what are considered to be variances of a size which potentially require investigation. Commonly:

1   The ratio of the variance observed to budget (standard) or actual cost. Choice of a ratio, the size of which if equalled or exceeded would make a prima facie case for investigation, is a matter for the company.
2   Ratios ignore absolute size: very large ratios are derivable from insignificant costs. Hence the absolute size of a variance may be considered a more important indicator of the need for investigation and a value chosen accordingly.

Of course each of these two criteria may give contradictory information if used in isolation: much unproductive work may result from a reliance on a ratio criterion (10 per cent, 15 per cent of standard cost, for example) if carried out without reference to the absolute size of a variance. Similar drawbacks attach to the use of absolute size alone. However, to attempt a joint criterion based on both elements would be no better a guide than perhaps saying look at all variances. Judgement founded on good experience must be used in conjunction with chosen criteria in this case.

Statistical control methods

Statistical control methods have been advocated. Support for them has been based on the parallel between the purpose of variance accounting and statistical quality control, namely the use of process defect rates and cost variance to indicate whether the underlying processes are in or out of control or are moving in the out-of-control direction.

The statistic used to define levels of in or out of control is measured in terms of the standard deviation. A series of observations of the performance of a process

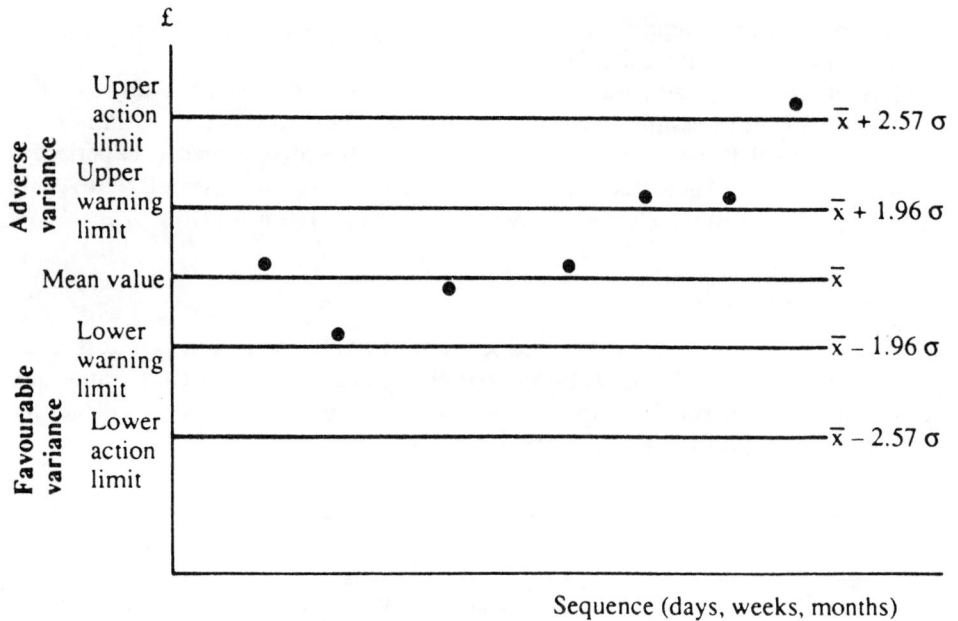

Figure 5.1   *Statistical control chart*

are made, say in relation to the actual usage of direct material in comparison with the prescribed standard. From the values obtained, the mean, variance and standard deviation may be calculated. Conventional statistical quality control charts identify warning limits, say at a level where the chance of the observation is 1 in 40 times, and action limits, where the chance may be set at 1 in 100 times. The standard deviation is used to measure these limits, but their selection is again a judgement for the company to make. A typical chart may appear as in Figure 5.1.

Figure 5.1 shows information on departures from standard plotted on a daily, weekly or monthly basis, with the situation initially apparently within the area which would be regarded as 'in control', then exhibiting a trend toward 'out of control' – firstly breaking through the warning limit (which should trigger at least preliminary investigation of the circumstances to reverse the trend) and finally going through the upper action limit (which demands that an investigation takes place, since the underlying situation is now deemed out of control). The underlying philosophy is simply that, since budgets and standards are substantially based on predictions of future conditions, it must be accepted that departures from them in the form of variances will occur more or less by chance and hence do not indicate that anything is seriously amiss. However, as the size of variance increases, the likelihood of it occurring by chance becomes progressively smaller, until at some stage (defined by managers) there is a presumption that something is going wrong and ought to be investigated. Investigation of variances does not follow automatically, since costs and benefits still need to be ascertained, though they could be among the considerations in establishing the scheme at the outset.

It is an appealing idea, which in practice appears to have attracted few adherents. Statistical schemes require quite long runs of data in order to establish the ranges within which outcomes may be normally expected to vary and hence to establish reasonable warning and action limits. The data must be consistent from one period to the next. In process and high volume manufacturing conditions both the quantity and stability of data factors are likely to be present, so that for production quality control schemes the basic data requirements are met. Standard cost and budget data are usually assembled to cover broad intervals of time, so that the number of measurements taken is much smaller per period than in the volume production case, leading also to the point that before sufficient information is accumulated, the underlying parameters may well have changed and data in one period are no longer comparable with those from preceding periods.

Although there is a distinction between standard cost and statistical quality control variances, a relationship remains. For example, examination of material purchase quality against specifications would produce the same outcomes – either the material is acceptable or not – whether measured in a quality control or standard cost variance analysis. The same could be said of many other SQC (statistical quality control) applications. The preference is also to catch departures from specifications (standards) at this point rather than waiting for them to be valued in order to produce cost variances, since they provide the opportunity to conduct investigations at an earlier rather than a later stage, much improving the chance of determining causes and reducing the possibility of future problems.

Important contributors to the idea of the adoption of SQC schemes have been Bierman, Fouraker and Jaedicke[10] and Dopuch, Birnberg and Demski.[11] In a further contribution Kaplan[12] extends (inter alia) the application of conventional statistical schemes to the use of cusum graphs. Here the cumulative sum of positive and negative variances is plotted, providing a graphical presentation useful in itself, since it helps to identify the point in time when an out-of-control situation may have developed. In order to give greater precision to the actual assessment, a V-mask may be calculated and added to the graph. The angle of the V-mask determines the sensitivity of the test of whether a situation is still within or has moved out of control, and this angle in turn is set by two parameters, 'a' and 'b'. Parameter 'b' is defined as a number of periods ahead of the most recent graph plot, while 'a' controls the angle of the V-mask and depends on a determination of the size of variance that would be considered indicative of a significant shift in actual against standard/budgeted out-turns. The cusum graph is illustrated in Figure 5.2.

The figure shows an in-control case, with the angle of the V-mask equal to the ratio of a/b. When the cusum plot cuts the mask, an out-of control case is signalled. It is a relatively simple technique to apply, though space does not allow further discussion here. Readers are referred to Lewis.[13]

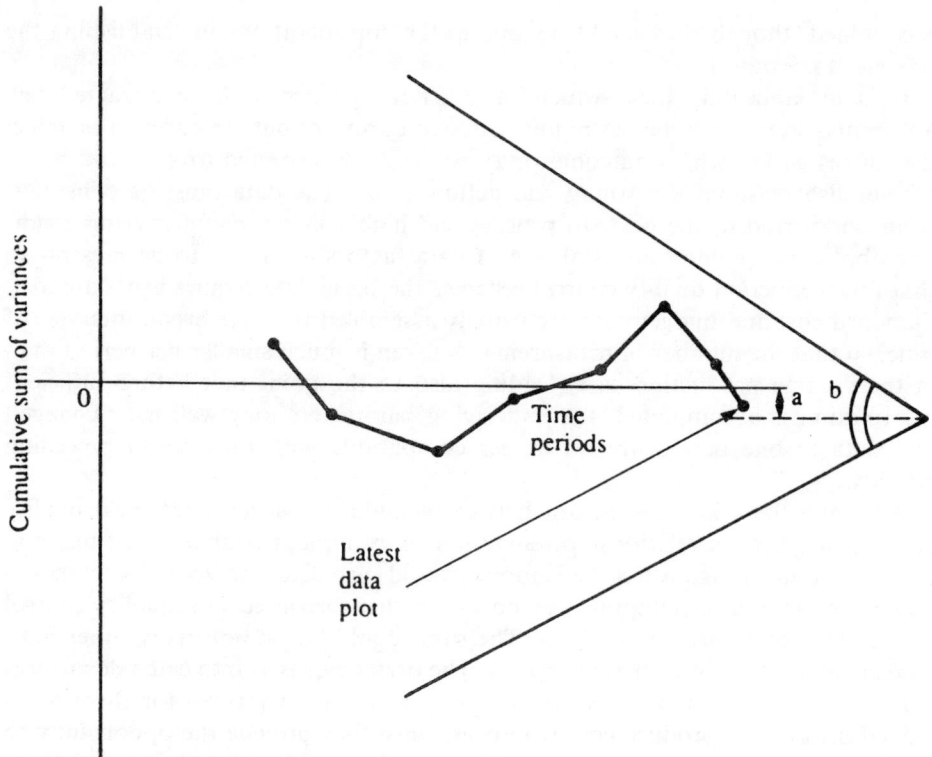

Figure 5.2   *Cusum graph*

Decision theory models

These deal specifically with the analysis of the costs and benefits of carrying out an investigation and hence can be used in conjunction with any of the three ways of identification of variances apparently worthy of investigation as listed above as a further evaluator serving a decision as to whether to proceed or not.

The basic model can be illustrated as a two-state model, i.e. a process is either in or out of control and the two actions possible are investigate the variance or do not investigate. In addition, information has to be obtained as to:

*   The prior probabilities that a process is in or out of control (effectively given by SQC-based schemes).
*   The cost of conducting an investigation and the value of likely benefits. The latter principally comprise the saving in costs otherwise incurred if control is not re-established.

This model may be shown as in Table 5.4.

If the following data is assumed:

Table 5.4 Decision theory model

| | State of process | |
| | *In control* | *Out of control* |
Decision	X_1	X_2
Investigate	– C	B – C
Do not investigate	0	0

where: C = cost of investigating
     B = benefit of investigating

p   = probability the process is in control = 0.9
(1 – p) = probability the process is out of control = 0.1
C   = £800
B   = £3,000

then the immediate decision would be not to proceed with an investigation, since the cost (C) at £800 is greater than the expected value of the benefit (1 – p) (B) = £300.

This decision model is about the most simple available, but nonetheless contains many difficulties. How does one estimate the cost of investigation before it takes place and before, possibly, having any idea of what may be wrong? This latter difficulty extends also to the estimation of benefits. Then there is the judgement as to the prior probabilities. Again, in the absence of evidence, how is it possible to assess them with any hope of accuracy? In the example given, were the probability that an observed variance indicating the process to be out of control to change from 0.1 to 0.3, the expected value of the benefit would become £900 and the decision becomes to investigate. Beyond these issues are ones concerning the attitudes of the decision makers towards the risk consequences of their decisions and the complexity of the decision model itself, i.e. a two-state, single period model, when several states and sequential effects may be a more accurate representation. Finally there is the question of actually taking action; waiting for all these models to be created and evaluated could well mean the passing of the most effective point in time for intervention to take place.

There is no evidence pointing to widespread use of models of this nature. Their most likely beneficial effects lie in the way they demonstrate the salient points needing to be addressed in the decision process and use as part of a management training programme. Thereafter, in the practical situation, managerial judgement takes over in actual decision making.

Conducting variance analysis

If information on variances is to be of any value, it must have reference to two main sets of conditions:

1   The actual presentation of the information, as regards speed and timeliness, relevance and accuracy.
2   The acceptance by managers of the validity of the plans, measurements and attributed responsibilities which are the basis for the derivation and application of variance analysis.

The factors referred to in 1 above are well understood, and only their interaction requires some further comment here. For successful investigation of current situations the general rule is to obtain variance data as soon as possible and hence there is a possible trade-off between accuracy and speed, certainly between fully costed variances and their presentation in physical usage units. For example, in the latter case it may be possible to provide data on actual against standard material consumption in units of volume or weight rather more rapidly than a standard or actual cost valuation of over or under usage. For the purpose of investigating the cause of excessive consumption against the standard amount, it is decidedly preferable to know about the occurrence of the event as soon as possible. This of course adds another facet to the process of deciding when it becomes worthwhile to conduct an investigation. On the other hand, certain variances have longer-term implications, perhaps being indicative of fundamental shifts away from the bases of current plans, as may be the case, for example, in the capacity utilization component of the volume variance. The appropriate response to such a situation is more likely to be founded on a build-up of these variances over time, which could ultimately call for a revision of the entire business plan, than one which presumes immediate correction is desirable and possible. Hence speedy action, within limits at least, is less likely to be a pressing need.

The question of the degree to which managers are able to exercise control over variances depends on how well responsibility and authority are identified in the managerial hierarchy. It is sometimes debated whether non-controllable variances should appear on the operating statements of individual managers, since they may detract from action which should be taken on those which are controllable, e.g. because of their size. On the other hand, there are likely to be some clear indirect links: it may not be possible, for instance, for a manager to control rates, depreciation charges insurances, service charges by direct action on those costs, but organizing and maintaining a throughput of goods as efficiently as possible will contribute effectively to the maximum absorption of those costs. It is a truism to say that all costs are controllable at some level in an organization's hierarchy, and in a responsibility accounting sense that point should be clearly identified. It is equally true, though, that inability on the part of managers to exercise direct control over an expense item does not mean it is necessarily uncontrollable in so far as their actions contribute to keeping down unit costs.

Relevance and accuracy may be considered also in the context of inflationary situations. In addition, there are situations where the underlying assumptions of budgets and standards are being progressively eroded by changes such as those brought about by increases or decreases in general economic activity, changes in the market for products and changes in the technology which produces goods and services.

Periods of rapid rises in resource cost, brought about by general inflation, which were experienced in the UK in the 1970s and early 1980s, rapidly undermine the meaning and significance of fully costed variances. The reaction observed in a number of companies to this problem was:

- To revise resource prices frequently and regularly, a common interval being quarterly.
- To concentrate on resource usage reports, on the grounds that price was becoming an uncontrollable variable.

It may be noted that companies dealing in commodities such as copper and coffee tend to suffer continually from the fact that these materials are unpredictably volatile in price. The custom and practice of trades affected by this volatility tend to be that prices charged to customers, eventually at least, will reflect the supplier passing on the commodity price increases or savings pretty well automatically. Except for merchants whose trade is solely as dealers in these commodities, most processor manufactures would not risk speculating on commodity markets, though they might take action to cover their transactions.

However, returning to the question of price changes brought about by inflation, it is clearly valid to try to ensure that the impact of the main body of controllable variances is not obscured by the less controllable, possibly dominating, impact of adverse price variances. *Less* controllable makes the point that even in these circumstances it would be wrong to ignore them altogether. Companies engaged in competitive situations, especially internationally, could well have to absorb at least some of these price effects, since they may not, perhaps because of exchange rate movements caused by differential inflation among competing countries, be able to maintain competitive market prices. Price variances are some measure of the problem faced.

Such changes may be presented as 'revisions variances' (CIMA terminology),[14] though the expression refers to the general range of resources used by an organization and to usage and volume as well as price variances. Such variances apply wherever conditions have changed sufficiently markedly from those underlying the original budget and associated standards to warrant budget reappraisal.

Over a longer period it has been observed in some companies (e.g. Crossways)[15] that standards and hence some budgets have been allowed to drift away from the reality of changing production and market scenes by clinging to concepts evolved for conditions which have ceased to exist. Most likely a series of ad hoc amendments will have been made to the original case, but without a great deal of care the lack of a fundamental review of developments leads to accounting reports being seen as irrelevant and consequently ignored. Instances of this occurring have been noted in cases where transfer to high technology manufacture with scarcely any direct labour base still leaves overhead being recovered on direct labour. Not only does this start to produce very high recovery rates, it also masks the deep change in the nature of the manufacturing process that has taken place, e.g. by apparently focusing on direct labour activity when this is really no longer significant. Attention as to the real problems has been misdirected.

Similarly shifts in the market with an increasing demand for product differentia-tion have possible knock-on consequences of some cost changes, shorter produc-tion runs and capacity loss. Standards based on the idea of production runs more suited to a past era of high volume mass production are again no longer relevant.

Besides the above issues, effective preparation of the groundwork for variance investigation must have reference to the possibility of interdependence between variances. This must lengthen the period required before publication to managers of various analyses. If attempts at responsibility shifting and the creation of an adversarial climate are to be kept to a minimum, then it is probably the accountants' responsibility to try to produce an objective report, incorporating reasoned explanations for the occurrence of events as far as possible. For example, at a simple level they may state that the use of a new or non-recognized supplier of materials or components, for whatever reason, may be a significant possible contribution to higher than expected material usage and lower than expected direct labour and/or machine or process efficiency. Obviously responsible managers' contributions to the explanation of given situations cannot be in any sense diminished by preliminary studies undertaken by the accountants, but management meetings to discuss variance reports can be put on a better directional basis as a result of them.

In organizations where priority has been given to the establishment of good inter-department relationships, much of the latter groundwork can be reduced; for example, in one company where departmental quality ratings are given considerable prominence, it is the practice for discussions to be arranged between representatives of departments when one believes that a fall-off in its quality standards may be in part at least due to faults coming through from a previous department. Owing to the environment created for the organization as a whole, departments see themselves as contributors to the company goals and not as independent islands, with the result that debates are conducted in a positive, amicable atmosphere which generally results in an agreed resolution of the problem (in so far as it is within their power to achieve it) and without much direction by the management accounting depart-ment. A further extension of this situation is that the realization of required standards of quality is not subject to a cost/benefit appraisal of input resources to a valuation of results, but is simply built into the product and costed at the specification level, in the expectation this will be achieved. This lessens any tendency to pass on sub-standard work solely for the purpose of fulfilling production quotas and getting products 'out of the door'. Variances, represented immediately by rejects and rework and in the longer term by guarantee/warranty claims and even loss of business, are kept to a minimum with little formal accounting input.

Clearly this situation links into the condition of ad hoc rules where a substantial body of literature exists on the topic of motivations and behavioural responses.

Managerial participation in budget planning and control

A superficial characterization of budget plans and a scheme of control in which variance analysis plays a significant role is that of the carrot and the stick.

Accountants are sometimes accused of wielding too much stick in a rather negative fashion. The body of literature devoted to this central aspect of management accounting is substantial indeed, far too great to even attempt to précis here. All aspects have received attention, from forecasting requirements through to setting budgets and standards, motivation, participation and reward schemes. Sometimes there is the accusation that this is just playing with buzzwords, but it is believed there is a general acceptance that the studies and analyses conducted do represent a reality which should be acknowledged in the procedures of any budgeting system. Among the many significant contributors are Cyert, March and Starbuck,[16] Hofstede in the aptly titled book, *The Game of Budget Control*,[17] Hopwood,[18] and Otley.[19] Emmanuel and Otley[20] provide an extensive list of papers and books devoted to this subject.

The results of this research show, among other things, budgets to be widely perceived as motivational devices aimed at obtaining desired levels of performance by the company through its management. Mere expressions to the effect that improvement is desired or required are considerably less successful in producing the improvement than are the use of quantified budgets as targets to aim for. At the same time it is recognized that simply presenting a budget as a target (take it or leave it) will not of necessity do much better. The key to the issue is seen as management's perceptions of budgets and its participation in their preparation. It is commonly observed that budgets should be both 'tight' and 'fair' in order to be accepted. Both are highly subjective concepts, likely to be perceived differently by different managers, but they encapsulate central elements by which managers will judge and respond to budgets they are working to.

If it is granted that the most successful route to establishing budgets and targets is via participation, consultation and mutual agreement, there will probably need to be some give and take between departmental/section managers on the one hand and planners/accountants on the other. The result should be targets which are within reach, but not too easily, and a consequential judgement they are equitable. Hofstede[21] makes three major claims as to how managers' participation in the budgetary process helps to secure a better performance from them:

- By ensuring a subordinate accepts the budget, which thereby becomes a motivational target.
- The process of participation produces clearer understanding of the circumstances behind setting the budget and thus produces more realistic standards.
- Given the clearer understanding, there is less chance of information being distorted and manipulated.

Even so, participation is held to be unlikely to attain what is aimed for in all managers under all circumstances.

The level at which a budget is finally set must be such that its attainment presents a challenge and hence is likely to give some satisfaction in its attainment. If it is set too far out of reach, especially if this is combined with a poor personal appraisal of the likelihood of its achievement, efforts to achieve it are expected to be either non-existent at the outset or become steadily and progressively extinguished. The nature and psychology of the managers themselves, whether they are uncertain or confident of their abilities, is also an important contributory factor to the establishment of budgetary targets in pursuance of acceptable corporate performance. Performance measures used in conjunction with budgets require similar considerations.

Finally it is recognized that, while satisfaction may well be found in the achievement of targets, the main motivational drive is the hope, prospect or expectation of the rewards for doing so. These include improved salaries, bonuses, perks, promotions and so on. Given a sound budgetary foundation, including the standards incorporated into many budgets, along the above lines, unless the surrounding business environment turns out markedly different from that which was envisaged, exceptional variances between actual and plan should be the exception rather than the rule. The objective, as with the quality example, is to get the plan as near right as possible in the first place, so that variances do relate to circumstances largely outside the control of the individual manager.

Conclusion

The activity of management accounting centres around the creation of planning budgets and their comparison with actual results. To achieve efficient control means close attention has to be paid to three major issues: creating a cost/benefit effective procedure to ensure plans are being followed and variances shown up by comparisons are investigated; ensuring standards and budgets are kept properly up to date to maintain their validity; and finally that the human and industrial relations aspects of the procedures are acknowledged and acted upon. After all it is the staff of the organization through whom the system is developed, maintained and progressed.

One of the benefits of new technology information systems is that information creation, capture and management should be much easier and more effective than in manual systems. There should certainly be fewer excuses about timeliness, speed of arrival of information and its accuracy than there has been in the past.

References

1. Solomons, D., The Historical Development of Costing. In Solomons, D. (ed.), *Studies in Cost Analysis*, Sweet & Maxwell, 1952.
2. Kaplan, R., The Evolution of Management Accounting, *The Accounting Review*, July 1984.
3. Scapens, R.J., *Management Accounting*, Macmillan, 1985, Chapter 8.
4. Emmanuel, C., Otley, D.T. and Merchant, K., *Accounting for Management Control*, (2nd ed.) Chapman & Hall, 1990, p. 174.
5. Tait, G., The Truth About Standard Costing, *Management Accounting*, October 1985.
6. Horngren, C.T. and Foster, G., *Cost Accounting – A Managerial Emphasis*, Prentice Hall, (6th ed.), 1986, Part 2.

7. Coates, J.B., Rickwood, C.P. and Stacey, R.J., Examination of the Differ-
    ences Between Academic Concepts and Actual Management Accounting
    Practices, Report to ESRC British Library Document Supply Centre,
    August 1987.
8. *Ibid.*
9. Coates, J.B. and Longden, S.G., *Management Accounting: The challenge of
    technological innovation*, CIMA, 1989.
10. Bierman, J., Fouraker, J.C.E. and Jaedicke, R.K., A Use of Probability and
    Statistics in Performance Evaluation, *The Accounting Review*, July 1961.
11. Dopuch, N., Birnberg, J.G. and Demski, J., An Extension of Standard Cost
    Variance Analysis, *The Accounting Review*, July 1967.
12. Kaplan, R., The Significance and Investigation of Cost Variances: Survey
    and Extension', *Journal of Accounting Research*, Autumn, 1975.
13. Lewis, C.D., *Industrial and Business Forecasting Methods*, Butterworths,
    1982.
14. CIMA, *op. cit.*
15. Coates *et al.*, *op. cit.*
16. Cyert, R.M., March, J.G. and Starbuck, W.H., Two experiments on risk
    and conflict in organizational estimation, *Management Science*, Vol. 7,
    1961.
17. Hofstede, G.H., *The Game of Budget Control*, Tavistock Institute, 1968.
18. Hopwood, A.G., *Accounting and Human Behaviour*, Prentice Hall, 1974.
19. Otley, D.T., Budget Use and Managerial Performance, *Journal of Account-
    ing Research*, Vol. 16, 1978.
20. Emmanuel and Otley, *op. cit.*
21. Hofstede, *op. cit.*

Questions

1 (a) The investigation of a variance is a fundamental element in the effective
        exercise of control through budgetary control and standard costing
        systems. The systems for identifying the variances may be well defined
        and detailed yet the procedures adopted to determine whether to pursue
        the investigation of variances may well not be formalized.
        Critically examine this situation, discussing possible effective approaches
        to the investigation of variances.
   (b) Explain the major motivational factors which influence managers in
        their actions to eliminate variances from budget.

                                                              (CIMA May 1987)

2 The ABC company is a large manufacturer of domestic appliance equipment.
   Internal accounting is based on a standard costing and budgetary control system
   introduced some 20 to 25 years ago in business conditions which could be
   described as a 'seller's market', with new product manufacture heavily based
   on a number of long-running standard lines. Since then greatly increased

competition, buyers' demands for product differentiation and greatly changed manufacturing technology (some of which is installed and operating in the company) have dramatically changed the company's business and manufacturing environment.

The results of a 4-week operating period in one of the production departments making component parts, are given below:

	Budget	Actual
Output (standard hours)	4,800	4,460
Direct labour:		
production time (hours)	4,000	3,900
attendance time (hours)	5,000	4,900
Direct materials used (kgs)	20,160	20,962

The direct labour production standard incorporates a 20 per cent efficiency factor. There is a standard downtime allowance of 20 per cent. Costs budgeted and actually incurred in the 4-week period are:

	Budget £	Actual £
Direct material	30,240	33,539
Direct labour	16,800	17,500
Indirect costs:		
Indirect wages of direct		
workers	2,500	3,000
Variable overhead	2,000	2,400
Fixed overhead	25,200	28,000

Variable overhead recovery is based on production time and fixed overhead recovery on standard hours output. You are required to: (a) Obtain all the relevant variances from the above data; (b) Comment on the variances in the light of the change in the business situation from one dominated by long production runs to the relatively shorter runs imposed in meeting the current demand for differentiated products; (c) Use the situation problems of standard setting in programmed and non-programmed decision-making circumstances.

(CIMA, MCA Specimen Question Paper)

3 Discuss whether cost trend analysis is a better approach to cost control in comparison to traditional standard cost variance analysis, where a company's main objective is to improve its profits in the main by driving down its costs (derived from visit to Ford Motor, 24/10/95).

4 In the new factory environment of advanced manufacturing technology, traditional standard costing and variance analysis has become less relevant, with much greater attention being paid to actual costs and how these are changing. Explain why this should be the case in advanced manufacturing technology and how cost control can be maintained in the absence of conventional variance analysis.

6

Activity based costing

Introduction

Activity based costing (ABC) is a topic which has attracted considerable attention since its inception – at least in its present form – during the latter part of the 1980s. Its emergence follows the appearance of Johnson and Kaplan's book,[1] which severely criticized traditional costing systems for failing to supply managers with information appropriate to the requirements of decision making, planning and control, including the strategic dimension (Kaplan,[2,3] Cooper,[4] Cooper and Kaplan[5]). The impression may well be gained that ABC is a new answer to the criticisms of 'traditional' costing as posed in Johnson and Kaplan.[1] However, the fundamental ideas of ABC have certainly been canvassed and applied before, though perhaps not so eloquently and well packaged (see, for example, Longman and Schiff,[6] and Staubus[7]). Staubus, for example, while primarily developing a very formal input–output costing system in the context of standard costs, emphasizes the need to have a detailed understanding of the nature and costs of the various activities identified within an organization. He also details the breakdown of what are known as 'cost pools' in ABC, such as transportation, purchasing, receiving, etc., into headings such as, for example, in purchasing: determination of possible sources, selection of the best source, traffic and routeing, issuance of purchase orders and so on, all of which are used in the ABC system.

The extent to which ABC systems have been promoted as being new and an almost universal solution to the shortcomings seen in 'traditional' systems, has also provoked criticism of ABC itself (see Piper and Walley,[8] Cooper[9] and Piper and Walley[10]). It is not the intention to indulge in an inconclusive debate here regarding the claims and counter-claims made for or against ABC, though it is probably fair to say ABC is still in a development phase, both as a subject and in the degree to which it has become established as a part of management accounting in practice. ABC itself was originally presented an overhead management system, but was popularized as a product costing system. Arising from it more recently however, are the ideas associated with Activity Based Management (ABM) and Activity Based Budgeting (ABB), regarded in at least some quarters as more useful to management than an ABC system itself.

Recent studies do give the impression that ABC systems are increasingly in use within companies, though the take-up rate may appear fairly slow: a survey of CIMA members published by Innes and Mitchell,[11] showed that only 6 per cent of those responding to their questionnaire had initiated an ABC system. A follow-up survey carried out by the same authors covering the same group (Innes and Mitchell[12]) showed that the proportion of users of either ABC or ABM had grown to 16 per cent by 1994. In a further survey of the UK's 1000 largest companies (Innes and Mitchell[13]), the authors found that out of 251 usable replies,19.5 per cent of respondents said they were currently using ABC and a further 27.1 per cent were considering its adoption. Many case studies have been published to illustrate the gains made by companies attributed to introducing ABC and associated cost management programmes, for example the Harvard Business School cases and those of Innes and Mitchell.[14]

Ultimately, implementation of ABC systems is said to be capable of generating multiple benefits for a company. Cooper[15] emphasized three important ones:

- more accurate product costs
- better understanding of the economics of production
- an understanding of the economics of activities performed by a company.

Innes and Mitchell[13] listed nine applications of ABC adopted by respondents who claimed to be using the system:

- stock valuation
- product/service costing
- output decisions
- cost reduction
- budgeting
- new product/service design
- customer profitability analysis
- performance measurement/improvement
- cost modelling.

Its application is of course, not limited to manufacturing industry: service industry, wholesale and retailing, public utilities and public sector organizations, all provide opportunities for the adoption of ABC systems (see Cooper and Kaplan[16]).

Altogether a large body of literature has been built up dealing with ABC and its subsequent developments, only a small part of which can be referred to here. Likewise it is not possible to become involved in detailed expositions of all aspects of ABC: the following introduces its more fundamental features.

The elements of ABC

ABC as a product costing system

Proponents of ABC make a number strong criticisms of traditional costing systems. Central to them is that volume of output plays an almost exclusive role in overhead recovery in the conventional case. This has resulted in an averaging of costs which can be quite misleading, especially when applied in a firm with multiple processes and products, which can lead to some products being subsidized at the expense of others, with consequential effects on matters such as product pricing, service and customer evaluation. ABC requires a fundamental reappraisal of the incurrence in particular of indirect costs, conducted on the basic premise that it is *activities* which consume resources and cause costs to be incurred. The result is that cost may be recovered to products through a much broader range of recovery variables than has traditionally been the case. In manufacturing for example, single bases such as direct labour cost or hours or machine hours content of products have conventionally been the bases for charging a substantial proportion of indirect cost to products, but are now regarded as being inadequate for accurate product costing where different markets, customers, quantity and quality of product demanded make very different demands on the activities of a business.

Making the assumption that direct labour (hours or cost) increase or decrease in relation to the volume of production, the use of direct labour as a singular factor in overhead cost recovery means that product costs are also closely related to the level of production volume. The same also applies to the use of machine hour rates, since machine operating time is also dependent on production volume. Certain costs may indeed relate to either factor through production volume, for example: power, overtime, some maintenance expenditures; but a whole range of others do not.

Frequently cited examples of costs which are considered non-volume related in the production context are set-ups, expediting, scheduling and material handling, together with expenditure on other service functions such as marketing, selling, distribution, information services and so on. Such costs are becoming an increasing proportion of total company costs.

The once pervasive (but certainly now declining) use of direct labour cost as a basis for recovering costs to products and also allocating certain costs to cost centres, can give the very misleading impression that reduction of direct labour time or cost will also result in a reduction of the amount of indirect expense to be allocated to departments and absorbed by products: to use the modern idiom, that direct labour cost 'drives' (i.e., causes) these other costs. In some instances this may be the case, but the objection is that it is applied indiscriminately to others as well where no such linkage exists. Consequently, attempts to reduce costs significantly by concentrating on a reduction of the direct labour base are simply misplaced and will not achieve the full level of savings apparently available.

The structure and mechanics of an ABC system

In place of the limited, volume related factors on which conventional systems are seen to rely, ABC proposes a far more extensive cost analysis. A series of cost pools are identified; to these are linked the cost drivers, i.e., the activities which determine the level of cost recorded in the individual cost pools. The chain of analysis is shown in Figure 6.1. The sequence can be extended to incorporate the intermediate manufacture of components and component assemblies.

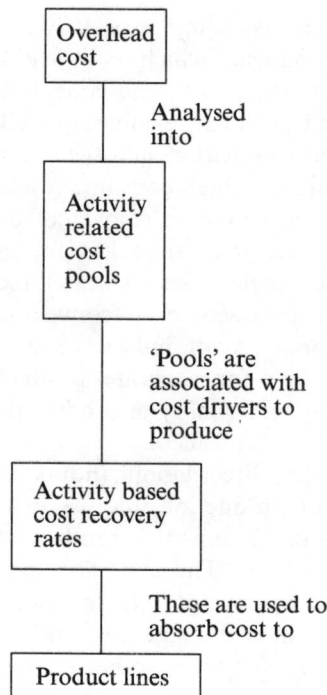

```
                    ┌──────────────┐
                    │ Overhead     │
                    │ cost         │
                    └──────┬───────┘
                           │   Analysed
                           │   into
                    ┌──────┴───────┐
                    │ Activity     │
                    │ related      │
                    │ cost         │
                    │ pools        │
                    └──────┬───────┘
                           │   'Pools' are
                           │   associated with
                           │   cost drivers to
                           │   produce
              ┌────────────┴────────┐
              │ Activity based      │
              │ cost recovery       │
              │ rates               │
              └────────────┬────────┘
                           │   These are used to
                           │   absorb cost to
              ┌────────────┴────────┐
              │ Product lines       │
              └─────────────────────┘
```

Figure 6.1

A diagrammatic presentation of a conventional cost flow system would appear little different in outline; but whereas in the latter systems, indirect cost is normally attributed to products through their initial allocation to departments (which could be thought of as pools), in the case of ABC, the initial allocation is to pools which represent activities such as machine set-ups, quality inspections, maintenance work and other service activities, as well as conventional activities such as machine running time. Activities are identified as events or transactions which are cost drivers and product costs depend on how much of these are consumed by individual products. It is the increasing refinement of the costing system brought about by this extension to the cost pools which marks out the ABC system in particular from its predecessors. The quality control process, for example, instead of appearing as part of works total overhead costs and recovered on the back of direct labour, may be identified as a separate cost pool. Within the overall pool, individual activities would need to be determined, which in turn would be linked to a cost driver, the factor causing the cost to be incurred in the first place, as illustrated in Table 6.1.

It should be noted that performance of the activity, quality control, includes work done by a number of different functions and departments, rather than work done within the confines of a quality control department.

Each product or service which requires the services of quality control must be examined according to the type of demand(s) it places on quality resources, so that it can be charged for them, using the quality cost driver rates.

Table 6.1   An illustration of some of the activities and cost drivers associated with the quality control process

Activities	Cost drivers
1 Checking inward supplies of raw materials and other goods	Number of different items received Frequency of receipt Number of checks required
2 Return of defective items	Proportion of substandard items
3 Checking process quality	Number of different types of check Frequency of checks
4 Checking finished product quality	Number of checks required
5 Supervision	Number of different departmental activities Number of people supervised

The illustration also indicates one of the problems with ABC: its complexity. The number of activities and cost drivers shown to exist within any function such as quality could be very extensive. There are no set rules to determine how detailed the analysis needs to become to produce a sufficient level of detail for product costing/decision making requirements. Only by bearing in mind the cost-benefit criteria – which itself would be by no means easy to apply – can some general guidance be obtained.

Certain practical steps can be taken with the objective of minimizing a potential proliferation of activities and cost drivers by looking for commonality of effect among differing cost drivers or by eliminating those with only a small cost impact (i.e., where accuracy loss is not significant) and adding these costs into other pools.

Where the same cause–effect relationship is found between the costs of a number of activities (say, within an overall cost pool) and a certain cost driver, then for product costing purposes they could be aggregated into a single 'homogeneous' cost pool. For example, within the overall 'personnel' activity, it may be found that the activities of pay-roll preparation and staff development and training are 'driven' by the same causal factor: number of employees. Hence, they could be added together and for costing purposes, recovered via the number of employees as the single cost driver. There is likely to be a cost-benefit trade off between having too many cost pools/cost drivers which would make an ABC system too complex, cumbersome and expensive to run and too few, which would diminish the sought-for improvements in the accuracy of the linkage of products to the resources they consume.

Cooper[17] offers some guidance on the question of the number of cost drivers needed and how they should be selected. In relation to the complexity of the product mix (and bearing in mind a perceived level of required accuracy), it is suggested that consideration of three factors will help decide on the number of cost drivers needed, while avoiding 'unacceptable' distortions in product costs:

Product diversity   The degree to which products consume resources in different proportions. It is demonstrated that where a high degree of such diversity exists, then the use of a broad cost driver such as direct labour hours or machine hours, can introduce significant distortions.

Relative cost of activities   A measure of how much each activity costs as a percentage of the total cost of the production process; inaccurate tracing of a cost which is high on this score introduces potentially a correspondingly large distortion . . . 'if an activity accounts for 20 per cent of the cost of a particular product, then tracing twice as much of that activity will cause reported product costs to be 20 per cent too high, but if the activity accounts for only 0.2 per cent, then the distortion introduced will be only 0.2 per cent'.

Volume diversity   This factor arises when products are manufactured in batches of different sizes. Where one product is produced at a much higher volume level than another, then it is argued that production, order and shipping batch sizes will differ significantly. In this case also, it can be demonstrated that using the traditional volume-only based cost driver will distort the costs of activities not affected by volume when these costs are attributed to products: some products will be overcosted, others undercosted. Cooper refers to 'high intensity' and 'low intensity' products, to describe the relative amount of non-volume related resources consumed, for example, the number of inspection hours.

The process of how to allocate costs to cost pools and thence via cost drivers to product costs is not, however, one which can be reduced to the application of readily available formulae. Nor is it one which is likely to be able to cope with all known costing problems, though comments on this issue are deferred to the conclusion. Establishing an ABC system requires careful analysis and grouping of activities and costs, for example according to their nature: whether they are influenced by volume of activity or by other support activities such as ensuring quality, controlling material movements, demand forecasting and resource planning, etc.

Each stage of analysis is accomplished by reference to existing records and a formal procedure of questioning managers as to how and why a given quantity of a particular resource is required for the performance of a certain activity. For example, ascertain why a purchasing department may require a certain number of people to progress orders or check invoices.

This part of the introduction of ABC to a firm is also a part of the cost management aspect of ABC. Many practical difficulties are encountered here in ascertaining verifiable and realistic information, not least being achieving the required degree of co-operation from company personnel. In the Edford case study, Coates *et al.*[18] found the company had had to make a careful choice of which department to work with on the proposed introduction of ABC, bearing in mind whether the department was likely to be co-operative and positive in its attitude toward the exercise and whether it was also likely to be able to demonstrate to top management and other departments, the benefits to be realized from the introduction of ABC. In order to keep the exercise on as neutral a basis as possible, these introductory stages are frequently carried out by consultants.

Cost behaviour analysis

ABC is said to improve cost control by specifically focusing attention on how and why cost comes to be incurred, the efficiency with which an activity is carried out and the time period over which control can normally be exercised (assuming a non-crisis situation!). Cooper[19,20,21] suggests a refinement of the commonly adopted fixed : variable classification of short run costs as follows:

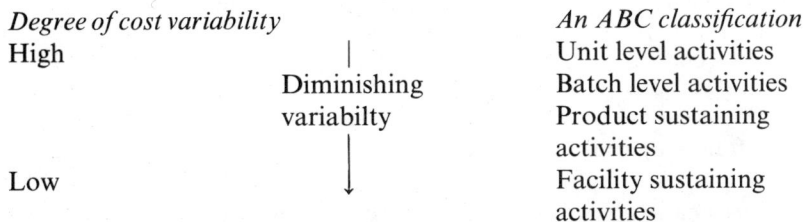

Degree of cost variability		*An ABC classification*
High		Unit level activities
	Diminishing	Batch level activities
	variabilty	Product sustaining activities
Low		Facility sustaining activities

The first and last categories in the classification list should correspond closely to those commonly thought of as containing variable and fixed costs such as direct material and plant management costs, respectively. However, the two intermediate categories are a refinement of this simple and rather rigid cost breakdown, stemming from taking an ABC approach. Batch sustaining activities include for example, set-ups, material movements purchase orders, whilst product sustaining activities include process engineering and product enhancement. This more extensive and penetrating cost analysis facilitates a more precise tracing of costs to products than would normally be achieved using the conventional short-term variable cost allocation methods for both batch and product sustaining activities, though problems will remain as before with facility sustaining activities.

The authors quote a case based on the machining shop of a large equipment manufacturer in support of an ABC analysis, where the company had allocated $13.38 of overhead to every 100 units of a simple drive shaft using a traditional overhead recovery system which employed three unit level bases: direct material cost, direct labour cost and machine hours . . . 'Underlying the cost system was the assumption that all activities were performed at the unit level and varied with the material $s, direct labour $s and machine hours being consumed. However, 40 per cent of the department's support costs were not used to produce products. Production of 8,000 shafts resulted in the recovery of $1,070 of overhead, but an ABC study showed that $1,700 of unit, batch and product sustaining resources were consumed.' Differences of this order are frequently cited in examples illustrating the impact of turning over to the ABC approach.

As an illustrative numerical example, the following illustration uses Question 1 of the CIMA June 1990 Management Accounting Control and Audit paper.

Question

XYZ plc manufactures four products, namely A, B, C and D, using the same plant and processes.
   The following information relates to a production period:

Product	Volume	Material cost per unit	Direct labour per unit	Machine time per unit	Labour cost per unit
A	500	£5	$\frac{1}{2}$ hour	$\frac{1}{4}$ hour	£3
B	5000	£5	$\frac{1}{2}$ hour	$\frac{1}{4}$ hour	£3
C	600	£16	2 hours	1 hour	£12
D	7000	£17	$1\frac{1}{2}$ hours	$1\frac{1}{2}$ hours	£9

Total production overhead recorded by the cost accounting system is analysed under the following headings:

Factory overhead applicable to machine-oriented activity is £37,424
Set-up costs are £4,355
The cost of ordering materials is £1,920
The cost of handling materials £7,580
The cost of administration for spare parts £8,600

These overhead costs are absorbed by products on a machine hour rate of £4.80 per hour, giving an overhead cost per product of:

A = £1.20
B = £1.20
C = £4.80
D = £7.20

However, investigation into the production overhead activities for the period reveals the following totals:

Product	Number of set-ups	Number of material orders	Number of times material was handled	Number of spare parts
A	1	1	2	2
B	6	4	10	5
C	2	1	3	1
D	8	4	12	4

You are required to:

(a) Compute an overhead cost per product using activity based costing, tracing overheads to production units by means of cost drivers.

(b) Comment briefly on the differences disclosed between overheads traced by the present system and those traced by activity based costing.

Commentary and solution

The question assumes the allocation of costs to various cost pools has already taken place, i.e., total costs for 'machine-orientated activity', set up costs, materials ordering, materials handling and administration for spare parts.

Essentially, the question then invited candidates to compare product costs using a single volume related cost driver – machine hours – with the selective approach of ABC using multiple cost drivers; finally, a comment on the differences was required.

In arriving at the product cost solution for the four products, A, B, C and D, new cost rates for the five activities are needed based on the given cost drivers. These are:

Machine hour rates	= £3.00 per machine hour
Set-up costs	= £256.18 per set-up
Material ordering costs	= £192.00 per material order
Material handling costs	= £280.74 per number of times material was handled
Spare parts administration costs	= £716.67 per part administered

It is worth considering the question of variability in relation to the above cost rates: they certainly cannot be regarded as variable costs in the same way that the total cost of direct material might be assumed to vary with output. They have to be regarded as budget rates, based on anticipated levels of the various activities, where a process of cost management has taken place or is expected to, to produce the total costs budgeted for each activity. Many of the support activities are unlikely to contain significant elements of truly (automatic) variable expense; so they will probably have to be managed to the levels required, fundamentally those which a business can afford and needs to support

The solution then proceeds to demonstrate one of the major claims for ABC, namely that utilizing volume based cost drivers alone will result in low volume products being undercosted and high volume products overcosted (i.e., both being within the same product mix):

Unit overhead cost structure

Product	Machine overheads £	Set-ups £	Material ordering £	Material handling £	Spares £	Total £	Old system £	Difference £
A	0.75	0.51	0.38	1.12	2.87	5.63	1.20	+ 4.43
B	0.75	0.31	0.15	0.56	0.72	2.49	1.20	+ 1.29
C	3.00	0.85	0.32	1.40	1.19	6.76	4.80	+ 1.96
D	4.50	0.29	0.11	0.48	0.41	5.79	7.20	− 1.41

The traditional system makes the false assumption that all overheads are related to volume and machine time. A and C are undercosted by the traditional system because it mis-allocates costs for small volume products. The activity based system recognizes the differences of relative input consumption between products, and traces the appropriate amount of input to each cost unit. Product B previously avoided its full share of overheads because of its low machine time, and may still do so if part of the £37,424 of machine-orientated overhead should be apportioned on some other basis.

Product D is overcosted because the traditional system loaded it with overheads attributable to activities concerned with A, B and C, as a result of using a volume based and machine-orientated rate, which failed to pay proper attention to activity costing.

Activity based management (ABM) and budgeting (ABB)

(Note: the terms activity based management and activity based cost management appear to be used interchangeably today, with the former appearing to be more widely adopted). Cost management was referred to in the previous section. It should be axiomatic that if product costing can be made more accurate, relevant and effective through the application of the ABC approach, then cost management and budgetary planning and control should be correspondingly capable of improvement. In many respects of course, ABC is a part of cost management in general, since the latter must be concerned with identifying how and why cost is incurred and how it can be monitored and controlled.

Criticisms of conventional cost management in practice generally refer to its narrow focus (for example, see Bellis-Jones and Develin 1992[22]); for instance, in manufacturing, emphasis has been on factory operations and over-simplistic, inadequate cost classifications such as the division of short-term costs into fixed and variable cost categories.

The concentration of attention on factory operations to the virtual exclusion of detailed analysis of selling, distribution and a whole range of other functional expenses, means not only the likely eventual distortion of product costs, but also an inability to manage the level of expenditure on these items effectively. Neglect of such costs and their associated activities may also have a knock-on effect on other expenses: Bellis-Jones and Develin[22] point out that an automobile industry study showed that 85 per cent of future unit product costs are determined by the end of the testing phase. Hence, there is a need to ensure that the various groups of people in departments such as design, purchasing and manufacture, work closely together in order that there is a full appreciation of the (cost) consequences of requirements being put forward and the decisions which are made.

As has been pointed out earlier, cost structures have been steadily changing over time due to factors such as changes in technology, conditions of employment, etc. The result has been a general increase in the proportion of indirect to direct (particularly, direct labour) expense, most noticeably in manufacturing. Costs, in the contexts of short-term planning and control, are widely categorized in conventional systems as fixed, variable, controllable and non-controllable. It is argued that the changes in cost structures have brought with them changes in the way costs behave; to stick rigidly and uncritically to unrevised cost categories/ classifications which have been in use for a long time will misdirect efforts at cost management as readily as lack of recognition of how true cost drivers distort product costs. Variable costs in particular are vulnerable to this in the short-run; direct labour is, in large measure, no longer related to volume of activity in a way which suggests that variation in the latter is automatically accompanied by proportionate increases or decreases in the former. Further, only a relatively small percentage of direct costs are likely to be controllable by management, in the sense of them being responsive to actions taken to secure an immediate change in their level (more especially a decrease).

Such action as may be taken by management will also generally require some time to become effective, for example, through achieving improvements in product design and manufacturing processes. The names given to different categories of cost can certainly be misleading if what is attributed to them is not kept constantly under review.

Cost management is based on a systematic process of continually searching for and quantifying the relationship between expenditure and the factor(s) which cause it to be incurred. Budgets are a mainly financial expression of revenue plans and the resources required to meet them: they should be based on efficient cost management.

However, budgetary planning and control as carried out in the conventional manner are nowadays widely criticized for reasons which go rather beyond inefficient cost management. Bellis-Jones[23] points to several widely perceived problems of conventional budgeting:

- A costly, burdensome routine.
- Reinforcing bad practice.
- 'Control' has become more of a 'constraint', suffocating management initiative.
- Managers settle too often for basing this year's budget on last year's.
- Budgets (as conventionally used) are poor at translating strategy into action.
- Conventional budgets overemphasize inputs at the expense of outputs.
- Non-financial performance measures not widely integrated into monthly performance reporting packages.
- Too inward looking – fail to recognize crucial role of cross-functional business processes.

Altogether, the budgetary planning and control process as it has been applied in the past, is seen as static and out of touch, not playing an effective role in today's business environment. The latter demands greater attention be paid to activities which drive cost, non-value adding activities, the fact that activities in departments are frequently driven by decisions taken at a management level higher than that of the budget holder, creating effective cross-functional linkages within the business, establishing relevant and effective performance measures, e.g., in relation to quality and customer service.

Activity based budgeting (ABB) is the name given to a refocused budgetary process, which incorporates the ideas/results of ABC and activity based cost management, and centres attention on planned output rather than building up budgets via extrapolations of historical inputs.

In this way, given that the purpose of budgeting is to determine resource requirements including investment needed to meet forecast customer demand (not solely 'quantity', but delivery, quality, etc.), Bellis-Jones[23] suggests the following outline scheme as appropriate to ABB:

Cost of resources supplied = Cost of resources used + Cost of excess capacity

Determining the left-hand side of the above equation, i.e., the people, equipment, premises required, is the function of budgeting. ABC is concerned with the right-hand side of the equation and therefore contributes to the budgeting of those activities which have cost drivers. In these cases, for individual cost/budget centres, the following equation may be used:

Forecast cost driver volume (a) × Cost driver unit cost (b) = Forecast activity cost (c)

The example is quoted where (a) is the number of new component designs and is the cost driver for a purchasing department negotiating with suppliers and is forecast for a given period to be 30; the cost driver unit cost is £2,360 per unit. Therefore:

$$\text{Forecast activity cost} = a \times b = 30 \times £2,360 = £70,800$$

Through the implementation of ABC, a clearer picture of how cost is generated and how it may be more effectively controlled is said to emerge, which develops data much more useful to budgetary planning and control than is considered to be the case in much of conventional budgetings.

Activity based management and decision making

Marginal, relevant and incremental cost analyses are concepts widely regarded as valuable aids to short-term decision making. It is claimed by Kaplan *et al.*[24] that there are dangers associated with their application in cases where spare physical production capacity is presently available, because used indiscriminately, they may lead to future capacity problems. Kennedy[25] takes up this point to demonstrate that ABM can be seen as a 'useful complement' to the relevant cost approach to decision making, since it would show more explicitly how short-term decisions will impact on resource requirements, particularly service support resources. The long term interests of a company are not necessarily best served by taking an incremental series of short-term decisions, though individually, each purports to show a contribution to profit. To quote Kennedy, the crux of the argument is that

> . . . 'where spare capacity exists in both production and support services any incremental work undertaken to utilize this spare physical capacity will result in very few incremental costs to the organization (due to their short term fixed nature) . . . nevertheless, the demands placed on support departments in servicing this incremental business may be disproportionate to those placed on the departments in the normal mix of activities'.

Only when applied to a 'single, unique problem' could the traditional relevant cost approach be relied on as an unambiguous decision-making tool.

If managers do not understand the relationship between particular orders and the demands these place on support services, the result could be infeasible production plans and/or unsatisfied customers, since some for example, may now find their orders being received late. Progress chasing, the old evil associated with unsound production plans, could well emerge leading to further dislocations and inefficiency. Kennedy maintains that 'fundamentally flawed' production plans should not occur 'unwittingly' where ABM is in place, since the underlying drivers of support activities would provide an understanding of various courses of action. In the long term, if there is no clear understanding of the relationship between production and support activities, then a production plan which specifies a product mix which places a disproportionate demand on certain activities, may well result in resources being diverted toward relieving these, rather than being used more effectively elsewhere.

There are possible links here with more formal contribution analyses rather than the simple selections based on single limiting factor analysis and to more complex schemes of cost allocation, based on the reciprocal cost method of distributing service department costs to production departments and subsequently on to products.

A general caveat then with respect to the behaviour of costs for decision making in ABC: it is clearly wrong to assume that traceability also indicates costs are avoidable in the sense they may be taken to be in marginal costing; the nature of the cost does not change just because it has been traced through an ABC analysis – a sunk cost such as depreciation remains a sunk cost however it may be traced. The question of avoidability of cost depends on the decision, the nature of the cost, the time span which the decision encompasses and possible interactions between other business sectors and products: a more complex but also more realistic decision-making scenario.

Business process re-engineering (BPR): a note

ABM and BPR are two closely related management tools. Hixon[26] distinguishes them on the basis that BPR deals with core processes only and is generally one-off, whilst ABM should be ongoing and is the 'management and control of enterprise performance using activity based information as the primary means of decision support'. A catch phrase sometimes quoted as indicative of the objectives of BPR is that it is about doing the right things right. ABM also addresses the question of ensuring the efficiency with which activities are performed and eliminating activities which do not create value; in this sense there seems little to differentiate ABM from BPR. Hixon believes that 'true' ABM has yet been undertaken by more than a few organizations, 'since more often than not it is used as a one-off performance improvement tool'. Semantics aside, both appear to aim for improvement of business practices through radical rethinking of how activities are performed, which may involve investment in new technologies in order to reduce costs, but which also must have regard to the integrated nature of the way a business conducts itself.

Conclusion

There are many useful insights and other benefits which are likely to emerge from a serious attempt to evaluate and implement ABC, whether it is regarded as old ideas in new clothing or not. Horngren[27] (despite misgivings!) credits ABC as having had a number of 'welcome influences on research and practice'. He lists the following:

- ABC has generated enormous enthusiasm about its basic ideas. Moreover, researchers are studying the actual cost accounting practices of companies in vastly greater numbers than before.
- ABC is the most highly-developed and expensive attempt yet to identify and link causes (cost drivers) with effects (changes in costs). It extends the cost accounting literature that has long warned about how broad averages may mislead.
- ABC entreats us to choose cost allocation bases with great care. In particular, we should be alert that costs are driven by many factors other than the volume of units produced or sold. Examples of non-volume cost drivers are the numbers of set-ups, engineering change orders, material movements, and products components.
- ABC has correctly advocated the use of multiple cost allocation bases that are appropriate cost drivers. ABC has criticized the overuse of direct labour as a cost allocation base, particularly when it is used as the lone base for applying indirect costs to products.
- ABC has stressed that executives manage costs by overseeing activities instead of products. The accounting for costs by activities highlights the interdependencies among activities in many departments or functional areas. For example, the total costs of a company may be affected by how design, engineering, manufacturing, and marketing activities interrelate.
- ABC has emphasized that product costs are affected by all functions in the value chain, not just by manufacturing alone. Inventory costs are incomplete measures of product costs for decision making.

- ABC has alerted managers to the existence of cross-subsidization among the product costs where there is a wide range of operating activities and a wide range of products. That is, case studies have demonstrated that existing cost systems using broad averages frequently load indirect costs too lightly on low-volume products and too heavily on high-volume products.
- ABC advocates are reluctantly starting to admit that the cost-benefit test must be met and that the complexities of a detailed ABC system may inhibit its use as an ongoing system. Mitchell[28] believes a 'strong case' can be made for ABC beyond the more cynical view that it represents an increase in the complexity of costing and management accounting by introducing an ever greater extension of the process of cost allocation. He also rejects the idea that ABC could be thought of as a 'cosmetic change', useful to meet pressures for 'new information which may point to a means of resolving difficulties'. He considers it is recognized that ABC has been making a positive, practical contribution to management accounting and discusses this with respect to applications in product costing for stock control, decision making, cost control and performance measurement.

Nevertheless, as Bromwich and Bhimani[29,30] point out, there are a number of costing issues which are not really resolvable by ABC, for example, that of shared inputs, where knowledge or specialized equipment is used by several products. Where several products receive inputs under these circumstances, it will not always be possible to find a cost driver sufficiently discriminatory to attach the appropriate amounts to individual products. They state that certain costs '. . . will not be amenable to ABC analysis for a variety of reasons specific to an enterprise and will, remain unattributable to the production of given goods and services. ABC as an accounting technique cannot overcome this problem fully'.

Other costs are linked directly to decisions and are discretionary up to the point in time a decision on expenditure is made, for example, research and development, and marketing expenditures. Once made though, these decisions result in expenditures becoming committed and hence in the normal course of events, unavoidable, for instance, a contract being signed with an agency to create a general advertising programme (not product specific) or contracts for the development of corporate facilities. They cannot be directly traced to products via activities.

One of the main weaknesses of traditional costing emphasized by ABC, the tendency in a mix of products to overcost the high volume and undercost the low volume items, may signal the wrong decision if the conclusion is to curtail the product range by eliminating at least some of the low volume items: the competitive strength of the company could be partly dependent on it being able to supply a wide range of products. Nonetheless, this is only a warning not to take action on information without a full appreciation of all the consequences – a warning which applies universally, not just to ABC.

It is valuable, however, to have a perspective on the way costing and management accounting have developed over time. Such a perspective provides a means to help judge the likely benefits or otherwise which it is suggested 'new' ideas will generate. Why, for example, has the at one time widely canvassed idea of zero-based budgeting apparently faded out of view, with relatively few claims for successful implementation, at least in the UK. Embracing 'new' ideas as they come along, without an ability to assess what they are really offering can be an expensive business. It also means it is not possible to apply the ultimate test of value, that of cost-benefit, impartially. As a last example on this point, at the 1991 European Accounting Association Conference, Coenenberg[30] stated that while he was an enthusiast for ABC, it was a system in practice in Germany since 1925 under the title of 'Prozesskostenrechnung'. Despite this, he also appears to recognize certain 'new' aspects in the modern presentation of ABC ideas (Coenenberg and Fischer).[31] Finally, it must be remembered there are a host of other factors with an influence on the kind of accounting techniques adopted in practice, for example: behavioural, organizational and political. Altogether, ABC, ABM and BPR are techniques still in the process of evolution so far as application in practice is concerned, though there is substantive theoretical appreciation of the processes themselves and their potential advantages and drawbacks for firms attempting to introduce them.

References

1. Johnson, H.T. and Kaplan, R.S., *Relevance Lost: the Rise and Fall of Management Accounting*, Harvard Business School Press, 1987.
2. Kaplan, R.S., Yesterday's accounting undermines production, *Harvard Business Review*, July/August 1984.
3. Kaplan, R.S., One cost system is not enough, *Harvard Business Review*, January/February 1988.
4. Cooper, R., Does your company need a new cost system?, *Journal of Cost Management*, Spring, 1987.
5. Cooper, R. and Kaplan, R.S., How cost accounting systematically distorts product costs, *Management Accounting*, London, April 1988.
6. Longman, D. and Schiff, M., *Practical Distribution Cost Analysis*, Irwin, 1995.
7. Staubus, G., *Activity Costing and Input–Output Accounting*, Irwin, 1971.
8. Piper, J. and Walley, P., Testing ABC logic, *Management Accounting*, London, September 1990.
9. Cooper, R., Explicating the logic of ABC, *Management Accounting*, London, November 1990.
10. Piper, J. and Walley, P., ABC relevance not found, *Management Accounting*, London, March 1991.
11. Innes, J. and Mitchell, F., ABC: A Survey of CIMA Members, *Management Accounting*, London, October 1991.
12. Innes, J. and Mitchell, F., ABC: A follow-up survey of CIMA members, *Management Accounting*, London, July/August 1995.
13. Innes, J. and Mitchell, F., A survey of activity based costing in the UK's largest companies, *Management Accounting Research*, Vol. 6, No. 2, June 1995.

14. Innes, J and Mitchell, F., *Activity based cost management: a case study of development and implementation*, CIMA, London, 1991.
15. Cooper, R., Implementing an Activity-Based Costing System, *Journal of Cost Management for the Manufacturing Industry*, Spring 1990.
16. Cooper, R. and Kaplan R., *The design of cost management systems*, Prentice Hall International, 1991, Chapter 7.
17. Cooper, R., The rise of activity based costing. Part 3: How many cost drivers do you need, and how do you select them?, *Journal of Cost Management for the Manufacturing Industry*, Vol. 2, No. 4, Winter 1989.
18. Coates, J., Rickwood, C. and Stacey, R., *Management Accounting in Practice*, CIMA, 1991.
19. Cooper, R.,Cost classifications in unit based and activity based manufacturing cost systems, *Journal of Cost Management*, Fall, 1990.
20. Cooper, R. and Kaplan, R., Profit priorities from Activity Based Costing, *Harvard Business Review*, May/June 1991.
21. Cooper, R., Activity Based Costing for improved product costing. In Brinker, B. (ed.) *Handbook of Cost Management*, New York., Warren, Graham & Lamont, 1994.
22. Bellis-Jones, R. and Develin, N., *Activity Based Cost Management*, Institute of Chartered Accountants, 1992.
23. Bellis-Jones, R., Budgeting and cost management = a route to continuous improvement, *Management Accounting*, London, April 1992.
24. Kaplan, R., Shank, J., Horngren, C., Boer, G., Ferrara, W. and Robinson, M., Contribution margin analysis no longer relevant/Strategic cost management: the new paradigm, *Journal of Management Accounting Research*, Fall, 1990.
25. Kennedy, A., Activity-based management and short-term relevant cost: clash or complement? *Management Accounting*, London, June 1995; Activity-based management and short-term relevant cost?, 2, *Management Accounting*, London, July 1995.
26. Hixon, M., Activity-based management: its purpose and benefits', *Management Accounting*, London, June 1995.
27. Horngren, C., Reflections on activity based accounting in the United States. Wissenschaft und Praxis – Gedankenaustauch zu actuellan Fragen. *Zeitschrift für Betriebswirtschaftliche Forschung.* Vertagsgruppe Handelsblatt. Düsseldorf, Frankfurt. March 1992.
28. Mitchell, F., A commentary on the applications of activity based costing, *Management Accounting Research*, 5, 1994.
29. Bromwich, M. and Bhimani, A., Management Accounting: Evolution not Revolution, Research Series, CIMA, 1989; Bromwich, M. and Bhimani, A., Management Accounting: Pathways to Progress. CIMA, 1994.
30. Coenenberg, A.G., Respondent to keynote lecture on activity based costing by R. Kaplan, 14th Annual Congress of the European Accounting Association, Maastricht, Holland, April 1991.
31. Coenenberg, A.G., and Fischer, T.M., Prozesskostenrechnung Strategische Neuorientierung in der Kostenrechnung, *Die Betriebswirtschaft*, Vol. 1, pp. 21–37, 1991.

Questions

1   'ABC is still at a relatively early stage of its development and its implications
for process control may in the final analysis be more important than its
product costing implications. It is a good time for every organization to
consider whether or not ABC is appropriate to its particular circumstances.,
J. Innes and F. Mitchell, *Activity Based Costing, A Review with Case Studies*,
CIMA, 1990.

You are required to:
    (a)   Contrast the feature of organizations which would benefit from ABC
    with those which would not.
    (b)   Explain in what ways ABC may be used to manage costs, and the
    limitations of these approaches.
    (c)   Explain and discuss the use of target costing to control product costs.
                                               (MCA, November 1991)

2   Many authors, e.g. Kaplan and Cooper; Johnson and Kaplan; Cooper, have
criticized the way in which 'traditional' management accounting systems have
attempted to allocate costs to products. Cooper is widely credited with
proposing the system of activity based costing (ABC) as an alternative
approach. In this system, 'cost drivers' attempt to link costs to the scope of
output rather than the scale of output. As a result, it is considered that ABC
will provide less arbitrary costs for decision making. You are required to:
    (a)   Discuss the criticisms of traditional management accounting which have
given rise to the idea of 'activity based costing'.
    (b)   Explain the meaning of the term 'cost driver' and discuss how the
concept may be considered to differ from ones previously employed to
distribute overhead costs to products.

3   Johnson or Kaplan argue that the 'primacy' of financial reporting creates
problems for the provision of accounting information of use to management.
It is claimed that the demands of financial reporting distorts management
information because the underlying generators of cost are not recognized or
revealed by financial accounts. You are required to:
    (a)   Discuss the above statement and explain how the requirements of
financial reporting may distort management (accounting) information.
    (b)   Apart from the problem of financial reporting referred to in (a), do you
consider traditional costing methods employed in business to obtain
departmental and product costs are generally suited to its requirements for
planning and control purposes? Give reasons for your answer.

4   Cost accountants must escape the confined thinking that costs vary with the
changes in the volume of production. There are many costs in the plants that
vary not with the volume of production but with other transactions/factors.
The reason why just-in-time (JIT) is so effective in reducing costs is that it
reduces such transactions. You are required to:
    (a)   Compare a traditional absorption costing system with the kind of

system being advocated in the above statement, explaining why it is thought 'cost accountants should escape the confined thinking . . .' etc.

(b)   What problems would be likely to be encountered in making the transition from a traditional absorption costing system to the new approach.

5   In the context of ABC, discuss the issues and problems that arise as a result of interaction amongst resources.

6   Bromwich and Bhimani state that '. . . activity based accounting cannot ensure the comprehensive traceability of costs to products'. What are the grounds for this statement and does it suggest a serious flaw in the case for introducing ABC into an organization?

7   Given that activity based costing succeeds in improving the traceability of costs to products, managers should nonetheless take care in using this information in relevant cost analysis for making short-term decisions. Explain why.

8   Compare and contrast the following quotations:
   (i)   'The usefulness of allocated overheads arises not from a need to satisfy costing objectives but for facilitating control' (Bromwich and Bhimani).
   (ii)   'I can't stand cost apportionments, they generate a lot of heat but not much light' (company finance director).

7

7

Assessing segmental performance

Objectives, rewards, measurement and motivation

One of the most intriguing aspects of business operations in recent years has been the attempt by management to motivate employees at all levels of the organization towards achievement of corporate organizational goals. Such approaches usually centre around formal performance appraisal reviews requiring the establishment of performance objectives and related criteria. Typically, in the UK and USA at least, these are reinforced by the application of reward systems, often of significant size in relation to basic wage rates. The application of these approaches to motivation, applied to corporate directors, have received considerable attention in the press in the 1990s, due perhaps to the sheer size of some incentive rewards and the lack of transparency of the merit and fairness of the incentive. The requirement therefore exists for the development of appropriate feedback mechanisms and performance criteria in relation to both individual managers and the units in which they serve.

Figure 7.1 attempts to illustrate the complex interrelationships between goals of investors, the corporation and individual managers, reward systems, performance evaluation systems and aspects of behaviour within and without organizations.

The distinctions between corporate goals and those of shareholders, directors, management at each level of the organization and employees, should be familiar to the reader. Naturally, as corporate goals are established by senior management, a greater congruence is likely to exist between corporate goals and those individual goals of managers than with the goals of other stakeholders in the business. That is not to say that corporate goals simply represent the agreed common goals of senior managers, for it is likely that senior management's perception of other stakeholders' expectations and the expectations of those external to the business, such as financiers and the stock exchange, will be considered and incorporated.

The linking of personal rewards of managers to their achievement of some or all parts of the corporate objectives of an organization is, as indicated earlier, a most popular approach to the motivation of managers at all levels. The establishment of such reward systems is dependent upon the establishment of suitable and relevant information systems and evaluation measures.

While formal evaluation systems might be expected to reflect the quantification of corporate goals, they frequently also incorporate elements of both an individual manager's personal goals and those goals assumed as necessary to meet external

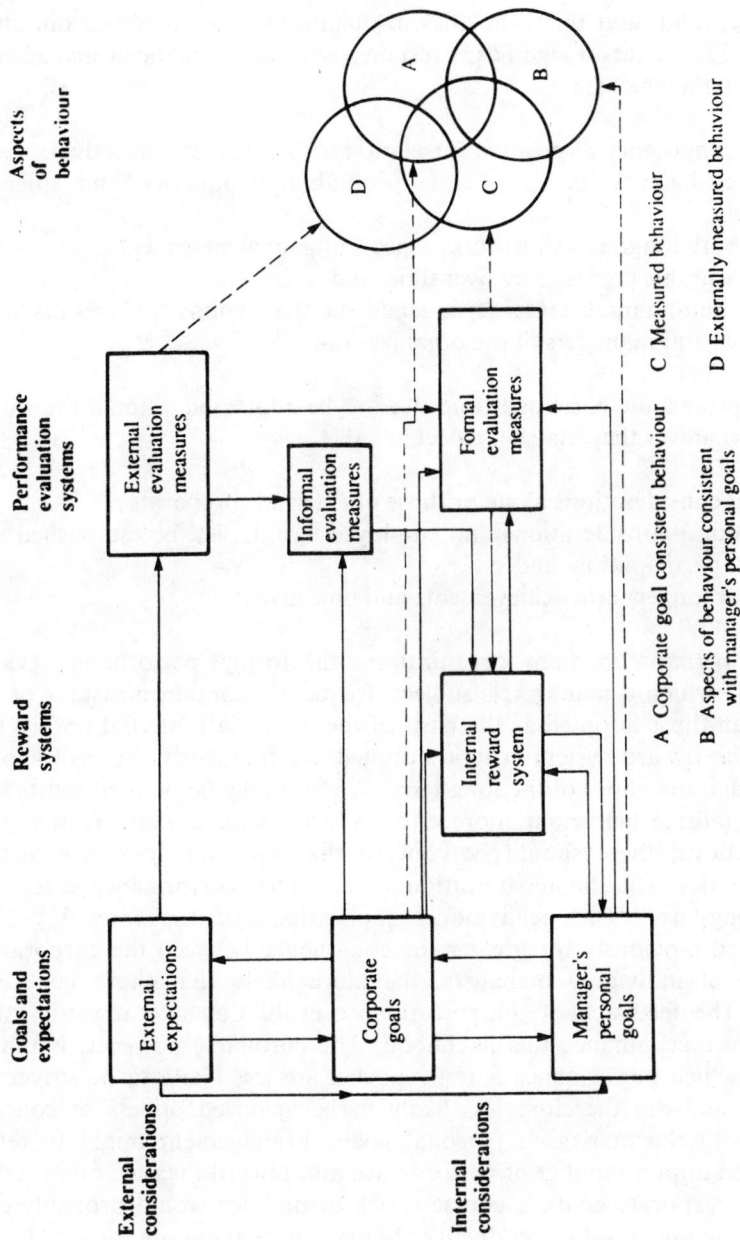

Figure 7.1 *Goal, reward, evaluation and behaviour relationships*

Aspects of behaviour

A Corporate goal consistent behaviour

B Aspects of behaviour consistent with manager's personal goals

C Measured behaviour

D Externally measured behaviour

Goals and expectations

Reward systems

Performance evaluation systems

External considerations

Internal considerations

External expectations

Corporate goals

Manager's personal goals

External evaluation measures

Informal evaluation measures

Internal reward system

Formal evaluation measures

expectations. The reliance upon financial or accounting measures as the basis for most evaluation criteria probably stems from the nature of corporate objectives on the one hand, and the difficulties in quantifying non-financial objectives on the other. This places a significant responsibility upon financial management to identify criteria which:

1   have a congruence or positive correlation with corporate objectives,
2   strike a balance between cost, profitability, liquidity and quantitative measures,
3   reflect both long- and short-term aspects of goal achievements,
4   are measurable consistently over time, and
5   have a minimum of interdependency on the actions and results of other segments and managers of the organization.

In this respect, some basic questions need to be addressed. Should the yardsticks adopted, whatever they may be, reflect:

1   internal considerations alone or those of external comparators;
2   behavioural considerations and employee morale, i.e. be established with or without participation; and
3   short- or longer-term achievements and objectives?

Curiously perhaps, in many organizations the formal performance evaluation methods to which a manager is subject, frequently contain measures of greater variety than those adopted as the basis of the (financial) internal reward system. Further, the reward system criteria adopted are frequently those of short-term measures and not those of the long-term. While it may be pointed out that quick rewards reinforce behaviour more effectively than those that are remote from specific actions, there should be concern that such an approach encourages suboptimization, e.g. the maximization of short-term performance at the expense of the long-term. The behavioural implications of the foregoing are not insignificant. Obviously the greater the congruence between the corporate goals and those of individual managers, the more likely that those goals will be achieved. The feedback of the performance evaluation and reward systems is likely to further enhance this likelihood. The corollary, however, is that goals regarding which performance is not reported are less likely to be striven for by managers, and are therefore less likely to be achieved, unless of course they coincide with the manager's personal goals. Management might therefore be tempted to adopt a number of performance and reward measures that reflect the totality of corporate goals, a course which in practice would probably be both impracticable and counter-productive. Management therefore faces a dilemma – the desire for a comprehensive, multi-faceted measure on the one hand and an easily understood, attention directing measure on the other – a choice of some significance to the success of an organization.

Centralization and decentralization

Centralization describes situations where the senior managers within an organization retain the authority to make decisions, with relatively few decision-making powers delegated to lower managerial levels. Such a situation may exist within small businesses with functional organizational structures (see Figure 7.2) where major decisions of a particular specialist nature are made by the appropriate functional head.

Decentralization exists where the authority to make decisions is delegated to lower levels of the organization. This usually is necessary where an organization's growth and complexity reach the point at which centralized decision making is no longer practicable, either economically or logistically.

The degree of decentralization adopted will depend upon the balance senior management makes between the perceived advantages and disadvantages in their particular circumstances.

Advantages of decentralization

Specialization

A manager may be responsible for a smaller and less diverse part of the organization than a manager in a centralized firm, and is likely therefore to have more detailed and specialized knowledge. This should improve the quality of decision making.

Timeliness

The spreading of decision making more thinly between managers should result in quicker and perhaps better results. Further, senior managers' time is released for more important strategic decision making.

Motivation

The delegation of authority is likely to have positive motivational impacts. The 'freedom' to make decisions which affect managers' personal performance is combined with the increased status this authority implies. Commitment to and responsibility assumed for decisions made are increased.

Personnel development

The devolution of authority provides an opportunity for managers to demonstrate their abilities both as managers and decision makers. Senior management is able to judge the suitability of junior management for more senior posts, without running the risk that a bad decision would be disastrous for the organization.

Segmental performance comparisons

The identification of separable parts of an organization with responsible managers enables each segment to be separately evaluated and compared against internal or external criteria.

Disadvantages of decentralization

Judging by the growth of decentralization in businesses, the disadvantages cannot be considered as weighty as the advantages. These are nevertheless significant and should not be too easily discounted by management. Disadvantages are believed to be:

Dysfunctional decision making

The opportunities for suboptimal behaviour are considerable, i.e. where the manager improves his or her own performance at the expense of the organization as a whole. This is particularly likely to occur when there is a lack of goal congruence between a manager and the organization.

Managerial rivalry

Managers may compete with each other in order to impress senior management, rather than working together for the good of the organization as a whole.

Loss of control

Senior management may lose control of the organization and, worse still, be unaware of this loss. Others may feel uncomfortable if they delegated authority.

Increased cost of control

The cost of management information systems to allow senior management to retain control of the organization and check that lower levels of management are using their delegated authority wisely can be high. There must be a danger of a costly bureaucracy developing purely to control subordinate management.

Lack of competent management

Can senior management select and/or train enough junior and middle managers of sufficient calibre to allow it to delegate the necessary decision making authority without loss of decision quality?

Risk orientations

To what extent will junior management exhibit similar risk orientations to that of their senior management? Might their lower seniority level discourage them from taking the risks seniors would like them to and hence ignore potentially profitable investments? On the other hand the reverse may be even more disadvantageous for the organization, i.e. a risk taken by a junior manager might have severe repercussions for the organization.

Diseconomies

Some decisions are best made centrally, perhaps because of economies of scale, the commonality of decisions or the sheer importance of the matter. The raising of finance, for example, is rarely delegated by senior management, even though control of it once it is raised may be delegated.

Divisionalization and segmentalization

Few organizations are totally centralized or decentralized. However, it would be wrong to equate centralization with small functional organizational structures. There are a number of very substantial companies with highly centralized organizations. Examples would include the major banks, many large retailers and certain governmental organizations.

The logical extension of the decentralization concept is the divisionalization of a business. This implies the segmenting of the total business into two or more (relatively) autonomous parts under separate management, each being responsible for its own corporate objectives and, in particular, profit performance (see Figure 7.2). Such an approach should, it is argued, enable large and/or complex businesses to gain the advantages of decentralization without the disadvantages. Of course decentralization can take a variety of forms between the extremes of functional and divisional organizational structures. Indeed the concept of segmentalization is applied in many groups to many levels of the business: frequently even relatively small parts of an organization are treated as if they were separate quasi-autonomous businesses. Generalizations can rarely be drawn. The degrees of centralization adopted by businesses, its breadth and depth within and across the organization and the amounts of responsibility devolved to each level are as various and as variable as there are organizations. A divisionalized structure is probably most suited, however, to businesses with a number of diverse activities where each can be identified as separable and independent.

Alternative bases for divisionalization

There are a variety of ways in which businesses might logically segment their operations. The more common of these are indicated below.

Markets and customers

It is argued that one of the most critical ingredients of success is the ability to identify and serve market needs. Many firms today therefore create separate divisions specializing in particular areas of the market or for particular types of customer. Thus a large engineering group might create separate divisions specializing in such different industry sectors as automotive, marine and aeronautic: or a service company might establish divisions specializing in commercial, industrial and governmental work.

A simple functional organizational business structure:

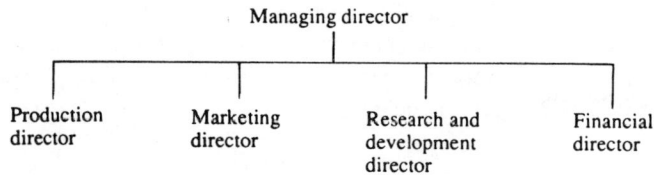

Managing director

| Production director | Marketing director | Research and development director | Financial director |

A simple divisional organizational business structure:

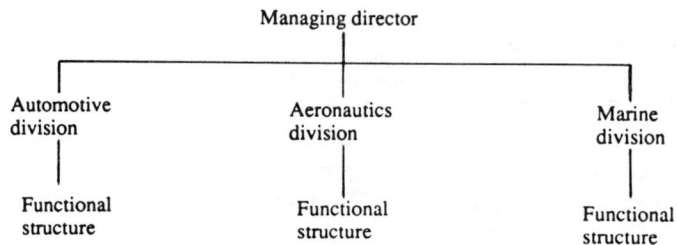

Managing director

| Automotive division | Aeronautics division | Marine division |

| Functional structure | Functional structure | Functional structure |

Figure 7.2 *Functional and divisionalized organizational structures*

Products or product groups

Where the products or services of a business are very different, requiring different business and operational skills, divisionalization by types of product or service would seem appropriate. Thus a manufacturing organization might distinguish between foundry, metal fabrication and electronics divisions, even if they might have, for example, some customers in common.

Technological

If the technological processes of making perhaps very different types of products, for very different types of customers, are similar, it would not be illogical to keep such processes together as one operation. This might occur, for example, where there are joint products such as in sugar refining where outputs are sold as animal feed, industrial sweeteners and as refined sugar to retail outlets.

Geographical

Segmentalization along geographical lines is perhaps the most common form of divisionalization, particularly within internationally oriented businesses. Divisions may be, for example, European, American, Asian, Australasian and Middle-Eastern, the European division being further split between say, the UK, Germany, France and other EU countries and non-EU countries. The UK could be further

Group A

```
                         Group A
           ┌───────────────┼───────────────┐
      Aeronautics      Automotive        Marina
           ┌───────────────┼───────────────┐
       America          Europe        Asia and
                                      Australasia
                          │
           ┌──────────┬───┴──────┬──────────┐
          UK       France     Germany     Italy
           │          │           │          │
       Products   Products    Products   Products
       ABCD       BCD         ABCD       ACD
```

```
                         Group B
           ┌──────────┬───┴──────┬──────────────┐
                                            Overseas
       Automotive Industrial  Foundry   ┌──────┼──────┐
           │          │           │   Europe America
       Products   Products   Products           Asia and
                                                 Australasia
```

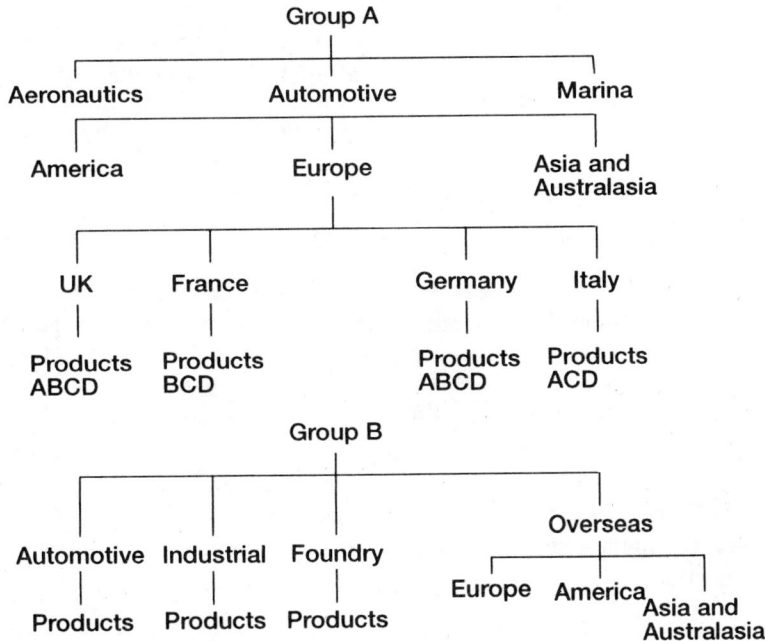

Figure 7.3   *Examples of mixed divisionalized bases*

segmented, perhaps between Scotland, N. Ireland, Wales, and North, South, East and West England. As business and competition cross national boundaries, the need to specialize in particular regions becomes increasingly important: the differences in social demands, culture, language, business ethos, law, etc. effectively demand that large organizations be prepared to segment geographically whenever practicable.

Of course, many large groups of companies segmentalize by means of more than one of these bases, either at the same hierarchical level of the business or using different bases at differing levels. Figure 7.3 gives examples. Group A is segmented at the highest level by market, at the next two levels by geographical region (continent and nations in which operations are centred) and then by type of product/product group. This approach is not untypical of many large multinational businesses manufacturing and selling a wide range of products. The example of Group B is of a large UK engineering business whose main divisions are separated by means of three different bases. In this specific case the foundry division provides products for both automotive and industrial divisions, as well as for customers outside the group, in these and other industries. As these were a significant proportion of group output, it was decided to retain foundry as a separate division. However, the overseas automotive and industrial divisions were deemed too small to warrant each having a separate representation and organization overseas. The amalgamation of these interests into the overseas division enabled local management selling in diverse markets to be more efficient. As overseas sales increase, however, pressure is being exerted to split representation again.

Observers of large businesses will be aware of the almost continual change of divisional/segmental structures of some companies, reflecting, for example, changes in the prosperity of different business sectors, a realignment for improved efficiency or perhaps a political power struggle within the hierarchy of the senior management.

Segments large and small

Although terminology is used very variously and loosely in business, the term 'divisions' is generally used to indicate the first or higher levels of segmentalizations of a large business. However, decentralization of some significance frequently operates in lower levels, with businesses being effectively treated as being just (smaller) subsets of a larger division – perhaps with different objectives, etc., but subsets all the same. As many of the approaches to performance measurement of large and small segments of an organization tend to be very similar, the following chapters will use the term 'segment' to imply any part of a business, be it the highest segment/division or the lowest, which a business wishes to assess separately.

Segments of management

One further matter must be addressed before alternative performance measures are examined. The foregoing has considered the segmentalization of a business, which might imply that management wishes to concentrate its controls in that direction. Discerning readers, however, will have realized that each segment of a business must have a manager responsible for it and that senior management would wish to measure the performance of segment managers separately and perhaps in a different way from that of the unit itself. After all, the manager of a successful segment which happens to operate in an area of high economic buoyancy might well not have performed that well himself and on the other hand a manager of a relatively unsuccessful segment might have performed miracles in saving the segment from abject failure. Further, it could and perhaps should be argued that while historic performance measurement may be of value in the evaluation of management, it can be of little relevance to the evaluation of the segment as such.

After all, the value of a segment is dependent not on its past performances but on its realizable potential, which can only be evaluated on an ad hoc, future-oriented basis.

In practice, however, common performance measures can be and frequently are applied to the evaluation of both the segment and the responsible manager. For this reason, while recognizing that most performance measures are directed at the measurement of management, such measures will be considered in general before distinctions are drawn as to their adoption and relevance to segments and managers.

Responsibility centres

The term 'responsibility centre' relates to the situation where managers are made responsible for the performance of some aspect of the business's operations. Further, the term implies that (a) the responsibilities and the criteria by which performance will be measured will be clearly stated, and (b) the requisite and necessary authority will be delegated. Although responsibility centres are usually synonymous with segments of the business, this is not a prerequisite. While the concept of responsibility centres is a simple one, the identification of clearly separate responsibilities is some times very difficult. Ideally, allocated responsibilities should not overlap those of other managers nor the decisions of one manager affect the results of another: likewise the measurement criteria should reflect that manager's actions over aspects which that manager can control. In practice, interrelationships and interdependencies in business are frequently such that the isolation of one responsibility centre from another is virtually impossible.

The essence of responsibility centres is that managers are responsible for the outputs of their centre in relation to the inputs into it. Management would therefore logically expect performance criteria to relate, as far as possible, the outputs to the inputs in some way appropriate to the operations of the responsibility centre.

Accounting approaches to this problem are to treat activity as one (or more) of the following:

- Cost centre.
- Revenue centre.
- Profit centre.
- Investment centre.
- Budget centre.

Cost centres

Cost centres are suitable in situations where a manager is responsible for the control of cost levels (whether or not there are revenue responsibilities), in relation to a given output. Cost centres can therefore be applied in a wide range of circumstances from large segments or divisions as a whole to any sub-segment of them down to the smallest responsibility centre to which costs are attributable. The rationale would be to identify some suitable expression of output of the cost centre to relate to the cost, so that unit costs may be determined. Trends in these unit costs, perhaps analysed by elements of expense, may be examined to stress cost accountability. Alternatively, unit costs may be compared with those of similar cost centres either elsewhere within the organization or outside.

Sometimes the outputs of cost centres are either not measurable or bear little direct relation to the expenditures. Examples might include research and development and many administrative departments, such as accounting, industrial relations and the secretariat. Such cost centres are sometimes referred to as discretionary expense centres and are usually measured by the amount of cost expenditure in relation to previous years, expectations or as a percentage of a general indication of activity, such as sales incomes.

Revenue centres

Revenue centres are principally intended to be applied to marketing and selling operations where the manager's responsibilities relate to the generation of income whether or not there are attributable costs. Such costs could be treated as a separate cost centre if so desired, although it is not uncommon to net these two elements, creating a 'revenue/expense centre', where the aim is to generate revenues but where some expenses will necessarily be incurred. Ideally, in an analogous manner to the calculation of unit cost rates for cost centres, revenues (as a measure of output) would be compared to related inputs and resultant earnings rates calculated. Examples might include sales per representative or sales per marketing £ expended. Such rates might then be compared with trends or past experience or other comparable revenue centres within or outside the organization.

Profit centres

Profit centres are applicable where the responsibility is to control both revenues and costs. Thus such a responsibility centre requires a diversity of managerial abilities – the skill to identify what will sell, to whom and at what price; to operate or produce efficiently; know what to make and how; to optimize resource utilizations, etc. – to operate a profit-seeking business effectively.

The term 'profit centre' is usually limited to situations where the manager does not have responsibility for the level of investment in the centre. In these instances profit levels would be related to such factors as sales outputs, cost, machine or labour inputs and these rates compared with trends over time or against other similar profit centres.

The advantage of the profit centre approach is that it can be applied to any profit-seeking activity, whatever the nature of the goods or services being produced and/or sold. It could therefore be used as a basis for comparison of apparently disparate activities.

Investment centres

Investment centres are profit centres where the responsibility is for profit and the related investment, i.e. both fixed and working capital. In such cases it would be expected that, in addition to the profit centre measures described above, profit would be related to the capital invested in the business, e.g. return on capital employed (ROCE/ROI) or measured as a profit after the cost of the capital employed (i.e. a residual income approach).

The investment-centre approach is popular today, presumably because the centre managers can be treated as if they were the managing directors or chief executives of the segment, as if it were an autonomous unit and not part of a larger organization. In practice the managers of most profit centres treated as being investment centres have some control over their working capital even if not over their longer-term capital.

Budget centres

Some might consider it inappropriate to discuss budget centres under the framework of responsibility centres. After all, budget centres are usually considered in the context of budgetary control. However, the application of budgetary yardsticks is so interwoven into the fabric of cost, revenue, profit and investment-centre approaches that to neglect it would be fundamentally wrong.

Budget centres, a slightly different concept to cost, revenue, profit and investment centres, compare actual performances with the budget for the same thing and the resulting variances are analysed with a view to identifying the need for (correcting) actions and to stress the need for control and accountability with the budgeted parameters. As such, budget centres are applicable very widely. Actual and budgeted performances are compared and thus budget centres can be applied to cost, revenue, profit and investment centres as well as being applied in their own right, i.e. where the performances are not measured in monetary terms at all but in such physical measures as labour efficiency and productivity rates, or visits, orders or new customers per sales representative. This topic is further covered in Chapter 9.

Selection of centre bases

As far as possible, segments of a business should be treated on as natural a responsibility basis as possible, i.e. if a segment has both incomes and expenditures, a profit centre basis is likely to be appropriate, while a segment which does not make sales would logically be measured as a cost centre. Shillinglaw[1] suggests that a centre's performance measurement should, as far as possible, be unaffected by actions elsewhere in the organization, and relate to facets of cost and revenue over which the centre manager has some measure of control.

In practice however, many responsibility centres within businesses are established on bases which to some greater or lesser extent are artificial and/or are affected by decisions elsewhere in the organization over which they have little or no control. The reasons for this contradiction of well known and understood managerial logic is probably that:

1   Situations arise, particularly in process industries, in which joint processing costs are common, where management wishes to segmentalize its organization on an approach other than on a technological basis (see page 117 *et seq.*). A transfer price or apportionment of joint costs to each segment is therefore necessary if each segment is to be treated separately.

2   The profit and investment centre approaches are increasingly acknowledged

or believed to have considerable advantages over cost and revenue approaches. It is argued that they offer a greater goal congruence with corporate objectives, profit is seen as a better motivation than cost control, and more segments of the organization can be compared on a compatible basis. Thus, for example the output of a natural cost centre might be valued at a transfer price to derive a figure of sales in order that the centre can be treated as a profit or investment centre.

3   Businesses have expanded through horizontal and vertical integration and acquisition, which has resulted in a perhaps significant degree of inter-company trading. It could be argued of course that these transactions are at a fair, arms length market price, but management must question whether such a transfer price is ever really fair or arms length, especially where segments of a business are in any way required or expected to trade with each other. Further, as the purpose of growth by merger or acquisition is presumably to gain the advantages of internal trading, it would seem illogical and suboptimal to permit responsibility centre managers the freedom to trade completely autonomously.

4   Centralized group services have increased in many large organizations, effectively creating a similar situation to (3) above. This may have been to gain economies of scale and an increase in negotiating power or simply to centralize control or gain a uniformity of approach. Such central services would probably include buying, computing, finance, personnel, training, property management, equipment supply and of course head office administration. Whether these central services are treated as cost or profit centres, if charges are made to other responsibility centres whether it be on a work done or simple apportionment basis the charge is effectively transfer price and therefore an uncontrollable cost from the user's point of view.

5   If a cost centre of an organization has spare capacity, management frequently wants to utilize this opportunity profitably by encouraging its sale (at a profit) to external businesses. A cost centre would then be in the position of being a cost centre for internal work and a profit centre for external work. Sometimes managements resolve this dichotomy of interests by changing such a cost centre into a profit centre, thus requiring internal work to be sold at a price to other responsibility centres. The distinction between internal and external work is therefore potentially resolved.

Thus in all these very common business circumstances a transfer price of some sort is required if a financial evaluation measure is to be applied. As the reader will readily understand however, the effect of this must be to cast doubt on the resultant measurements of responsibility centres and of their management. If the transfer price is high the seller is advantaged and the buyer disadvantaged and vice-versa if the price is low. Transfer pricing from a control viewpoint will be considered later.

Finally, it should be pointed out that there is no logical reason why, in suitable circumstances, a responsibility centre could not be treated as a cost, revenue, profit and investment centre *and* as a budget centre for cost, revenue, profit, investment and (some measures of) physical performance. Obviously there would be duplications of performance, but each would allow senior management to examine more closely performance in each element as well as overall. The more the views, the better the understanding, perhaps.

Transfer pricing

Unfortunately, in large and segmented organizations the measurement of performance based upon cost, revenue and profit criteria is made difficult by the inevitable lack of complete autonomy of the parts of the business; one part of the organization will receive from and/or provide goods or services to others. If therefore management wishes to measure the total monetary value of inputs and outputs from parts of the organization, it becomes necessary to place a price upon the transfers from one segment to another.

It is however likely that even without the existence of profit and cost centres, transfer prices would be needed for other managerial purposes such as encouraging efficiency and economy. To elaborate, if goods and services were received and provided without a charge, managers would not be motivated to be economical and efficient with resources or keen to generate greater output for others. Further, it would be difficult for managers to make good decisions for the organization as a whole if they were unaware of all the cost and revenue elements.

The objectives of transfer pricing can therefore be summarized as being to:

1   provide a basis for the financial control and evaluation of managerial and unit performance;
2   motivate managers to be both economic and efficient with resources and achieve better results;
3   enable and encourage managers towards optimal decision making.

Unfortunately, no transfer pricing method achieves these three objectives simultaneously.

An aspect which should not be forgotten is that transfer prices could be set in order to manipulate profit into those parts of the world with lower taxation regimes – and in some situations, cash between countries. Multinationals will no doubt try to establish their organization structure in such a way as to reduce their taxation burden – but within the rules – i.e. avoidance and not evasion. Countries' revenue authorities do talk with each other and exchange information; the penalties for breaking national rules are severe, and businesses tend to adopt a 'whiter than white' approach. International transfer pricing will be discussed in later paragraphs.

Transfer pricing method

The principal transfer pricing methods can be summarized as:

1   Market price
    Although this method is popular in practice, market price may be difficult to ascertain with any degree of confidence.

2   Cost-based prices
    Cost may be interpreted in different ways of course: actual or standard cost; variable cost; incremental cost; total cost; fixed cost per annum (buying a supplier's capacity) plus variable cost per unit; etc. A profit margin may be added if desired, but how much?

3   Negotiated price
    Negotiation may approximate to market price – if managers are autonomous. Where autonomy is constrained, i.e. the buyer and/or the seller does not have complete freedom to trade (or not) with other units within a group, negotiation is less likely to lead to a price considered fair by all parties. If a group of companies has grown, by acquisition or otherwise, in order to gain the benefits of synergy, it would be, perhaps, illogical to permit units to trade externally when the opportunity exists internally.

4   Group imposition
    Top management may dictate prices or act as arbiters where negotiation fails.

5   LP shadow prices
    Prices resultant from linear planning (analogous to marginal costs) can be seen as the incremental cost of additional operations. These are rarely found in practice.

Variations on these themes are possible of course. Two interesting methods seen in practice are:

6   Cost plus profit share
    Under this approach, transfers are made at cost – total or marginal – and margins on the ultimate sale are shared amongst the segments according to an agreed formula.

7   Dual prices
    Here, a group acts as an intermediary between buyer and seller, i.e. buying from the supplier at one price and selling to the receiver at another price. This enables the group to achieve different transfer price objectives for buyer and seller, albeit at the cost of additional administration and the need to net off the difference in group profit reporting.

The impact of transfer pricing

The impact of these alternative methods on reported financial outcomes are likely to be affected by the circumstances of each segment.

1 How large the proportion of inter-organization purchases or sales are in comparison to the total for each segment (the larger the proportion, the more the impact and potential distortion the transfer pricing method may have on reported performance).

2 Whether or not managers have the freedom to trade outside the organization should they wish. The more freedom to trade outside the organization is restricted, the more significant the transfer price will have on managerial and unit performance measures.

3 The existence of alternative suppliers or customers and the difficulty in obtaining market price knowledge. Pseudo profit centres, i.e. those where the segment is not truly operating freely, are more likely to lead to managerial demotivation and distorted performance measures. Market prices for many inter-company transfers do not exist or are difficult to obtain. How many competitive quotes, for example, are needed to establish a market price? To what extent are quotes from suppliers who do not expect to receive orders or who are desperate for work, likely to constitute a market price?

The efficacy of transfer prices

The efficacy of these alternative methods in achieving each of the objectives of control information, motivation and optimal decision making might be argued as below.

1 To provide good control information on a unit or manager's performance, the transfer price should reflect the situation where there was complete autonomy. Thus market price, where it exists, could be said to satisfy this criteria. Negotiation and cost plus methods may approximate this price level. Alternatively, in some circumstances, from a top management perspective, controllable costs may be appropriate.

2 To motivate managers, transfer prices probably need to be seen by them as fair. How managers react is always difficult to predict and is likely to depend on circumstances. One could argue that arms length market or negotiated prices are likely to be considered fair, as might total standard cost plus. However, it all depends on a manager's reactions and the reader should think of circumstances where each method might be considered unfair.

3 To enable managers to make optimal (non-parochial) decisions, it is likely that some detail of price make-up would be needed. In particular, the marginal/variable cost, fixed cost and profit components of the transfer price are likely to be required. Transfer price methods most likely to aid optimal

decision making would include marginal (and LP) cost, with or without fixed cost knowledge. Profit component knowledge may or may not be useful knowledge. Prices without component analysis such as, for example, market or negotiated prices are unlikely to lead to optimal decision making – from a total corporate viewpoint at least. For organizations with units in other countries, optimality would need to include international taxation and currency considerations.

International transfer pricing

While transfers of goods and services between business segments in the same country are at the sole discretion of top management, transfers between units in different nations is subject to the laws of each country in which the organization operates. Such laws are principally in the area of taxation, and currency control; the revenue authorities are, for example, very aware that multinationals have the potential to switch profits to those countries with generous taxation regimes, leaving little or no tax to be paid in those countries that generate the wealth. To safeguard national interests, most countries have rules which allow the Revenue to share information with other countries and to make assessments on and penalize companies they believe are abusing the rules. Typically too, the onus is on the companies to demonstrate that they are not breaking the rules rather than the burden of proof being on the Revenue. In fact, very few cases are taken to trial, most organizations preferring the anonymity of an agreed settlement, thus also avoiding the high legal costs involved.

The rules in most countries are that companies should adopt the most appropriate method. Businesses would be wise to gain approval for their method before adoption, rather than become embroiled in post event justification. The Organization for Economic Cooperation and Development (OECD) has published guidelines on transfer prices, the essence of which most countries have accepted. These rules state that transfers between countries should be at :

1 Arms length (market price), but if that is not ascertainable, at
2 Ultimate selling price less (the seller's normal margins) or if not,
3 Total cost plus (the seller's normal margins), failing which companies may use,
4 Any other method (agreed to by the Revenue).

In an international context however, revenue authorities expect that transactions will be, or approximate to, the price at which completely independent companies would trade. A corporate taxation director recently commented that 'the overriding accepted rule is the "arms length standard". Tax authorities will generally expect the best method to be applied in approximating an arms length situation.' For many international inter-company transactions, an arms length price is difficult to approximate, and the application of OECD guidelines far from straightforward. Examples would include the definitions of cost and profit margins, compensation for risk, currency movements, joint and shared costs, indirect taxes, joint ventures and management charges. In particular, tax authorities are generally wary of management negotiated prices. In situations where the OECD framework methods, 1, 2 and 3 above, do not derive a method considered arms length enough, the IRS in the USA are believed to favour either the 'any other method' of profit split approaches or comparable ROI (where the company needs to demonstrate that a price will give them a fair return on the investment in each country of operations). Advance Price Agreements (APAs), i.e. prior approval of a transfer pricing system, are increasingly popular among large multinationals with significant trade in the USA. However, most tax authorities are simply not staffed sufficiently to give such approval. Retrospective transfer pricing adjustments, i.e. where the revenue authorities disagree with the pricing method used by a company in the past, almost invariably result in double taxation.

The onus is very much on the business to demonstrate that they are complying with the laws of each country. It is important that companies can demonstrate, through documentation, that they have analysed the alternative pricing methods, which, for them, might approximate to an arms length price. Penalties for abuse are, potentially severe. Most companies attempt to be 'whiter than white' while still reducing the taxation burden within the rules. Organizations would be wise to ensure that their system is acceptable to the revenue authorities of the countries in which they operate, especially if their system falls under the 'any other method' category. The fact is however that some countries offer transfer pricing havens to attract businesses to operate in their countries, and that 'double taxation agreements' do not exist between all countries.

Those wishing for more details would benefit from reading *International Transfer Pricing*, Coopers and Lybrand, Published by CCH International, 1993.

Practical considerations

No system is perfect. Top management should select a transfer price policy that best responds to the organization's needs and problems. In practice, the senior management of organizations tend to believe that transfer pricing, affecting a relatively small element of total costs and revenues, is not important. Research indicates however that for some segments of organizations, transfer pricing can have a significant influence on financial performance measurement (see Rickwood, Coates and Stacey, Managed Costs, *Accounting and Business Research*, Autumn 1987). A further finding of this paper was that management often design or change their transfer pricing policy to influence managers towards particular decisions. Such an approach has the advantage that senior managers are not seen to be overtly interfering in a decision and hence managers' autonomy is apparently preserved!

Reference

1. Shillinglaw, G., Guides to Internal Profit Measurement, *Harvard Business Review*, Vol. 35, No. 2, April 1957.

Questions

1   ABE Ltd and KIM Ltd are two newly established divisions of RAT plc. They operate as independent trading units, though some of their final product markets overlap.

Their managing directors each agreed an initial plan based on a 20 per cent per annum charge for capital by RAT plc. The plan showed both divisions to be capable of meeting the 20 per cent target.

During the first year's operation ABE Ltd secured a contract to supply items to LO plc, a company not within the RAT group and a direct competitor in KIM Ltd's market. KIM Ltd could have bought the same supplies from ABE Ltd but preferred to buy from a supplier outside the RAT group.

In the first year of operation LO plc secured a 5 per cent increase in its share of the market at the expense of KIM Ltd. A major factor in LO plc's success was considered to be the superiority of ABE Ltd's product over those of its competitors.

KIM Ltd and LO were initially expected to have a 50 per cent share in the final product market, the latter being KIM Ltd's sole market outlet.

The key elements of the budgets agreed at the outset by ABE Ltd and KIM Ltd are:

	ABE Ltd	KIM Ltd
Initial investment in plant and equipment (£m):	10	15
Cost of capital charge	20%	20%
Expected new cash flows in £m		
First year	1.9	3.2
Years 2–8 pa	2.9	4.2

Assume that:
1   The operating efficiencies of KIM Ltd and LO plc are broadly the same.
2   The 5 per cent increase in the market share made by LO plc results in a pro rata 5 per cent increase in ABE Ltd's net cash flow.

You are required to:
   (a)   Evaluate the two divisions' expected performance as seen by RAT plc at the time of their establishment.
   (b)   Evaluate the actual performance of the two divisions in their first year of operation, giving a reasoned interpretation of the outcomes.
   (c)   Discuss the performance measures applicable to assessing the success or otherwise of the divisions. Identify further issues which may be deemed relevant but beyond the information given you in the questions.
   Note: Taxation is to be ignored.

2   (a)   Discuss the nature of the problems presented for the creation and

transmission of planning and control information at (i) the top management level, and (ii) the division level, when a previously centrally managed organization decided to reorganize the management of its operations into a group of autonomous divisions.

(b) Many indicators may be used to assist in the appraisal of the performance of divisions within a company. However, they must be designed to ensure that divisions' activities are directed toward the achievement of corporate goals. Discuss the above statement and support your answer by reference to particular performance measures.

3 Residual income and return on investment are commonly used measures of performance. However, they are frequently criticized for placing too great an emphasis on the achievement of short-term results, possibly damaging long-term performance. You are required to discuss:

(a) the issues involved in the long-term:short-term conflict referred to in the above statement;

(b) suggestions which have been made to reconcile this difference (CIMA November 1988).

8

Assessment criteria

Behavioural implications

In reading this chapter, a few salutary points should be remembered. Management accounting, perhaps all accounting, is aimed at changing behaviour. Why else is information produced, if it is not to generate a response? This is particularly true in the field of performance measurement. 'What you measure is what you get,' and 'Tell me how a man is measured, and I'll tell you how he will behave,' are quotes attributed to Robert Kaplan[1] for example. Every measure will tend to encourage certain behaviour, perhaps to the detriment of other desirable outcomes.

Responsibility assessment criteria

The alternative types of responsibility centre address different aspects of managerial controls and therefore require different measures of performance. The balance of this chapter will consider performance criteria suitable for profit and investment centres and the following chapter cost and revenue centre criteria. Budget centres have been considered in preceding chapters but their particular relevance to cost, revenue, profit and investment centres will be reintroduced as necessary.

Profit and investment centre criteria

As indicated earlier, most profit centre managers have at least some responsibility for and impact upon the investment in their profit centre and it might therefore be fair to treat them as an investment centre[2,3]. Such evidence as there is of business practices in Britain and the USA indicates that investment centres are more common than profit centres. This was certainly the experience of the authors in a small sample of divisionalized organizations visited in the generation of case studies between 1983[2] and 1986.[3,4]

There is absolutely no reason why an investment centre manager could not be assessed as a profit centre manager as well, although, as will be explained later, this could lead to some conflicts between the various performance measures. A consideration of the situations in which a profit centre approach might be preferred to that of an investment centre approach, together with an examination of appropriate performance measures for a profit centre, will be addressed later in the chapter.

The immediate concern here is with possible criteria for the evaluation of investment centres, and the alternatives, variations, advantages and disadvantages and their relevance to the control of responsibility centres.

Return on investment

There can be no doubt that return on investment (ROI) or return on capital employed (ROCE) as it is often termed, particularly when used as an internal measure for the evaluation of investment centres, is the most popular and widely used performance criterion for investment centres (and inter-firm comparisons). There would appear to be an intuitive and inescapable argument for drawing together as a ratio (usually expressed as a percentage) two of the most critical aspects of business management – the main objective of profitability and the perhaps major resource constraint of capital availability. If these factors are critical in measuring the business as a whole, surely they must be equally important to each investment centre within the business, if for no other reason than to encourage and emphasize goal congruence. Not only does ROI draw together two such important elements, but the resultant percentage facilitates the comparison of the performances of different investments; one business with another, or one investment centre within a business with another or an investment centre within one business to that within another. In principle, it also allows businesses of different sizes or in different lines of business to be compared.

   ROI is frequently seen as being at the apex of a pyramid of ratios. While it is not intended to examine the pyramid as such, it is perhaps germane to examine the two ratios which it is frequently suggested are the constituent ratios forming the next stage down the pyramid, i.e.

$$\text{ROI} = \frac{\text{Profits}}{\text{Investment}} = \frac{\text{Profits}}{\text{Sales}} \times \frac{\text{Sales}}{\text{Investment}}$$

$$= \text{Profit margin} \times \text{Turnover of capital}$$

These two ratios demonstrate that ROI can be affected by improvements in profit margin and/or sales volumes for a given level of capital invested, or of course a mix of both, i.e. an increase in either will bring an increased return but so too could a decrease in one, if the other increased disproportionately to compensate. For example, a 20 per cent ROI obtained by a 10 per cent profit margin and a TOC of 2 per cent would be improved if, when profit margins are reduced to 9 per cent, sales volumes and therefore TOC increased by more than 10 per cent, say to 2.4. Thus 9 per cent × 2.4 = 21.6 per cent ROI as long as capital invested does not also increase (as it might if sales volumes increase by 20 per cent).

   In spite of its popularity as a performance measure, ROI can be interpreted in a large variety of ways, and has a number of inherent limitations which are frequently overlooked or ignored by management. These aspects merit careful consideration.

What profit?

Which figure of profit should be used in the ROI ratio? Should it be operating profit, trading profit, net profit before loan interest or after, before tax or after ... or something else instead? Obviously, each has its merits and would give perhaps a different perspective on the business and its management. It depends just what one wants to measure, with what one wishes to compare and why. In comparing one company with another a shareholder might consider net profit after tax to be a sensible profit measure. After all, that is the profit figure available to the shareholder for distribution as dividend or for growth. But would this be a sensible basis to compare the divisions and segments of a business with each other? Possibly. But if taxation planning is considered to be the prerogative of senior management, a pre-taxation basis might be more logical. Similarly, if capital sourcing is a centralized activity, perhaps profit before loan interest would be more appropriate.

However, this assumes that, even for investment centre performance measurement within an organization, a measure of profit compatible with that used in the financial accounts should be used. But why should internal performance measures be restricted to those used in the financial statements? Why should they be prepared to a format and manner proscribed by law and standard accounting practices, and which accountants recognize as having severe limitations as meaningful informative data? Are the traditional accounting conventions really relevant for such measurements? Do we really want internal performance measures prepared in a prudent way? Should not reality be the aim for such purposes? Why should we stick rigidly to the historic cost convention which can provide such meaningless and incomparable data? Surely here is an opportunity to introduce current cost and value data into an internal measurement? Should not internal performance measures concentrate as far as possible upon attributability of costs and revenues, i.e. reflect those aspects which are directly attributable to the investment centre but exclude those which are little more than a sharing out of corporate costs? Likewise, in measuring a manager's performance, should the emphasis not be upon those aspects the manager can control in some meaningful way, while excluding general cost apportionments?

These aspects will be considered shortly but a similar questioning of the assumptions in the investment element of the ROI ratio is also required.

What investment?

A questioning of the investment/capital employed element of the ROI ratio in a similar manner to that of the return/profit element is necessary.

- Do we want to continue using financial accounting conventions?
- Should the emphasis be upon shareholders' funds alone or include loan capital and other creditors over one year?
- What figure of capital employed should we use – fixed assets alone, pre- or post-depreciation, or plus current assets or plus net current assets?

- Should assets remain at historic cost or be increased to reflect current costs of replacement or some other interpretation of value?
- How are shared fixed assets to be dealt with? Are they to be apportioned between investment centres?
- Can working capital be directly attributed or must this too be apportioned? How much of this capital is truly attributable to investment centres or controllable by investment centre management?
- How can the anomalies of leased assets on and off balance sheet compared to asset ownership be reduced or eliminated for comparison purposes?
- Should the investment base used be that for the beginning or end of the period or an average?

As with the profit measure, the investment measure must depend upon circumstances: what one wants to evaluate why and with what the comparison is to be made. A shareholder may well be interested in profits after loan interest pre- or post-tax, compared to shareholders' funds. However a comparison of the same profit figures with the total of shareholders' funds and loan capital would surely be illogical (in which case a profits before loan interest would be more appropriate). Yet in inter-firm comparisons, different capital gearing may make shareholders' funds a poor indicator of managerial utilization of funds. Or would it? And what basis is relevant for a business's investment centre performance? Gearing differences might make shareholders' funds an anomalous figure, so perhaps fixed assets plus current assets or working capital should be used. Or . . ?

ROI inconsistency

ROI can be a ratio that lacks consistency with real performance over time, and can therefore be a misleading measure. Consider the following simplified example.

Arnold Freighter decides to set up in business as a road haulier. He buys a lorry costing £60,000, which he estimates has a business life of four years with little or no residual value. His policy is to depreciate the vehicle on a straight line basis. He expects steady sales of £50,000 pa and operational costs, excluding depreciation of £25,000. A. Freighter's accounting data would appear as in Table 8.1.

What is the ROI likely to be in each of the four years? Assuming that it is intended to use net profits as shown before taxation, the question remains as to which capital-employed figure to use – that at the beginning of the year, end of the year, or an average. Different figures result, as in Table 8.2.

The distinction between the three alternatives is a matter of choice, of policy. There are arguments for using each of them. If capital changes significantly, year on year, an average may be more appropriate but practices across industry are very variable.

The principal point to be made however, is that the ROI percentage increases over time even though the assumptions of work done/sales volumes are the same over time. The danger therefore is that, if this ratio is used as a control measure,

Table 8.1   A. Freighter – profits and capital employed

| | Years | | | |
	1	2	3	4
Profit statement	£000	£000	£000	£000
Sales	50	50	50	50
Operating costs	(25)	(25)	(25)	(25)
Depreciation	(15)	(15)	(15)	(15)
Net profits	10	10	10	10
Capital employed				
Vehicle at cost	60	60	60	60
Depreciation	(15)	(30)	(45)	(60)
Net book amount	45	30	15	0

Table 8.2   A. Freighter – ROI based upon different CE bases

| | 1 | 2 | 3 | 4 |
ROI based on CE	%	%	%	%
at beginning	16.7	22.2	33.3	66.6
at end	22.2	33.3	66.6	infinity
average	19.0	26.7	44.4	133.3

the impression might be gained that performance is improving significantly over the years when it obviously is not.

Additionally as the ROI percentage increases over time from quite low to perhaps very high figures, managers are likely to become increasingly disinclined to propose new capital investments which would depress the ROI evaluation of their performance. Even if the depression would only affect the short term, managers with an eye to promotion or salary increases in the shorter term may be influenced to defer investment as long as possible. Thus, the currently attained ROI percentage effectively becomes the minimum acceptable return for any further investments.

Residual income

An increasingly popular alternative to ROI is the application of the residual income concept. This measures the net income of an investment after deducting an amount representing the required rate of return on the capital invested in the business. The required rate may represent the minimum required by the organization, perhaps some target or expected level of returns, or in some businesses, the weighted average cost of capital of the organization. In this latter case the sum of the residual incomes of all segments of the business could equate with the business's net profit after loan interest.

Table 8.3 ROI and residual income calculation for business segments

	Segment A	*Segment B*
Capital invested	£3,000,000	£10,000,000
Annual profit	£540,000	£1,400,000
ROI percentage	18%	14%
Required return (10%)	£300,000	£1,000,000
Residual income	£240,000	£400,000
(at 10% required return)		

The argument for residual income (RI) is that it encourages investment centre managers to explore any investment with the potential of obtaining a return in excess of the business's required rate of return. As mentioned earlier, this motivation does not always exist where ROI is used as performance measure, particularly if the percentage is high with an ageing capital base. An illustration of the residual income approach is shown in Table 8.3.

It could be argued that, even if the ROI percentages shown were a consistent annual measure, not prone to increase over time, if ROI were the main preference measure, investment managers of A and B are likely to act suboptimally from the business's viewpoint. Suppose A and B identified new investment propositions for £1m with a return of 17 per cent and 15 per cent respectively. The manager of B is likely to propose such an investment as it would increase his segment's ROI performance measure and if the required rate of return is 10 per cent, this would be good for the business as a whole. The manager of A however is unlikely to propose such an investment, even though it has a higher return than that identified by B, because it would depress his segment's ROI performance of 18 per cent – an action which would not be in the business's best interest. At worst, A is being encouraged to be beautiful (in ROI terms), even if small! If, however, residual income was the performance measure of A and B, both segments would be likely to propose the £1m investments.

This does mean however, that the judgement of management in setting the required rate of return can be of critical importance to the operation of the residual income performance measure and to decisions made. If, for example, the required rate of return had been set not at 10 per cent, as earlier, but at 13 per cent or 16 per cent, very different performance measures would result (see Table 8.4).

The repercussions are significant. From a control viewpoint, the relative performances of A and B vary with the requirements for return. Is segment A performing better than B or not? Is it sensible to argue that if the required return of the business is 10 per cent, B is performing better than A, while at required returns of 13 per cent and 16 per cent the reverse is true? After all, if the required rate was 10 per cent, the manager of B would argue that, even though their rate of return on capital was lower than that of A, by taking on investments with returns over 10 per cent he has increased corporate profits to a greater extent than A. A, it could be argued, has perhaps ignored opportunities to expand and

Table 8.4   Residual income for differing rates of required return

	Segment A	*Segment B*
Capital invested	£3,000,000	£10,000,000
Annual profit	£540,000	£1,400,000
ROI percentage	18%	14%
Residual income		
at 10% return	£240,000	£400,000
at 13% return	£150,000	£100,000
at 16% return	£60,000	£(200,000)

obtain an increase in residual income. Was this a good decision? Apparently not if capital is freely available at a rate of 10 per cent or less.

What then should the required rate of return represent? Ideally, as RI could be considered as an abbreviated NPV approach from an economic decision-making viewpoint, the opportunity cost of additional sources of capital should be used.

However, once expenditures have been made, it would be more logical to apply a rate approximating to the opportunity value of those assets acquired. Because (a) this rate may be difficult to determine, (b) using two different rates is likely to lead to confusion, and (c) changing the rate used to reflect changes in opportunity can distort performance measurement over time, businesses tend to adopt one rate and stick to it over time. This should mean of course that business management ought to take a long-term view of opportunity cost in its industry(ies). It should be noted however that if the availability of capital is effectively nil then the residual income measure is irrelevant and profit maximization alone is relevant.

Finally the reader should be aware that RI is as prone as ROI to the increase of the performance measure over time, given the use of traditional accounting depreciation techniques. If A. Freighter, for example, was a segment of a business using residual income at a 10 per cent required rate of return, the performance would appear as in Table 8.5.

Suppose however, that the investment was less profitable than as shown. Say that periodic net profits were only £5,000 pa and resultant residual incomes were £(1000), £500, £2,000 and £3,500 in each of the four years. Bearing in mind the negative RI in the first year and a second year of only £500, would A. Freighter have proposed the investment?

Discounting approaches

Annuity depreciation is an attempt to equalize the effective annual cost of asset purchases over time, i.e. to spread the cost of asset depreciation and the required rate of return on the capital expended to buy the asset, equally over each year of the asset's life. Perhaps the most obvious analogy is that of a building society mortgage on a house, where repayments are made in equal instalments over time.

Table 8.5 A residual income example showing improving RI over time for A. Freighter

	Years			
	1	*2*	*3*	*4*
Profitability statement	*£000*	*£000*	*£000*	*£000*
Sales	50	50	50	50
Operating costs	(25)	(25)	(25)	(25)
Depreciation	(15)	(15)	(15)	(15)
Net profits	10	10	10	10
Required profit	6	4.5	3	1.5
Residual income	4	5.5	7	8.5
Capital employed				
Vehicle at cost	60	60	60	60
Depreciation	(15)	(30)	(45)	(60)
Net book amount	45	30	15	0

Note that the required profit is based in this example upon the *opening* balance of *depreciated* assets. Different depreciation assumptions will therefore affect the notional profit requirement.

In the early years, repayments represent mostly interest and a small amount of capital. In later years, the interest element declines and the capital repayment increases. To illustrate, a simple example is shown in Table 8.6 continuing the A. Freighter residual income approach example shown in Table 8.5. The equal annuity rate of £18,930 required to repay £60,000 over four years at an interest rate of 10 per cent may be calculated from the formula illustrated below:

$$A = I \times \frac{(1 + r)^n \times r}{(1 + r)^n - 1}$$

where

A = annual investment
I = invested sum
r = required rate of return, expressed as a decimal
n = number of years (life of asset/projected)

Thus for example using the figures as in Table 8.6

$$A = 60{,}000 \times \frac{(1 + 0.1)^4 \; 0.1}{(1 + 0.1)^4 - 1} = 60{,}000 \times \frac{1.4641 - 0.1}{1.4641 - 1} = £18{,}930$$

In year 1 only £12,930 of this is depreciation while in year 4 £17,210 is depreciation (see Table 8.6).

Annuity depreciation enables the RI performance measure to reflect a consistent figure over time (rather than a rising one) when margins before depreciation are at a constant level. Of course, if gross margins vary, so will the RI but that is presumably a relationship that management is not unhappy to reflect in resultant residual income levels. The point is that the total cost of buying equipment in terms of depreciation and interest remains constant.

Table 8.6 A. Freighter – residual income calculation using annuity depreciation and cost of capital of 10%

	Years							
	1		*2*		*3*		*4*	
Profitability statement	*£000*		*£000*		*£000*		*£000*	
Sales	50		50		50		50	
Operating costs	25		25		25		25	
Gross margin	25		25		25		25	
Annuity costs:								
Depreciation[(ii)]	12.93		14.22		15.64		17.21	
Interest[(i)]	6.00	18.93	4.71	18.93	3.29	18.93	1.72	18.93
Residual income[(iii)]		6.07		6.07		6.07		6.07
Capital employed								
Cost	60.00		60.00		60.00		60.00	
Depreciation	12.93		27.15		42.79		60.00	
Net book amount	47.07		32.85		17.21		0	

Notes (i) 10% of opening book amount.
  (ii) The balance between the interest charge and the annuity repayment of 18.93 (£000) pa.
  (iii) NPV of 6.07 (£000) for 4 years @ 10% × 19.240 (£000)

A further advantage is that the resultant RI is consistent with the NPV approach to capital investment appraisal. In our example, the NPV of the original investment at 10 per cent (£25,000 in four annual instalments less £60,000 invested) is £19,240, the same as the NPV of £6,070 in four annual instalments shown in Table 8.7. Thus annuity depreciation offers management the potential to measure investment centre performance by the same criteria that its expenditures were (probably) approved by. Further it should continue to encourage investment centre managers to put forward proposals which are expected to beat the company's required rate of return and/or opportunity cost. However, it may not show consistently positive residual incomes if cash flows from the investment are erratic and therefore investment centre managers may be deterred from proposing such an investment.

However, annuity depreciation is apparently rarely adopted in practice. The reason is probably because the effect of low depreciation in early years goes against both managers' instinctive belief about depreciation and the accounting prudence principle of asset valuation, in as much as depreciation is lower in the early years and therefore the net book amount is likely to be higher than the asset's potential resale value (although the going concern concept could counter this argument).

Valuing assets at net present value

An interesting variant of the annuity depreciation approach values investments at their NPV, using the required rate of return. Thus in the A. Freighter example

Table 8.7 A. Freighter – residual income calculation using the NPV value of the vehicle as the basis for depreciation.

| | Years | | | |
	1	*2*	*3*	*4*
Profitability statement	*£000*	*£000*	*£000*	*£000*
Sales	50	50	50	50
Operating costs	(25)	(25)	(25)	(25)
Gross margin	25.000	25.000	25.000	25.000
Depreciation	17.075[(i)]	18.78	20.65	22.275
Profit before interest	7.925	6.22	4.35	2.275
Interest	7.925[(ii)]	6.22	4.35	2.275
Residual income	—	—	—	—

Value at start: $(25 \times 0.909) + (25 \times 0.826) + (25 \times 0.751) + (25 \times 0.683) = 79.225$
Value at end of year 1: $(25 \times 0.909) + (25 \times 0.826) + (25 \times 0.751) = 62.150$
Value at end of year 2: $(25 \times 0.909) + (25 \times 0.826) = 43.375$
Value at end of year 3: $+ (25 \times 0.909) = 22.725$

(i) Value at start £79.225 less value at end of year 1 £62.15.
(ii) 10% of the value at start of £79.225, adjusted slightly to allow for rounding of discounting.

(Table 8.7) the vehicle would be valued at its NPV of £19,240. This vehicle could therefore be sold by the group to the A. Freighter investment centre at £19,240. The management of A. Freighter would then, for performance evaluation purposes, depreciate and charge interest on £19,240 reducing periodic residual income to nil. Thus Table 8.7 indicates the performance statements. The advantage of this approach is that

1 investment managers would be more careful in putting forward exaggerated cash flows for favoured investments,
2 managers' performance against investment proposals are consistently measured, and
3 irregular cash flows would still allow a consistent residual income (of nil) to be produced.

However, the authors know of no example of this approach in practice, which perhaps is not surprising, as it is not likely to motivate managers to propose new investments when resultant RI would not increase. Further, the method would require a separate set of managerial records from those of the financial accounts.

The cash flow approach

The lack of use of the discounting approach as an aid to performance measurement, in spite of its academic attractions, probably results from the difficulty accountants would have in explaining the logic, and indeed, the reversal of normal depreciating policies, to management and perhaps auditors. If, however, management like the principle of the approach but see it as being difficult to sell, there is a development of it which has the attraction of simplicity and indeed a link with financial accounting principles.

If the reader looks again at Table 8.6, they will see that, once the investment decision is made, annuity costs (of £18,930) are a constant charge against annual gross margins, i.e., profits before depreciation and financing charges. As this margin is under the control of management, would it not be logical simply to measure this controllable feature? Further, as one value of the discounting approach is its congruity with the DCF, why not measure margins before annuity costs on a cash flow basis, i.e. simply measure cash flow from operations and working capital management. A little thought will perhaps persuade the reader that such a measure is likely to be congruent with corporate goals, managerial goals, DCF appraisal principles, and the corporation's cash flow statement! 'Cash is king', as one company phrases it.

Accounting conventions and policies

The principal reason for the ROI etc. inconsistencies is of course that a depreciating figure of capital employed is used as the denominator in the ROI ratio. This might be logical if the asset's service potential was decreasing year on year (in the A. Freighter example, reducing by 25 per cent each year). However, while an asset may well be decreasingly useful over time, because (a) it reduces in efficiency as it wears, and (b) it requires more frequent stoppages for repairs and maintenance, and therefore has reduced availability (and increased costs of maintenance), such is not likely to reduce utilizability as substantially as most assets' depreciation rates would imply.

It should be pointed out that the anomalies stem partly at least from the use of financial accounting conventions and policies. Consider the profits and ROI over time of, say, a sum of digits or reducing balance depreciation method had been adopted. The financial statements might (at worst) appear as in Table 8.8.

Of course no account has been taken of increasing repairs and maintenance and reducing utilizability over time. However, it would appear that such a system is likely to provide even bigger variations in the ROI percentage over time than a straight line approach.

The above examples have all been based upon the original assumption that the vehicle will have a four year life and no residual value. It would not be surprising if these estimates were somewhat pessimistic, based upon the need to be prudent and conservative in calculating profitability for financial accounting purposes. Suppose a more realistic assumption is that the vehicle will last five years and will have a residual value then of £5,000. Depreciation then would be £55,000 over five years or £11,000 pa on a straight line basis. In these eventualities, if the vehicle lasts for years the financial figures when compared to the original assumptions might appear as in Table 8.9.

Different figures of ROI emerge of course, but increasing at a lower rate, simply because a less conservative/more realistic view of depreciation is taken.

Table 8.8   A. Freighter – ROI using sum of digits depreciation

| | Years | | | |
	1	2	3	4
Profit statement	£000	£000	£000	£000
Sales	50	50	50	50
Operating costs	(25)	(25)	(25)	(25)
Depreciation	(24)	(18)	(15)	(6)
Net profits	1	7	13	19
Capital employed				
Vehicle at cost	60	60	60	60
Depreciation	24	42	54	60
Net book value	36	18	6	0
ROI% based on opening CE	1.7%	19.4%	72.2%	316.7%

Table 8.9   A. Freighter – contrast between 4- and 5-year assumptions of asset life

| | Years | | | | | Profit on sale |
| | 1 | 2 | 3 | 4 | 5 | |
	£000	£000	£000	£000	£000	£000
Net profits						
original	10	10	10	10	25	5
revised	14	14	14	14	14	0
Capital employed[(ii)]						
original	60	45	30	15	0	
revised	60	49	38	27	16	
ROI%						
original	16.7%	22.2%	33.3%	66.6%	infinity	
revised	23.3%	28.6%	36.8%	51.9%	87.5%	

(i)   Profit on sale of assets = sales value less WDV. Does this become a below the line or above the line profit? A central or a segmental profit?

(ii) Capital employed using straight line depreciation, taking the opening figure for each year.

This is particularly important if assets are to be retained beyond their book life, as ROI percentages in later years could appear to be very high indeed.

One possibility to reduce the anomaly would be to use an undepreciated figure of fixed assets for capital employed calculations. This would give a constant figure in this example of 16.7 per cent. However, as in practice assets do become less utilizable and more costly to repair over time, this approach would probably lead to a reducing ROI over time, even if other efficiencies, e.g. excluding utilizable vehicle capacity, remained the same.

Some observers might argue that the increasing ROI percentages are not likely to happen in practice, as most businesses own more than one fixed asset: if, for example, the business owned four vehicles, one purchased each year, every year the total figures would be made up of one vehicle each of 1, 2, 3 and 4 years old and therefore a consistent percentage over time would arise. This of course would essentially be true if businesses replaced assets regularly and equally year on year. Some business may well do so of course, but an examination of the accounts of businesses shows clearly that this is by no means a universally adopted practice. The financial director of one large asset leasing/ rental business has abandoned the ROI percentages as a performance measure for his investment centres because, in his words, 'they are meaningless ... they go up over time and when we replace assets to modernize our equipment in response to customer demands for the latest models, the percentages go back down again'.

Depreciation is not the only element affected by accounting policies and conventions. Consider, for example, alternative stock valuation approaches and the treatment of goodwill and R&D expenditures. Are the accounting conventions adopted for external financial statements appropriate for internal performance measurement purposes? For inter-firm comparisons, figures have to be taken in the form in which they are available, but within a business, it is possible to adopt a different approach to attempt to reflect reality, or at least, policies that are not overtly prudent and conservative.

Historic or current cost

The historic cost convention underpins most businesses' external financial statements, although revamped current cost financial statements are provided nowadays by a few companies. Historic costs is one accounting convention, however, which tends to be ignored in the preparation of many aspects of management accounting data such as budgets and standard costs – the principal exception regrettably being segmental performance measurement. Perhaps this follows from the felt need to segmentalize not only the organization but its objectives and financial measures as well.

Some drawbacks of an historic cost measure in an inflationary period can perhaps be illustrated by considering again the A. Freighter/ROI example. Table 8.10 takes the original figures but assumes an annual 10 per cent increase in operating costs, vehicle costs and selling prices.

This results in net profits increasing at a rate of over 20 per cent because (a) depreciation remains static, being based on the original cost of the vehicle in spite of its replacement cost increasing annually and (b) gross margins are increasing in line with inflation. This simply makes the ROI percentage increase even faster than when there was no inflation.

If however, inflation adjustments were made to the performance measurements in a similar way to those adopted for the published financial statements, performance criteria would be at least no less steady than if there were no inflation, thus reducing the possibilities of invidiously comparing different segments with very

Table 8.10 A. Freighter – effects of inflation upon ROI%

	Years			
	1	*2*	*3*	*4*
Profit	*£000*	*£000*	*£000*	*£000*
Sales less operating costs	25	27.5	30.25	33.275
Depreciation	(15)	(15)	(15)	(15)
Net profits	10	12.5	15.25	18.275
Capital employed (as originally)				
Vehicle at cost	60	60	60	60
Depreciation	15	30	45	60
Net book amount	45	30	15	0
ROI%	16.7	27.7	50.8	121.8

different effective inflation rates. Bearing in mind that most companies have this information available for external disclosure purposes, why should management feel it needs even less information than that provided to shareholders?

Asset hire or ownership

One fundamental problem in comparing the relative performance of investment centres within an organization (or indeed of entire businesses) has been the differences in practice on the ownership of assets. One business/segment may have decided to buy the assets it uses, another business/segment to rent, hire or lease business assets whenever possible. In such situations, the former is almost certain to have a much lower ROI than the latter, particularly in the earlier years, given relative similarity in other respects. Consider again the A. Freighter example, this time with a working capital of £10,000, compared with an otherwise identical operator, B. Freighter, which hires its vehicles at an annual cost of £21,000. A comparison of operating ROI is shown in Table 8.11. In this particular case A. Freighter's ROI is worse than B. Freighter's until the last year. Thus A may appear less profitable than B simply because of its asset financing practices/policies.

If, however, a residual income approach were adopted, a different, perhaps fairer view, could be obtained. Table 8.12 illustrates this using again a 10 per cent required rate of return. In this particular case the measured relative profitability is reversed, A looking better than B in all but the first year.

The extent to which businesses own or hire/lease assets varies considerably even in the same industry. Even within particular organizations, different practices may exist, although many would consider the financing decision to be the prerogative of head office finance. This is particularly so where leased assets are considered to be an 'on balance sheet' item, i.e. where the asset is treated for financial accounting purposes as if it were owned; the capital cost and related depreciation are separated from the interest element of the lease, which is written

Table 8.11   A. Freighter – comparison of ROI-owned and hired fixed assets

| | Years | | | |
| | 1 | 2 | 3 | 4 |
	£000	£000	£000	£000
A. Freighter				
Profit statement				
Sales	50	50	50	50
Operating costs	(25)	(25)	(25)	(25)
Depreciation	(15)	(15)	(15)	(15)
Net profit	10	10	10	10
Capital employed				
Vehicle at cost	60	60	60	60
Depreciation	15	30	45	60
Net book amount	45	30	15	0
Working capital	10	10	10	10
Total capital employed	55	40	25	10
RIO Percentage	4	18	25	40
B. Freighter				
Profit statement				
Sales	50	50	50	50
Operating costs	(25)	(25)	(25)	(25)
Hiring charges	(21)	(21)	(21)	(21)
Net profits	4	4	4	4
Capital employed				
Working capital	10	10	10	10
ROI percentage	40	40	40	40

NB   ROI based on asset figures at the beginning of the period. Working capital being treated as an opening balance.

off in the accounts over the leasing period. In such a situation the financial accounting policies may well be reflected in the management performance measures and thus any anomaly between owned or leased assets is effectively removed. Additionally, the financial gearing of the business as a whole will be affected.

However, by no means all hiring/leasing contracts are 'on balance sheet'. A distinction can be drawn between financing and operating leases; in the lessee's accounts, the former lease will be treated for accounting purposes as if the asset was owned, the latter as a hire charge. For some segments/businesses, property is a substantial part of their fixed asset expenditures, while others rent or lease their business premises. In such cases, ROI and RI measures can still result in invidious comparisons between investment centres.

Table 8.12 Comparison of residual incomes – owned and hired fixed assets

| | Years | | | |
	1 £000	2 £000	3 £000	4 £000
A. Freighter				
Profitability statement				
Net profit[i]	10	10	10	10
Required return[ii]	7	5.5	7	2.5
Residual income £000	3	4.5	6	7.5
B. Freighter				
Profitability statement				
Net profits[i]	4	4	4	4
Required return[ii]	1	1	1	1
Residual income	3	3	3	3

Notes
(i) Figures ex Table 8.5
(ii) 10% of opening capital employed for A. Freighter, e.g. in year 1, 10% of 60 + 10 = 70.
(iii) 10% of capital employed of £10,000 working capital.

Apportionments, attributability and controllability

Profit concepts

When making comparisons between external businesses, the alternative profit concepts available to the analyst are somewhat limited – essentially to those available in published data, which, with few exceptions, relate to some variation of net profit. Indeed all examples of investment centre performance used in this chapter have consistently used net profit as the profit measure.

It is necessary however to consider the value of net profit as the basis for both segmental and managerial performance measurement across all investment centres within a business. The investment centre approach can be applied within businesses to segments both large and small: from large divisions of conglomerates to small sections of operating units. Should such different segments be measured on the same basis, even if both are treated as investment centres, or can some appropriate differentiation be found? Some investment centre managers have the ability to control most, if not all, of the costs, revenues and investments constituting their performance measure: others may have relatively little control over perhaps significant aspects of cost, revenue and investment. Should both these managers be measured by similar criteria or should some differentiation be considered to reflect their different situations?

Measuring segment or management

As indicated earlier there must always be a danger that a business segment and its management become so associated in the minds of senior management that the performance of the segment is effectively treated as being the performance of its managers. It could be argued that, if the manager's responsibilities are to manage an investment centre, the requisite duties are effectively analogous to those of the segment's objectives and that therefore the same measure should be applied to each. However, as indicated earlier, good managers may be responsible for poorly performing segments, perhaps if the industry as a whole is in, say, a slump or a highly competitive state. In these circumstances, the manager may be performing very well indeed. In contrast, a manager of a higher performing segment may be failing to manage the segment as successfully as he might. Additionally, the risk orientation of the business must be considered in relation to the return: a business in a high risk industry or one which adopts a high risk profile could be expected to have higher returns than those in low risk industries or with a low risk profile.

It is surely apparent that the measures applied to the manager need to be different from those applied to the segment. But in what respects should the measures differ? Suggestions over recent years (see Solomons,[5] Shillinglaw,[6] Amey and Eggington[7]) have concentrated on distinguishing between controllability in the measurement of managers and attributability in the measurement of investment centres.

Controllability and attributability

It would be reasonable to assume that management would wish to measure an individual manager on the basis of those aspects of the business the manager is able to control which presumably would reflect the autonomy and decision-making authority delegated to the manager. Although, as discussed earlier, this will vary from centre to centre, for an investment centre manager significant aspects of revenues costs and investment are likely to be included.

The controllability approach suggests therefore that a variety or range of profitability measures be considered. Investment centre managers may then be evaluated by the profitability and/or non-financial measures which best suit their delegated authority and ability to control.

The attributability approach follows a similar reasoning and suggests that differing degrees of attributability of costs may be relevant for different management comparison control and decision-making purposes.

Shillinglaw[8] has suggested four profit concepts:

1   Sales margin, i.e. total revenues less total variable costs.
2   Controllable profit or sales margin less all the division's fixed costs controllable by the manager.
3   Contribution margin or controllable profit less all other costs directly traceable to the division.

4 Net profit, or contribution margin less some share of general management and service centre costs.

As he points out, no one of the four profit concepts is 'best'. None is superior for all purposes. Each has a value for differing control and/or decision-making purposes.

Sales margin concentrates on sales volume and price and production efficiency responsibilities. 'Controllable profit' emphasizes the profit margins controllable by the manager while 'contribution margin' measures profit on attributability bases – attributable that is to the business segment.

Net profit, however, is described by Shillinglaw[9] as appearing to be a logical basis on which to judge investment centres but summarized as the least useful of the four concepts. Its usefulness for both evaluation and guidance is destroyed by the arbitrary allocations of extra divisional expenses that must be made in order to derive a net profit figure.

Emmanuel and Otley[10] adapt the approach of Amey,[11] Solomons,[5] and Amey and Eggington[7] and suggest a wider range of profit classifications (Figure 8.1). Their first two profit concepts are similar to those suggested by Shillinglaw[8] though with sales margin called controllable contribution. Thereafter, two alternative sets of profit concepts are adopted, one relating to profit attributable to the segment (traceable profit, net profit and net profit after tax) and the other profit controllable by the manager (controllable residual income before and after taxes and net residual income after taxes).

The principles on which these profit concepts are based are well accepted in accounting texts, although Amey[11] suggests that 'in the interests of achieving the firm's overall objective, divisions should not ... have the power to determine their own capital investment'.

The academic argument against apportionments and far more emphasis on attributability and controllability is by no means accepted in business. In those companies of which the authors have recent experience,[3,4] the willingness to view profit measures in more than one way is common, although most businesses retain the net profit concept as either the main objective for their investment centre managers or to remind them of those costs which are incurred on their behalf, even if they are not directly attributable or controllable. This widely held view in business today makes the point that if investment centre managers are not regularly reminded of their segments' non-attributable/controllable costs, there is a danger that they will ignore them from an operating decision viewpoint. However, for control, it should surely be argued that these costs can only be managed at a senior level and therefore should not be included in investment centre management's routine control information. If they are, there must be the danger that managers' attention is distracted away from the aspects they can control, or that their energies are given to arguing the unfairness of these charges, with demotivational effects. Do investment managers think like that? Some certainly do. The important aspect, however, is that the segmental/management performance measures used and the detailed information given to those managers should be agreed upon by senior management and not left to be decided by default.

```
Sales to outside customers                              XXX
Internal sales                                          XXX
                                                        XXX

        Less   Variable costs of goods sold
                  externally and internally            XXX
               Variable divisional expenses            XXX

               Controllable contribution               XXX
        Less   Controllable divisional overhead        XXX

Controllable profit                                     XXX

Less  Depreciation and              Less  Depreciation and
      expenses on                         controllable
      divisional fixed                     fixed assets           XXX
      assets              XXX
      Non-controllable                Expenses (e.g. leases)
      divisional                         relating to controllable
      overheads          XXX             fixed assets             XXX
                                       Interest on controllable
                                          investments             XXX
                         – – –                                   – – –

      Traceable profit   XXX         Controllable residual
                                         income before taxes      XXX

Less  Allocated central             Less  Depreciation on
      expenses           XXX               non-controllable
                                           fixed assets           XXX
                                       Allocated central
                                          expenses                XXX
                                       Interest on
                                          non-controllable
                         – – –             investments            XXX

      Net profit         XXX         Net residual income
                                        before taxes              XXX

Less  Taxation on                   Less  Taxation on
      divisional income                   divisional
                         XXX               income                 XXX

      Net profit after tax          Net residual income
                         XXX           after taxes                XXX
```

Figure 8.1   *Alternative forms of divisional profit measures (adapted from Emmanuel and Otley, 1985)*

The investment base

The same arguments which apply to controllable and attributable profit also apply to the investment base. If investment centre management or segments are to be fairly measured, the investment base must be as appropriate as the profit concept. Thus, for any given manager, controllable profit can be related to controllable investment, and, for any given segment, attributable profit can be related to attributable investment.

In administrative/accounting terms this may of course require some changes in the information system, which would need to identify, as far as practicable, the fixed and current assets of each investment centre. While fixed assets and the depreciation may not be too difficult to identify with particular segments, the same may not be true of current assets. Are debtors recorded and controlled centrally? Can the actual debtors of each segment be identified, especially where segments have the same customers? Are stocks held locally and/or centrally? Is cash considered to be a controllable item at segment level or are any such surpluses controlled centrally? Are creditors relatable to each segment or are they controlled centrally?

Of course the information system would ideally need to reflect asset controllability as well as attributability, but in many, perhaps most, cases these are likely to be similar. However, this does raise the question of just how controllable by investment centre managers are the fixed assets? Can the manager, for example, identify a surplus asset and either physically or book-wise have it excluded from their accountability and returned to a central pool? It is not uncommon in building and contracting industries, for example, to have a central plant and equipment stock through which management can change its fixed asset investment levels according to requirements. Not only does each investment centre manager recognize his accountability for such fixed assets, but he/she is thereby encouraged to return surplus fixed assets rather than have them standing idle. This makes them available to other investment centre managers, and economies in plant and equipment cost and utilization are therefore improved.

One specialist haulier known to the authors has a pool of vehicles which are attributed to the segment that operates them. They are controllable in that vehicles not required in the long term are appropriated elsewhere and extra vehicles required are either transferred to the segment or bought for it. This forms a controllable investment base perhaps, but the costs are perhaps not controllable! It is central management's policy to place newer vehicles in the busier segments of the business and older ones in the less busy. A busy segment therefore usually has disproportionately high depreciation and fixed asset investment costs than one that is less busy. Of course the advantage of lower repair and maintenance costs and higher utilization rates helps to compensate, but the effect on the busy segment's profitability is almost certainly negative.

The other side of the coin, however, is that, if attributability and controllability are practised, the problems of apportioning the fixed assets of the business to each investment centre is unnecessary. Such apportionments can be time-consuming, arbitrary and frequently the cause of discontent among segment managers. Apportionments will not be seen as fair by those who feel they are adversely affected by them.

However, if central management is interested in comparing the performance of investment centres with organizations outside the business, it may be necessary for some apportionment of fixed assets to be made. If not, the controllable and/or attribute investment base is unlikely to be comparable with the data available on these external entities.

Short-term measures, long-term goals

By definition, an investment centre is a business entity, small or large, responsible for profitability and investment. As a large proportion of investment is likely to be of a long-term nature – fixed assets, new products, new markets, etc. – the appropriate performance measure should logically be a long-term one, at least in part.

Profitability indices such as ROI and RI are potentially capable of reflecting long-term performance of past decisions but not recent or current decisions. The measures are for a particular period but not of the future. They are therefore effectively short-term measures which if overemphasized as a measure of performance can only lead to short-term decision making, dysfunctional in the longer term. The potential for such decisions will be apparent from the foregoing.

It could be proposed of course that those ROI and RI measures be applied only to longer-term profitability by using, for example, three or four year rolling/average profitability indexes. But this is likely to be both impractical and misleading. Is a new manager to he held responsible for the decisions of his/her predecessors? If a manager expects to be in a particular post for only two or three years before being promoted or leaving for pastures new, of what relevance is a long-term measure, even if a fair one were found? Would errors of judgement affecting the long term not be as apparent as with shorter-term performance measures?

It is the use made of this profitability index which is the critical factor. If it is not overemphasized, but perhaps used as just one of a range of measures, the impact upon managers' behaviour should not be dysfunctional. If businesses place an undue emphasis on such profitability indices, adverse behavioural effects aimed at achieving short-term results will surely be encouraged. Worse, those managers who do take a longer-term view at the expense of shorter-term performance may well not be allowed by the company to survive long enough to be judged upon the long-term benefits. Further, that manager is likely to have missed out on the rewards of shorter-term performance in terms of personal salary and promotion. Those who gain promotions are perhaps more likely to be those who achieve short-term results than those who strive to achieve such in the longer term.

Is therefore the concentration by management on profitability indices which are not seen by managers as fair or relating to attributable and controllable features likely to have demotivational effects on investment centre managers? Will such controls simply discourage managers from long-term planning and decision-making and cause them to settle for the achievements of shorter-term performance measures? If senior management closes its eyes to this problem, it is quite likely, perhaps inevitable, that those managers who achieve senior management status are those who will have been motivated towards shorter-term measures and therefore will not see any need to change the control measures. Naturally, once this situation is reached, it is likely to be self-perpetuating.

Profit centres

As discussed earlier, a profit centre is the term used for 'a segment of the business entity by which both revenues are received and expenditures are caused or controlled, such revenues and expenditure being used to evaluate segmental performance'.[2] The presumption therefore is that the manager is responsible for both the sources of supply and the sale thereof. Sources of supply may well include the manufacture or the buying in of goods or operation of services; 'sale' is likely to include decisions as to markets (perhaps within constraints so as not to trespass on the allotted areas of other segments of the business and the marketing mix – pricing, promotion, product design and perhaps distribution networks). The autonomy, however, that profit centre managers are given may well be restricted by internal trading requirements – the sourcing of goods and service supplies and the sale to selected customers, including probably the prices of any such trading. A profit centre does not relate profit to the level of investment in the segment, although of course its manager's decision making may well have investment repercussions, if only on working capital. Thus performance measures must be of profitability unrelated to investment per se.

The profit measure

Essentially, a profit centre's performance is judged upon the level of profit earned and the trend thereof, perhaps related to some aspects of output, e.g. profit as a percentage of sales, or as a percentage of input (profit per vehicle, machine or employee). The profit to sales percentage is by far the commonest measure, although this is usually used in addition to the growth trends in absolute amounts of profit.

However, in the same way that the ROI measure was questioned as regards its components, 'what return?' and 'what investment?', so here the challenge must be made concerning 'what incomes?' and 'what costs?'. In other words, 'what are the profits?'.

In fact, interpretations of profit for profit centre purposes are similar in many respects to those considered earlier for investment centre purposes. Operating and trading profits, and net profits before loan interest, are logical measures, but not of course after loan interest or post-tax, as these have capital gearing implications. The relevance to these interpretations of profit of accounting conventions and policies, including that of historic versus current costs and the hiring versus leasing argument, are also important considerations in profit centre performance measurement.

Such profit concepts as controllable contribution margin, controllable profit and traceable profit, discussed earlier, probably have at least as great a significance in profit centre measurement as they may be appropriately tailored to the specific responsibility aspects of profit centres, large and small, within a business. The arguments for these approaches will not be repeated here, except to suggest that the arguments against their use on investment centre measurement are less strong in a profit centre context. While it could be argued that a net profit figure is needed to compare against total invested capital, no such objective exists in profit centres, where net profit is of no special significance. Hence some interpretation of controllable or attributable profit before apportionments could be expected to be more popular in practice within profit centres than investment centres.

The contradiction between the short- and long-term nature of profitability measures is also relevant to profit centre performance assessments.

The added value concept

The added value concept, probably more appropriate to profit centres than investment centres, is an increasingly popular measure of profitability. Although various methods of calculations are used, the basic theme is that profitability is measured by the differences between sales and the cost of bought-in goods (and sometimes services). The difference is the amount of value added to the material inputs by the operation of the business, the bulk of which is usually the employment of staff, whether direct or indirect. This concept is particularly useful in situations where the sales value of items can be high or low, depending primarily on the cost of material inputs. If the sales value does not vary proportionately with resource inputs such as direct labour or machine time, sales value and such measures as profit as a percentage of sales are poor and inconsistent indicators of performance. In such circumstances added value can replace profit as a profitability measure in absolute terms or as a ratio in relation to resource inputs such as machine labour hours or be the base against which some interpretation of profit is compared.

Profit to sales percentage

This ratio simply expresses the size of the profit to the output, expressed at sales value, and together with turnover of capital forms the first two elements of the ROI pyramid of ratios. The components effectively being compared of course are the levels of sales revenues and costs (sales − costs = profit), and it could thus be argued that the measure is soundly based. As with all performance measures, however, there is always a danger that the profit to sales ratio will, in motivating a manager towards its achievement, cause dysfunctional behaviour. In this case the emphasis of the ratio is on the size of profit margin. This may be achieved by a number of actions which to some extent pull in different directions, e.g. cost reduction, increased volumes and increased prices.

Cost reductions achieved by improvements in efficiency is an excellent means of increasing the sales margin, because it need have no repercussions elsewhere and gives the profit centre more flexibility for pricing in periods of high competition or low industry activity. If, however, cost reductions are achieved by a reduction in the quality of the product and/or service available to the customer, any increases in margin may be short-lived.

Changes in the volume of output can sometimes have a significant effect on the measured unit cost and therefore on resultant sales margins, as fixed costs spread more thinly across larger volumes. If sales volumes are increased without a reduction in sales prices, higher margins should result. If the higher output levels require additional fixed cost expenditures, the long- and short-term aspects may again be important in that incremental fixed costs resultant from increases in output may not be easily removed if volumes subsequently decrease. If volumes are increased by a reduction in sales prices, however, significant longer-term implications may ensue. Will reductions invite retaliation from competitors? For how long will the additional volumes be retained? What are the longer-term prospects in the market and in particular the effects upon the profit centre?

If prices are increased to achieve higher margins, this may or may not prove a desirable action. If the centre's prices were low for some or all customers, a change in price may well have no serious long-term effect on volume. The danger of increased prices is that the higher margins are achieved on small sales volumes. Although of course smaller volumes, by increasing average unit costs, can decrease resultant margins, it is quite possible that a profit centre can unconsciously become a high price/low volume business, with resultant lower levels of total profit. No doubt for this reason the objective of increased sales volumes is frequently linked with the profit to sales percentage measure. It is perhaps the fear of the opposite effect, i.e. achieving volumes by low prices (what is sometimes called chasing marginal business), that makes the profit to sales percentage so popular.

As would be expected, the sales price:volume:cost:profit relationship is of critical importance in managing profit centres. The major concern, however, must be that in the achievement of higher margins, profit in relation to investment is not also optimally achieved. If higher margins are achieved by lower prices and increased volumes, additional investment may result either from an earlier than expected exhaustion of fixed assets or the need for incremental capacity. If higher margins are achieved at the expense of lower volumes, the danger is more of a contraction in longer-term volumes and market share, resulting in lower total profitability with a fixed investment base.

Profit growth objectives

The objective of profit growth in absolute terms is frequently used as a profit centre measure, either as the principal measure or in conjunction with profit/sales or other ratios. If capital investment is effectively fixed, profit maximization, i.e. making the best of what you've got is the obvious and optimal business objective and therefore performance measure. However, as capital is unlikely to be fixed in the longer term, the measure would be logical only as a short- or medium-term indicator.

Measures which compare profit with resources inputs such as employees or equipment may be seen as a surrogate for ROI, i.e. resources could be seen as financed by the investment. Their use in practice, however, tends to be limited to that of an ancillary measure, and they are unlikely to be used as a measure of prime importance except perhaps in businesses where management expertise or specialist equipment are in scarce supply and are effectively limiting factors as far as profitability is concerned.

Why profit centres?

Profit centres tend to be used relatively rarely in practice, the extension into an investment centre being considerably more popular and in many cases more logical. Although investment centres may also be measured as a profit centre, i.e. in profit to sales percentage and sales growth terms, profit centres tend to be used where the investment centre approach is seen to be either less relevant or inapplicable to a particular segment. *Budgeted* profit centres however are very popular indeed, and in particular, profit as an absolute sum and as a percentage of turnover.

When a company makes an investment in plant and equipment, especially if it is flow- or process-oriented, say a steel mill or motor assembly line, such an investment is effectively a sunk cost, with relatively little sale or alternative use value. The object therefore must be to use that equipment as profitably as possible. In such circumstances ROI, whether it be high or low, is of little relevance to decision making or control except in a post-audit of investment sense. The treatment of the segment as a profit centre may therefore be more appropriate, in that it directs management's attention to the one objective whereas ROI may add concern over the investment (which is effectively more relevant from a decision-making point of view) and worry the managers unnecessarily.

The owning or hiring/leasing of assets was discussed earlier as a problem of investment centre performance measurement. If one segment owns and another leases assets, their respective performances as investment centres are likely to differ, perhaps considerably. In many industries there has been a trend away from the ownership of business assets towards the hiring and leasing of operating assets, the sale and perhaps leaseback of property, the discounting of debtors and towards obtaining stocks just in time by requiring suppliers to hold stock or by having such on a sale or return basis. Although there have been some tax advantages in these actions, the principal benefit has perhaps been in the areas of cash flow – the release of funds for other parts of the business.

The effect of these actions is that many businesses effectively have relatively few owned assets and therefore capital invested either in some or all of the segments of their business. When this occurs, the investment centre approach is not, effectively, an available option, but as the profit objective remains, a profit centre approach is the only logical responsibility centre basis.

An example of this is the Central Freight Co. This haulier operated a large number of depots situated in large British conurbations, each of them treated as an investment centre. Even at this time there were anomalies between owned premises old and new, and rented premises. As the business expanded, the pressure on capital and liquidity became significant. Operating assets, especially vehicles, were frequently leased if cash was not available, and this soon became the normal means of acquiring such assets. Further, in order to release capital some depots with a high market value were sold and either leased back or moved to a rented site. The attributable fixed assets of many depots therefore became negligible, while others were little changed. In such a situation ROI was of little relevance as a basis for comparison across the group or indeed of trends over time and against other similar organizations. Although the investment centre concept had effectively broken down, the profit centre concept was unlikely to be an acceptable alternative basis in such circumstances. Comparison was impossible between depots when some rented and others owned their property and therefore had no rental, or between those which leased vehicles and those which operated owned assets now depreciated perhaps wholly or only to a small extent.

If a profit centre approach was to be adopted all equalization of ownership/rental/leasing was required. Corporate divisions were established to own all operating assets and property. Assets were then rented/leased back to the depots on a 'going rate' basis. Thus all depots were treated in a similar fashion, but the capital base per depot had disappeared. Profit performance measures of profit percentage of sales and sales volume growth were established. Interestingly, however, some responsibility for investment remains. New operating assets can be applied for and surplus assets reassigned to other depots, such actions being reflected in the charge made for assets used. Stocks are under depot control although much of these are on a sale or return basis. Debtors are considered to be a depot responsibility, although debt collection is organized centrally, and only slow payers are referred to depot management for collection. Poor working capital control is therefore not reflected in the profit centre performance measure, which might therefore encourage a laxity in this area. However, management performance is also assessed via a number of performance measures, including those for stock and debtor control.

Budgeted profit and investment centres

It can be argued that many of the deficiencies of profit and investment centre measures discussed in this chapter can be remedied or ameliorated if a budget centre approach is adopted, i.e. if segments are measured against a budgeted level of performance. Thus, for example, the increasing ROI percentage over time is not a problem, it is argued, if such is compared against a budget for the increase, which might reasonably be anticipated (as the asset depreciates).

As discussed earlier, to compare one profit or investment centre's performance against another's may well be illogical if each segment is operating under different circumstances – industry, location, market etc. – certainly in the shorter term. To be fair, a segment's performance needs to be compared against a comparable parameter, of which a budget may be the most applicable and appropriate. The popularity of budgeted profit and investment centre measures can be seen as an acceptance of the need for budgets as a comparator, but in some respects it is applied somewhat illogically. If a budget makes allowance for the special circumstances of a segment, what is the logic of comparing such a profit budget against capital employed whether actual or budgeted? Indeed, is not the logical measure controllable or attributable profit or residual income? The asset base in the shorter term is surely irrelevant, even if, say, working capital is considered to be controllable or attributable. Surely such can be better measured by separate, more specific, measures?

As a control measure therefore, while budgets add an extra dimension to the measurement of profit and investment centres, the use of the same ratios/ comparisons in a budget:actual context may not be so logical. However, the projected ROI over, say, the five years of a segment's corporate plan may be a very useful measure for decision making and be the basis for a longer-term post-audit of the performance of a segment or, in particular, its management, especially if the budget incorporated new developments or the ideas of new management.

Non-financial criteria

The foregoing has concentrated upon the financial aspects of performance, appraisal and control. Non-financial measures should not, however, be forgotten. An amusing, but highly effective article by Robert Bittlestone of Metapraxis in June 1991,[12] likened the predominance of financial measures to accountants measuring car speed in dollars; 'What speed are we doing, Jim?' 'Hold on a minute, Bob. The figures are just coming through now. This is just a flash estimate, we don't have the full results yet, but it looks as if we're doing about $55'. Silly? Well, hopefully it reminds accountants that their love affair with financial measures is not shared by everyone, nor is it relevant in all situations. Performance measurement today goes well beyond the purely financial.

Key results analysis

In 1952, The General Electric Co. (GE) in the USA, following extensive decentralization of its operations, recognized the need for an improved system of management control and evolved a set of eight 'key result areas' for the measurement of divisions (not managers), as follows:

1 Profitability, defined as residual income,
2 Market position, measured in terms of market share,
3 Productivity, recognized as being difficult to define, but broadly based on the inputs of capital and labour versus outputs of sales, added value, or other suitable measure.
4 Product leadership, i.e. being a market leader in product innovation and development.
5 Personnel development, i.e. the bringing-on of staff to fill vacancies, allow expansion, etc.
6 Employee attitudes, i.e. employee attitudes which might influence future behaviour and thus objective achievement.
7 Public responsibility, an ethical objective to stakeholders – the public, shareholders, customers, suppliers, employees – and the environment in general.
8 Balance between short-range and long-range goals, of survival and growth over 5, 10, 15 and more years.

The company's planning, budgeting and forecasting programme then incorporated these key result areas before reviewing the recent and present levels of achievement, setting standards for each department, planning their achievement and establishing their periodic reporting.

As will be apparent, such a multi-faceted approach may have considerable merits in (i) recognizing the breadth of organizational objectives, and (ii) being widely adaptable to a variety of managerial situations. Its implementation, however, may be fraught with difficulties.

Definition

The most obvious problem perhaps is that of clearly and unambiguously defining the objective. 'Market share', for example, may be defined in many ways and 'public responsibility' may be definable in only general terms.

Measurement

If performance is to be appraised, achievement must be measured. The extent to which the GE key result areas may be objectively evaluated is likely to vary considerably, some elements being relatively simple to establish performance measures for, others far less so. Given a definition, profitability and productivity may be easily measured, with evaluation of market position and product leadership being rather more complex. But how would one measure personnel development, employee attitude and public responsibility? The use of subjective judgement is likely to be an essential ingredient in the evaluation of the non-quantifiable and perhaps some quantifiable performances.

Objective ranking and suboptimality

Objectives such as those proposed may to some extent be mutually exclusive: market position may be achieved at the expense of profitability; productivity while risking employee attitudes; personnel development at the expense of long-term goals. This problem may be mitigated perhaps by establishing a hierarchy of or ranking of objectives, e.g. (i) Profit, (ii) Market position. . . . Alternatively, each objective may be given a weighting, reflecting top management's perceived valuation of each facet's importance. In doing so, a minimum achievement level of each element may be established, below which superior performance in other areas will not be considered sufficient compensation.

A divisional measure?

The key results areas established by GE were specifically aimed at measuring the performance of divisions and departments and not necessarily their management. However, as discussed earlier, the separation of the performance of a segment and its management is not always clear. There are, and always will be, behavioural implications in measuring performance.

In a subsequent study at GE, Meyer, Kay and French[13] concluded that:

- Criticism has a negative effect on the achievement of goals.
- Praise has little effect one way or the other.
- Performance improves most when specific goals are established.
- Defensiveness resulting from critical appraisal produces inferior performance.
- Coaching should be a day-to-day, not a once a year activity.
- Mutual goal setting, not criticism, improves performance.
- Interviews designed to improve an individual's performance should not at the same time weigh his salary or promotion in the balance.
- Participation by managers in the goal setting procedure helps produce favourable results.

Most managers have responsibility for a wide range of activities, some of which may not be easily measured objectively. The fact that financial measures are objective should not necessarily imply that they are appropriate as the sole or prime criteria. Non-financial indicators and even subjective judgement may be at least as important as financial criteria, depending upon the objective being measured. Evaluation complexity or difficulty should not be an excuse, merely a challenge.

Benchmarking

A phenomenon of the early 1990s was the growth in popularity of benchmarking as an aid to business improvement and performance measurement, practised and accepted across the range of business functions. The concept, though far from new, caught the mood of business, following on from concepts such as JIT, total quality management, change management and continual improvement. Its focus was simply that, in setting standards of quality and performance that a business should aim to achieve in everything it does, by comparing itself, i.e. benchmarking, in every single facet of a business's operations, against the best – the best at each activity the business engages in. Thus, a distribution unit of a toy manufacturer may compare itself with the business with the best distribution service of any industry worldwide. The more traditional basis of comparison of the best in one's own industry has severe limitations, although of course it can be instructive. While the basis of comparison may be similar, competition makes the inner workings of another business difficult to access, ideas are not necessarily 'new', and are not likely to lead to competitive advantage – just reduced disadvantage. Different and perhaps more instructive lessons can be learnt by seeing how other types of organization resolve similar problems – not so much lateral thinking as lateral viewing! Such benchmark firms may be more willing to discuss their practices as the firms will not be in competition with each other and the firm itself may learn from the comparison.

It is important to recognize that benchmarking is not simply a new performance measurement tool. Its principles can be, and are applied in all aspects of business – marketing, selling, distribution, manufacturing, operations, finance, administration – and all types of organizations – service, manufacturing, retail and the public sector – and are aimed at real improvement. Performance measurement is essentially a side benefit, though of course, a potentially important one.

The balanced scorecard approach

A complementary development of this theme is the balanced scorecard approach developed by US consultants Nolan, Norton and Company Inc. with Robert S. Kaplan of Harvard Business School, published in the *Harvard Business Review*, Jan/Feb 1992. Its concept has much in common with that of the General Electric Co. in the early 1960s (see Key results analysis as discussed on page 158) in that it attempts to address the need to perform, and therefore measure performance, across a wide range of managerial duties, related to the business's strategic and tactical needs.

The approach is that goals and appropriate performance criteria are established in respect of four inter-related areas of business, crucial to success:

1   **The financial perspective**, i.e. satisfying the shareholders, the goals and measures for which will be essentially financial and shareholder value oriented in nature
2   **The customer perspective**, i.e. customer service goals relating to those, usually non-financial, factors that concern customers, such as quality, time, performance and service.
3   **The internal business perspective**, i.e. what the company must do internally to meet customer and shareholder financial expectations. Examples may include cycle times, quality, efficiency and employee skill levels.
4   **The innovation and learning perspective,** i.e. continued improvements, product and process innovation and value creation, necessary to achieve both customer and internal business perspectives.

As the reader will have noticed, this is a total business concept, and it is perhaps fitting at the end of this chapter to remind ourselves that performance achievement is necessary in all facets of modern business. The challenge is to find performance criteria that are appropriate to the goals of each manager and sector of an organization. Measures may be financial or physical, quantified or subjective, short or long termist in effect, used singly or with other measures; at the discretion of both managers and managed, it is to be hoped that the choice(s) made are both goal congruent with organizational and personal objectives and motivational to those being measured.

References

1.   Kaplan, R.S. and Norton, D.P., The Balanced Scorecard – measures that drive performance, *Harvard Business Review*, Jan/Feb, 1992.
2.   Coates, J.B., Smith, J.E. and Stacey, R.J., Results of a Preliminary Survey into the Structure of Divisionalized Companies, Divisionalized Performance

Appraisal and the Associated Role of Management Accounting. In *Management Accounting Research and Practice*, ICMA, 1983.

3. Coates, J.B., Rickwood, C.P. and Stacey, R.J., Examination of the Differences Between Academic Concepts and Actual Management Accounting Practices. Report to ESRC, British Library Document Supply Centre, August 1987.

4. Rickwood, C.P., Coates, J.B. and Stacey, R.J., Managed Costs and the Capture of Information, *Accounting and Business Research*, Vol. 17, No. 68, Autumn 1987.

5. Solomons, D., Divisional Performance Measurement and Control. Richard D. Irwin Inc., 1965.

6. Shillinglaw, G., *Managerial Cost Accounting*. Richard D. Irwin Inc., 1961.

7. Amey, L.R. and Eggington, D.A., Management Accounting – a Conceptual Approach. Longman, 1973.

8. Shillinglaw, G., Guides to Internal Profit Measurement, *Harvard Business Review*, Vol. 35, No. 2, March/April 1957, pp. 82–94.

9. Shillinglaw, G., *Managerial Cost Accounting, op. cit.*

10. Emmanuel, C.R. and Otley, D.T., *Accounting for Management Control*. Van Nostrand Reinhold (UK), 1985.

11. Amey, L.R., *The Efficiency of Business Enterprises*. Allen and Unwin, 1969.

12. Bittlestone, R., Financial Perestroika on 1–95, *The Soft Machine*, June 1991.

13. Meyer, H.H., Kay, E. and French, J.P.R., Split Roles in Performance Appraisal, *Harvard Business Review*, January/February 1965.

Questions

1   (a)   What are the potential strengths and weaknesses of the profit centre approach to performance appraisal?

    (b)   Why has the popularity of cost centres declined in recent years in favour of profit centres?

2   'The linking of budget performance to an individual's reward package is a natural development of control via budget centres.' Consider this assertion and identify the positive and negative aspects of such an approach.

3   IVY plc manufacture invalid vehicles in Birmingham, England, for sale worldwide. The vehicles are marketed in Britain and Eire by the UK division; in Europe by the Europe division, based in Switzerland; and in North and South America by the Americas division, based in New Orleans.

    Although there is currently only one model, the need to comply with safety and other requirements of overseas countries creates substantial additional manufacturing costs over and above those of the basic UK model.

    Vehicles are sold overseas at estimated cost price. Although it is difficult to record all the additional costs of overseas models, this is estimated by reference to the time and materials book onto production batches. These are added to the standard product costs of the UK model. In both cases, overheads are recovered at the budgeted blanket overhead recovery rate, currently 200 per cent of direct labour.

Included in the Budgeted Profit Statement attached are assumptions regarding tax rates and currently exchange rates in the UK, Switzerland and the USA.

Expert advice received is conflicting, reflecting the current state of uncertainty in politics, oil prices, the British and world economies and therefore currency exchange rates. Likely scenarios are briefly as follows:

1 The US dollar will lose 10 per cent value against European currencies and US sales volumes reduce by a similar percentage.
2 The £ sterling will lose 20 per cent value against the US dollar and 10 per cent against European currencies. Overseas sales will increase by a similar percentage in both cases.
3 A change in British government influences a 25 per cent £ sterling currency reduction against European and US currencies and will result in the introduction of exchange control and currency regulations.

Matters for consideration
(a) Which performance measures should IVY plc consider for the evaluation of its three divisions?
(b) Invalid vehicles are currently sold within the group at standard/estimated cost. Which transfer price method would you recommend:
    1 to facilitate the performance measures chosen?
    2 in order to maximize after tax profits for the group?
    3 in order to maximize liquidity
      (i) overseas, and
      (ii) in Britain?
(c) What legal and operating constraints need to be considered?

4 If ROCE has so many inherent deficiencies, why do you think it is so popular among senior managers?

5 (a) Consider the difficulties in applying key results analysis to the performance evaluation of segmented managers.
  (b) Why might it be desirable in spite of these difficulties?

6 As a junior consultant with Stokes Consultants you have gleaned the following information about a client company, Central Freight. The new managing director of the Elco Group has expressed concern about the relevancy and adequacy of the operating statements and appraisal measures both for Central Freight's internal purposes and as a basis for the management and control of CF by the Elco Group. He has given Stokes Consultants a wide ranging brief to examine and criticize the existing approach and to recommend such

IVY plc
Budgeted profit statement

	UK division		Europe division		Americas division		Consolidated Group Total
Sales volume	3,000		5,000		3,000		
	Total £000	Per unit £	Total £000	Per unit £	Total £000	Per unit £	Total £000
Sales – internal	24,900						44,000
Sales – external	10,500	3,500	20,000	4,000	13,500	4,500	44,000
	35,400		20,000	4,000	13,500	4,500	44,000
Cost of manufacture (all in UK)							
Variable costs:							
materials	12,600		6,000	1,200	3,600	1,200	12,600
labour	6,600		3,000	600	2,100	700	6,600
Fixed costs	13,200		6,000	1,200	4,200	1,400	13,200
Total	32,400		15,000	3,000	9,900	3,300	32,400
Cost of sales	(24,900)		15,000	3,000	9,900	3,300	
Selling and admin. costs	2,100	700	3,500	700	2,100	700	7,700
Profit before tax	900	300	1,500	300	1,500	500	3,900
Effective tax rates	35%		20%		45%		
Assumed Exchange Rate To £ sterling			2.75 Swiss Francs		1.40 US dollars		
Capital employed	13,200		2,000		1,500		16,700

MEMO ONLY (Cost of manufacture section for Europe and Americas divisions) alternatives as it thinks fit. However, he expects that any alternatives or changes proposed will be appropriate and that the likely implications of their imposition will be clearly stated.

Central Freight

Central Freight, a subsidiary of the Elco Group, is a large goods haulage company. It is organized on a regional basis, each region consisting of a number of operating depots which provide the services/products of the company. Regional and company head office staff act as a backup to and control of the depots.

Before 1974 the company offered only a general haulage service, although it also operated a separate 'contracts' company. However, following a change in strategy of the organization, it was decided to add 'new products', hopefully synergistically, stemming from a conversion of their main general haulage product. As a result each depot was then able to offer the following products:

1   *Contracts* – where an organization's road haulage function is taken over by Central Freight.
2   *General haulage* – a national service, although now on a much smaller scale, previous haulage work having been converted to other products, especially contracts.
3   *Warehousing* – a storage facility to other companies, perhaps related to distribution or general haulage products.
4   *Property* – the rental of surplus storage space to a third party.
5   *Truck rental* – the hire of trucks of various sizes and types either on a self-drive basis to individuals and organizations.
6   *Engineering* – the maintenance workshops for the company's fleet, surplus capacity being sold to the marketplace.
7   *Distribution* – the distribution of goods either held in Central Freight's or client companies' warehouses, which could involve a 'breaking of bulk' service.
8   *Rescue* – roadside assistance to commercial vehicles on motorways and elsewhere and providing an on-the-spot repair service, or bringing a vehicle into the engineering depot for more serious repairs.
9   *Trailer rental* – the rental of trailers with or without the truck rental.
10   *Miscellaneous*, covering any items of income or expenditure not covered under any other head.

A depot may have had any or all of these products, depending upon local demands. Thus in any one area one product may predominate, while others may be insignifcant or non-existent.

Each depot was treated by the company as a budgeted investment centre, as in turn were each of the products within each depot. Additionally, performance was compared with that budgeted for the investment centre as a whole and for its component parts.

While depot managers had an overall responsibility for all products within their depot, some products, depending on their nature of significance within the depot, also had individual product managers. Thus the engineering product invariably had an engineering manager, owing to the specialist nature of the product, while other products were managed directly by the depot manager with some assistance from subordinates.

Each product and depot, as indicated above, was expected to sell its services to the market at a profit, according to the local market conditions at any point in time. However, a considerable amount of inter-region, inter-depot and inter-product group (intra-depot) trading occurred. While wishing to retain the profit motivativation for such internal trading while encouraging (in theory requiring) the use of such facilities (rather than that of outside suppliers), fixed internal charge rates were agreed centrally for some products. These rates were designed such that intra-depot trading had the lowest margins, with increasing margins for inter-depot and inter-region transactions, the latter still being lower than the current market price, or at least no lower than a favoured customer.

The above resulted in the investment centre's revenues being generated from four different sources in terms of price structure, i.e. sales to other products within the same depot, sales to other depots in the same region, sales to other regions and sales to the general market. The proportions of these sales were largely dependent upon the particular location of a depot, the extent to which it had a variety of products, spare capacity for sale to the outside market, etc.

There were also directives on a number of expenditure items over which profit centres had little or no control. These included rates of pay (and to an extent the hiring and firing of staff) and the source and/or price of a number of expenditures such as fuel, tyres and insurance. Capital equipment was authorized at regional and/or company level, depending upon the size of expenditures proposed. There were also company policies regarding such factors as depreciation rates and the apportionment of depot, regional and head office overhead expenses across depots and product investment centres.

Operating statements

A periodic trading statement was produced for each depot, analysed between the ten product investment centres. This statement analysed revenue into eight categories of sale, as follows:

1　External sales – to own customers
2　External sales – to own customers, storage only
3　External sales – transportation work subcontracted to another depot, e.g. backloads
4　External sales transportation subcontracted to outside contractors
　　= Total customer revenue
5　Internal sales transportation work for other depots, e.g. backloads
6　Internal sales – intra-depot/products revenues
7　Internal sales – inter-depot revenues
8　Internal sales – inter-company revenues
　　= Total revenues

Expenditures included the costs of inter-group services, subcontracting and the various operating expenses of each investment centre, including depreciation, and *shared* depot overheads. The margin between these expenditures and revenue was defined as the 'gross operating profit'. Thereafter apportioned charges were subtracted to provide a 'trading profit or loss', which was then expressed as a percentage of (i) capital employed and (ii) revenues.

Capital employed itself contained a number of appointments, being composed of (a) directly attributable fixed assets, i.e. those assets which could be specifically identified with a particular product investment centre, (b) fixed assets directly attributable to a depot (though apportioned to product investment centres) and (c) working capital and regional and company head offices fixed assets, apportioned over depots and thence product investment centres. In outline therefore a depot operating statement appeared as follows:

Table 1

Revenue:
Sales to outside customers
Sales to outside customers – storage only
External sales – transportation work subcontracted to another depot, e.g. backloads
External sales – transportation subcontracted to outside contractors
= Total customer revenue
Internal sales – transportation work done for other depots, e.g. backloads
Internal sales – Intra-depot/products
Internal sales – Inter-depot and sales inter-company
= Total revenues

Expenditure:
Subcontracting – own company
Subcontracting – other contractors
Total subcontracting
Vehicle hire charges – medium- to long-term
Vehicles hire charges – short-term
Drivers' wages
Depot and warehouse wages
Fuel and lubricants
Tyres
Other operating expenses
Vehicle and equipment maintenance depreciation
Insurance and damages
Licence duties
Direct property charges
Direct property depreciation
Direct branch management and administration
Direct branch miscellaneous
= Total operating expenses

Gross operating profit: Apportioned property charges
                         Apportioned property depreciation
                         Apportioned branch management and admini-
                           stration
                         Apportioned branch miscellaneous
Net activity profit: Regional company/group head office expenses
                         Trading profit/loss
                         Trading profit as a percentage of revenue
                         Capital employed (£)
                         Trading profit as a percentage of capital employed

The above was compiled on a four-weekly basis showing a total for the
depot as a whole and for each of the product investment centres. A number
of regions introduced incentive schemes based upon the achievement of
budgeted profitability and other 'key target areas', particularly the level of
debtors and certain cost ratios such as the fuel and maintenance costs per
mile.

Management appraisal
Management was assessed primarily on actual return on capital employed
and profit percentage to revenue figures against budget, as well as certain
physical/cost centre ratios such as maintenance cost per mile and fuel cost per
mile.

Some regional acountants produced a league table for senior management
based upon the ROCE figures of the depots within their region. Although not
published as such, depot managers were usually made aware of their relative
position in the table: those at the bottom end of the table could expect more
'attention' and 'visitations' than other depots, while those at or near the top
received relatively fewer.

Profit as percentage of revenue was considered to be of secondary
importance to the ROCE ratio. Its trends were followed and considered to be
an important indicator of the pricing practices adopted and of the present
and future market situation. Low margins were in general considered with
extreme concern.

7 Residual income and return on investment are commonly used measures of
   performance. However, they are frequently criticized for placing too great an
   emphasis on the achievement of short-term results, possibly damaging long-
   term performance. You are required to discuss.
   (a) the issues involved in the long-term:short-term conflict referred to in the
        above statement;
   (b) suggestions which have been made to reconcile the difference
                                                        (CIMA November 1988)

9

Assessing performance – expense and service centres

Introduction

The significance of responsibility centre concepts for good organizational and managerial control was introduced in Chapter 7. This has enabled the management and monitoring of performance of operating units set up as profit or investment centres to be examined. Expense and service centres represent those parts of a business which service directly or indirectly the business's profit or investment centres or expend resources that provide benefits for the business as a whole. The former may well be termed service centres and the latter expense centres. They possess features which pose different issues for control which this chapter will examine. While the outputs of a profit or investment centre are quantifiable in monetary terms in relation to monetary inputs, thus providing a ready measure of performance, i.e. profit, the same is not true of expense and service centres.

Although inputs to service and expense centres may be measurable in monetary terms, ready measures of their outputs are not likely to be available. Indeed it may sometimes be difficult, impracticable or impossible to quantify in any meaningful way the outputs of some centres, let alone measure the qualitative aspects of the service provided. In a number of cases, not all such outputs are tangible. How, for example, would an organization quantify employee morale, pride or disaffection? Safety may be an essential factor in success but there may be no ready way of placing financial value on it.

Expense or cost centres

A distinction is sometimes drawn between expense and cost centres. Anthony, Dearden and Vancil argue, for instance, that 'The cost centre is an accounting entity, a device for accumulation of costs to be charged to products or services; the expense centre is an organizational entity'.[1] Although terminology in accounting is often applied very loosely, the distinction raised is an important one. The cost centre approach is an accounting measure to control those parts of an organization whose outputs are not expressible in monetary terms. As such, it may be equally applicable to the measurement of both service and expense centres. Distinction, however, needs to be drawn between various types of expense centre, e.g. engineered, committed and managed costs.

Engineered, committed and managed costs

- **Engineered costs** are those for which an input/output relationship may be defined, e.g. the direct material and labour costs of manufacture may be expected to have a direct relationship to output volumes.
- **Committed costs** are costs which have already been incurred, of which depreciation is the best and most obvious example.
- **Managed or discretionary costs** are those categories of expense incurred at the discretion of management at a point in time, and may vary quite widely in size. The right amount of expense, say, on research and development is impossible to determine on any scientific or engineered basis, and management must use its judgement in deciding what level to authorize. One view is that most costs are managed costs, to the extent that managerial decisions are made to determine their level. This may even apply to labour costs in operating cost centres which are often determined in fact not by the volume of output but by the level of labour the management perceived would be necessary to meet the anticipated level of output. Once actual production activity commences, labour costs may not vary. However, volume of activity is very significant in determining their level in these cases while expense and service centres are likely to lack such an explicit basis for determining the levels of managed and discretionary cost to take on.

Effectiveness and efficiency

In establishing measures of expense/service centres' performance a distinction needs to be drawn between those that measure effectiveness and those that measure efficiency. Effectiveness is a measure of performance outputs against objectives, while efficiency is a measure of the creation of outputs in relation to inputs. The danger of course is that expense/service centre managers may achieve efficiency at the expense of effectiveness. The implications for managerial control therefore are to identify measures for the evaluation of such responsibility centres which encourage the desired *balance* between effectiveness and efficiency, i.e. between efficiency and the supply and usage (by other managers) of a service provided.

The word balance is emphasized, because the pressures for effectiveness and efficiency may pull in different directions. Consider, for example, a plant maintenance department. It may be effective at reducing machine breakdowns and keeping machine downtime to a minimum by employing large numbers of maintenance engineers, even if from time to time they are underemployed or overservicing equipment – 'Rolls-Royce' service maybe but surely they are unlikely to be *efficient*. For that they may need perhaps to provide, say, a 'Sierra', 'Cavalier' or even a 'Mini' service, reducing staff to a sensible minimum, so that all are kept fully stretched and occupied, though at the expense of some effectiveness in terms of machine downtime. Of course line/production/operational management would probably prefer the Rolls-Royce service, as that would make their job easier, but senior management is likely to be looking for both efficiency and effectiveness. That balance needs to be defined, however.

Cost centres and control

Cost centres are parts of an organization to which costs are attributed for purposes of management and control. If possible, some suitable expression of output of the cost centre is established, compared with the costs, and cost rates per unit of output calculated. These are then compared with the cost rates of previous years or of cost rates of similar units elsewhere in the organization. The control implications of cost centres vary between the circumstances under which each operates, i.e. whether or not service or expense costs may be allotted or are chargeable to beneficiaries of the service or expense. Control can be exercised over engineered costs by the measurement of cost rates (the relation of physical outputs to cost inputs), the objective being that of rate reduction within some parameters of the minimum desired/specified quality of goods or service. Managed costs, however may not be controlled in such a manner; the relation between outputs and inputs is not meaningfully calculable. The levels of expense must therefore be at the discretion of management.

Control of engineered costs

As indicated earlier, engineered costs are those where there is a specific and specifiable relation between the outputs and the cost inputs, i.e. those costs which lend themselves to standardization via methods and work-study engineers. Most but not all variable costs are of this nature, as (i) by definition there is a linear relation between the cost input and the volume of output, and (ii) engineered standards for such costs usually can be created. Such costs lend themselves neatly to the cost centre approach. Cost rates can be derived and compared with those of previous years, other similar cost centres, or budgeted/standard cost rates.

Although the term engineered costs may give the impression that such are necessarily manufacturing oriented, it must be stressed that this need not be the case. Any cost, whether it be in manufacturing or service organizations or segments, where the output/input relationship exists, can be treated as an engineered cost. Nor necessarily need methods and work measurement techniques be applied, although these techniques are increasingly applied to non-manufacturing/service-oriented situations though not without some difficulties, owing to the varied nature of the work in many non-manufacturing business segments.

Control of committed costs

Committed costs are those which will be expended by an organization to maintain a minimum level of competence if normal activities ceased for a period (such as a strike). Consistent with the description introduced in Chapter 1, these costs are fixed since they cannot change in relation to volume. Such fixed costs would include the depreciation on fixed assets, property costs (rent, rates, repairs and maintenance), equipment cost (repairs and maintenance to maintain workable capacity) and such minimum organizational costs as minimum staffing levels, especially key staff and senior managers.

These costs are not controllable in the short term, although of course the utilization of them may be. In the short term therefore control can perhaps be best achieved by excluding such costs from routine reports or making it clear in reports that such costs are provided for information only. In the longer term, however, no cost is committed permanently. Control can be exercised (i) by carrying out a post-audit of capital expenditure authorizations to learn from past decisions and to indicate the need for future decisions, and (ii) by considering the desirability or not of retaining/reducing/removing existing levels of committed costs, e.g. by selling assets representing any excess capacity.

Control of managed/discretionary costs

Managed or discretionary costs are those which are neither committed nor engineered and which therefore, by definition, are expended at the discretion of management. Such expenditures are a considerable problem to management in that there is no way of knowing how much expenditure on such costs is warranted in terms of the benefits it would bring, nor of the relative benefits of one such expense type over another, e.g. of £1m on research and development and over £1m on promotion.

This might be interpreted as implying that these costs could be reduced or eliminated should the organization hit hard times, suffering profitability, liquidity and survival problems. Curiously, while this may be true of some discretionary costs, particularly in the short term, and is a practice exhibited by many management groups, the very reverse may be the case in respect of other costs. Thus, for example, management might reduce expenditure on research and development when resources were low, without sufficiently damaging the short-term results, but at the risk of the long-term prospects. Should management, however, reduce marketing and promotion costs when market size or market share falls? Perhaps the very reverse would be more rewarding in both the short and longer term. It would be a gamble of course, but that is in the nature of such discretionary costs. The output for a given input is not predeterminable in any scientific sense: output forecasts from experts are likely to be best information available to assist such decision making.

Discretionary cost decisions are usually made as part of the budgetary process, as a matter of policy/tactics. While the actual expenditure decision may take place subsequently, as the expense is presumably an integral part of the plan, actual expenditure is unlikely be deferred – unless of course management decides to rethink the strategies/tactics of the business.

Control over such costs is necessarily of a somewhat different nature to that of engineered and committed costs. It must reflect as far as possible the decision-making processes, assumptions and decision data. Decision practices in relation to managed costs are likely to be made on one or more of the following bases:

1   Treating past years as the norm, adjusting annually for inflation.
2   Treating the expenses as a percentage appropriation of budgeted or previous years' sales.
3   Treating the expenditure of competitors as the norm either in absolute or percentage terms.
4   Consideration on a 'what we can afford basis', as a residual of the budgetary process, i.e. sales less committed and engineered costs and the profit requirement.
5   Evaluation on a case by case basis, using past experience and expert opinion to answer such questions as the following. Why spend any money at all? What alternative ways are there of obtaining the same objectives? What are the estimated costs, benefits and liabilities of each, and what priorities should be given to each alternative?
6   Negotiation, as part of the budgetary process, on the basis of any of the other approaches.

Such expenditures, once agreed, are effectively budgeted fixed costs, although some would argue that if such expenses are authorized on the basis of a fixed percentage of sales values, they are thereby variable costs. Control, it may be argued, can be established by a comparison of actual with budgets, and depending on whether the budget is considered to be a maximum, minimum or a guide, variances may be examined accordingly. However, in all but the fifth decision base outlined above, the authorization itself is the only yardstick and must be considered somewhat arbitrary. Higher or lower levels of budget might well have been agreed, and therefore neither an overspend nor an underspend against budget is necessarily good or bad. Control therefore is purely a measure of managers' ability to manage their expenditure within the agreed budget. That is not to say, however, that comparisons with expenditure levels of other companies are completely arbitrary. It must surely always be reasonable to question why competitors spend more or less on discretionary costs.

However, in situations where discretionary expenditures are evaluated individually (the fifth basis outlined above), more points for control are likely to exist. The opinions offered by line managers in the formation of the budget can be the yardstick against which actual events, performances, costs, etc. can be compared. Thus, for example, in the case of the S Company,[2] discussed in Chapter 7, the marketing assumptions put forward during the budgetary/tactics process in deciding between alternative marketing strategies/tactics were used subsequently to control the costs and outcomes. In this instance it is believed the commitment by marketing managers to their estimated input/output relationships encouraged them to ensure, as far as they were able, that the results matched those forecast.

The potential outputs of some managed costs may be better known than others. The aim for control purposes must be to engineer as many or as much managed costs as possible. Expenditures on such areas as research, management training and public relations are probably among the most difficult areas to control, as the outputs are not only impossible to predetermine but also to measure in respect of past expenditures. The control of managed costs as regards both effectiveness and efficiency of quality and quantity of expense and outputs must therefore remain subjective, but that is no reason not to exercise such controls as are possible.

Recovery of service costs

It is difficult to plan and control any part of an organization whose goods or services are not sold to a customer outside the organization. There are no market forces which indicate the profitability of the segment and the outputs are not easily expressible in monetary/financial terms. A number of organizations resolve this quandary by establishing transfer prices for the segment's goods and services.

Imputed transfer prices

Where these transfer prices are above cost, a pseudo-profit or investment centre is created. However, where the price is at or below cost, a cost centre is established.

The reasons for the charging or allotment of costs tend to be negative in that they stem from the problems believed to exist if the costs were not charged or allotted. Many management groups believe that if recipient managers are not aware that they will be charged for a supply, they will use it uneconomically. This may be perhaps by demanding more or of a higher quality than they really need, or simply by being wasteful in its use in an unplanned manner. Further, as it is difficult for management to know what volume and quality of service to provide, a charge acts as a surrogate for a market price and, in effect, regulates the demand. Internal users are able to calculate the cost of the service supplied internally and compare this with its value. The internal price can be assessed against the price of an external supplier so that the efficiency of the internal supplier, the expense centre, can be compared against more objective data. Of course such a system also has the advantage of deriving data to calculate a total product/service cost of the business.

Although we are primarily concerned here with the control of the supplying cost centre, the control upon the recipient cannot be ignored. Thus a distinction needs to be drawn between charges based upon some realistic measure of consumption or usage and those of an arbitrary apportionment nature. In the former case there is an implication that control is likely to be exercised more meaningfully than in the latter case.

Charging on consumption

If a measure of consumption or usage is available, the input cost of the cost centre can be compared with total usage to derive a cost rate as a basis for evaluation. Likewise the recipients may be more readily controlled in respect of their consumption. However, this control may only be fair if the calculation base of the charge is consistently calculated. In principle the charge and the suppliers' cost rate should not be affected by the demands, actions and efficiencies of other segments of the business or factors that cannot be anticipated or lie beyond the centre's control.

Thus, for example, the charge per unit to users should not increase if the total demand in a period falls, nor because the costs of the supplier are higher than anticipated. On the other hand, management would certainly want to know the reasons for the change in demand and the effect on cost rates both in the short and long run. For those reasons, budget cost rates are used in many organizations as the basis for charges, perhaps reflecting the fixity and variability of costs, actual cost rates being compared with the (flexed) budgeted cost rates of the supplying cost centre.

Although charging on a usage basis has a number of advantages, in some circumstances it may be counter-productive. Many large groups, for example, operate an internal consultancy service and have found that charging for their services on a usage basis dissuades some managers from using the service, an event which senior managers neither intended or desired. Possible alternatives are not to charge at all or to charge a fixed (apportioned) rate whether the service is used or not.

Apportioned charges

Charges of a fixed nature not reflecting consumption may, however, have adverse effects. Why should a manager control the usage of a service if the charges made to the using segment will not increase? Further, those managers who believe that their charges are inequitably high might be demotivated, blame all their segments' ills upon such perceived inequality and be diverted from their real problems.

However, many management groups believe that any such demotivating effects are overstated and that recharging of costs, even on an arbitrary basis, provides a positive motivation (i) in that the user will demand a good service, and (ii) that the supplying managers attain a higher status (in their eyes) not dissimilar from that of managing a profit centre. Again, the use of budgeted costs as the basis for charging, reflecting fixed and variable cost elements, is popular among businesses for the reasons outlined earlier.

In terms of a control on the supplying managers, however, the recovery of costs via apportioned charges may mislead management into believing that the cost centre is paying its way. In fact of course the effect of apportioning costs to user segments is, per se, no control at all. However, if the fact of charging persuades users to criticize the service, and thereby create an environment under which improvements are encouraged and made, a control of a sort may be achieved.

Management is likely to seek alternative means of controlling such cost centres. If costs had a direct causal relation with some measure of output, the need for apportionments would presumably not arise, for they would be chargeable on a consumption basis. If possible therefore, management should consider alternative bases – bases, which, having no direct causal link, can be viewed as a surrogate for them. Such activity levels might include numbers of units sold, sales value, standard hours produced or worked, customers' enquiries or orders received, purchase requests received, and invoices received or issued. Actual cost centre costs may then be related to those measures to derive unit cost measures for comparison and, thereby, control. Such an approach is not possible for many cost centres, particularly where the costs are committed or managed, and must therefore be controlled by other means.

Service centre to service centre charges

The discussion so far has considered only the charging of service and expense centre costs to production centres, whether established as cost or profit centres. Attention must also be given to the situations where service and expense centres contribute to the work of other service centres. The charging between centres can become complex particularly where the relationship is reciprocal. In practice this is not at all uncommon. The personnel department is unlikely to restrict its provision of services to production departments only. Similarly the cleaning services department, which may make substantial use of personnel in meeting its recruitment needs, for example, might be expected to extend its services to the personnel offices.

Three types of approach can be considered: the first is to ignore all allocations between service or expense centres; the second and third are known, respectively, as the step method and the reciprocal method. Each can be illustrated by a simple example:

> Company A has four cost centres, Boilerhouse, Canteen, Track D, Track E. Two (Boilerhouse and Canteen) are service centres while the remaining two (Track D and Track E) are production centres. For an accounting period, the total costs incurred by the Boilerhouse are £21,000 and by the Canteen £17,500. The services of the Boilerhouse are considered to serve the other centres in the proportions 4:3:1 for Track D, Track E and the Canteen; those of the Canteen serve the other centres in the proportions 2:2:1 for Track D, Track E and the Boilerhouse.

The first approach considers apportioning the service centre costs to the two production centres only. It can be supported on the basis that all apportionments depend upon arbitrary assumptions (here, the relative proportions of usage of the centres' services) and that the costs and intricacy of carrying out any more complex approaches adds no useful information and is therefore wasted. The calculations are very straightforward with the costs of the Boilerhouse being split 3:2 and those of the Canteen 2:2 between the two production centres:

	Track D £	Track E £	Total £
Boilerhouse (4:3)	12,000	9,000	21,000
Canteen (2:2)	8,750	8,750	17,500
Apportioned costs	20,750	17,750	38,500

In using the second approach, the step method, a decision must be made on the order in which costs will be apportioned from service centre to service centre. This is entirely subjective. It may be decided that the Canteen costs should be apportioned as the first step, then the Boilerhouse as a second step as follows:

	Track D £	*Track E* £	*Boilerhouse* £	*Total* £
1st step				
Canteen (2:2:1)	7,000	7,000	3,500	17,500

The total costs of the boilerhouse become £21,000 plus £3,500 which equals £24,500. In apportioning these costs as the second step, re-apportionment back to the canteen is ignored, so the result becomes:

	Track D £	*Track E* £	*Boilerhouse* £	*Total* £
1st step				
Canteen (2:2:1)	7,000	7,000	3,500	17,500
				(3,500)
2nd step				
Boilerhouse (4:3)	14,000	10,500		24,500
Apportioned costs	21,000	17,500		38,500

While the amounts apportioned to each production centre have changed, all the costs of the service centres (£38,500) have again been apportioned to the production centres.

Although this method is dependent upon the arbitrary ordering of the centres, the third approach attempts to overcome this by considering the effects of reciprocal re-apportioning. The result can be established mathematically by using simultaneous equations. In this case the total cost after apportionment of the Boilerhouse should include a fifth $(1 \div [2 + 2 + 1])$ of the total cost of the Canteen and the Canteen should include an eighth $(1 \div [4 + 3 + 1])$. Representing the Boilerhouse cost as £B and that of the Canteen as £C, the relationship can be expressed (amounts in £000s):

$B = 21 + \frac{1}{5}C$ i.e. $40B = 840 + C$

$C = 17.5 + \frac{1}{8}B$ i.e. $8C = 140 + B$

Adding and simplifying gives $39B = 980$

so that £B = £25,128 and £C = £20,641.

These costs include re-apportionment, and only that part applicable to production centres needs to be apportioned to those centres:

	Track D £	Track E £	Total £
Boilerhouse £B ($\frac{4}{5}:\frac{3}{5}$)	12,564	9,424	
Canteen £C ($\frac{2}{5}:\frac{2}{5}$)	8,256	8,256	
Apportioned costs	20,820	17,680	38,500

If the proportions of the usage of each service centre are accurate, this approach is mathematically correct. However, given that, usually, the amounts cannot be measured precisely, the level of mathematical precision achieved may not be justifiable. Moreover, in this case the equations were simple to solve, with only two service centres and two unknowns. With only a few more unknowns, the problem will be beyond the scope of solution without the aid of computers. Practical situations, involving many service centres, produce very substantial mathematical problems which would not be justified by the mathematical complexity. Comparison of the results in the example show that the change of approach produced little change in costs. Indeed, in this case, the simplest method was closer than the step method to the reciprocal approach.

Revenue centres

The revenue centre concept is a marketing measure/control. The implication is that marketing/sales segments are measured on their sales volumes and values. However, such could be a dangerous application of this approach, as managers might be encouraged to obtain sales at almost any price. However, if sales prices are fixed, and are not at the discretion of sales management, the measure could be practicable, although the mix of products sold might distort the value of the revenue centre measure.

Perhaps a more rational approach would be to attribute the contribution or gross margin of sales to the revenue centre rather than the sales value as such. In such a situation flexibility could still be devolved to sales management without its objective being incongruent to that of the business as a whole. Indeed such an approach could be developed into a revenue/expense centre, where marketing and sales managers are measured on the net contribution created, i.e. the contribution from the sale of products/services less marketing and selling expenses. Thus marketing management could itself authorize, say, some promotional expenditure which it believes would generate more additional contribution than its cost, and be itself measured on the net effect of its decisions.

This perhaps attractive idea could, however, lead to problems if marketing/ sales managers expanded their sales volumes by selling marginal business. They would also of course need to be aware of the organization's productive capacities, the relevant range under which product contribution is calculated and incremental effects on fixed costs and liquidity resources, e.g. of additional working capital as sales volumes increase. The problems for control in such situations is not likely to be one of measurement as such. As outputs are known in terms of sales volume and resource inputs identifiable, performance measures are calculable and practicable. However, what may not be so easy is to draft performance measures in such a way that the actions of marketing/sales management are congruent with that of the organization as a whole, its segments and its *resources.*

Budgeted performance measures

The successful application of the cost centre approach to the control of services, engineered, committed and managed costs relies substantially upon the use of budgets, i.e. the budgeted cost centre approach. Additional or alternative measures in the control of services and cost centres may be available through the application of budgeted performance measures.

Budgeted performance measures may also be expressed in terms of physical, non-financial indicators, such as machine downtime rates, scrap rates, distribution response rates and enquiry/order conversion rates. Their advantage is that (i) managers may well feel that such indicators are more realistic than monetary expressions, which in any event can be distorted over time, (ii) such may be possible in situations where financially oriented cost rates are impossible or inapplicable, and (iii) budgeted performance can address facets of a segment's objectives that are not measurable in financial terms.

References

1. Anthony, R.N., Dearden, J. and Vancil, R.F., *Management Control Systems: Cases and Readings*, Richard D. Irwin Inc., 1965.
2. Coates, J.B., Rickwood, C.P. and Stacey, R.J., Examination of the Differences Between Academic Concepts and Actual Management Accounting Practices. Report to ESRC, British Library Document Supply Centre, August 1987.

Questions

1 (a) How would you assess the performance of the maintenance department of an organization of your choice?

   (b) How, and why, would your view differ if it was allowed to sell its spare capacity to other organizations?

2 (a) By what measures may the operations of the research and development function be controlled?

   (b) How would you assess the long-term performance of the R&D function?

3 'Charging, even if arbitrary, for the assumed consumption of service centres is the only means by which management can dissuade other managers from

misusing the service.' To what extent and why would you agree or disagree with the statement?

4   What are the arguments for and against the recharging of service and expense centre costs?

5   Contrast the methods by which committed and managed fixed costs may be controlled.

6 Why are 'budgeted performance centre' measures (as against budgeted cost or profit centres) an important element of multi-variant performance analysis?

10

Management accounting in the service industries

Introduction

Textbooks normally devote little attention to the particular case of management accounting in service industries; it appears to be assumed that in the main, the principles and techniques prescribed for manufacturing industry can be transferred into service organizations with little amendment. Very broadly speaking, this is probably true, but it does overlook the adaptations and developments which may be needed to suit particular cases in what is a very varied sector of the economy.

Taken as a whole, service industries represent a far larger proportion of the national economy than do manufacturing industries: in 1983 the latter represented 24.8 per cent of gross domestic product at current factor cost; by 1993 this had fallen to 21.7 per cent. The GDP share of service industries on the other hand, rose from 60.7 per cent to 70.6 per cent over the same period; the 'financial intermediaries' sector alone rose from 19 per cent to 24.5 per cent of GDP over the same period, thus representing a greater proportion of GDP than manufacturing. The range of businesses encompassed by the service sector is, of course substantial, the following merely giving some indication: professional firms such as lawyers and accountants, hotels and tourism, telecommunications, financial services, education and healthcare (which receives more detailed attention in Chapter 11 of this book). A number of the organizations involved are or have been nationalized or regulated; some are commercial profit making perations, others do not have a profit making objective. These variants and changes in status have exerted their own influence on the development of costing and management accounting in the organizations concerned. Generally though, service industry has been later and slower than manufacturing to introduce these techniques; in healthcare and education for example, they are very recent arrivals as tools of management.

Most of the commonly used (in manufacturing industry) concepts and techniques of costing and management accounting are potentially applicable in some combination or other to all service industry organizations. Thus one could expect to find instances within service industries of the application of job and mass production costing; full and marginal costing; actual and standard costing; budgetary planning and control; contribution analysis; activity based costing; transfer pricing; performance measurement; investment appraisal and strategic financial analysis. The basis and purpose of their use would also be the same in service industry companies as in manufacturing. The two industry types are not entirely distinct, since there are 'service industry' elements in manufacturing and vice versa. There are though, a number of important features of service company businesses, which exert a more specific influence on the design and operation of their cost and management accounting systems. Some of the principal ones are:

- The products of a service industry are predominantly intangible and therefore cannot be held in inventory, though work in progress stocks may well exist in a way similar to manufacturing industry. This characteristic also makes them difficult to value, since much depends on the value customers perceive they have gained from the consumption of a service.
- The outputs/products of a service industry may not be so readily identifiable or homogeneous as would normally be the case in manufacturing.
- The labour or people cost content of a service industry is likely to be high relative to manufacturing, if only because the direct material cost of output will be correspondingly low. The indirect nature of labour cost is also is also likely to be more pronounced in a service industry, though the proportion of indirect labour cost is also increasing in manufacturing industry as a result of technological developments.

Such features as those outlined above do not require a new methodology or conceptual base for management accounting to be applied to service industry, they merely exert special requirements of their own. For example, lack of inventoriable product actually simplifies both financial reporting and management accounting. On the other hand, real-time consumption of services has implications for capacity planning, pricing and cost management somewhat different to companies in manufacturing industry: since services cannot be stored, then means other than holding stock will have to be devised in order to make the best use of capacity, for example, differential pricing to attract different classes of customer at different times of the day. Performance measurement in relation to both the supply and maintenance of the quality of a service will also be affected; if, for example, there is a high labour content of a service product, the problem of maintaining consistent quality in the provision of the service occurs both with respect to a single individual over time and an individual in comparison with others. This is much less of a problem for a manufactured product where technology can often ensure that there is an almost 100 per cent consistency in the quality of goods supplied. Service industries though can similarly benefit from their increasing use of technology as in the case of the widespread use of automated teller machines (ATMs) by banks.

   The difficulty of defining an output or product for a service industry can be illustrated in respect of the purchase of a ticket for travel say by road, rail, sea or plane. To the person purchasing the ticket it may seem to be a single product, but in reality the purchase covers much more than just transport from A to B: it includes the standard of seating and a host of other services such as waiting room accomodation, stewards, baggage handlers, skilled drivers/pilots, restaurant services and so on. The sale of a ticket thus covers multiple outputs so far as the provider of the service is concerned. Further difficulties arise in that the latter may not be solely dedicated to a single type ticket purchase and hence some process of allocation between different classes of ticket purchase may be required. Additionally, many of the costs incurred in the provision of any single output may be also indirect to it, creating yet another cost and resource allocation problem. Pricing in the transport industry has become very sophisticated in relation to market differentiation, as can be seen in the many ways that the same journey can be priced according to different times of day, different days in the week and different kinds of customer. A 'journey' also illustrates the attribute of non-storability of service industry products: a journey not taken at a particular time cannot be stored; nor for example, can unsold theatre seat tickets. Differential pricing can be observed in many other service type situations, such as hairdressing, hotels and consultancy.

The attribute of intangibilty of a service introduces the need for organizations to undertake continuous monitoring of customer perceptions of the value of the service they receive. Hotels for example, routinely request customers to complete questionnaires relating to how satisfactory they have found an hotel's services, however short the stay, in an effort by management to determine how well they are meeting the requirements of customers (each of whom will probably have different expectations of the service they are buying) perceived to constitute their market and hence the acceptabilty of their service and prices; the questionnaires also provide information which will assist in the planning and control of hotel operations.

Given the great range in type, size and complexity of the organizations which constitute the service industry sector of the economy, it is not feasible to attempt a description and analysis of each. The following therefore discusses only a limited number of applications: universities, banks and hotels, in order to illustrate some of the particular aspects of management accounting in a number of very different service industries. As already noted, healthcare receives special consideration in Chapter 11.

Universities

Although their main functions are generally recognized to be teaching and research, the output of a university is rather elusive and difficult to define from either a student or a societal point of view. Since the mid-1980s, however, as part of a process intended to lead to changes in the structure of funding for individual institutions, considerable effort has been put into determining ways of measuring both the quality and quantity of the teaching and research 'outputs' of universities. External groups of assessors have been appointed to monitor and evaluate both the teaching and research excellence of the various institutions. Their evaluations will place institutions on scales of achievement which it is intended should facilitate comparison between them. According to the rankings attained, institutions may and do find that their funding by central government will be increased, remain constant or be reduced. This is taking place against the background of general reductions in government funding for universities, which has occurred year by year for well over a decade and which has been accompanied in many cases by significant increases in the number students a given institution has to accept. In comparison with the former times of quinquennial funding reviews and, what may be regarded now, of funding budgets comfortably rising period by period, universities must pay much closer attention to all aspects of their operations: outputs and the raising and spending of funds. Under the former regime, there was little cost control beyond the attempt to balance the books overall; the distinction between teaching and research activities and their financial consequences was largely blurred; departments of all kinds cross-subsidized each other, but without knowing where surpluses or losses occurred or, of course, their extent.

It would be fair to say that until recently, such management accounting as was undertaken in universities was a rudimentary affair consisting of little more than the distribution of broad budgets to faculties and departments and monitoring budget and actual expenditures. Little attempt was made to quanitify or evaluate outputs; the consequences of any financial mismanagement do not seem to have been particularly severe. Today, this has largely changed; resources are very restricted and management accounting techniques have been adopted to help plan, control and provide information for decision making in universities in much the same way as it would be used (or should be) in private enterprise (CIMA[1]).

Two ideas figure prominently in the change: Total Quality Management (TQM) and the Trading Company Model (TCM), the latter being essentially a profit centre model though variously described by different institutions.TQM has helped in the definition of an output of a university and its constituent departments by specifying what should be achieved and to what standard; TCM is intended as an internal resource distribution and control mechanism, dependent in part at least on attainment of standards laid down in the TQM schemes.

TCM embodies the management accounting system which is aimed at enabling universities to target objectives and monitor resource usage much more closely than in the past. In summary, its objectives may be expressed as to ensure over time that:

- the university maintains a sound financial position,
- each department receives a reasonable and fair allocation of resources,
- resources are made available for special non-departmental projects.

Broadly speaking, universities comprise three groups of departments:

- central services, such as finance, personnel, registry, public relations, estates, the vice chancellor's office;
- service departments serving both academic and non-academic departments (including the above), such as library and information systems, staff training and development, reprographics etc.;
- academic faculties/departments, for example, maths, physics, languages.

The exact configurations and groupings will vary from university to university, but there is as complex an interrelationship between the first two groups and the third as would be likely to be found amongst the sections of a firm in manufacturing industry: central service departments both provide services to and receive them from other service departments as well as providing services to academic departments. The same kinds of intra-organization transfer pricing questions naturally also occur: should transfer charges be levied at all; how far down the organization should transfers be made; on what basis; at what price and what are the consequences for departments if such transfers mean their accounts show a loss?

Universities need to know their cost structures and cost behaviour – at its simplest level, the distinction between fixed and variable costs; activity based costing techniques could be used to determine causal cost factors, if it were considered a cost-beneficial approach. Costs could be allocated/apportioned between service departments and between service and other departments using the standard methods of direct or step re-allocation or through determining a reciprocal services base. There would also be possibilites for the use of standard costing in at least some departments, for example, reprographics. So, in building up cost budgets for its various cost centres, a university is faced with exactly the same choices as a manufacturing firm: to go for a costing system which, as realistically as possible, reflects the costs of running individual sections of the organization as opposed to the use of purely arithmetic devices to share out total costs incurred between them; to go for simplicity as opposed to complexity; to use contribution analysis rather than full cost distributions and so on.

Accounting for the costs of library services

Several services are normally found within a library:

- book loans
- inter-library loans
- journals
- access to database information services
- support by information specialists

Each of these could be subdivided further, but in essence it would appear a relatively straightforward task to assign costs to the various services listed: counter staff to book loans etc. Some difficulties arise because staff are not necessarily dedicated to single areas of service: in many places the practice of multitasking library assistants is actively adopted, but a time-based analysis could help solve this problem by simply recording average time spent by staff in each designated area. Library overhead costs such as its senior management, heating, lighting, maintenance, etc., would probably have to be apportioned to user groups pro rata on some basis such as the number of staff in the user groups.

A more interesting aspect of accounting for the library lies in how to charge out its costs to user departments. The simplest solution for a TCM model would be to do so directly to academic departments on some basis such as unweighted student numbers, i.e. ignoring the differential income brought in by different types of student and the differential costs imposed on the library by meeting the requirements of different types of student and staff teaching and research require-ments. A more refined approach would seek to identify users of the service more directly and precisely. The costs of using databases such as Datastream, Fame, Lexis, etc. could be attributed to the user department(s); the acquisition costs of books, journals, periodicals, etc. can be attributed similarly; even certain staff costs may be directly identifiable as supplying a quantifiable amount of service to given sections of the university, e.g. science faculty, engineering and so on. The purpose of such analysis, which can have considerable set-up costs, is clearly to identify the sections of the organization which drive library costs and to include these costs in their budgets, to be set against the income they generate. It will have to be regularly reviewed to allow for changes in patterns of usage.

However, agreements on the way costs are to be charged and received requires a definition of what standard of service is being provided: the outputs which constitute a library service have to be spelt out in some detail in what is frequently called a 'service level agreement' between the supplier and user of a service (see Abbott[2]). For example, a library may make available a CD-ROM service across a local network allowing interactive electronic access, for which users will be charged. In order for users to feel they are getting the level and standard of service which would justify the charge they receive, performance indicators may be specified relating say to network downtime, which could establish service targets for example that access should be available say 95 per cent of total available time.

A more detailed illustration of a proposed specification for the management of the library book collection, which is normally called 'collection maintenance', is reproduced in Table 10.1 with the kind permission of the Aston University Library and Information Services Department. The ideas of Total Quality Manage-ment are clearly apparent in the illustration.

The latter is regarded as a 'standard service' along with some fourteen others, covering such matters as the provision of study and photocopying facilities. Beyond these there are 'tailored services', designed to meet particular needs associated with specific teaching and research programmes such as journals specific to the needs of identified departments.

Both service provider and customer have responsibilites related to the operation of the scheme: the provider, amongst other things, undertakes to provide customers with regular feedback on costs, performance and the take-up of services and to alert customers to actual or potential changes in these factors; in turn, amongst other things, the customer will provide appropriate and timely information to the service supplier on information needs and changes in these requirements.

The charging of the library costs to the departments follows the standard and tailored service breakdown, with the former being a more general re-apportion-ment of library costs amongst user departments on the basis of their student load figures, whilst the latter will rely on more precise costing of services, for example time logged by library staff on carrying out work for individual departments.

Altogether, the system developed is very detailed and brings together both

Table 10.1   Collection maintenance

Definition and scope	Reshelving of material returned from loan/used within the library/new material. Shelf checking and tidying; shelf guiding; stock moves; repairs of worn out materials.
Objective/aim	To maximize the availability and accessibility of stock by ensuring that material is well guided, that it is correctly and quickly shelved, and kept in good repair.
Customer entitlement	Open access principle (except for a limited amount of short loan material and items in store, such as PhD theses).
Cost elements	Staff time: shelving assistants; library assistants; reprographics costs; staff time involved in producing shelf guides. Staff time involved in stock moves.
Quality standards	Shelving to be carried out accurately and with maximum speed. Guiding to be accurate and self explanatory.
Performance indicators	Speed and accuracy of shelving. Number of requests for guidance to shelves.
Performance targets	All unshelved materials to be reshelved within 24 hours. 100 per cent accuracy of shelving to be aimed for. All areas to be tidied systematically once a term. Shelves should not be packaged more tightly than 80 per cent occupancy per metre average.

quantitative and non-quantitative factors in order to establish an acceptable standard of library service in agreement with customer departments, which contains specified means for monitoring performance and which contains the mechanisms by which library costs are to be charged to customers. It is a model which is applicable to other service areas in the university, as well as being one which could be adopted in other not for profit organizations.

Apart from the initial investment in establishing schemes of this nature, they also entail ongoing costs in recording and monitoring the actual operation; a factor to be weighed in deciding the cost-benefit of a scheme. Service level agreements are quasi-legal documents, since both parties to the agreement sign them and they serve as a basis to help resolve future disputes, underlining the need for a sound monitoring process.

It would be possible to envisage some form of standard costing, in some sectors of a university's activities, for example, courses could be costed out at a number of standard lecturer hours times the standard lecturer cost per hour. Most universities also have a reprographics department, dealing with photocopying, document binding, etc.; capacity can be defined in terms of either machine or labour hours and a standard cost rate per hour can be calculated according to forecast/budgeted workloads; cost centres could be created if there are large differences in the value of equipment in use or in labour skills. Jobs are thus readily priced depending on the facilities used and time taken to complete them. A normal variance analysis could also be carried out.

In the TCM, departmental expenditures are built up through identification of direct departmental costs together with transfer charges for the use of the services of other departments. How detailed the system should be is entirely a matter for the judgement of the individual institution.

Accounting for departmental income:

Service departments generate their income through the system of cross-charging, but it is academic departments which directly generate most of a university's income. This would include income from:

*   teaching (per capita income based on the number and type of student)
*   tuition fee only and overseas students
*   research (contract income from research councils and other funding bodies)
*   consultancy
*   miscellaneous income (e.g. from conferences, donations and other forms of gifts).

Income and expenditure accounts can now be generated for designated sectors of the university, such as individual departments (service and academic), faculties and the whole institution. Decisions with respect to departments, for example, whether they should be encouraged to expand or contract, can now be based in part at least on whether their activities result in a profit or loss. A format for the operating statement of a social science faculty could be drawn up as shown in Figure 10.1

| | Academic departments | | | |
	Economics	Accounting	Psychology	Politics
Income				
Undergraduates				
Postgraduates				
Research				
Miscellaneous				
Total income				
Expenditure				
Direct				
Academic staff				
Support staff				
Indirect				
Transfers from academic related service departments				
Total expenditure				
Contribution to central costs				
Apportioned Central Service charges				
Total surplus/(loss)				

Figure 10.1   *TCM pro-forma operating statement*

In summary, the TCM is a model which potentially helps a university pinpoint where it is being most successful and where it needs to either strengthen or cut-back on activites, objectives entirely parallel to the use of management accounting in a manufacturing setting. A great deal is dependent though on a searching review and analysis of the resources needed to deliver the specified levels of service throughout the organization. The existence of a clearly identified income stream for academic departments puts pressure on these specifications to be as realistic as possible. It is a model also relevant to other types of educational institution, including other colleges and schools, as well as individual institutions such as libraries themselves. Like all such systems (i.e. those using apportionments of joint costs) considerable care has to be exercised in the use of the data produced. A university would not necessarily benefit from closing a 'loss making' department for instance.

Banks

The banking sector of the economy today includes a variety of institutions, for example, the clearing banks, merchant banks, former building societies, branches of overseas banks. Each specializes in some degree in different types of business. The following concentrates on the major UK clearing banks, which have experienced and are continuing to experience extensive changes in the character of their business and how it is conducted. Much of this stems from the two factors of rapid technological change and greatly increased competition, each factor reinforcing the other, compelling banks to pay much greater attention to the way they market their products. Change has been accelerating since the early 1980s with a momentum which shows no sign of abating just yet. The subsequent discussion therefore represents an interim picture of the direction which these traditional institutions are taking, rather than one which focuses on any status quo.

The fundamentals of business conducted by the clearing banks remain much as they always have been: funds raised from depositors on varying terms are employed as investments in liquid assets, loans and advances and longer-term investments such as gilt-edged securities. The total profit margin earned by a bank depended (and to an extent still does) on the differences between borrowing and lending rates. To these traditional investment activities, banks have added further wide ranging financial services, for example, in selling various types of insurance and in mortgage lending, as well as offering more refined services to investors and businesses through the acquisiton of merchant banking arms (for example, Barclays Bank acquired Barclays de Zoete Wedd in 1986. A regulatory framework exists through the Banking Act of 1979.

The changes referred to however, have forced banks to define the nature of their business and its products/services more closely to obtain a better understanding of profitabilies and the way costs are incurred. As a banker at one interview put it: 'previously the bank was there for people and businesses to come along and do business with it; now the bank has to actively seek out what services it should provide and how these are to be delivered to customers.' The latter part of the quote portrays the transitional state which these banks are still in, though they are not necessarily all following the same business philosophy.

Sloane,[3] commented, that 'there can be little doubt that banks in general have been slow to understand how to subdivide products and delivery systems to selected groups of customers at acceptable profit and risk'. This statement has been well borne out by the heavy charges for bad and doubtful debts and large provisions for anticipated losses which banks had to make in the early 1990s; TSB's accounts for 1991 and 1992, for example, show charges for bad and doubtful debts of £654m and £597m respectively against profit before charges of £607m and £637m, though the situation has considerably improved since these two years. Prior to this time it appears that management accounting systems may well have been inadequate, though little detailed published information is available. Judging from journal articles, the lack of a management accounting presence seems to be true of both sides of the Atlantic, see for example Sharma.[4]

Management accounting in a clearing bank

Services provided by a bank extend from something comparable to mass production in the case of retail banking to jobbing where for example, investment plans may be tailored to the needs of individual clients. Costing systems would vary accordingly. Banks, like any other business, also need to know their cost structures and how their costs are likely to behave as business rises and falls, both overall and within defined sectors of activity. The basic cost characteristics appear to be:

- a high proportion of what would normally be termed fixed costs (in the short run), related to: buildings, equipment (a component of cost increasing in proportion as computerization is extended ever more widely) and staff (with wages and salaries still accounting for around 70 per cent of total cost);
- few costs of significance which vary directly with the volume of activity other than interest;
- product complementarity;
- the existence of joint costs arising from products' use of common facilities – staff and equipment.

Product and business sector profitability

As implied by the earlier Sloane quotation, banks have only recently begun to analyse and segment their business on profitability lines; risk–return analyses are an even more recent innovation, not yet fully understood or implemented. Some of the common groupings for purposes of profitability studies are:

- defined business units, such as branches, divisions, service functions;
- geographical areas served;

```
                    ┌──────────────────┐
                    │    Main board    │
                    └──────────────────┘
                             │
                             ├── Central services:
                             │
                             ├── Administration
                             │
                             │
                             │
                             ├── Personnel
                             │
                             ├── Corporate planning
                             │
     ┌───────────┬───────────┼───────────┬───────────┐
┌──────────┐ ┌──────────────┐ ┌──────────────┐ ┌──────────────┐
│UK domestic│ │International  │ │Investment/   │ │Services      │
│banking    │ │division      │ │merchant      │ │division      │
│division   │ │              │ │banking div.  │ │              │
└──────────┘ └──────────────┘ └──────────────┘ └──────────────┘
     │              │                │                 │
┌──────────┐ ┌──────────────┐        │                 │
│ Branches │ │Geographical  │        │                 │
│          │ │area          │        │                 │
└──────────┘ └──────────────┘        │                 │
     │              │                │                 │
  ├Retail        ├Europe         ├Securities      ├Cheque clearing
  └Corporate     ├Retail         ├Insurance       ├Personnel
                 ├Corporate      ├Fund raising    ├Management services
                 └Investment     └Loans           └IT
```

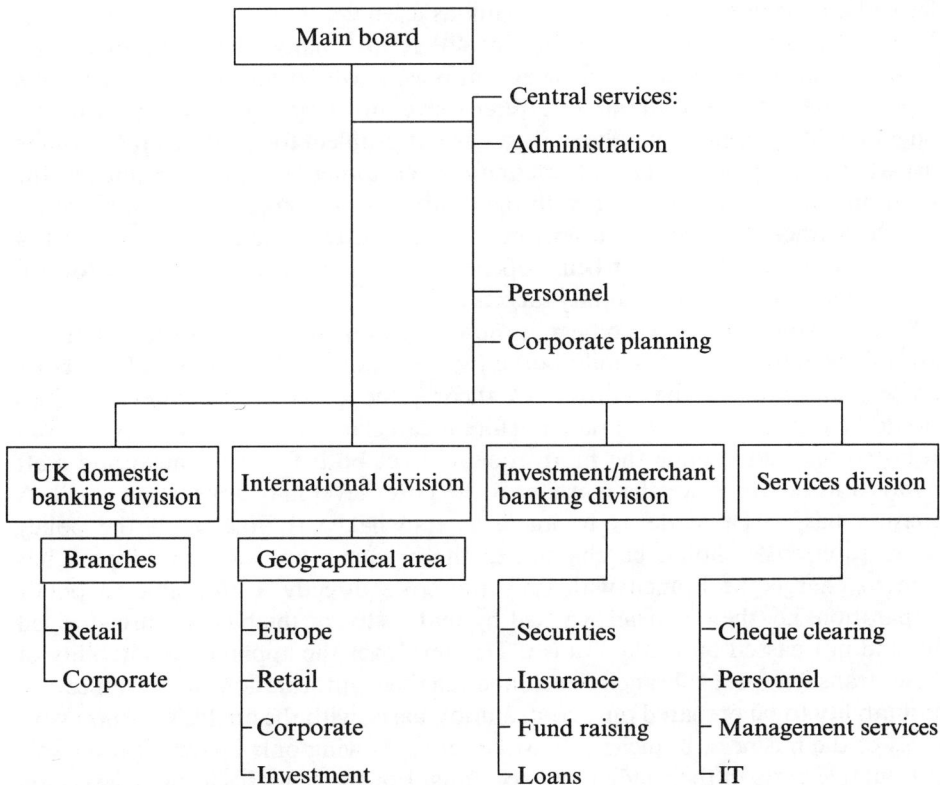

Figure 10.2 *Traditional organization chart*

- customer groupings and perhaps individual customers;
- products/services, though these may be difficult to define as discrete items.

There are the usual considerations with respect to specifying what a profitability study aims to achieve; for example, is it to promote business in areas shown to be more profitable than others, including the type of customer a bank would wish to attract; is it for motivating branch personnel and so on? The illustrative organization chart shown in Figure 10.2, which is not unrepresentative of how a bank might have been structured until recently, would, together with appropriate information systems, enable a bank to analyse the profitabilty of the main sectors of its business operations. A clear definition of 'profitability' however, is not an entirely straightforward matter.

Individual bank branches are frequently designated as profit centres. They are expected to generate new business for the bank by attracting new customers to open accounts, by selling insurance and so on. In order to motivate branch staff to realize these objectives, attention has to be paid to factors which will help generate such motivation. For example, the attraction of new accounts may be deemed a desirable objective for the bank as a whole, though it is not clear what the benefit to it will be in financial 'profit' terms: many customers have 'free' banking, but maintenance of their accounts is a cost to the bank; further, loan opportunities at an acceptable risk–return level utilizing funds from deposits no longer readily present themselves. So, a current problem for banks is to determine just what is the profitabilty of attracting new customers to open accounts; in the meantime, to provide a branch with the motivation to persuade customers to do so, when otherwise it may see only costs, banks often credit the branch with a notional value of an account being opened as recompense and to help it toward the achievement of its profitability targets.

Selling insurance to customers is now commonplace at branches, but the cost of the activity is not wholly borne by the branch: other sectors of the bank devise and draw up the policies. In theory, the costs of the latter activities should be transferred to the branch before it can claim to have made a profit, but to do so may undermine the motivational effect both for the branch and staff involved in selling, since the margins at the latter level may appear too small. A decision has to be made as to made as to what part, if any, of the policy preparation costs should be charged to the branch. One solution adopted has been to charge the branch with only the costs directly attributable to policy preparation, i.e. the overheads carried by that sector of the business are stripped out and not passed on to the branch. This improves the apparent profitability of these transactions at branch level and enables information with respect to profitability to be prepared on a contribution basis, with the analysis of successive levels of the business, branches, divisions, etc., showing only income less directly attributable costs in their individual accounts. For the bank itself, these levels are then progressively consolidated upwards to derive the profit for the bank as a whole.

In one of the banks visited, contribution based management accounting analysis was a feature of the management accounting system. It showed that in general, only directly identifiable costs would be charged from one part of the bank to another, whether the transaction in question related to inter-branch or division or head office services. Full-cost transfer charges were rejected.

Budgets were also prepared throughout the organization, but only a few items could be 'flexed'. The most important of these was probably the cost of borrowing money from Group Treasury. This was at London inter-bank offer rates (LIBOR) based on a one-month rolling average and was a cost which changes with levels in interest rates in general. A continuing problem for the bank has been that at the moment every £ lent is at the same cost, resulting in the cross-subsidization of one type of borrower by another: a high risk account is only charged at the same rate as a low risk account. One of the tasks of management accounting has been and continues to be to assist in the investigation and quantification of factors such as risk, so that this can be properly reflected in charges to customers.

Other changes are envisaged in staff performance measures, for example, amongst branch staff selling insurances. These staff are currently expected to achieve certain targets, but are paid according to grade rather than sales achievements; this leads to cross-subsidization between staff as to their effectiveness. A future aim is to reduce this cross-subsidization by relating pay more directly to performance.

Overall bank performance continues to be viewed in conventional terms with earnings per share and return on equity playing key roles at the corporate level. For the time being, branches retain their status as profit (contribution) centres. However, certain changes envisaged in the way the bank of the future may be structured and operated, briefly outlined below, may result in their being judged on the quality and speed of delivery of services, customer complaints, etc. rather than on financial outcomes alone.

A reported case study

Cobb *et al.*[5] examined the changes in the management accounting system of the UK division of a multinational bank, brought about by the 'dramatic changes' in the banking world since the 1980s. Identified as principal external pressures were:

- globalization of markets
- increase in competition
- a 'plethora' of new products
- increasing technological sophistication
- large bad debt write-offs

From a position in 1989, where the division had only one simplistic management accounting report (in contrast to 'many' financial reports), the study details how the MAS was changed in order to meet the above pressures. Briefly, the report used up to 1989 provided summary results only: 'no product cost or profitability information'. Costs were not a focus for the bank, it was revenue and market share that mattered. There was no balance sheet information, but some non-financial data such as headcount by department was given. Since then, as a response to both internal as well as external pressures, there has been a consider-able broadening of the information produced by the MAS; by 1993 the following items had been incorporated:

- product group costing
- responsibility accounting
- participative budgeting
- provision of cost information to managers
- provision of decision-making information
- the beginnings of cost management

The authors point out the process of improving the information provided was not complete at the time of writing. As an example, the cost of foreign exchange dealing was cited as being known in aggregate, though the cost of a particular transaction or type of transaction was not, 'hence the individual product profit-ability and customer profitability cannot be assessed'. Clearly, there was some way to go in developing a comprehensive MAS which would be able to cater for important information demands.

To achieve the required improvement, attention had to be given to costing methodology, in particular, cost allocations. The latter were to be based as far as possible on cost drivers, aimed at avoiding arbitrary allocations. All departments were covered by this examination of the bank's costs '. . . every cost from back office staff costs to audit, photocopying and messenger costs. For example, telex, swift and chaps charges . . . were allocated on deal volumes'. Value for money studies were conducted to reduce costs and in 1991 the UK division participated in a benchmarking exercise, which compared it against an average of 14 other banks. '. . . It included factors such as cost against volume, transaction processing costs per transaction, average number of details per front office and back office staff member, systems and premises costs and the relative automation of the processing deals'.

The bank first attempted to introduce ABC in 1991 (ABC is discussed in more detail in Chapter 10). It was initially viewed (as has often been the case), as a product costing system, rather than a cost management system. The authors took the view that this was one of the reasons why 'no progress was made in the implementation of ABC between 1990 and 1993 in the Division', though factors such as increased pressures on reduced staff are acknowledged as likely contributory factors.

Joint costs may pose a relatively greater problem for banks than manufacturing industry in general, but otherwise, it is clear from Cobb *et al.*[5] that the objectives of management accounting in this service industry (and in all probability, in many other service industries) largely mirror those in manufacturing. The main feature distinguishing the two is the comparatively late start by banks in developing their MASs into modern systems capable of dealing with rapid changes in their business environment.

The future in banking?

As mentioned at the beginning of this section, banks and banking in general is in a state of rapid change, a state likely to continue for some time yet. Until this period of change finally reaches a degree of equilibrium, it is difficult to be prescriptive about the role and opportunities for management accounting within, in this instance, a traditional clearing bank.

In contrast to the organization chart of Figure 10.2, the new philosophy behind the reorganization of banks is to supply services to potential customers in as attractive and efficient manner as possible. Figure 10.3 outlines in concept, the kind of organization structure which may evolve.

The organization is now seen to focus on its main customer groupings. Operations will be structured to meet the requirements of these customers in respect of the services themselves and how they are best delivered. Corporate HO is likely to be slimmed down to a small group which monitors results and develops strategy.

Appraising customers and their value to a bank is a complex task. As noted,

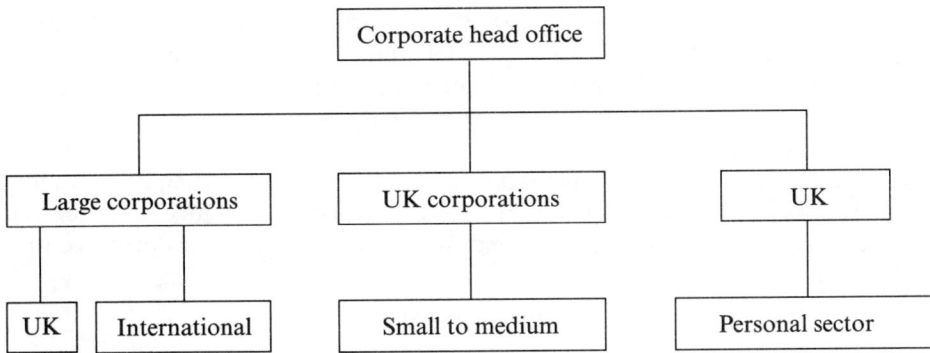

Figure 10.3   *Conceptual outline for a clearing bank in the future*

many customers do not pay for the administration of their accounts and many credit card holders likewise pay little or perhaps nothing for a certain period of credit. Banks have to determine what the value to them is of attracting particular types of individuals, groups of customers or businesses to hold accounts with them: what are the probabilities that they will eventually move on to taking profit generating services after opening an account; what returns will they produce? The extent of cross-subsidization amongst account and card holders (income from one class being used to subsidize the costs of providing free services to others) will need to be addressed more deeply. The problem of defining what is a product or service on offer is clearly seen, since services taken by customers are frequently jointly determined, but taken in varying proportions.

These are just some of the issues a bank will need to resolve in the future. Whereas the role for management accounting, when related to the organization of the kind illustrated in Figure 10.2, differed little in principle to that of a manufacturing company with a range of goods on offer, it must now relate more closely to questions of marketing and customer analysis and the provision of new measures of performance. Similar trends, however, are also discernible in manufacturing.

Hotels

Hotels represent a section of service industries in which there is a clear opportunity to apply the techniques of management accounting to their full extent: sectors of the business are well delineated and products/services are reasonably well defined entities. The industry ranges from small units, privately owned, to large multinational corporations, such as Trusthouse Forte. In the large organizations, there will be additional operations beyond those associated with an hotel alone, for example, Grand Metropolitan (as at September 1994) had an eyeware and eyecare division, as well as subsidiaries such as Haagen-Dazs and Burger King. This section, however, concentrates purely on hotel operations.

Individual hotels are often designated as investment centres, whilst the main revenue generating activities within an hotel, namely accommodation, restaurant and beverages (bar facilities) would form natural profit centres. Larger hotels may offer conference accommodation either with or without overnight accommodation and franchised shop premises, also definable as profit centres. In addition, they may provide a wide range of facilities for guests, such as swimming pools, saunas, fitness rooms and so on, though the latter of course are often not revenue generating themselves and hence do not always appear as profit centres in their own right.

Cost characteristics

Apart from the raw materials for the restaurant and bar operations, laundry services and guest supplies, costs of running hotels are predominantly of a fixed nature in the short run at least. They are also highly labour intensive. Increasing use of part-time labour has introduced some flexibility into staff costs, but not to the extent of their becoming directly proportional to the volume of business. Heating and lighting also vary to a small degree with business levels, but the remaining important costs, such as depreciation of buildings and equipment, business rates and rents and maintenance, are generally regarded as fixed expenses in the short run.

Management accounting and costing objectives

In general these objectives are the conventional ones of information required for planning, control and special decisions. However, the industry is tailor-made for the application of contribution-based pricing, using a standard marginal or incremental costing approach. The need for this kind of analysis has been heightened by intense competition within the industry; one of the clearest examples of its application is to price-setting for periods when capacity can be expected to be underutilized, principally at weekends and during winter periods. Pricing strategy is obviously not wholly dependent on costs: hotel location, the type of custom it normally attracts, the degree to which an hotel can segregate its market, also need to be taken into account.

Figure 10.4 shows a cost–revenue analysis for an hypothetical hotel group, involving three profit centres: accommodation, restaurant, beverages.

The benefit of a contribution analysis in this case is the same as in other applications: it presents management with a clear picture of how much individual sections of the business are contributing to overall hotel profits, without the distortions caused by applying full absorption cost rates to them. Additionally, costs are more clearly related to those sectors where they arise and matters such as responsibility for and controllability of cost can be more accurately evaluated. Consequently, the common approach of designating sections of an hotel as profit centres can be more reliably employed to assist management to develop the hotel's services in an appropriate direction and the ability of central management to compare the performance of individual hotels in the group is also facilitated.

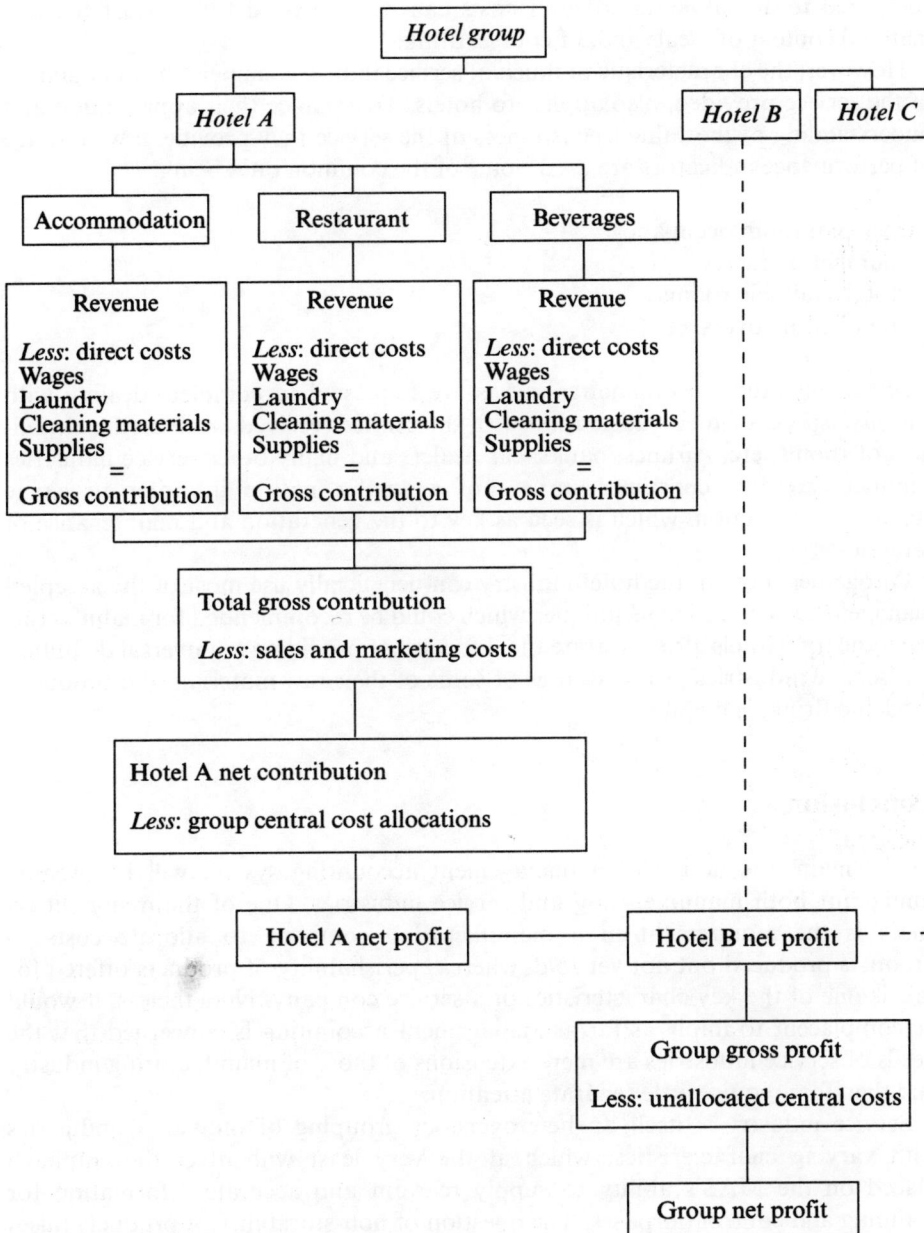

Figure 10.4   *Cost-revenue analysis*

Standard marginal (or full) costing and budgetary control can also be readily employed throughout the hotel industry. Capacity utilization can be forecast and compared to actual; standard unit costs can be developed for at least the raw material content of meals and, of course, drink.

However, the characteristic of much of service industry, namely the intangibility of the service provided, also applies to hotels. To enhance their appreciation and understanding of the value to customers of the service they provide, a wide range of performance indicators are used, some of the common ones being:

- per cent room occupancy
- number of guests
- total available rooms
- number of covers, etc.

together with the questionnaires guests are requested to complete dealing with various aspects of their satisfaction with the service received, such as the cleanliness of rooms, etc. Airlines, banks, car dealers and many other service industries conduct extensive consumer surveys of a similar nature in order to gauge customer satisfaction, which is seen as key to the generation and maintenance of revenues.

Altogether though, the hotel industry can beneficially use most of the accepted management accounting techniques which could be recommended for manufacturing industry. Hotels also illustrate the difficulty of providing a universal definition for 'service industries', since storage of some of their raw materials and products, food and drink, is possible.

Conclusion

In the main, the design of a management accounting system will be broadly similar for both manufacturing and service industries. One of the major differences is the requirement in a manufacturing company to allocate costs to products produced but not yet sold, whereas perishability of products offered for sale is one of the key characteristics of a service company. Nonetheless, it would be complacent to imply as far as management accounting is concerned that the needs of service industries are mere extensions of those of manufacturing industry and therefore require little separate attention.

Service industry is itself an heterogeneous grouping of individual industries with varying characteristics, which at the very least will affect the emphasis placed on the MAS's ability to supply relevant and accurate information for planning and control purposes. The question of non-storability of products raises special interest in product pricing schemes, as can be readily seen in the sales of theatre, railway and airline seating, as well as hotel accommodation. This is reinforced by the high fixed cost structures (not, of course, an exclusive feature of service industry) of, for instance, airlines and hotels, which in turn focuses attention on decisions prior to commitments to expenditure being made and to how costs are to be managed. Joint costs and understanding the functions of support departments are also aspects which may assume a greater significance for a service company than one in manufacturing, leading again to a difference of emphasis in the nature of information supplied by the MAS to management.

References

1. Berry, R.H., (ed.) *Management Accounting in Universities.* CIMA, London, 1994.
2. Abbott, C., Service Level Agreements. Proceedings of a workshop held in Stamford, Lincolnshire. Ed. Ashcroft, M. Capital Planning Information Ltd, 52 High Street, St Martin's, Stamford, Lincolnshire PE9 2LG. June 1994.
3. Sloane, L.J., Accounting in British Banking. Framework Series in Accountancy. CIMA, London, 1991.
4. Sharma, V.S., Determining product profitability. *Bankers' Magazine*, March/April, 1992.
5. Cobb, I., Helliar, C. and Innes, J., Management accounting change in a bank. *Management Accounting Research*, June 1995.

Further reading

1. Fitzgerald, L., Johnston, R., Brignall, S., Silvestro, R. and Voss, C., *Performance measurement in service industries.* CIMA, London, 1991.
2. Collier, P. and Gregory, A., Management accounting in hotel groups. CIMA, London, 1995.
3. Ward, K., *Financial management for service companies.* Pitman Publishing, London,1993.

Questions

1   If education can be regarded as a product, what are the direct costs to a university of providing education for a student?

2   It is often said that product costing for service companies is in principle the same as in manufacturing companies. However, given that in many cases service companies do not have to 'manufacture' inventoriable products, their costs do not flow through inventory accounts as they would in a manufacturing company. So strictly speaking they have no product costs. Give some examples of the kind of service companies to which the above statement may apply and discuss the implications for product costing in such cases.

3   The reprographics department provides services to many departments of Lowlands University. One of these, external relations, considers that due to

the continually rising charges from reprographics, it would do better to buy-in printing services from outside.

The normal load of the reprographics department in a four-week period is 400 service hours. Also on a normal basis, external relations would require 50 service hours. In the latest four-week period, the actual hours supplied and demanded were below normal at 350 and 47 hours respectively. It was because the reprographics department bases its charges to customer departments on actual hours and external relations' actual usage has fallen during the period in question, that the latter department was considering buying the service outside.

The reprographics department budget cost (based on 400 hours) and actual costs (based on 350 hours) is given below:

Cost classification		Budget £	Actual £	Variance £
Material supplies	V	3,600	3,200	400
Operators	V	2,400	2,200	200
Indirect labour	V	1,000	980	20
Equipment depreciation	F	1,600	1,600	—
Supervisory staff	F	1,400	1,400	—
Premises	F	700	740	(40)
Total		10,700	10,120	

V = variable cost; F = fixed cost; () = unfavourable variance.

Although reprographics does not make a special charge for it, the equipment used for much of the work for external relations is more expensive than that used for other work within the university.

(a) Examine whether external relations' view of its charges from reprographics is justifiable and explain how the problem may have arisen.

(b) Comment on the possible effects of the situation described by the last paragraph above.

11

Budgeting and performance measurement in public sector organizations

Introduction

In the UK, general government expenditure (GGE) accounts for over 40 per cent of the gross domestic product (GDP); in 1995/6 the ratio of GGE to GDP was estimated to be 43 per cent.[1] Public sector organizations possess a variety of social, economic, political and legal characteristics. The profit motive which generally drives commercial enterprises has traditionally been absent from many public sector organizations. The absence of the profit yardstick in respect of both planning and control makes it considerably more difficult to establish acceptable requirements for resources, acquire them and measure performance. However, in the period since 1979, there have been many changes in the structure and management of the public sector including privatization; compulsory competitive tendering; internal markets and devolved management. Just as important is the emergence of a new management culture brought about by the exposure of parts of the public sector to competition and market force mechanisms. It is no longer true to say that commercial accounting techniques have little application in public service provision. On the other hand, business is adopting additional, less tangible, performance measures previously associated with the public services. Many businesses now measure the level of customer service provided and the speed and accuracy of the provision of information, or give an additional measure of success beyond profit based measures, such as growth in sales, reputation in the community and so on. In other words, it is not the case that one set of management accounting techniques and performance measures applies to commercial enterprises and another totally separate set to public sector services. This chapter deals with two aspects of control and audit in the management of public sector organizations: budgeting and performance measurement. Emphasis is placed on local government and the National Health Service, but many of the principles also apply to a myriad of other areas of public service provision.

Budgeting in public sector organizations

Incremental budgeting

A number of authors (for example, Pendlebury,[2] Jones and Pendlebury,[3] Butt and Palmer,[4] Coombs and Jenkins[5] and Glynn[6]) have characterized the 'conventional' budgetary procedures in local authorities as the incremental approach – last year's allocation plus or minus a sum for next year, depending on factors such as the expansion of services, limitations on resources, expectations of inflation. It is a practice common in the public sector, but is not unique to them. It is frequently justified on the grounds that it maintains the level of service previously provided. On the other hand, this equally may be seen as one of a number of weaknesses:

1   That little or no attempt is made to see whether the bulk of the funding is justifiable: it is assumed that because a sum was spent on an activity in the past, it is ipso facto also a justification of future expenditure of at least broadly the same amount.
2   It is a self-perpetuating system which, while making life generally easy for all concerned, is likely to lead to complacency and must eventually extinguish any spark of critical evaluation faculty that may once have existed.
3   The existing situation is regarded as static rather than dynamic. Priorities may change continually and maintenance of the status quo could in effect be drawing funds away from potentially more valuable budget areas.
4   The approach considers the annual budget but neglects long-term objectives. Continuing past expenditure activities may commit the organization to future expenditure which will restrict future choices.

Incremental budgeting often forms part of a financial planning system. Such systems encompass a number of years' plans for which expenditure guidelines are issued. The typical annual cycle for a local authority would be

June	Medium-term forecast preparation.
July	Medium-term forecast to management team and policy committee.
August	Budget procedures and guidelines finalized.
September	Capital programme preparation starts.
October	Revenue estimates preparation starts.
November	Budget (capital and revenue) to management team and leadership.
January	Policy committee examines in light of guidelines.
February	Committees may reconsider estimates. Policy committee finalizes estimates.
March	Council approve estimates.

Local authority planning systems have been hampered in recent years by the introduction of community charge and council tax capping which at a late stage in the process restricts the level of a local authority's tax.

Under a financial planning system, the annual budget is seen as the first year of a multi-year rolling programme as in the government's expenditure plans. Typically, base expenditure; inflation; committed growth and new growth are specified. Committed growth includes the full year effect of developments brought on-line in the previous financial year. New growth is growth in service expenditure which is at the organization's discretion. Where incremental budgets form part of a financial planning system, the criticism of neglecting long-term objectives may be invalid. Nevertheless, the justification for the base budget is largely unquestioned and there is no attempt to monitor efficiency and effectiveness – the emphasis is on input; output measures are usually absent.

In the public sector it is often difficult to obtain reliable and objective measures of resource consumption and the benefits produced; value judgements play a significant role in determining what resources are required or are adequate. Under these circumstances then, what was apparently deemed acceptable last year, plus or minus a little, clearly offers a seductively simple and seemingly reasonable point of departure for next year. However, there has been a demand for a more rational form of budgeting. Two concepts originating in the US – zero-base budgeting (ZBB) and planning programming budgeting systems (PPBS) – provide a much more rational, corporate approach. In recent years, UK public sector organizations have also attempted to ensure a more efficient budgeting system by increasing budget delegation, for example, local management of schools (LMS). These concepts and approaches are examined below.

Zero-base budgeting (ZBB)

Introduction

The Chartered Institute of Management Accountants[7] defines ZBB as:

> A method of budgeting whereby all activities are re-evaluated each time a budget is formulated.

Each functional budget starts with the assumption that the function does not exist and is at zero cost. Increments of cost are compared with increments of benefit, culminating in the planned maximum benefit for a given budgeted cost.

In contrast with the creeping incrementalism referred to previously, there is no longer any presumption that simply because an activity has existed in the past it should continue to do so in the future. Expenditure justification starts from the zero-base and comparisons of costs and benefits take place at sequentially defined levels of activity/service from that point. Hence its principal attraction may be seen to be the maintenance of a continuing pressure on spending departments to commit themselves to a programme of thorough re-appraisal of the value of their activities. Instead of adding or subtracting a little from a previously budgeted or actual amount of expenditure, as though this in itself is an acknowledged and therefore justified point to build on for the next round of budget preparation, ZBB forces managers to address the fundamental question of whether an activity is necessary at all and even if this is conceded, at what level it should operate – in theory a complete break with what has happened in the past.

Viewed simplistically, it might seem that ZBB opens up the possibility of ad hoc budget approvals taking place without any coherent, cohesive planning framework to hold them together, especially as the process is commonly referred to as 'bottom-up' budgeting, and everything is up for re-appraisal at the start of each new round. In practice, however, although budgets are indeed seen as being developed from the basic activity levels upwards, it should be a process taking place within the broader planning mechanism aimed at securing and supporting the achievement of management's overall strategic objectives for an organization, so that budget approvals are part of a well defined total plan.

ZBB is, at least so far as its formal name is concerned, a fairly recent introduction as a planning tool, credited to the United States Department of Agriculture in 1962.[8] It seems likely though that the idea has been applied earlier, though not referred to as ZBB. Indeed it is probable that this continues to be the case at present, since there is no compulsion to refer to the particular style of budgeting as ZBB.

It is likely that the ZBB approach is adopted without any questioning of the need in many situations; new business enterprises, disposals and acquisitions of existing business, expansions and contractions of business, are obvious cases where a zero-base approach to budgeting may well be taken in practice if not in name. Equally changes in the levels of economic activity, more particularly significant downturns, will in all likelihood bring about a zero-base attitude, with a thorough re-appraisal and justification of all expenditure in a drive for economy. However, recorded applications of ZBB in the UK appear to be relatively few, suggesting that the practice has not been adopted widely here in spite of its apparent value. Perhaps the differentiation between use and non-use lies in whether it is a concept fully integrated into an organization's regular budgetary cycle. In the examples cited in the previous paragraph, the events are irregular and the process thus becomes one of occasionally conducting a special exercise. By contrast, a thoroughgoing ZBB programme means budgeting is permanently placed on this footing. In turn the operation of such a scheme demands substantially greater administrative resources, particularly in terms of managers' and accountants' time, certainly more than traditional incremental budgeting, which possibly accounts at least in part for its failure to be adopted here on a widespread scale.

Zero-base budgeting in operation

The focus of attention of ZBB is the functions of an organization which are regarded as necessary if it is to achieve the success it aims for.[9] Although the budgets are created from the bottom up, they are examined and filtered in accordance with organization objectives. It is the responsibility of top management to see that units are given sufficient knowledge of their objectives, and that

Function head

Division 1   Division 2   Division 3

Department 1   Department 2   Department 3

Operating
unit 1

Operating
unit 2

Operating
unit 3

Decision
packages

Decision
packages

Decision
packages

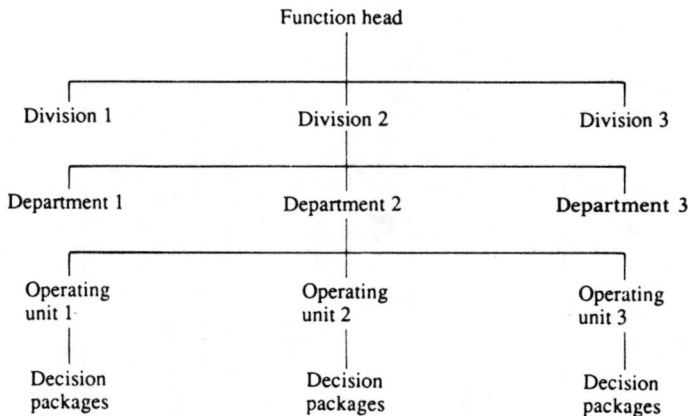

Figure 11.1 *Function hierarchy*

they and senior managers understand the assumptions of the plan it is aimed to achieve. The latter should be set, of course, within the context of the organization's strategic development plans.

The mechanics of operating a scheme require a clearly recognized organizational framework, built around well defined functions. As a total entity, an organization will be composed of several functions and each of these in turn will be examined on a zero-base; it is not just individual activities which come under scrutiny, but functions as a whole will need to justify themselves.

Figure 11.1 illustrates a typical function hierarchy. The first-line 'decision packages' on which ZBB is founded are shown at the base. Assume that the function is within a large local authority and represents one with a responsibility for road construction, repairs and maintenance and road clearance. Then, following the line from the head of the function through the hierarchy:

1   Divisions could correspond to districts within the authority.
2   Departments represent various aspects of the main function, e.g. new road construction, maintenance, liaison with such other services, e.g. telephones, traffic control.
3   Operating units represent individual units within the departments designated to particular aspects of the work, e.g. major/minor road construction, surveillance of major roads, flyovers and so on.

Each of the sections could demonstrate its operational capacities at varying levels of activity and this information would be contained in the decision packages. The departments and districts, and ultimately the function itself, are the 'decision units' whose budgets are eventually to be determined. The administration of a ZBB may thus be summarized as requiring:

1   A statement of objectives of an organization and its functions.
2   Identification of decision units.

Table 11.1 Incremental decision packages

	Package numbers			
	1	2	3	4
Definition of level of output/activity	Minimum required to maintain a presence	Poor standard of service	Current service level	Improved standard of service
Incremental cost (£)	30,000	20,000	20,000	15,000
Cumulative total cost (£)	30,000	50,000	70,000	85,000
Comment	No more than keeps service together. Emergency cover only.	Emergency cover provided. Only 40% coverage of other demand within specified time period. Long backlog develops.	Emergency cover provided. Other demands met to 75% within time limits. Backlog of demand exists.	As with 3, but 100% of normal demand within specified time limits.

Table 11.2 Decision package ranking

Rank	Description	Package number	Incremental cost (£)	Cumulative total cost (£)
1	OU1	2 of 4	50,000	50,000
2	OU3	1 of 4	80,000	130,000
3	OU2	2 of 4	90,000	220,000
4	OU1	3 of 4	20,000	240,000
5	OU4	1 of 4	30,000	270,000
6	OU2	4 of 4	10,000	278,000
etc.				

3   Identification of decision packages.
4   A system for ranking the selection of decision packages.

Continuing the example of the local authority roads function:

1   **Function objectives** may be defined on the following lines: to ensure that (i) the provision of road capacity within the authority is sufficient to ensure a smooth, free flow of traffic; (ii) that construction of new roads is to the highest standards; and (iii) that road repairs are completed to an accepted standard, and within a specified time period of a maintenance need being reported.

2   **Decision units** are units for which the budgets are prepared. They stand above the level of operating units. In principle the selection of the levels at which decision units should be identified is on the grounds that too great a level of aggregation of activities will make it difficult to single out individual features, while too great a level of disaggregation will materially affect the cost of information preparation. In the example, the departments might well serve as the lower level of decision units. Each unit will require clear objectives to work to and will be in the charge of a responsible manager.

3   **Decision packages** are often referred to as the 'building blocks' of ZBB. Jones and Pendlebury[10] cite two types of decision package:
   (a)   *Mutually exclusive:* packages which identify alternative ways of operating the unit to which they relate, including that of doing without it altogether.
   (b)   *Incremental:* various levels of resource/cost input are measured against the realization of various levels of output. Table 11.1 provides a generalized illustration of this process.

4   **Ranking decision packages.** Once the packages are completed, within each decision unit, starting at the lower levels, it will be necessary to rank the packages in priority order for selection. The process is illustrated in Table 11.2.

The 'descriptions' (Table 11.2) would refer back to those given to the specific packages within the operating unit: so, for example, four packages were identified in the case of each of the operating units listed and first priority was given to package number 2 (from the four listed) in operating unit 1. This is followed by package number 1 from unit 3 and so on. It should be noted that, provided the funds are available, higher numbered packages may be added to the list; in the above example package number 3 from operating unit 1 is ranked fourth, automatically incorporating the level of service defined in package number 2 already accorded first priority. If available funds amounted to £240,000 then this would be the level to which operating unit 1 would work. The filtering out of the decision packages would take place upwards in line with the priorities seen for the individual decision units.

If a ZBB approach were adopted within a commercial company, the rankings would probably be established more objectively than within non-trading areas of the public sector, since cost-benefit trade-offs can probably be quantified with a greater degree of precision and certainty. In the not-for-profit organizations, especially those in the public sector, the ranking is certain to be a more subjective process, with political value judgements likely to play a major role in determining priorities.

Conclusions on ZBB

ZBB is a very formal system. It differs from the normal budgetary process in that detailed budgets are prepared at the lowest defined level of activity in a way which shows several levels of outcome starting from the zero-base, rather than from a point attained in an immediately preceding period. Instead of targets and budgets being pushed downward through the management hierarchy, here they are built upwards within a framework of known organizational objectives, with successive levels of management receiving increasing quantities of information leading to the agreement of a conventional master budget. The link to the master budget also shows ZBB to be part of the short-term tactical planning process.

The clear merit of ZBB is to force a detailed re-evaluation of what a function is able to achieve in order of preference in line with its objectives. In reality, many areas of the public sector are locked into expenditure programmes by past legislation or political necessity. ZBB's main disadvantage is probably its own administrative cost and feasibility. In theory, it should be a permanent part of a budgeting cycle. Treated as a once-off blitz procedure to haul organizations back to an acceptable level of performance from a previously unacceptable one runs the obvious risk of a drift back to inefficiency once the pressure is relaxed. Nevertheless, a once-off blitz is better than no scrutiny of the base budget. A ZBB approach is implicit in ad hoc efficiency reviews now quite common in the public sector. Such reviews may be instigated by external bodies such as the Audit Commission which undertakes reviews in local government and the National Health Service or as a result of internal management action. A further fairly common method of ensuring that the base budget is scrutinized is to operate a system of option budgets. Option budgets do not incorporate the full decision package approach, but nevertheless do embody some ZBB principles and enable the priorities of the department to be tested. Under an option budget, budget heads would be required to identify their response to various percentage reductions/increases in their financial budget, perhaps ranking their responses within each reduction/increase. A further measure to encourage managers to question their base budget is often provided through budgetary arrangements which enable managers to retain a reasonable percentage of planned savings in their budget for use on service development.

Planning, programming and budgeting systems (PPBS)

Introduction

Anthony and Young[11] suggest PPBS contains three central ideas: 'first, it is a formal programming system; second, it uses a program budget as contrasted with a line by line item budget; and third, it emphasizes benefit/cost analysis'. PPBS represents one of the first moves in the public sector away from incremental budgeting towards a more formal approach both in programme structure and analysis. In contrast to incremental budgeting (and also to zero-base budgeting), it is a centralized, top-down process which seeks to define clearly the objectives and sub-objectives of the various activities for which an organization may be responsible and set their achievement on to a longer-term basis. In this way it has the appeal of a rational/logical planning procedure. However, it is commonly thought[12] that the day of PPB systems has come and gone, indeed that few, if any, examples really exist that it ever had a true application. It is possible that there may be a subconscious impact on the planning systems operated within organizations induced by the exposure to the idea of PPB, but this would be difficult to prove. It is an attempt to change the way budgetary planning is done within the public sector which is thought to have failed. However, since the *concept* has the appeal of rationality, it is probably one worth keeping alive.

Background to PPBS

The 1960s was the period during which, especially within the US federal government, efforts to introduce PPB systems were actively pursued. By the early 1970s these efforts were waning, and indeed by the mid-1970s the officially inaugurated programme of the US government and experimentation with the ideas at state and local levels both within the US and UK appear to have ceased. Against the attraction of the ideas constituting PPB it is of more than academic historical interest to try to appreciate why it did not have greater success.

The PPBS framework

The contrast between PPB and the traditional incremental budgeting already referred to is best summarized as the difference between a clearly stated, planned set of long-term objectives whose resource implications have been carefully evaluated, to the case where the future is seen as more short-term, largely dependent on the extrapolation of past developments, with relatively hazy objectives, especially in the long term, both within individual activities and activities relative to each other.

Establishing PPBS

This requires the identification and evaluation of:

1   The goals of each of the main spending programmes within an authority.
2   Each of the sub-goals whose individual achievements are an integral part of the successful accomplishment of one of the main goals. These are generally referred to as the *programme categories*.
3   The activities which in turn constitute the means by which each of the sub-goals is to be realized. These are referred to as the *programme elements*.

The starting point of determining a budget for any spending programme is agreement on what it is intended it should accomplish, not simply over the annual budget cycle period but with respect to the time properly needed to realize the goals. Not only does this give clarity of purpose, it should also provide greater stability during the period of its execution, with less susceptibility to short-term pressures for changes of direction of the kind likely to be brought about by the ever-changing political complexion of authorities (though here is also the most likely key to the failure of the idea to gain adherence).

A simple example of a PPBS structure is given in Jones and Pendlebury[13] and is reproduced here with permission. It deals with flood protection in the context of coastal local authorities in England and Wales. Jones and Pendlebury[14] describe and illustrate the goals, programmes, programme categories and elements along the lines of a PPB system.

Coastal local authorities have responsibility for flood protection and, in order to meet this responsibility, might well have programmes aimed at 'sea defences' and 'surface water drainage'.

The beneficial impacts of flood protection relate to the avoidance of the loss of agricultural production caused by flooding, and also the avoidance of damage to property. Providing the areas at risk can be adequately estimated it ought to be possible to express the benefits of flood protection in monetary amounts. The benefits would therefore be measured in terms of the economic consequences of avoiding crop spoilage, or livestock losses, or domestic and commercial property damage. Ideally, of course, measures reflecting the benefits of protecting human beings from death or injury, or benefits concerned with 'quality of life' or 'peace of mind' should also be included. However, the more easily measurable economic benefits offer a starting point.

For each of the basic programmes of 'sea defences' and 'surface water' there will be a variety of programme categories. For example, the programme categories for the 'sea defences' programme might include:

Table 11.3 Example of programme elements presentation showing the costs and related benefits of each programme element

Programme category 'Soft sea defences' Programme elements	Cost / benefits Monetary measures (in Year 0 prices) represented by X. Physical measures represented by Y. Year 0 = current year						
	− 1	0	1	2	3	4	5
1 Existing soft sea defences							
1.9 Estimated costs							
Estimated benefits:	X	X	X	X	X	X	X
1.1 Agricultural area offered protection	Y	Y	Y	Y	Y	Y	Y
1.2 Financial benefits of 1.1	X	X	X	X	X	X	X
1.3 Urban area offered protection	Y	Y	Y	Y	Y	Y	Y
1.4 Urban population offered protection	Y	Y	Y	Y	Y	Y	Y
1.5 Financial benefits of 1.3 and 1.4	X	X	X	X	X	X	X
1.0 Total financial benefits	X	X	X	X	X	X	X
2 Extensions to soft sea defences							
2.9 Estimated costs							
Estimated benefits:	X	X	X	X	X	X	X
2.1 Agricultural area offered by protection	Y	Y	Y	Y	Y	Y	Y
2.2 Financial benefits of 2.1	X	X	X	X	X	X	X
2.3 Urban area offered protection	Y	Y	Y	Y	Y	Y	Y
2.4 Urban population offered protection	Y	Y	Y	Y	Y	Y	Y
2.5 Financial benefits of 2.3 and 2.4	X	X	X	X	X	X	X
2.0 Total financial benefits	X	X	X	X	X	X	X

Source: Pendlebury, M. and Jones, R., *Public Sector Accounting*, Pitman, 1992.

- Hard sea defences – concrete and steel defences
- Soft sea defences – earthbanks, groynes, dunes, etc.
- Dredging of estuaries
- Tidal barriers

The *programme elements* and the related costs and benefits for the 'soft sea defences' programme category could then be expressed as in Table 11.3.

Each programme element would be similarly treated and evaluated; these are added to give the total costs and benefits of each programme category, leading on to the total for the category (here, flood protection) as a whole. The evaluation should be based on costs and benefits in financial terms as far as possible. In the example certain items such as loss of crops, livestock, damage to property could be given a financial value, but others such as 'peace of mind' for residents living in areas threatened by flooding would be much more difficult to appraise. Indirect measures, such as anticipated improvements to property values, may be used as surrogates for direct measures. In the final analysis certain items may not be amenable to direct or indirect measures, but could be judged significant or not, depending on the extent to which schemes can be appraised on land data alone.

This type of cost-benefit evaluation is the same as for ZBB in principle. The key difference between the two systems appears to be the reorganization likely to be required for PPBS in order to realize clear, specific long-term objectives for an activity. The aims, objectives, evaluation procedures and criteria for programme elements follow, being transmitted downward through the organization. In contrast, the conditions for ZBB to operate do not demand such organizational change, and the planning framework may be correspondingly less specific. Nonetheless it would seem possible for a PPB system to incorporate a ZBB approach.

Advantages of PPBS

Given the apparent unpopularity of the concept in application, 'advantages' may be thought to be limited. Looked at objectively, however, there would seem to be some substantial potential gains:

1 It focuses on the provision of clear long-term policy aims and objectives.
2 Activities to be linked in achieving a programme are identified and brought together.
3 Waste is reduced by removing duplication of activities.
4 It promotes the evaluation of resource allocation through the use of cost-benefit appraisals.

Altogether it offers a coherence to the planning process, particularly in central and local government, which could improve the level of service enjoyed from a given level of resource input by having a distinct long-run objective and avoiding the waste caused by continually chopping and changing programmes and duplicating effort.

Conclusions on PPBS

The lack of success of the PPBS approach in the US and by central and local government in the UK was apparent by the late 1970s. Despite its rational approach to budgeting a number of problems proved insurmountable.

The complexity of programme structures leads to severe practical problems. The need to reorganize departmental activities into matching programme areas not only affects traditional empires, but it is also not easy to split the costs of services which spread diffuse benefits to a number of programme areas. For example, the provision of school meals has benefits relating to education, social welfare and health. Party politics may lead to uncertainty in relation to programme objectives with differing emphases placed on the various aspects of programmes due to different political views. The problems are further exacerbated by the dearth of relevant information and the limited cognitive ability of human beings – the inability to foresee the full consequences of major changes in policy makes the movement towards goals in small sequential steps much more attractive.

However, although PPBS is not adhered to rigorously in any area of the public sector today, its ideas are valuable and elements of it can be seen in recent initiatives. In 1982 the Financial Management Initiative (FMI), was introduced for use in central government departments. The FMI called for all managers at all levels to have:

> A clear view of their objectives and means to assess, and wherever possible measure, outputs or performance in relation to those objectives.
>
> Her Majesty's Government, 1982.[15]

Although some departments implemented the proposals admirably, notably the Department of Customs and Excise,[16] progress was not uniform across all departments. In 1988, the Efficiency Unit of the Prime Minister's Office issued the *Next Steps* report.[17] The report pointed out that 95 per cent of civil servants carried out service delivery or executive functions and the report proposed the establishing of executive agencies to carry out these executive functions. Strategies, objectives, budgets and targets were to be set for each agency and then the manager would be free to run the agency to meet the strategies, objectives, budgets and targets. The thirty-two Executive Agencies that had been established by 1990 were surveyed by Pendlebury *et al.*[18] who found that the vast majority had identified specific and measurable targets and performance indicators.

Devolved budgets to facilitate competition

Introduction

The principle of creating budget and responsibility centres as far down the organization structure as possible has already been discussed in Chapter 3. In the public sector, budget devolution has been pursued in recent years in the health service, local government and central government in order to improve control and consequently efficiency. In the health service budgets have devolved from district-wide functional budgets to unit budgets and clinical directorate budgets.[19] In local government, management and responsibilities have been decentralized for many services (education, social services and so on); similarly the *Next Steps* has brought about extensive devolution of budgets in the Civil Service. An impetus to increasing devolution has been provided through the introduction of many public sector services not previously regarded as trading services to competition or quasi-market mechanisms, for example, direct service organizations for local authority services and healthcare provision in the NHS internal market or 'managed competition'. This has been achieved by the separation of purchaser and provider elements of the service. Competition, it is argued, will stimulate efficiency in the provision of public services and make them more responsive to consumers; indeed such services will only remain in the public sector if public sector providers can effectively win clients.

The above developments require budgets to be devolved to distinct management units. The extent of budget devolution will depend to some extent on the nature of the competitive environment, for example under local management of schools, certain items are excepted from the general schools budget whereas under direct service organization arrangements and the NHS reforms where competition includes competing on price with private sector provision, the devolved budgets must include all the costs associated with service provision.

Local management of schools (LMS)

Under LMS each school is given a delegated budget.[20] In determining the delegated budget for each school, deductions are made for mandatory and discretionary exceptions from the general schools budget (GSB). Mandatory exceptions include capital expenditure and government grant related expenditure. Discretionary excepted items fall within two categories: those which are not subject to any limit such as central administration and those where the total amount held back by the local education authority (LEA) must not exceed 10 per cent of the general schools budget (7 per cent from April 1993), for example, structural maintenance and special educational needs. For this second category, the practice of whether or not items are delegated to schools varies among LEAs. The aggregated schools budget (ASB) is allocated to each school on the basis of a formula determined by the LEA and approved by the Secretary of State. At least 75 per cent of the ASB must be allocated on the basis of the number of school pupils weighted by age. The remainder of the ASB is allocated on the basis of other 'reasonable' factors such as type of fuel used, floor area, etc. The amount allocated to each school is known as its budget share. This budget is then allocated by the school to a number of subjective headings and spent according to the needs of the school. The governing body has the formal authority for spending decisions, but in practice this is delegated to the headteacher.

Under the Education Reform Act 1988, a school may opt out of local authority control and receive its funding directly from the Department of Education and Employment. These schools will receive the funds that they would have received from the local authority under LMS together with an amount which is deemed to cover its share of the costs of the services retained and funded by the local education authority. Such schools will have complete autonomy over which advisory and administrative services it should purchase and from where they should be bought. In April 1995, there were 1049 opted out (grant maintained) schools in operation. This number represents 4.3 per cent of the 24,000 state schools in England.[21]

The pilot schemes of devolved financial management in schools[22,23] showed encouraging results with schools able to create and keep within their budgets as well as being able to generate earnings and to spend more on books, materials and so on. Effectiveness in achieving targets was displayed, as was efficiency in the conversion of resource inputs into outputs.

Direct service organizations (DSOs)

In 1980, the Local Government Planning and Land Act[24] required local authorities to set up direct labour organizations for construction and maintenance work; the DSO would obtain its income through competing with other providers for the work of the local authority. In the 1988 Local Government Act[25] the principle of compulsory competitive tendering (CCT) was extended to cover a wide range of DSOs: grounds maintenance; management of sports and leisure facilities; refuse collection; street cleansing; schools and welfare catering; other catering; vehicle maintenance and cleaning of buildings. When these services are provided by local authority employees, they are required to be organized as separately accountable DSOs. Similar opportunities for competitive tendering exist in central government and the health service; in 1983 all health authorities were required by the DHSS to develop competitive tendering programmes for the provision of domestic, catering and laundry services.

When public sector service provision is in direct competition with the private sector, the cost of central support services must be included in the devolved budget in order to ensure 'a level playing field' for all competitors. Support services are internal activities of a professional, technical and administrative nature. In local government support services cover managerial and professional services; office services; office accommodation; central expenses; and democratic processes. The recommendation of the Chartered Institute of Public Finance and Accountancy[26] (1991) is that the costs relating to local elections, council meetings, members' allowances, accounts and budget preparation, estimating and accounting for local taxes, precepts and grants and certain of the costs of senior officers, should be specified to a 'corporate management' heading and not allocated to service departments and DSOs. Support services which derive from the provision of discrete services to service departments and DSOs such as legal advice, purchasing, financial management advice and so on, should be charged to service departments and DSOs. However, these charges should not be retrospective, arbitrary apportionments, but based on service level agreements.

Support service users should specify as far as possible their requirements in advance, rather than be given what the support service provider thinks is needed. The term 'service level agreement' implies that both parties know as far as possible what is expected of each other. Thus the position is envisaged where any agreement may be based on an agreed cost, a day-work rate, a unit rate for a defined service, or the cost of an agreed number of staff working on a function. Such arrangements must be capable of examination by review agencies such as audit.[27]

Consequently, many service departments are introducing trading accounts. Under this system, should a support service fail to secure enough business through its service level agreements with its users and it does not alter its expenditure accordingly, the trading account will go into deficit. The government plans to increase the scope of DSOs to cover finance and other central support services.

The introduction of competition into public sector services has therefore increased budget devolution; the DSO holds the budget responsibility for the full cost of the service provided. The DSO must budget in competition with outside providers and in order to ensure in-house provision remains competitive, the support services of the organization must also be justified. The introduction of competitive tendering in local government and health has brought about major changes in the provision of services and has resulted in cost savings. In 1991, it was reported by McGuirk[28] that out of 47 refuse collection/street cleaning contracts awarded in London 19 had been awarded to private contractors. Presumably each outside contract awarded showed significant savings over the most efficient in-house tender possible. In 1987, the National Audit Office[29] estimated that total annual savings from competitive tendering for domestic services laundry and catering in the NHS amounted to over £70 million.

The NHS under 'managed competition'

The National Health Service and Community Care Act 1990[30] created a market approach to healthcare provided through the NHS – the creation of the 'internal market' or 'managed competition' (Figure 11.2). Under 'managed competition' hospitals earn their revenue according to the services they supply rather than a global allocation.

The Act requires hospitals (directly managed NHS hospitals, NHS trust hospitals and private hospitals), to compete for contracts for healthcare provision. By April 1994, 95 per cent of hospital and community services were provided by the NHS trusts. District health authorities (DHAs) are the main purchasers and therefore hold the budget for the majority of funds available in the hospital and community health services, but GPs with large practices have the opportunity to become fundholders to purchase selected hospital services. Both the numbers of GP practices within the scope of the scheme have expanded rapidly.[31] DHAs and GP fundholders buy care from the most efficient provider, public or private and within or outside the district, thus 'money follows the patient to wherever the best care can be acquired most efficiently'.

Three forms of contract are possible: block contracts; cost and volume contract; or cost per case contracts.[32] Under a block contract the DHA or GP pays an annual fee to the hospital for access to a defined range of services, i.e. funding a level of capacity. Under a cost and volume contract the hospital receives a sum in respect of a base-line level of activity, defined in terms of a given number of treatments or cases, beyond that level, funding is on a cost per case basis which is agreed in advance. Cost per case will be used for hospital referrals which do not fall within either of the two previous forms of contract.

The Department of Health's approach on the pricing of contracts was set out by the NHS Management Executive in October 1990:[33] contract prices must be based on full cost with no planned cross-subsidization. Operation of the market therefore requires hospitals to be attributed all the costs associated with healthcare provision. As with DSOs above, the problems of attributing central support costs must be addressed. Prior to 1991, central administration costs covering district and regional headquarters expenditure (finance; supplies; person-

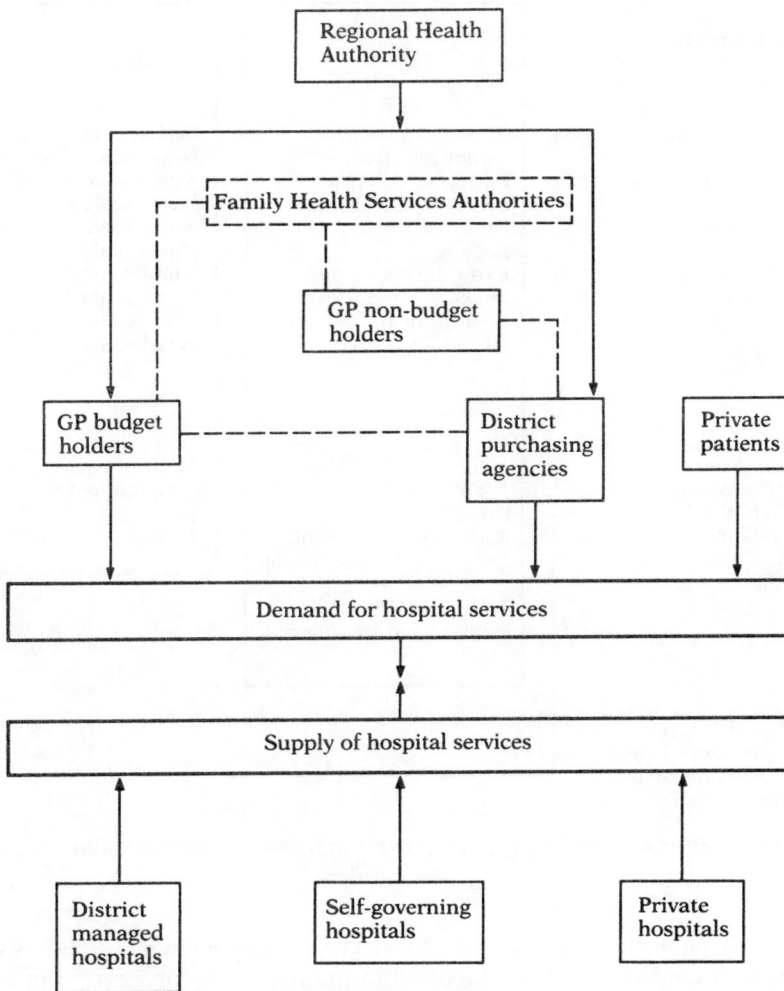

Key:
—————— Reflect 'non GP budget' services only

Figure 11.2 *The internal market for hospital services*

nel; planning and so on) were not attributed to hospitals.[34] Central administration cost and hospital general service costs must be attributed to contracts. Budgets had traditionally been structured by function: nursing services, pharmacy services, sterile supplies, etc. In the 1980s budgets had devolved to unit level and in a number of hospitals, ward and department budgeting had been developed.[35] There had been a number of attempts to involve clinicians in budgeting. Clinicians, it was argued,[36] determined the resource use of the service departments whilst functional budget holders remained accountable for the costs, e.g. X-rays and pathology investigations. In some hospitals, in particular the six pilot hospitals of the Resource Management Initiative (RMI), budgets had developed

Surgery directorate

	Pact *(General surgery II)*	Ward *(Martha)*
1 Pact management budgets General surgery I General surgery II ← ENT Ophthalmology Urology Urodynamics Paediatric surgery Endoscopy	Salaries and wages Senior registrar Registrar Senior house officer House officer Locum Extra duty payments Medical secretaries Medical records staff	Salaries and wages Nurse scale G Nurse scale F Nurse scale E Nurse scale D Nurse scale C Nurse scale B Nurse scale A Agency nurses Ward receptionist

2 Ward management budgets
Sarah Ward
Martha Ward
Evelyn Ward ←
Luke Ward
Patience Ward
Stoma Care Nursing
	Non-pay
	Medical and surgical
	  equipment
	Drugs
	Radiology consumables
	Laboratory -consumables
	       -on call
	Travel and subsistence
	Printing and stationery
		Non-pay
		Medical and surgical
		  equipment
		Dressings
		Drugs

3 Assigned functions
Surgery central costs
Audiology department
Optical services

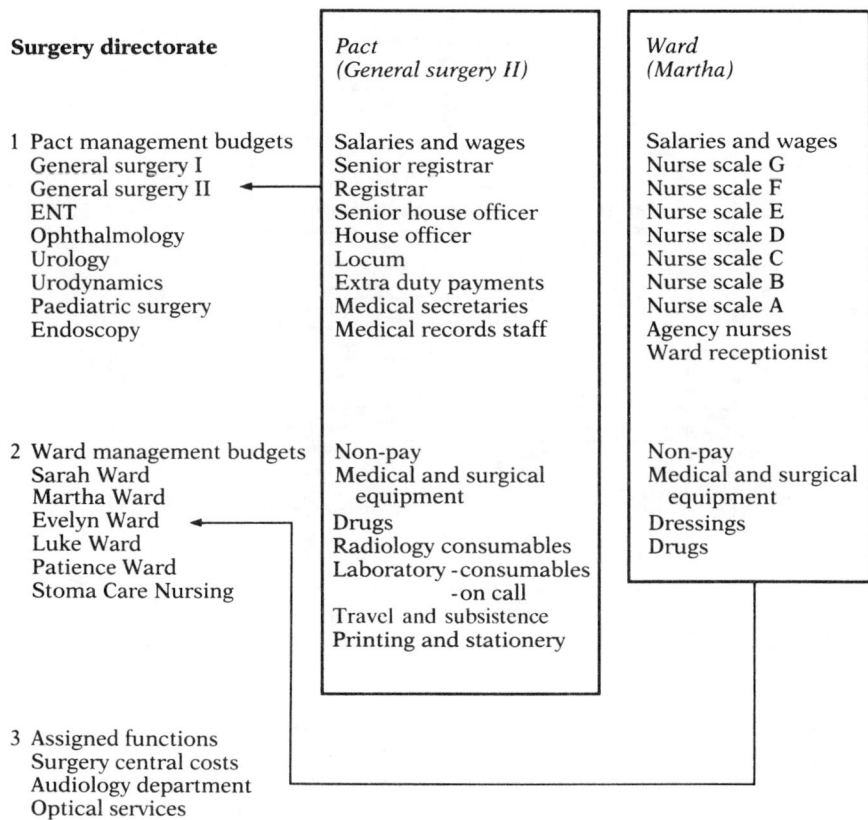

Figure 11.3   *Hierarchical budget report structure – surgery directorate, Guy's Hospital*

according to clinical directorates (natural groupings of clinical areas within a hospital) with clinicians actively involved in the budgetary process.[37] Figure 11.3 shows the budget report structure for the surgery directorate at Guy's Hospital, one the RMI pilots.

The internal market requires budgets to be developed according to product lines. In 1991–92, the first year of operation of the internal market, contracts were largely block and healthcare provision was only specified according to specialty.[38] Hospitals followed the lead of the resource management pilot hospitals and organized budgets into clinical directorate structures. As contracts become more refined (movement to cost and volume contracts with healthcare provision specified according to treatment groups), budgets will be devolved to smaller clinical areas.

The internal market injects competition into the provision of healthcare. As a hospital or clinical directorate budget is no longer fixed, but rather determined by the contracts which it wins, efficiency should be encouraged. Efficiency could be achieved through the exploitation of spare capacity; stimulating expansion of facilities to reap economies of scale, or through the reduction of input costs. However, the transaction costs necessary to operate the market are considerable.

Conclusions on devolved budgets to facilitate competition

The introduction of competition or quasi-market arrangements has necessitated budgets to be devolved to smaller management units. Considerable success has been reported in the operation of LMS, DSOs and other competitive tendering arrangements. Competition in healthcare is difficult to achieve and there is some evidence that little use is made of more sophisticated information.[39,40] Although devolved budgets have generally resulted in considerable financial benefits, the necessary systems are complex and costly to operate. It is difficult to disentangle the extent to which the benefits result from competition or from devolved budgetary arrangements. The process has enabled greater participation in the budget process, more realistic and responsive budget setting and improved control. In particular, central service costs are open to scrutiny – those at the 'sharp end' cannot be subjected to commercial pressures without those at the centre also having to justify themselves in a similar way.

Performance measurement in the public sector

The nature of performance measurement

In the commercial sector, an organization measures its performance primarily in terms of its profitability. The profit figure, particularly expressed as a ratio of capital employed, has become the ultimate test of the success or failure of a business. This approach seems sound in principle as profit indicates how well the business produced goods, and how much the customers were willing to pay for them. In practice, however, many firms operate in markets which are not competitive and given the array of alternative accounting treatments available in arriving at accounting profit, the profit figure is usually only a starting point for the financial analyst.

In the public sector, the profit measure is generally not available, although commercial targets have been set in recent years for many services previously regarded as non-trading, for instance many DSO services in local government and healthcare under internal market arrangements; these targets are considered towards the end of the chapter. Measuring performance for many areas of the public sector is fraught with difficulties: in order to measure performance it is obviously necessary to be able to define performance. However, the performance of a local authority, a health authority or even a single service, is a complex, multifaceted concept and hence a definition of performance is extremely difficult to derive.

The Audit Commission provided a framework for describing performance by defining value for money (VFM) and promoting economy, efficiency and effectiveness, the framework as originally defined is shown in Figure 11.4. Nevertheless, there are often difficulties in measuring both inputs and outputs and relating the latter to the achievement of an imprecisely defined objective. To give some examples:

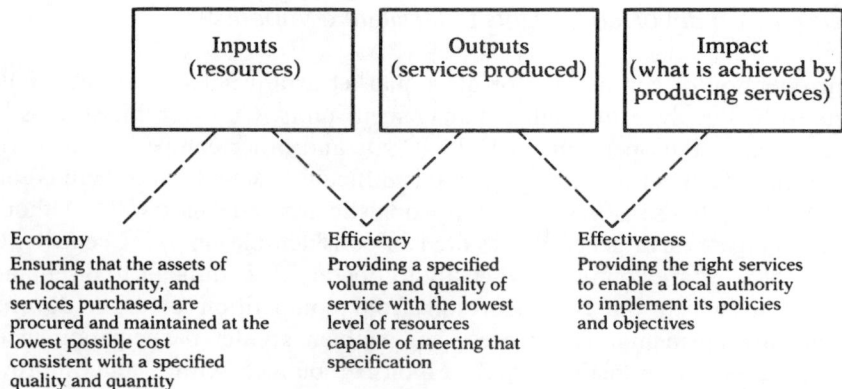

Figure 11.4 *The three Es as defined by the Audit Commission in 1986*

- It is difficult to give precise meaning to qualities such as health, welfare and education.
- Benefits from expenditure may not arise altogether immediately, but be rather diffusely and imprecisely spread over a period of time, this clearly applies again to health as well as to most normally recognized social services.
- Additionally, a number and variety of benefits may arise from expenditure programmes. A healthy population could be more generally economically productive; campaigns to reduce smoking, if successful, produce not only a healthy population, but save costs in the provision of health services, reduce working days lost, and improve output.
- The benefits claimed will frequently be difficult to measure in monetary units. This applies to the success of the armed forces in preventing war, and to measuring the final outputs of many traditional social services such as those instanced above. In the pursuit of law and order, for example, several services may at times combine to prevent problems, with police, fire and ambulance services acting together on many occasions. It would be difficult therefore to ascribe individual benefits to individual services even if they were measurable.

Performance measurement in the public sector has received increasing attention over the last decade as the Government has sought to make the public sector more performance orientated. It is possible to go beyond the 3Es and consider other important dimensions, e.g. excellence (the enhancement of quality services); empowerment both of consumers and employees; environment ('green' issues) and so on.[41] Performance indicators, value for money auditing and return on assets have all been employed to assess and motivate public sector management.

Performance indicators

As highlighted above, in considering performance measurement in the public sector, it is important not only to consider the resources input, but also the services produced (intermediate outputs) and the impact (final outputs or

Table 11.4   Input/throughput/output taxonomy

	Chemotherapy for cancer
Inputs	Beds, staff, drugs, laboratory services, etc.
Intermediate outputs	Patients treated, number of chemotherapy sessions, survival post-treatment, malignancy removed
Final outputs	Normal lifestyle, re-admissions, quality of life, death

Source: Adapted from *Outcome and Performance in Health Care*, H. Roberts, 1990

outcomes) of these services. An example of the input/throughput/output taxonomy is illustrated in Table 11.4.[42]

One response to the problem which was instigated prior to the Audit Commission's work in this area and indeed which forms the basic data for the VFM approach is the development of performance indicators. Performance indicators (PIs) are quantified measures designed to reflect some aspect of the operational performance of an entity.

In developing performance indicators, the first step is to clarify what the service is trying to achieve, it is appropriate to consider what is currently done, with what effect and at what cost. In establishing an ongoing system of performance monitoring, key indicators need to be developed.

> These should strike a balance between having too many indicators, and thus losing focus, and having too few, with the result that the indicators do not reflect those aspects of behaviour which allow management to make an informed decision.
>
> (Jackson and Palmer, 1989)[43]

Jackson and Palmer then go on to describe the common 'tools of the trade' with illustrations (see Table 11.5).

In 1981 the Secretary of State for the Environment[44] required local authorities to produce a minimum number of specified unit cost statistics in their annual reports. For example, for each service, the net cost per 1000 population and the manpower per 1000 population must be shown. These must be supplemented by further statistics such as, for the education service, the pupil/teacher ratio and the cost per pupil. Performance indicators are not absolute measures; they can only be judged by making comparisons. Performance can be compared with plans; standards; past performance; other sections in the same authority; other authorities; or similar services provided by the private sector.

Table 11.6 is taken from Birmingham City Council's Annual Report and Accounts 1990–91. The Authority compares its performance statistics with those of similar metropolitan authorities. The performance indicators are useful in highlighting areas worthy of further investigation.

The Department of Health has been working on performance indicators (PIs) since 1981. Numerous indicators are also produced for government departments and nationalized industries.

Table 11.5   Examples of performance indicators with illustrations

Performance indicator		Example
Cost indicators (economy)	e.g.	Annual cost per aged person in residential home.
Productivity indicators (efficiency)	e.g.	Number of library books issued per library assistant per hour.
		Yield per VAT visit.
		Ratio of laboratory technicians to clinicians.
Time targets (efficiency/ effectiveness)	e.g.	Turnround time for dealing with applications for government grant.
Volumes of service (crude measure of efficiency/ effectiveness)	e.g.	Number of housing repairs.
		Number of vehicle licensing applications processed.
		Battalion training days.
Quality of service indicators (effectiveness)	e.g.	Percentage of library users satisfied with library services.
		Number of complaints received from public on street cleaning.
		Speed of completing housing repairs.
Demand (or take-up rate) for service indicators (effectiveness)	e.g.	Acres of recreation land per 1000 population.
		Number of bathers in municipal pools.
		Additionality created by government grant.
Availability of services (effectiveness/equity)	e.g.	Availability of library services to all locations/ age groups.
Outcome (or impact) of policy indicators	e.g.	Reduction of unemployment levels through vocational training scheme.

Source: Jackson and Palmer 1989

Unit costs

The cost per unit of service, derived by dividing the cost of the service by the number of units served (such as the gross cost per secondary school pupil), is often used to compare performance over time or between different providers. However, there are a number of problems associated with such comparisons:

- The definition of the cost unit. It should be directly relevant to the costs being expressed. Costs per head of population are often meaningless, not all the population generally receives the service being measured, for example, education or social services. In the health service there are difficulties in deriving a cost unit which adequately reflects the differing case-mix in hospitals.
- Difficulties of comparison due to accounting practices. For example, in local government there are wide variations in the accounting for capital expenditure and central administration costs.
- Difficulties in ensuring that like authorities are compared. For this reason profiles of authorities are compiled and authorities are grouped into families.

Table 11.6 Birmingham City Council Annual Report 1990–91 Education Performance Statistics

	Birmingham		Metropolitan average		Leeds		Liverpool		Manchester		Sheffield	
	1986–87	1989–90	1986–87	1989–90	1986–87	1989–90	1986–87	1989–90	1986–87	1989–90	1986–87	1989–90
Gross cost per pupil (£) – secondary education	1374	1841	1389	1913	1278	1750	1516	2093	1721	2230	1508	2000
Pupil : teacher ratios – primary and nursery education*	21.9	21.8	21.6	21.4	21.8	19.2	20.9	21.2	21.0	NA	20.7	20.5
School meals – percentage of total cost covered by income	26.3	35.1	26.0	41.5	28.6	41.9	17.1	24.1	14.0	45.4	22.9	55.8
Pupils receiving free meals as a proportion of school roll	31.9	21.4*	28.2	12.5*	21.3	12.4*	39.7	NA	48.8	NA	27.0	NA

* Estimate from CIPFA statistics

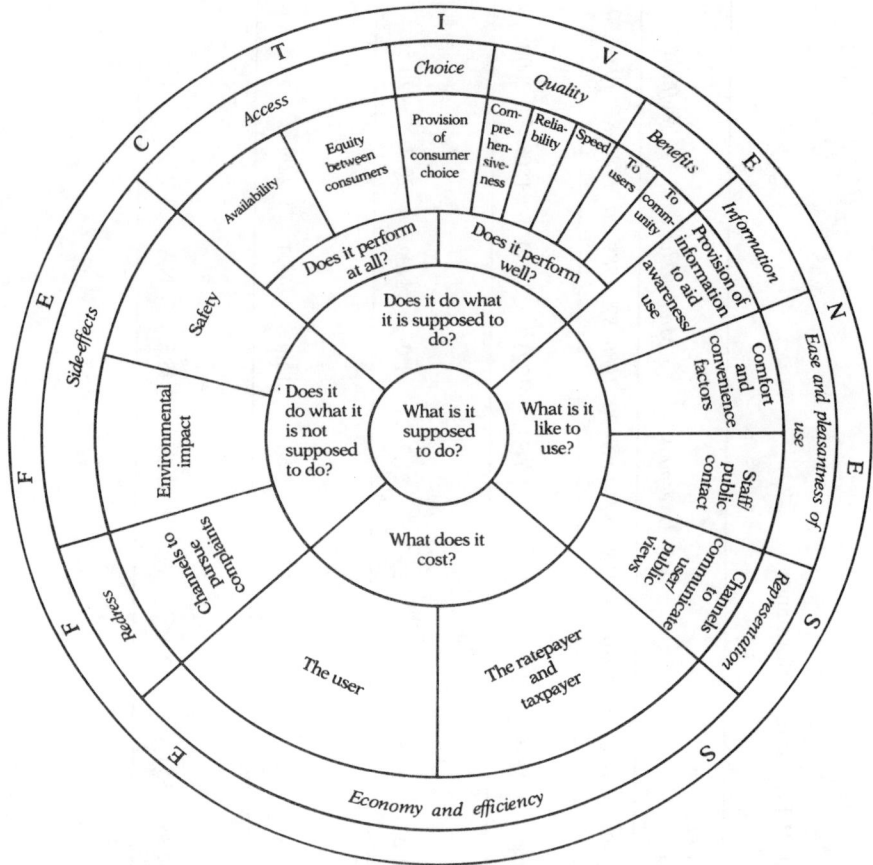

Figure 11.5   *The Service Wheel*
Source: National Consumer Council

- Unit costs are the average (mean) cost; they may disguise a wide variation.
- Unit costs are about economy and efficiency; they say little about the quality of provision and its effectiveness.

Quality of services

In more recent years, the views of consumers and citizens have become increasingly important. 'Customer care', 'a public service orientation' and 'putting people first', are all terms now widely used in the public sector. The National Consumer Council's Service Wheel, Figure 11.5,[45] provides a consumer criteria for performance evaluation. Thus useful indicators of quality from a consumer perspective may include: availability of service; accessibility; reliability; and response times to requests.

In order to obtain the necessary data, negative performance indicators are needed such as the number of complaints (a negative PI often monitored by the regulatory bodies of the recently privatized utilities). Consumer satisfaction surveys form another important source.

The Government's Citizen's Charter[46] puts still further emphasis on this area, for example school attendance statistics and exam performance are published. The 1992 Local Government Act required the Audit Commission to draw up a set of indicators for measuring the performance of local authority services. In 1995, the Audit Commission[47] published a major series of documents which represented a mass of data on comparative performance of every local authority in England and Wales across a wide range of dimensions.

Conclusions on performance indicators

Performance indicators (PIs) have become increasingly prolific in the public services over the last decade. PIs now cover most areas of the public sector and include not just statistics on inputs, costs and outputs but also service quality data and further dimensions. This approach to performance measurement is not without problems itself, particularly as regards how to obtain an impression of what the totality of the performance indicators convey. PIs do not provide a comprehensive measure of overall performance as profitability does in the commercial sector. Nevertheless, they can provide useful signals to areas worthy of investigation if they are compared over time or with broadly comparable operations; such information forms an important element in VFM studies.

Value for money auditing

Although a part of public sector audit practice for some time, it is probably only since the 1970s that the promotion of value for money to a specific goal has taken place in government. In 1973 the issue of an Audit Code of Practice, aimed at local authority auditors, required them to ensure that accounts being audited did not contain any significant loss arising from waste, extravagance, inefficient financial administration, poor value for money, mistake or other cause. This rather general exhortation has since been strengthened considerably, amongst other things, by the Local Government Finance Act of 1982 and the National Audit Act of 1983.

A requirement of the 1982 Finance Act was that the local government auditor should ensure that not only are accounts properly prepared by authorities, but also that they have made *proper arrangements for securing economy, efficiency and effectiveness in the use of their resources*. It was a requirement made against the background from the mid-1970s of increasingly constrained resources available for public sector activities, the application of cash limits and demands for greater disclosure and accountability by local authorities.

The Local Government Act of 1972, stated that local authorities could choose to appoint private accounting firms instead of the district auditors to audit their accounts, but although auditing remained principally a verification process

Measuring performance
Performance is measured at four main levels

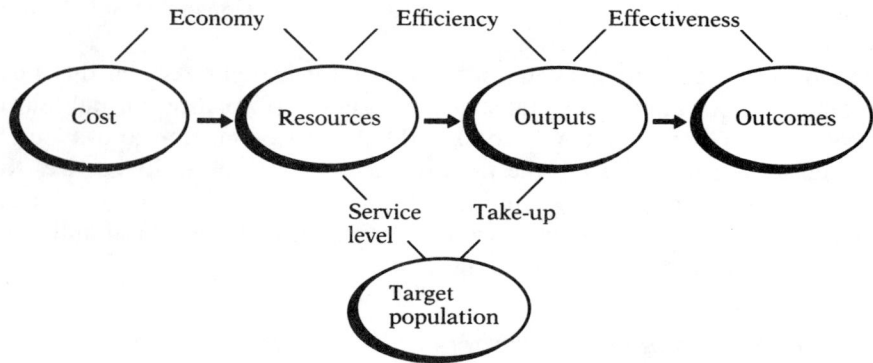

Figure 11.6 *A development of the three Es model of performance*

Source: Audit Commission, *Managing Services Effectively – Performance Review 1989*

concerning legality, amounts spent and procedures followed, matters such as wasteful spending were to be investigated. Following the 1982 Finance Act, the Audit Commission was set up in 1983 as a single independent body not only to oversee auditing within local authorities but also with the wider role of improving management within authorities. Central to the latter is the value for money audit. The ambit of the Audit Commission was extended to health authorities under the NHS and Community Care Act, 1991.

Once again a precursor to the application of an idea within the UK can be found in the USA, where 1972 saw the publication of the Standards for Audit of Governmental Organizations, Programs, Activities and Functions. These were revised in 1981. All US government audits are covered by the standards, and they contain reviews of economy, efficiency and effectiveness among the objectives of such audits. Pendlebury and Jones[48] point to the US example as a clear influence on developments in the UK.

Economy, efficiency and effectiveness

The original definitions used by the Audit Commission have been stated earlier, in Figure 11.4. The definition of effectiveness as 'providing the right services to enable the local authority to implement its policies and objectives' was criticized for two reasons. First, for not addressing the impact or consequences of local authority activity and, second, because it begs the question of how authorities state their objectives (for example, the objectives may be expressed merely as a volume of service to be provided rather than an impact).

Effectiveness and quality were embodied much more clearly in the redefined basic model in 1989,[49] Figure 11.6. The model now contains four dimensions of measurement: cost, resources, outputs and outcomes. The three Es are defined as follows:

- **Economy measures**
  'the cost of acquiring resources such as staff, premises or supplies.'
- **Efficiency measures**
  'the outputs achieved in relation to the resource inputs.'
- **Effectiveness measures**
  'measures . . . of the final outcome of a service in relation to its output.'

Efficiency is now stated in descriptive rather than objective terms. However, the major change is in the broader definition given to effectiveness. In addition, target (or catchment) populations have been included in order to provide two further measures: level of service and take-up, this latter measure providing an indication of service quality.

Outcomes have to be established in order that effectiveness may be evaluated, which could be an extremely difficult task in some cases. Economy and efficiency measures have to be developed in line with programme objectives: quality and cost factors are of major importance in the study of economy while efficiency – in essence a concept relating output of goods and services to a quantity of resource inputs on a standard and actual basis – requires careful attention to the development of measures of standards of performance, which in turn is not always likely to be a straightforward task.

As a brief example, consider the provision of residential care for the elderly. To operate *economically*, the quality of resources needed to provide a defined and acceptable standard of care has to be assessed. The auditor then has to ensure that these resources have been acquired at minimum cost. This cannot be done to any absolute standard, since it must take into account local conditions, e.g. shortages of particular grades of staff, which may arise for a variety of reasons in different parts of the country.

To operate *efficiently*, authorities would need standards they could aim to achieve, subject to special local conditions. In the example the principal measure of efficiency would be the number of people given accommodation (the output) compared to the resource costs (inputs). Achieving efficiency against a standard obviously depends on examining the number of residents and the level of costs.

To operate *effectively*, the desired outcomes of the exercise have to be defined, a problem which could be particularly difficult to resolve in the case of the present example, probably centred on the 'quality of life' provided for the residents.

Achieving value for money

The Audit Commission is a self-financing body whose members are appointed by the Secretary of State for the Environment acting jointly with the Secretaries of State for Health and for Wales. The Commission appoints auditors for all local authorities and health service bodies in England and Wales. It has as one of its main duties to undertake or promote studies to improve economy, efficiency and effectiveness in local government and the NHS. In 1994–95, the spending of local government and the NHS are estimated to be over £73 billion and £32 billion respectively.[50] Thus there is the prospect of realizing substantial savings through the three Es concept. In addition, central government has conducted similar studies through the Rayner Reports and the National Audit Office: the 1983 National Audit Act required the Comptroller and Auditor General to review the three Es in central government departments, while the Monopolies and Mergers Commission has a similar remit for nationalized industries. However, the prime responsibility for value for money lies with management.

The Commission recommends some 40–50 per cent of auditors' time should be spent on reviewing the arrangements for securing VFM within authorities and to undertaking specific VFM projects focusing on particular services or costs. Guidance for auditors is available in the form of statistical 'profiles' of different authorities. The profiles are compiled by using families (or clusters of authorities having similar demographic and socio-economic characteristics). They are designed to help both the authority and the auditor to identify those elements of costs or those services on which attention should be concentrated. In addition, there are Audit Commission Special Studies discussed below as well as audit reports from district auditors and auditor firms.

Figure 11.7 illustrates the Audit Approach, a systematic breakdown of the approach to VFM work, showing how the various aspects are identified and relate to each other. VFM is probably most closely identified with the special studies branch, because of the publicity these receive, but the figure clearly shows a broad approach to securing improvement in local authority management. The Audit Commission[51] also provides a working framework which identifies the interrelated elements within an organization whose achievement will add up to the realization of value for money measured against objectives to be attained (Figure 11.8).

Reference will have to be made to outside political influences as well, but the points listed below Figure 11.8 (page 230), serves as a starter guide on issues to be covered in a VFM audit. As an example, Figure 11.9 illustrates how this guide was used in a special study by the Commission of a central transport organization.[52]

More direct expression of guidance to auditors may be on the following lines:

1   Identify the intended outcomes of policy.
2   Examine organization structures with particular reference to (a) below.
3   Examine how well subordinate managers understand and implement policies laid down for them to follow by top management.
4   Examine information and information sources to see how well managers are served in making appropriate decisions.
5   Examine performance indicators as to their validity for measurement in given policies, programmes, departments.
6   Examine the results of the application of performance measures.

The translation of these guides into the conduct of a VFM audit takes the auditor beyond the traditional financial audit. Some of the methods and techniques which could be employed are:

• Input-based review, where the emphasis is on costs attributable to specific

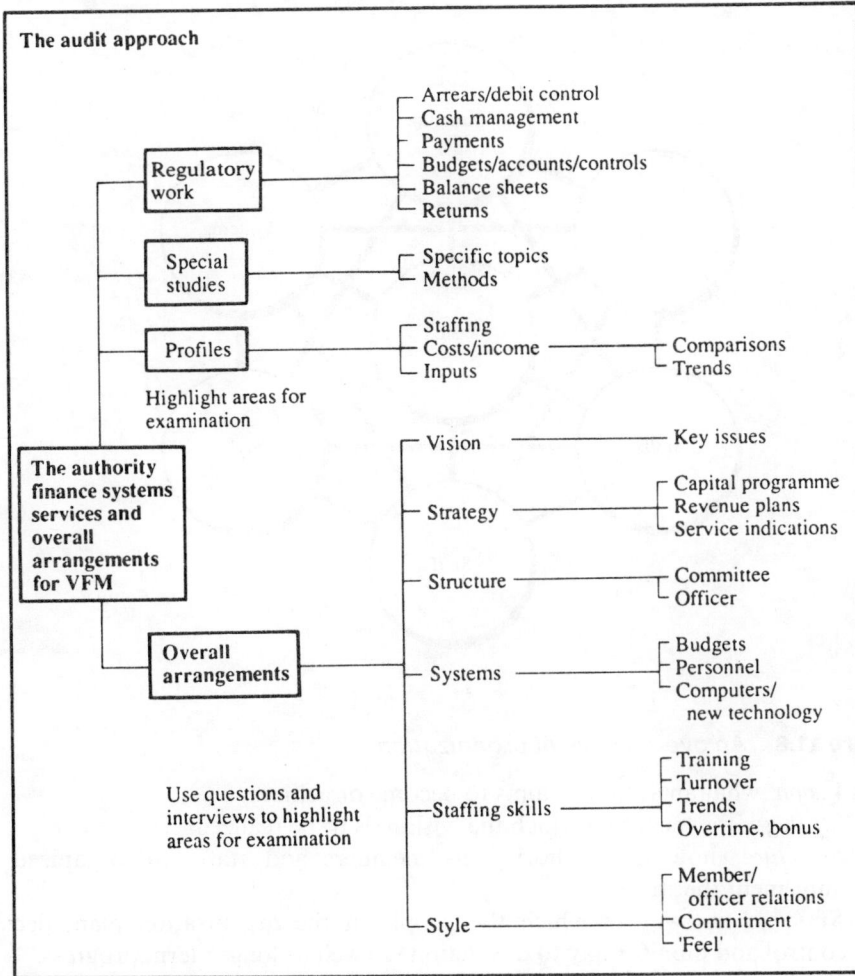

Figure 11.7 *Arrangements for securing economy, efficiency and effectiveness*

activities and on making cost comparisons with, amongst other things other areas' functions, previous years and the private sector, to try to keep costs at the most economical level and make managers more cost-accountable. There are a number of bodies from which data for this kind of comparison study may be obtained, such as the Chartered Institute of Public Finance and Accountancy (CIPFA), Local Authorities Management Services and Computer Committee (LAMSAC) and the Centre for Inter-firm Comparisons (CIFC).

• Systems-based review, where the emphasis is on the process (of the service or function) and the way in which it is organized, to try to establish the most efficient arrangements and to ensure that the system is relevant to current requirements and is being operated correctly.

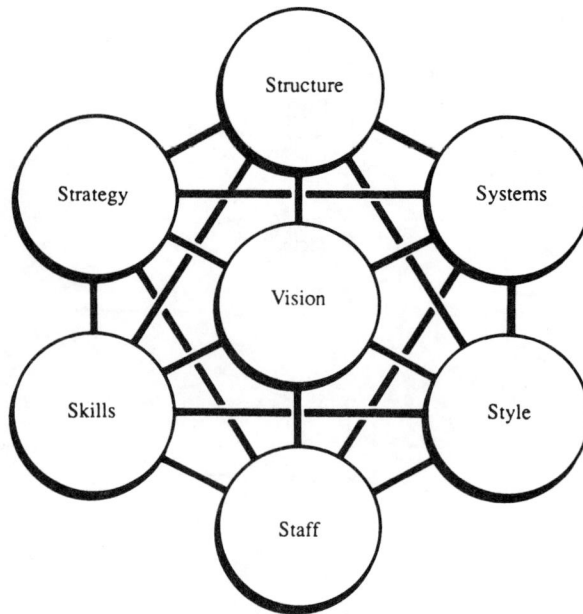

Figure 11.8   *An overall view of organization*

(a)   *Vision:* what an authority aims to become or achieve.
(b)   *Strategy:* the means by which the 'vision' is to be realized.
(c)   *Structure:* how the authority, its members and staff, are organized to implement the strategy.
(d)   *Systems:* the way in which the people in the organization plan, decide, control and monitor day to day actions as well as longer-term progress.
(e)   *Staffing and skills:* the way in which the critical resource in every authority – people – is acquired, trained, deployed, motivated and rewarded.
(f)   *Style:* the 'way we do things' and the way members, officers and employees relate to each other and to those they are to serve.

- Output-based review, where the emphasis is on the outputs produced by the entity and on defining them, measuring them and comparing them with the desired outcomes in order to establish the most effective arrangements. Determination of acceptable performance measures must be a part of this review in the light of the difficulty likely to be experienced in measuring achievements.

Table 11.7   Proposed indicators of vehicle maintenance performance 1984–85

Indicator	Practice	Unsatisfactory practice
Days off the road per annum		
– cars and light vans	6	12
– medium vans	10	15
– heavy goods vehicles up to 7.5T GVW	15	25
– heavy goods vehicles over 7.5T GVW	20	30
– refuse collection vehicles	25	35
Annual maintenance cost per weighted vehicle	£700	£850
(Parts cost included in above Maintenance cost)	£250	
Weighted vehicles per workshop employee		
(all grades)	30	
Weighted vehicles per fitter	40	
Booked hours per weighted vehicle p.a.	41	
Weighted vehicles per bay	35	
Bay utilization	70%–80%	
% Maintenance contracted out (counties)	15%	
Safety check intervals (normal mileage, excl.		
Special HGV)	12 weeks	

Audit Commission special studies

Each year a number of activities are selected for detailed examination. Development of target and performance indicators represents the central objective of the special studies work; these indicators are standards by which authorities may judge their success or otherwise with respect to meeting the three Es' criteria. There are no absolute values, since the circumstances of individual authorities will vary on different issues, e.g. the age structure of the population resident within a district or the degree of industrialization. Following studies conducted over a number of authorities, the Audit Commission publishes details of the approaches it considers may lead to the adoption of sound management practices.

In conjunction with the management scheme for a central transport organization illustrated in Figure 11.9, a list of indicators which may be used in measuring performance in one area of transport management, vehicle maintenance, was devised and is reproduced in Table 11.7.

The two columns of Table 11.7 labelled 'Practice' and 'Unsatisfactory practice' are yardsticks by which authorities can judge their own efficiency: the former of course represents what may be regarded as a sound performance level, while the latter, if recorded, would indicate poor performance and inefficiency in resource utilization. The concept of a 'weighted vehicle' illustrates the way in which comparative standards may be derived. Each type of vehicle operated by authorities in general is given a weight, which reflects the 'typical' extent of maintenance

Vision	Provide a central transport organization that will provide service departments with vehicles 20 per cent cheaper than if obtained on contract hire

Strategy	Structure	Style	Systems	Skills/staffing
● Offer a 'contract hire with maintenance' service to the users ● Use available scale to negotiate better purchasing discounts on new vehicles and spare parts. Spread overheads over the whole fleet ● Check internal hire rates against private firms. Users free to go outside if consistently cheaper to do so ● Pool all reserve vehicles (except police and fire) ● Maintain vehicles owned by police and fire (in counties) ● Seek arrangements with neighbouring authorities for maintenance of out-stationed vehicles and pooling reserve specialist vehicles ● Contract-out for vehicles and maintenance where more economic to do so (e.g. for specialist maintenance work, vehicles with irregular demand)	● Central control of all transport provision and maintenance. ● Maintenance treated as a separate cost centre with transport ● Use outside garages for maintenance where appropriate ● In countries, locate workshops close to the main users' depots	● Run like a commercial hire firm. Non-bureaucratic approach ● Treat user department as 'customers' ● Liaise with neighbouring authorities ● Market services to neighbouring authorities and health authorities ● Council Committee agrees budget and main programme but avoids involvement in details	● Computerized management information system – utilization – fuel consumption – maintenance ● Individual vehicle costing on a whole life basis ● Easily administered bonus scheme, based on vehicle availability ● Regular checking of internal charges and costs against – contract hire – spot hire – private garages ● Workshop manning levels based on support man hours	● Lean, professional staffing (two or three central staff in a district, no more than ten in a county). Assign the following responsibilities*: – procurement and disposal of vehicles – customer liaison/sales manager – utilization officer to co-ordinate spot hiring and secure utilization of 1,500 hours/year – information officer – maintenance manager, with a target of £700 per weighted vehicle ● – Transport manager 'buys-in' central services (e.g. financial and legal) from Treasurer etc. * Usually, not full-time posts

Figure 11.9 *Overview of a successful transport organization*

work it requires, and from this information it is possible to assess the total number of maintenance hours which would be required to support a vehicle fleet's operation. The accompanying report also points out the need to record reasons for poor labour utilization, such as ineffective working, undeclared lost time and so on, in order to effect proper control.

A further illustration is taken from the Commission's special study of energy management within authorities.[53] Energy costs were noted to be large, with wide

Table 11.8   Normalized performances indicators

Category of building	Standard hours of use per annum	Yardstick of efficiency *kWh/m²/annum*	Indicator of poor efficiency
Primary school, no indoor pool	1,480	180	320
Primary school with indoor pool	1,480	230	440
Secondary school, no indoor pool	1,660	190	300
Secondary school with indoor pool	2,000	250	390
Special school, non-residential	1,570	230	490
College of further education	2,530	230	370
Special school, residential	8,760	380	820
Adult training centre	2,150	250	620
Elderly persons' home	8,760	450	680
Day centre/day nursery	2,200	330	590
Residential home (e.g. children's home, hostel, home for handicapped)	8,760	380	820
Sports centre, no pool	4,700	220	410
Leisure/recreation centre with pool*	4,800	900	1,400
Swimming pool/baths†	4,000	1,250	1,750
Library/museum/art gallery	2,540	200	440
Offices over 2,000 m²	2,600	230	390
Offices less than 2,000 m²	2,400	200	400
Transport depot, operating approx. 2,500 hours per annum	2,500	270	520
Sheltered housing	8,760	270	430

* Pool area less than 20% of total area.
† Pool area more than 20% of total area.

Source: Consumption data on about 3,200 buildings from 30 authorities analysed in the special study.

variations in authorities' performance in energy management. Opportunities for saving £135 million p.a. were considered to exist given that necessary investment and management action was undertaken.

Energy costs are of course very much related to the type and standard of buildings managed by authorities, and these vary considerably across individual authorities. In order to produce standards and comparisons, it was necessary therefore to devise a uniform indicator by which energy consumption could be measured and which allowed for factors outside the immediate control of the authority, e.g. the number of hours of use, the degree of exposure of the building to the elements, the prevailing weather conditions in the locality and the floor area of the building.

The resulting measure, termed a normalized performance indicator (NPI), expresses energy consumption as kWh (kilowatt hour) per square metre of

Category of building	kWh/m²/annum
Primary school – no indoor pool	
Secondary school – no indoor pool	
Library, museum, art gallery	
Office less than 2000 sq. metres	
Sports centre – no pool	
Offices over 2000 sq. metres	
Primary school – with pool	
Special school – non-residential	
College of further education	
Adult training centre	
Secondary school – with pool	
Transport depot operating 2500 hours per year	
Sheltered housing	
Day centre/nursery	
Special school – residential	
Residential homes e.g. children's hostel, home for handicapped	
Elderly persons home	
Recreation centre with pool (pool area ≤ 20% total area)	
Swimming pool/baths (pool areas > 20% total area)	

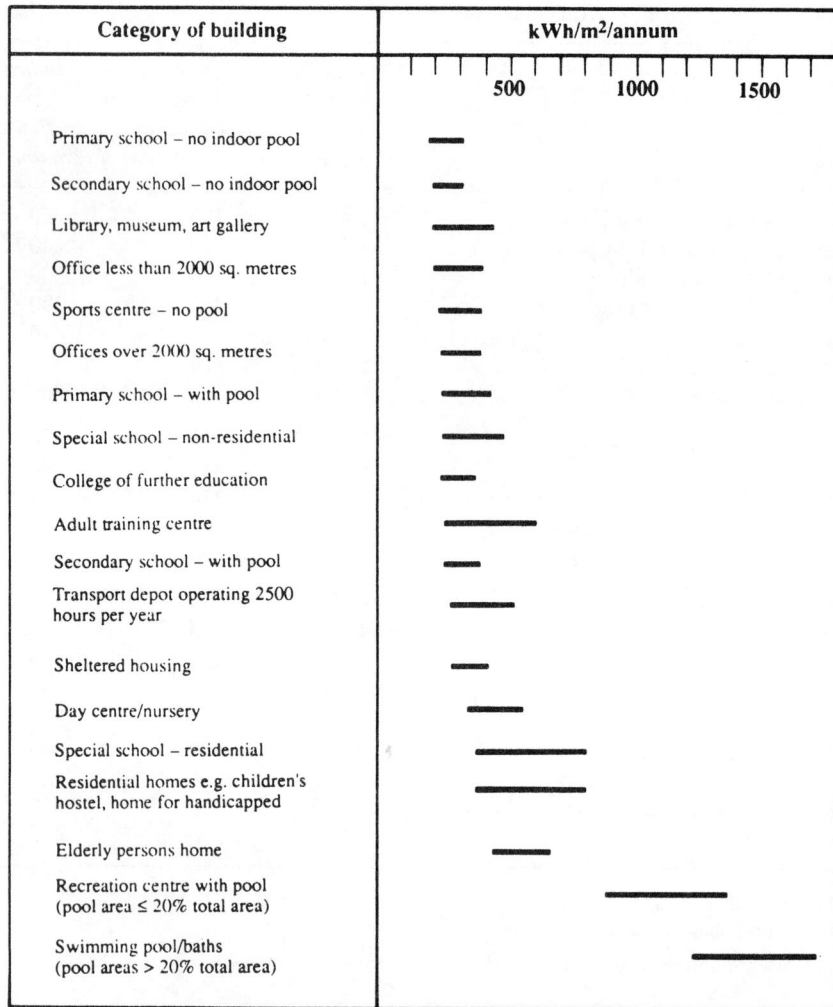

Figure 11.10 *Range in normalized performance indicators for different categories of building (normalized performance indicator kWh/m²/annum)*

floorspace per annum, adjusted to average hours of use, normal exposure and average weather. Figure 11.10 and Table 11.8 show the range (defined as 0.68 of a standard deviation on either side of the mean value) in NPIs for a set of buildings commonly found within local authorities (Figure 11.10) and against a measure of standard hours of use per annum, a yardstick of efficiency and an indicator of poor efficiency (Table 11.8).

Dorset County Council was used as an example to illustrate the potential benefits of an energy-saving programme, which showed a reduction of 23 per cent in energy used over a five-year period and cumulative savings always exceeding cumulative investment, making the programme self-financing throughout.

The first special study undertaken within the NHS examined day surgery.[54] The Audit Commission study focused on a 'basket' of twenty common operations. The study concluded that if all district health authorities used day case treatment to the same extent as the 25 per cent that use it most, an additional 186,000 patients could be treated in England and Wales every year at no extra cost. It is through studies such as these, as well as direct audit work, that information is fed back into authorities in a way which shows the potential for improvement in particular areas where it arises.

Problems of VFM auditing

These are numerous, as will have become clear to readers already. They arise in the main from the immense range of applications and in particular from the difficulties in arriving at objective evaluations of concepts such as outcomes and 'output'. Some aspects are described as follows:

- Outcomes are particularly difficult to measure. They may relate to the long-term impact of an activity which other factors will also be influencing. For example, the outcome of a health treatment may be affected by family care, wealth and nutritional status.

- Outputs may be hard to define and measure. With hospitals, residential homes, and educational establishments it is easy to measure the number of people processed and produce a cost per person (e.g. £150 per person per week) to measure efficiency. But people are not identical. In a hospital a patient for heart surgery is more expensive than one having tonsils removed. Young children and incontinent geriatrics are more expensive to keep in homes than fit retired people. Medical students cost more than history students.

- Emphasis on unit costs suggests that throughput should be increased to keep unit costs down. This can usually be done by sacrificing quality. Graduates can be produced very cheaply if there is very little tuition or examining. A social worker could easily deal with two or three times as many clients, but the value of a five-minute visit by a social worker once a month may be negligible. An apparently efficient organization, with low unit costs, may be lowering the quality of its output and failing to achieve its desired outcomes.

- Effectiveness is much more difficult to define and measure. Often objectives are not clear, and may be conflicting. A police force could be thought more effective if it succeeded at crime prevention than if it prosecuted large numbers of offenders and vice versa. The outcomes of an education system may not be adequately assessed in terms of numbers of examination successes. In seeking a measure for effectiveness these measurable achievements may be given undue emphasis at the expense of less measurable achievements. The danger is that it may be assumed the only things that count are the things that can be counted.

- As costs are easier to define and measure than outputs or outcomes, VFM auditors may tend to concentrate on costs. Emphasis on costs in practice may lead to undue stress on the organization's own revenue expenditure, to short-term decisions rather than long-term implications, to too little regard being given to capital expenditure, the best use of assets and to costs to society. A unit in one area (a hospital ward, or a home) may be closed down, but this could result in greater costs being incurred elsewhere. Further social work visits could result in more children being taken into care or more people returning to crime and prison. It is much more difficult to assess these longer-term costs to society.

- Even efficiency is not a clinically neutral concept. If any job is very narrowly defined, it is usually possible to find a cheaper way of doing it, by employing lower grade staff for example. But most jobs contain more than narrow definitions might imply (hospital cleaners for example tend to talk to patients, pass important information to nursing staff and do other odd jobs). Most jobs require flexibility in changing circumstances. Relatively untrained staff who are perfectly capable of fulfilling the minimum requirements of a job, for example, may be quite inadequate in changed circumstances, which may lead to disaster in an emergency.

- In commenting on effectiveness the auditor is in danger of concerning himself with policy issues. It may appear legitimate to comment on the effectiveness, for example, of regional aid policies, but even here policy questions are raised. It may be sensible to subsidize motor manufacturers moving to unemployment blackspots in Scotland or elsewhere, but the use of equivalent incentives for construction related to North Sea oil (which cannot go elsewhere) may not be a very effective policy or an efficient use of resources.

- VFM auditors are inevitably dependent on those who work within an organization to supply them with the information they need to prepare their reports. Internal management may be reluctant to supply them with information likely to lead to critical reports. Many management accountants are well practised in supplying suitably partial explanations which satisfy external auditors who have little real knowledge of the organization they are examining, or of the extent and limitations of information produced.

Conclusions on VFM auditing

The introduction of a clear framework for assessing value for money in the public sector greatly enhanced performance measurement. However, application of VFM auditing has numerous problems and there has naturally been a tendency to dwell on the more easily quantifiable. The approach requires extensive resources and it will obviously take a considerable time before comprehensive coverage is achieved. Although VFM auditing has highlighted extensive potential savings, the responsibility for securing VFM rests with the managers of the organizations.

Return on assets

Following the 1978 White Paper[55] on nationalized industries, many nationalized industries were set targets as a percentage return on assets by the minister. Subsequently, the profitable nationalized industries such as gas, water and electricity have been privatized and are currently operating as regulated industries in the private sector. However, the requirement to earn a return on public sector assets has been extended to local government and the NHS. This requirement to earn a return on assets equates public sector performance to the commercial sector where return on capital employed is often referred to as the primary business.

Local authority DSOs

The 1980 Local Government Planning and Land Act required separate annual accounts and reports for direct labour organizations' activities analysed over four categories:

1 General highway work.
2 Major new construction work costing £50,000 or over.
3 Minor new construction work costing under £50,000.
4 Maintenance work.

Each category was set a required rate of return, namely, 5 per cent calculated on a current cost basis. Local authorities keep their accounts on the historical cost basis using a finance capital approach to capital maintenance whereby the source of finance determines how assets are accounted for. Thus the surplus on the direct labour organization (DLO) revenue account has to be converted as shown in Table 11.9.[56]

The Act also required competitive tendering for the vast majority of DLO work. Financial accounts have to be prepared within six months of the end of the financial year and any local authority which fails to achieve its target for three consecutive years for the same category of work is required to produce a report. The Secretary of State has the power to stop the local authority from carrying out further DLO work of all or any description.

The 1988 Local Government Act extended competitive tendering and required rates of return to a number of further direct service activities (see page 215). The required rate of return is again 5 per cent on capital employed calculated on a current cost basis, but there are exceptions, for example building, cleaning and leisure services management, where the objective is to at least break even. In practice, the return on assets has frequently been much higher than 5 per cent.

Table 11.9   Rate of return on direct labour organizations: an illustration

Surplus on DLO revenue account*			x
Add back:†			
	Interest charges		x
	Principal repayment to loans funds		x
	Renewals funds contributions		x
			x
Deduct:	Current cost depreciation	x	x
	Stock adjustment	x	x
Current cost operating surplus			x
Capital employed:‡			
	Land		x
	Vehicles, plant and equipment		x
	Stock		x
			x

Notes:
* Based on conventional local authority accounting practices.
† Conventional local authority capital charges.
‡ At current cost.

Source: Accounting Code of Practice for Direct Labour Organizations (CIPFA, 1985).

The returns achieved by the DLO and other DSOs of Birmingham City Council in 1990–91 are shown in Table 11.10.

The rates of return achieved by DSOs are extremely wide. In 1981–82, the first year of operation of DLOs, one in eight failed to achieve the required return, but one in three had a return over 20 per cent and several were over 100 per cent.[57] A recent survey of Scottish regional DLOs found that rates of return on new construction work under £50,000, ranged from 7 per cent to 465 per cent for individual DLOs in the period 1984/5 to 1988/9.[58]

Table 11.10   Birmingham City Council: return on assets achieved by DSOs in 1990–91

Direct service organization	*Return achieved*
DLO General highways	14.2%
Maintenance	12.8%
Education and welfare catering*	178.7%
Other catering	259.0%
Grounds maintenance	24.7%
Vehicle maintenance†	5.8%

* Commenced operation 1 August 1990, therefore only 3.33 per cent return required.
† Commenced operation 1 January 1991, therefore only 1.25 per cent return required.

The NHS internal market

Under the NHS internal market or 'managed competition' outlined earlier (see page 216), hospitals compete for healthcare contracts. The contract prices must be based on cost including capital charges. Previously, the cost of capital items had been merely recorded as capital expenditure in the year of acquisition. The NHS Management Executive[59] stated that capital charging was introduced to provide real economic incentives for using those assets more efficiently and to create a 'level playing field' between the NHS and the private healthcare sector. Directly managed hospitals incur capital charges on all of their assets in excess of £5000 (increased from £1000 on 1 April 1993): these charges consist of current cost depreciation on all assets excluding land plus an interest charge (6 per cent laid down by HM Treasury), on the value of all assets. Capital charges are paid by the directly managed hospital to its regional health authority. Trust hospitals retain depreciation; this together with accumulated surpluses will be a source of funding for subsequent capital acquisitions. Trust hospitals do not make an interest payment but are required to earn a target rate of return (6 per cent) on the current value of their net assets.

Capital charges were found immensely difficult to compile for the first year of 'managed competition', 1990–91.[60] If the market is allowed to operate unfettered, such charges could make hospitals with high current asset values uneconomic and consequently lead to their closure; the capital charges of one inner London hospital were 39 per cent of the hospital's total costs.[61]

Problems in applying return on assets

In applying target rates of return on public sector assets, the Government has been attempting to ensure that the public sector competes with the private sector (which must generate a return on its capital employed to be commercially viable), on an equal footing. It follows that services will only continue to be provided by the public sector organization, if the service cannot be provided more efficiently by another public sector organization or the private sector – performance must at least match that of its competitors. The target rates of return are deemed by the Treasury to be comparable to the returns achieved by private sector organizations. It would therefore appear from the returns found above, that public sector provision is often extremely efficient! However, there is also evidence that DLOs have been able to circumvent competition requirements; Lapsley and Llewellyn[62] refer to a number of practices uncovered by auditors:

• The imposition of unreasonable contract conditions.
• Non-acceptance of the lowest tender.
• Fixing overhead rates which inflate costs on work not subject to competition and reducing overheads on jobs which are competed for.
• Artificially dividing work into small job lots so as not to exceed the threshold for mandatory competition.
• Aggregation of maintenance work to form a single multi-trade job.

Even if the competition requirements are operating 'fairly' considerable difficulties exist in applying such performance targets. The Audit Commission concluded in 1987[63] that the 5 per cent return was inappropriate for DLOs because:

* Private firms may accept lower than 5 per cent real returns especially during recessions.
* The balance sheet can be manipulated to show a low level of capital employed. It is often difficult to attribute assets to individual DLO categories, e.g. multipurpose depots, and the replacement cost of specialist assets is subjective.
* The capital invested is relatively small and therefore return on capital employed is not particularly relevant.

Lapsley and Llewellyn[62] also point out the inappropriateness of a single financial measure as a means of measuring performance. They argue that DLOs are complex organizations with distinct public interest aspects to their operation and suggest that their assessment should be broadened to include:

* Performance indicators (e.g. response times for repairs).
* Social indicators (e.g. accident and safety statistics, training and employment).

They conclude 'not withstanding the more commercial ethos of their operations, it is the interests of the local community which DSOs seek to serve and which should predominate'.

These points are applicable to all local authority DSOs not just DLOs.

In the NHS, similar problems are likely to be experienced. Many hospitals will not be operating in a competitive environment and the attribution of costs to individual contracts may be arbitrary.[65,66] In the inner cities where hospitals are less likely to be able to exert monopoly power, the market may not be allowed to determine hospital closures. For example, a Commission was established in 1992 to consider the future distribution of hospitals in London.

Conclusions on return on assets

The introduction of target rates of return on capital employed to public sector services, has made such services subject to the primary commercial performance measure. The introduction was largely to ensure parity between public sector providers and their private sector competitors rather than to measure performance per se; performance was to be tested by the regime of competing for contracts. As discussed earlier competition has produced cost savings and, therefore, provided that service quality has been maintained, improved performance.

Nonetheless, it is unlikely that the returns achieved by public sector organizations in local government and health can be used confidently as performance measures and their applicability as a sole performance criteria is inappropriate for public sector organizations serving the public interest.

Summary

The public sector expends a sizeable proportion of the UK's economic resources. The nature of the services provided by the public sector is such that it is often difficult to establish satisfactory methods of planning resource use or measuring performance. In recent years, the differences in management and operation between the commercial sector and the public sector have been narrowed. The effects of compulsory competitive tendering, internal markets and devolved management, can be seen to have introduced a more commercial approach to both budgeting and performance measurement. On the other hand, commercial organizations often have budget areas which are not profit orientated (e.g. public relations), and are taking a greater interest in the quality of their services leading to the application of performance measures previously more at home in the public sector. Hence there is not one set of budgeting methods and performance measures applicable to the public sector and a further set applicable to the commercial sector.

Nevertheless, the diffuse nature of public sector services does require a different emphasis of approach. Budgeting even in the 1990s is not generally undertaken in a competitive environment: techniques such as ZBB and PPBS provide rational alternatives to the customary incremental method and while not adopted fully have permeated into practical improvements. Performance indicators and value for money auditing provide a logical basis for assessing performance when the profit motive is lacking. Attempts have been made to emulate the private sector's primary performance measure, but return on assets has generally been shown to be an unsatisfactory indicator of performance for public sector organizations.

References

1. HM Treasury, *Financial Statement and Budget Report, 1994–95*, HC 31, HMSO, 1994.
2. Pendlebury, M., *Management Accounting in Local Government*, CIMA, 1985.
3. Jones, R. and Pendlebury, M., *Public Sector Accounting*, Pitman, 1992.
4. Butt, H. and Palmer, R., *Value for Money in the Public Sector. The Decision Maker's Guide*, Blackwell, 1985.
5. Coombs, H.M. and Jenkins, D.E., *Public Sector Financial Management*, Chapman and Hall, 1991.
6. Glynn, J. *Public Sector Control and Accounting*, Blackwell, 1993.
7. *Management Accounting, Official Terminology*, CIMA, 1991.
8. Jones and Pendlebury, *op. cit.*, p. 78.
9. Lyden, F.J. and Miller, E.M., *Public Budgeting, Program Planning and Implementation*, 4th edition, Prentice Hall 1982, Chapters 11 and 17.
10. Jones and Pendlebury, *op. cit.*
11. Anthony, R.N. and Young, G.W., *Management Control in Non Profit Organizations*, Irwin, 1984.

12. Jones and Pendlebury, *op. cit.*, Lyden and Miller, *op. cit.*
13. Jones and Pendlebury, *op. cit.*
14. *Ibid.*
15. HMSO, *Efficiency and Effectiveness in the Civil Service*, HMSO, 1982.
16. Killikelly, T., Management accounting developments in the customs and excise department, *Management Accounting in the Public Sector*, Pendlebury, M. (ed.), CIMA, 1989, pp. 234–59.
17. Efficiency Unit of the Prime Minister's Office, *Improving Management in Government: The Next Steps,* HMSO, 1988.
18. Pendlebury, M., Jones, R. and Karbhari, Y., Accounting, for Executive Agencies in UK Government, *Financial Accountability and Management*, Vol. 8, No. 1, Spring 1992, pp. 35–48.
19. Ellwood, S., *Cost Methods for NHS Healthcare Contracts*, CIMA, 1992.
20. HMSO, *Education Reform Act 1988*, HMSO, 1988.
21. Department for Education, Statistics of Schools in England, *Statistical Bulletin 8/94*, 1994.
22. Burgess, T., Cambridgeshire's Financial Management Initiative for Schools, *Public Money*, Vol. 6, No. 1, June 1986.
23. Audit Commission, *Delegation of Management Authority to Schools*, HMSO, June 1988.
24. HMSO, *Local Government Planning and Land Act 1980*, HMSO, 1980.
25. HMSO, *Local Government Act 1988*, HMSO, 1988.
26. CIPFA, *The Management of Overheads in Local Authorities*, CIPFA, 1991.
27. CIPFA, *Accounting for Support Services*, CIPFA, 1987.
28. McGuirk, T., Is the Private Sector Cleaning Up on CCT?, *Public Finance and Accountancy*, August 1991, pp. 15–17.
29. National Audit Office, *Competitive Tendering for Support Services in the National Health Service*, HMSO, 1987.
30. HMSO, *The National Health Service and Community Care Act 1990*, HMSO, 1990.
31. NHS Executive, *GP Fundholding: list of goods and services*, HSG (95) 19, 1995.
32. Department of Health, *Funding and Contracts for Hospital Services, Working for Patients*, Working Paper No. 2, HMSO, 1989.
33. NHS Management Executive, *Costing and Pricing Contracts.* EL(90) 173
34. Ellwood, S., Competition in Healthcare, *Management Accountancy*, April 1990, pp. 24–28.
35. Perrin, J., *Resource Management in the NHS*, Chapman and Hall, 1988.
36. Griffiths, R., *NHS Management Inquiry*, DHSS, 1983.
37. Ellwood, S., *op. cit.*, p. 41.
38. Ellwood, S., Costing and Pricing Healthcare Contracts, *Management Accountancy*, November 1991, pp. 26–28.
39. Ellwood, S.M., Costing for Contracting Rules, *Public Money and Management*, Vol. 15, No. 2, 1995, pp. 41–47.
40. King, M., Lapsley, I., Mitchell, F. and Moyes, J., *Activity based costing in Hospitals – a case study investigation*, CIMA, 1994.

41. Jackson, P.M. Reflections on performance measurement in Public Service Organizations. In Jackson, P.M. (ed.) *Measures for Success in the Public Sector*, CIPFA Public Finance Foundation, 1995.

42. Roberts, H., *Outcome and Performance in Healthcare*, Public Finance Foundation, 1990.

43. Jackson, P. and Palmer, B., *First Steps in Measuring Performance in the Public Sector: A Management Guide*, Public Finance Foundation, 1989.

44. Department of Environment, *Local Authority Annual Report*, HMSO, 1981.

45. The National Consumer Council, *Measuring Up*, 1986.

46. UK Government, *The Citizen's Charter*, Command 1599, HMSO, 1991.

47. Audit Commission, *Local Authority Performance Indicators*, Vols. 1, 2 & 3, HMSO, 1995.

48. Pendlebury and Jones, *op. cit.*, p. 222.

49. Audit Commission, *Managing Services Effectively – Performance Review*, 1989.

50. HM Treasury, *op. cit.*

51. Audit Commission, *Improving Economy, Efficiency and Effectiveness in Local Government in England and Wales*, Audit Commission Handbook Vol. II, December 1984.

52. *Ibid.*

53. Audit Commission, *Saving Energy on Local Government Buildings*, November 1985.

54. Audit Commission, *A Short Cut to Better Services: Day Surgery in England and Wales*, October 1990.

55. White Paper, *The Nationalized Industries*, Command 7131, 1978.

56. CIPFA, *Accounting Code of Practice for Direct Labour Organizations*. CIPFA, 1985.

57. Sparrow, C. and Kirwan, M., Measuring Performance of DLOS, 1983, p. 14–16. Reported in *Public Finance and Accountancy*, August 1983.

58. Lapsley, I. and Llewellyn, S., Accounting and Regulation in Local Government: The Case of Direct Labour Organizations, *Public Money and Management*, Vol. 11, No. 4, Winter 1991, pp. 43–51.

59. NHS Management Executive, *Capital Charges Manual*, 1990.

60. Ellwood, 1992, *op. cit.*

61. *Ibid.*

62. Lapsley and Llewellyn, *op. cit.*

63. Audit Commission, *Competitiveness and Contracting Out of Local Authority Services*, Occasional Paper No. 3, 1987.

64. Lapsley and Llewellyn, *op. cit.*

65. Ellwood, 1992, *op. cit.*

66. Ellwood, S.M., *Cost-based pricing in the NHS Internal Market*, CIMA, 1996.

Questions

1   A public health clinic is the subject of a scheme to measure its efficiency and effectiveness. Amongst a number of factors, the 'quality of care provided' has

been included as an aspect of the clinic's services to be measured. Three features of 'quality of care provided' have been listed:

Clinic's adherence to appointment times
Patients' ability to contact the clinic and make appointments without difficulty
The provision of a comprehensive patient health monitoring programme

Suggest a set of quantitative measures which can be used to identify the effective level of achievement of each of the features listed.

(CIMA November 1989)

2   Problems are said to arise from the absence of a profit measure when measuring the efficiency and effectiveness of not-for-profit organizations.
(a)   Explain why the lack of the profit measure may cause the problems referred to.
(b)   Discuss whether similar problems may extend to support service activities in businesses which do have profit making as a main objective.

3   Discuss how NHS costing systems can take account of the hospital case-mix problem.
How could activity based costing assist cost-based pricing in the NHS?

12

Strategic management control and appraisal

Introduction

The interrelationships between goals, reward systems, performance evaluation systems and aspects of behaviour internal and external to organizations were illustrated in Chapter 7. In presenting this, Figure 7.1 showed external considerations impacting on the goals and the performance evaluation system. While a number of earlier chapters have given attention to performance measurement, the focus of attention has been on the achievement of efficiency and of corporate objectives which were largely taken as given. In system terms, the organization was to some extent treated as closed by isolating the external impact on the determination of goals and strategies from the control mechanisms. This chapter attempts to give emphasis to the external considerations on management controls. Attention is directed at both the operation of the accounting control systems and the use of information about the external environment which is vital to performance in competitive activity.

It was suggested in Chapter 2 that a critical requirement of control systems for managing in a business context was the need to cope with uncertainty. Systems theory identifies a range of responses to change, only one of which is to attempt to resist it by adopting a policy of rigidity. A range of more responsive approaches may be more successful given the rate of change currently faced.

Internal controls for risk and uncertainty

One of the significant arguments put forward for the adoption of decentralized structures in large organizations is their ability to cope with the increased uncertainty associated with the diversity of activities and environments which they face. Local management teams are given delegated responsibilities which allow them to use their local knowledge and perception of changes. The appointment of local managers enables them to acquire specialist knowledge of the particular conditions in which they can expect to be operating and competing which would be beyond the capacity of a highly centralized management.

Decentralization of this type appears to offer considerable advantages to the diversified business. However, if the benefits are to be realized, it is necessary for incentive systems to be in place which will motivate local management to use the advantages in promoting the corporate goals. Conditions of uncertainty permit gains to be made by those with the ability to make better predictions of future conditions and who act in accordance with those predictions. Realizing this in the decentralized organization requires a management control system which encourages local managers to utilize their entrepreneurial skills and local knowledge in proactive ways. This does not appear to be fulfilled by performance measures which are based on past performance against pre-set budgets and the use of divisional performance measures of the type described in Chapters 7 and 8 may go some way to addressing this.

However, this concentrates on only one aspect of the relevance of uncertainty for business management. The earlier discussion also recognized that the expectations of others, not part of the internal management of a company, are likely to be important in assessing its success. Financiers and stock markets were specifically mentioned. Financial markets research has drawn attention to two particular attributes of overall company performance that are valued by the investment community. These are return and risk which are both incorporated into portfolio theory and capital asset pricing models. Investors are taken to desire return but to be risk averse. To the extent that company objectives are dependent upon promoting investor wealth, internal control systems will need to encourage the use of forecasting to obtain perceptions of the future and to manage exposure to risks.

Research[1] in 12 large divisionalized manufacturing companies in the UK investigated the focus of accounting control systems in these companies identifying how they addressed the issues of change. The view obtained from company managers was that financial markets' concern with risks was revealed in a particular intolerance of surprise. Poor performance was less disturbing when early warning of the outcome was provided. This reflected the view that the credibility of a company's management was undermined when they were unable to predict the successes or failures they faced. This view was important in shaping the control systems operated in a number of the companies studied. It is consistent with the observation made by Simons (1990):[2]

> . . . management control systems are used not only to monitor that outcomes are in accordance with plans but also to motivate the organization to be fully informed concerning the current and expected state of uncertainties.

This background to the considerations of uncertainty can be taken to suggest that control systems might be required to (i) rapidly identify potential change and transmit this to senior managers, (ii) to encourage local managers to apply their perceptive abilities in meeting this, and (iii) to exercise control even when it is the local managers who are the subject of the control who possess the key information to assess this view of performance. Jones *et al.* refer to this as 'Surprise Management' reflecting the comments that they had received in a number of the companies in the research that an objective of the accounting control systems was to create a no surprise environment.

A feature in eight out of the twelve companies studied was that 'they reported actual outcomes, not only against budget, but against [monthly] forecast figures . . . The updating of forecasts . . . was identified as of particular significance.' The basis for the significance is also revealed. There were incentives to avoid failure to meet budgets since this could result in loss of bonuses. However, failure to meet forecasts was perceived as much more serious and as potential grounds for dismissal. Further, in some companies, it was expected that any changes in forecasts were expected to be signalled informally before being reflected in the formal reporting system. Local management were under considerable pressure to continuously monitor their environment for changes and to give early notice of any impact this may have on their performance.

Placing stress on forecasts in this way modifies the nature of the control system which is being operated. Managers were motivated to reveal their perceptions of the future. There were incentives to deter a tactic of forecasting low when bonuses were judged not by actual outcome alone but by assessing forecast against budget so that overachievement of forecast which resulted in meeting the budget would not entitle the manager to the full bonus. Instead of control being a feedback loop focusing on past achievement against plans, it becomes a feedforward system with some of the resulting advantages identified in Chapter 2. Management in large organizations can be seen to be concerned with more than the internal environment. The strategic action of monitoring externally takes on appropriate significance. In practice, comparison is not only against internal targets which have been given attention in earlier chapters, but also against the performance of other companies.

Inter-firm comparisons

Businesses, whether independent limited companies or public limited companies, divisions, subsidiaries or operating units, find it both necessary and beneficial to compare themselves with similar organizations, particularly those with whom they directly compete. The purposes of such comparisons are likely to be:

- With a view to improving business performance, and to identify those areas of their business which are comparatively/relatively weak and with scope for improvement.
- To examine the business as others would, to understand more clearly:
  (i)   The likely prospects, potential and costs of raising equity and/or loan finance.
  (ii) The organization's relative attractiveness (or otherwise) and the potential threats of takeover bids, disposal or closure.
  (iii) How customers, suppliers, trade unions, employees and others might view the status of the business in respect of their interest in it.
- As an aid to strategic and managerial planning, to identify the relative strengths and weaknesses of the business, particularly in relation to those of competitors both present and prospective. Further, to relate these to perceived opportunities and threats in the formulation and selection of strategic and tactical alternatives.

Inter-firm comparisons tend to concentrate, in the first instance, on financial data through the analysis of published reports and accounts, using ratio analysis and industry/governmental statistics. While, in the present chapter, this aspect of comparison will be considered first, in practice other, less publicized sources of information may be just as important.

Financial ratio analysis

Financial ratio analysis is usually illustrated in texts using skeletal analysis concentrating upon:

- Operating performances, in the areas of profitability, cost control and asset utilization, using a pyramid analysis of the ROCE ratio.
- Financing and liquidity ratios, concentrating on equity and medium- and short-term borrowed capital sourcing and gearing.
- Investment return ratio.

These ratios may then be compared with alternative yardsticks of:

(a)   Past periods, in order to demonstrate trends.
(b)   Data of other companies.
(c)   Industry or governmental indices.
(d)   Budgets for the same period (which are only likely to be available to the managers within a business and not to outsiders).

The art of financial analysis lies in the selection of sufficient suitable and comparable ratios and yardsticks, and the interpretation of these measures *as a whole* – a process which has been likened to the examination of a patient by a doctor, i.e. selecting relevant questions, taking measurements (temperature, pulse, etc.), identifying symptoms and making a diagnosis. It should be remembered, however, that, as in the medical analogy, (a) good diagnoses can usually only be made from a variety of corroborating evidence, (b) relevant experience of similar situations in the past is an invaluable aid, and (c) symptoms usually lead to probable diagnoses at best, certainty being a rare commodity in most instances.

Limitations of ratio analysis

The usefulness of financial ratios may be limited by:

- The differences in accounting policies adopted by companies in areas such as fixed asset depreciation and revaluation, stock valuation, bad debt provisions, R&D and goodwill write-offs, and profit recognition.
- Differences and changes in asset ownership, renting and leasing practices.
- Difficulties in consistent interpretation of ratios over time and between organizations.
- Changes in the value of money over time.

- Differences in the trading environments over the periods being compared.
- Window dressing of financial statements to hide short-term fluctuations.
- Difficulties in deciding on a suitable yardstick and the direction of change, i.e. while a higher ROI or EPS can generally be considered good, a higher acid test ratio is more difficult to interpret.
- Historic performance only being of relevance if it can reasonably be considered as relevant to future activity.

Internal or external comparisons

The yardsticks relating to external business are limited, the amount, content and format of data which businesses are required to divulge to others being partly stipulated by law, partly influenced by accounting standards and partly by the quotation requirements of stock exchanges. Additionally, of course, information is given confidentially to government and trade organizations, aggregated with that of other organizations and made valuable in statistical or general terms only. While information gleaned from reports and accounts tends to be mainly financial, that available from trade and governmental statistics often includes both financial and quantitative data, often statistically analysed into, for example, quartiles, deciles, means, etc. Such quantitative data, otherwise held confidentially within a business, may then be usefully compared with these statistics as a further and perhaps very different perspective on the performance of an organization. The accuracy of source data, its comparability with that of other businesses and the delay before such statistics are available are considered by many to reduce any value such data may have as comparators, but this is probably an overly negative view.

The value of physical and quantitative information, even if limited to that within an organization, e.g. trends over time and against budget, is considered by many to be a useful, even vital explanatory and indicative adjunct to the financial comparisons and ratios available within the organization and in relation to external entities.

Adjuncts to ratio analysis data

No ratio analysis of an organization's financial statements would be complete without an attempt to refine the diagnosis reached by the search for additional and/or corroborative evidence from other public sources. These are likely to include:

- The report that comes with the accounts and in particular the directors' report (and the chairman's report if given). This in any event contains the minimum data prescribed by the Companies Acts as well as other, gratuitous data. Copies of the report and accounts may be obtained from Companies House when registered, but earlier copies may be obtained for public companies by the purchase of shares in that business.
- Share ownership, which entitles the shareholder to attend the AGM and

question the directors and auditors regarding the conduct of the business and the content of the annual accounts.

- Prospectuses, prepared either in the raising of new finance or in compliance with stock-exchange flotations, contain information which may not be available elsewhere.
- The press – financial, national, trade and local.
- Bankers, brokers and investment advisors have sources of data not available to others and are in the business of analysing this data in order to advise their clients and customers.
- Audit rating organizations such as Dunn & Bradstreet.
- Statistical and market research of trade associations (although these may only be available to contributors).
- The PR and marketing literature of organizations; their products, current, new and deletions; and the price lists, including perhaps discount structures, etc.

The reader may well add other items to the list, particularly those related to businesses in a specific industry or market sector. The point must be made that sources of data which can corroborate or refute analyses of financial statements are an important and integral aspect of meaningful ratio analysis. It is as vital that an organization is as aware as possible of these sources. A business is not judged solely by its financial statements: it is the package of information available to the outside world which influences the judgement made of the business.

Assessing competition

As indicated earlier, one of the prime uses of inter-firm comparisons by businesses is the need to identify their own strengths and weaknesses in relation to that of their competitors as part of long-term planning. The foregoing inter-firm comparisons can provide some useful insights into a competitor's business. However, there is likely to be a real barrier to a meaningful analysis of many competitors, which are like operating units, subsidiaries or divisions of a group, their operations, finances, assets and profitabilities being aggregated with those of other parts of the group. In those circumstances, while some segmental information is required to be given in the annual report, e.g. sales and profitability by the main sectors of a group's business, such information tends to be of minimal value in the investigation of a competitor. However, it could also be argued that where a competitor is part of a group of companies, it is the group as a whole which provides at least some of the strengths (or weaknesses) of the competitor. For example, whatever the balance sheet finances of a competitor, in practice it is the ability and willingness of the group as a whole to raise finance efficiently that is the real strength or otherwise of that business. Thus it might prove harder to win a war of attrition against a competitor which is part of a large group that operates in the aero engines market. For this reason many analysts discriminate against its main American competitors, which are part of very large conglomerates, such as General Electric Co.

It is quite conceivable, however, that such strength could be quite illusory in some situations. Would a group support a cash-hungry business if its forecast profitability over the next few years was poor? Might this not depend upon alternative demands for resources from other parts of a group? Is a competitor which is but a small part of a large group's portfolio of companies more vulnerable to cash constraints, closure or disposal than if it were independent, larger or part of a larger group? On the other hand, large groups, and particularly conglomerates, frequently demonstrate a reluctance to support operating units or divisions which are either cash-hungry or have low, short- or medium-term profitability prospects, particularly if, or as a result, they do not fit into the group's long-term product strategies.

The investigation of a competitor tends to be a complex task. Moreover, it could be argued that any such financially based analysis is likely to be of less relevance to the design of business tactics and strategies than that of a competitor's operational capabilities and plans. In an increasingly complex business world, confidentiality and secrecy are scarce commodities. Diligent investigators have a variety of means of gaining information about their competitors' capabilities and activities – 'tapping the information grapevine'. These information sources are likely to include:

1 Broker, banker, credit agency and inter-firm comparison reports, bearing in mind that each may well receive information not directly available to others.
2 The press, bearing in mind newspapers and periodicals appear able to attract disclosures of confidential information from disaffected, injudicious, publicity-seeking or simply greedy employees.
3 Trade association and chamber of commerce meetings, exhibitions and promotional material.
4 Equipment and material suppliers, advertising media and agencies.
5 Market research, including perhaps observation of a competitor's operating units. One business before a takeover bid employed investigators to sit outside its victim's premises, logging comings and goings and interviewing employees when entering or leaving.
6 Visiting the competitor's operations. While simply walking into a competitor's premises is less easy in this security-conscious world than it used to be, many organizations are prepared to show visitors around. This might apply to the general public, students, customers, suppliers, outside maintenance staff, etc.
7 Buying in expertise, i.e. the employees of competitors or their business advisers.
8 Nefarious activities such as bribery, bugging and industrial espionage in general.

An illustration of a competitor assessment is provided by the Stapylton company of which the following is a resumé:[3]

S, a wholly owned subsidiary of a very large international group, was a manufacturer of hygiene and cleaning materials sold directly to retailers, principally supermarket chains. One major quality product with a good market share was sold with distinctive packaging at a premium price in competition with own label and other named brands. Competition arose from a major competitor, L, whose major product had been losing market share. S collected competitive awareness information by a variety of means: weekly surveys by sales staff of retailers, the collection of competitor's and retailers' advertising material, monthly market survey reports, regular contacts with suppliers both of equipment and raw materials and various financial reports. This information was used in a routine way in regular management meetings where consideration of competitors was a recurrent agenda item.

A small Scottish retail chain had been threatening not to stock the brand. In order not to lose the customer, L gave the retailer advance information about its product repackaging and reduced selling prices. This information was then used by the retailer to attempt to lever lower prices from S. S already had a good idea of L's operational capabilities, gleaned over time from equipment suppliers and certain customers during 'own-label' negotiations. L's production methodology, although different to that of S's main product, was very similar to that used by S for 'own label' production. This enabled S to forecast reasonably accurately the cost and revenue structure of the L product. Although L was part of a small group, the data could be cross-checked against the annual report and accounts, as L's product range was dominated by the product of interest. Additionally, indicators of capital investment plans and labour changes were usually outlined in the group's directors' report. This data was further cross-checked against the investment analyst reports of specialist stockbrokers.

In order to judge their response, S needed to establish:

(i)   Whether L's operating capabilities had changed. Discussions with processing and packaging-equipment manufacturers indicated no change in these areas. This was confirmed by the sales literature given to the Scottish retailer, and enabled S to estimate L's product's variable and prime costs.
(ii) What costs L was expending on operating charges and, in particular, in advertising costs. The latter was indicated partly by L's own literature and partly by advertising agencies hoping to persuade S to match L's expenditures.

This additional information, together with that already obtained, effectively enabled S to produce a financial model of the L operation and deduce from this its management's thinking, the volumes and market shares needed to justify its strategic response. S had put itself into a significantly better position to consider and evaluate its response. Alternative tactics and strategies were considered and their likely impacts upon both S and L evaluated both as a means of maintaining a competitive advantage and to better anticipate any further reaction from L to S's responses.

The authors have become increasingly aware over recent years that corporate assessments are an increasing part of the industrial and commercial scene. For example, competitive assessment is used in strategic and tactical planning, and managerial, valuation and profitability assessments in takeover and divestment situations. As the Stapylton example indicates, however, it is necessary to obtain confirmatory evidence whenever possible, as most sources of information will not be completely reliable. The greater the confirmatory evidence the greater the certainty and the more confidently the data can be used. When important decisions are at hand, businesses cannot afford too many guesses. Finally, while businesses are obviously concerned with investigating those other businesses they are interested in, they should not forget that the reverse may be true – they are being investigated and evaluated, too!

References

1. Jones C.S., Rickwood, C.P. and Greenfield, S.M. *Accounting controls and management philosophies*, ICAEW, 1993.
2. Simons, R. The Role of Management Control Systems in Creating Competitive Advantage: New Perspective, *Accounting, Organizations and Society*, 1990.
3. For the Stapylton Company case, see Coates, J.B., Rickwood, C.P. and Stacey, R.J., Examination of the Differences Between Academic Concepts and Actual Management Accounting Practices, Report to ESRC, British Library Document Supply Centre, August 1987; and Rickwood, C.P., Coates, J.B. and Stacey, R.J., Managed Costs and the Capture of Information, *Accounting and Business Research*, Vol. 17, No. 68, Autumn 1987.

Questions

1   Why are inter-company comparisons of doubtful value today as bases for comparison?

2   Why are governmental statistics of little value as a basis for performance appraisal of any one company?

3   (a)   List and explain the means by which you would investigate the affairs of a potential takeover target.
    (b)   What role in the appraisal should the financial team play and why?

4   What routine information would you expect to gather on your competitors if you were:

(a)   a large retailer
(b)   a large manufacturer of consumer products, or
(c)   a small manufacturer of industrial products?

13

Internal audit and control

Internal control

A pervasive theme found throughout this book has been that of control. The management of any organization is charged with the responsibility of ensuring adequate control exists. To be effective, controls should ensure that the entity's activities maintain a degree of co-ordination, that activities are complementary and that the individual pursues the goals of the organization, suppressing, if necessary, their own interests. In this context internal control and internal audit play a vital part.

Internal control is defined as 'the whole system of controls, financial and otherwise, established by the management in order to carry on the business of the enterprise in an orderly and efficient manner, ensure adherence to management policies, safeguard the assets and secure as far as possible the completeness and accuracy of the records'.[1,2]

Types of control

Internal control defined in this way covers a broad range of management functions. This is amplified by the Auditing Practices Committee (APC), which identifies eight types of control[3] which may be commonly found:

- *Organization.* This provides the general structure for control, identifying the location and extent of authority and responsibilities within the structure and defining reporting channels and the existence of control mechanisms.
- *Segregation of duties.* The separation of duties and responsibilities for the recording and the processing of a complete transaction provides a prime form of control, reducing the risk of error or deliberate manipulation without the existence of collaboration. It permits the checking of one individual's work by another. The APC indicates that the following functions should be separated: 'authorization, execution, custody, recording and in the case of computer-based accounting systems, development and daily operations'.[4]
- *Physical.* These are the security measures and procedures which restrict direct and indirect access to assets to authorized personnel. They play a role in relation to the custody of assets, particularly those which are readily exchangeable, valuable, or portable.
- *Authorization and approval.* This control specifies the individuals responsible for approving transactions and the extent of their authority.

- *Arithmetical and accounting.* As part of the recording function, these controls check the correct and accurate recording and processing of transactions verifying the proper authority is present. Examples include reconciliations, control accounts, trial balances, document controls and check totals.
- *Personnel.* The quality of control systems is dependent upon the competence and integrity of those who carry out control operations. This control factor requires attention to be given to selection, training and qualifications of personnel, as well as personal qualities, including honesty, reliability and conscientiousness.
- *Supervision.* 'The supervision by responsible officials of day-to-day transactions and the recording thereof'.[5]
- *Management.* In addition to day-to-day supervision, management should provide control through analysis and review of management accounts, including comparison of achievement with budgets, by other special reviews and through the provision of internal audit procedures.

Use of controls

These controls may be utilized in various combinations, and what is appropriate will vary between organizations with, for instance, company size, the nature of the business and the assets, the volume of transactions and the geographical distribution and remoteness of company operations. The effect of increasing numbers of people within an organization is to decrease the degree of personal contact with management and increase the need for formal controls. Segregation of duties is likely to be more extensive in large organizations; those controlling large quantities of cash or other valuable exchangeable assets will find more need for controls which provide for the security of its assets. The senior management of the organization will need to consider the extent of the risks faced by the organization and to install the control systems appropriate to the particular situation, taking into account the system's costs.

The function of the system of controls instituted by management is to enable an organization:

(a) To operate in an efficient and orderly manner.
(b) To safeguard its assets.
(c) To check the accuracy, reliability and completeness of records.
(d) To permit the preparation of financial and other reports.
(e) To ensure compliance with the law.
(f) To promote pursuit and observation of management policies.

It may be useful to classify controls as either administrative or accounting controls.

- *Administrative controls* are particularly concerned with the achievement of objectives and implementation of policies. Attention is directed to the provision of a suitable structure, including the division of managerial authority and job descriptions, channels of communication and reporting responsibilities.

- *Accounting controls* aim to achieve accountability and provide records. They cover the recording of transactions, establishing responsibilities and maintaining authority, including that for assets. Specific procedures are applied to: cash and cheques; stocks including work in progress; sales and debtors; purchases and creditors; investments; fixed assets; capital expenditure; debt and equity capital.

Limitations of controls

It must be recognized that, whatever the extent of the internal controls in operation, the resulting control system cannot be regarded as 100 per cent effective, automatically achieving efficiency and accurate reports and providing full protection for assets. The APC identifies a number of ways in which controls may fail.[6]

1 Segregation of duties avoided by fraudulent collusion, especially by those in authority.
2 Authorization controls abused by the person in authority.
3 Competence and integrity of personnel undermined by pressures from inside or outside the organization.
4 Human errors of judgement or interpretation due to misunderstanding, carelessness, fatigue or distraction undermining the effective operation of internal controls.

Internal audit and the internal auditor

When we considered internal controls, reference was made to internal audit as a key element. This managerial function plays an important part in the maintenance of all other controls. This is evident in the definition of internal audit provided by CIMA: 'It is a control which functions by examining and evaluating the adequacy and effectiveness of other controls'.[7] Similarly the APC definition includes reference to internal audit's role in 'examining accounting and other controls on operations'.

The CIMA definition extends to identifying the scope of internal audit: 'originally concerned with the financial records the investigative techniques developed are now applied to the analysis of the effectiveness of all parts of the entity's operations and management'. The work of the internal auditor may have originally been restricted to the checking of accounting and other records to identify mistakes, and disclosure of errors continues to be a part of the important controls which ensure duties are carried out in accordance with policies and instructions. He/she continues to provide protection for the organization and its assets.

However, the internal auditor's independent position and access to all parts of an organization enable him or her to perform a wider role. He/she is able to provide an integrating service, particularly with knowledge of the accounting system, which itself plays an important co-ordinating role. He/she no longer limits attention to narrow compliance but is concerned with promoting efficiency in the implementation of policy. He/she can make use of his/her broad organizational perspective to identify corporate risks and opportunities.

Status and capacity

It is important that the internal auditor is given the appropriate status to enable him/her to carry out these functions. He/she is responsible to senior management, and if he/she is to have the authority required to support his/her access to all parts of the organization, he/she needs to be able to report any findings to senior management. However, it must be recognized that the role is one of reporting and recommending; it is not the internal auditor's job to make and implement decisions to change an organization's operations. The basic capacity of the internal auditor has its foundations in the protection of the organization through the prevention and detection of error and of fraud and waste and the monitoring of information systems to ensure relevant information is being provided and transmitted to those who require it.

To fulfil this capacity the internal auditor will need to:

(a) Ensure provision of adequate internal controls and recording systems.
(b) Review the reporting procedures.
(c) Examine records and reports, testing for errors by detailed investigation of transactions and balances.
(d) Report on any fraud or misuse of resources revealed.
(e) Review economy, efficiency and effectiveness of operations.
(f) Review implementation of corporate policies, plans and procedures.
(g) Undertake special assignments.
(h) Support statutory audit requirements as appropriate.

In the context of statutory requirements, the need for internal audit is made explicit in certain cases, notably for local authorities. Here the Accounts and Audit Regulations[9] require the responsible financial officer to 'maintain an adequate and effective internal audit', and grant right of access to all relevant documents and to explanations necessary for the conduct of the audit.

The internal role extends into many other areas and should be seen as complementing the other approaches to internal control adopted by an organization. In the case of Kimco[10] the internal auditors carried out a major managerial role, utilizing their links with activities across a highly decentralized corporate group. This group had adopted a divisionalized structure, delegating substantial responsibility to the managers of each of its many operating subsidiaries. Financial controls were the main formal mechanism for internal control, making use of performance measures reflecting those identified in Chapters 7, 8 and 12.

Since the group pursued a policy of acquisition and disposal of subsidiaries, it was concerned to establish a system of control which motivated and monitored subsidiary performance in a manner consistent with group financial performance while avoiding any distortion of internal transfer prices which would cause potential difficulties if divestment of a subsidiary took place. The autonomy of the subsidiaries was maintained by allowing them to negotiate transfer prices freely on an arms-length basis. However, internal audit provided an important check on the application of transfer prices to the company's internal trading policies.

The activities of internal audit are generally associated with action after the event. In the Kimco case, the internal audit function provided an important on-going role which facilitated co-ordination across the group. The accounting function in business organizations often occupies a unique role serving not only a staff function within operating units, providing financial input into management at that local level, but also as a key part of the communication network across the group. Such communications are often financial, notably the regular, perhaps monthly reports. The internal audit function maintained links on all parts of this network which placed them in a special position to get insights in all parts of the group's activities. Their audit role gave them authority which resulted in a concern for them to be included in the early signalling outside the local operating unit of important developments identified within the unit. They contributed to the surprise management controls identified in the previous chapter. Links with the accountants in the group made the internal auditors a suitable location for the organization of the training and development of the accounting personnel. Their position was further strengthened since, making use of their knowledge of accountants employed within the group, they were advisors on promotions and appointments to accounting positions.

Internal and external audit

The existence of a sound internal audit function contributes to the conduct of external audit, which is defined as 'A periodic examination of the books of account and records of an entity carried out by an independent third party (the auditor) to ensure that they have been properly maintained, are accurate and comply with established concepts, principles, accounting standards, legal requirements and give a true and fair view of the financial state of the entity'.[11] It is usually carried out in compliance with the statutory obligation.

The APC provides guidance on the factors which the external auditor should take into account when assessing the extent to which he/she can rely on the work of the internal auditor. The factors comprise:

'(a) the degree of independence of the internal auditor from those whose responsibility he is reviewing
(b) the number of suitably qualified and experienced staff employed in the internal audit function
(c) the scope, extent, direction and timing of the tests made by the internal auditor
(d) the evidence available of the work done by the internal auditor and of the review of that work
(e) the extent to which management takes action based upon the reports of the internal audit function'.[12]

These factors provide some good indicators of effective internal audit as well as signifying how internal audit can reduce the costs of external audit by its support of that activity. The more the internal audit function is relied upon by the external auditor, the more significant the reductions in the level of tests that must be carried out by the external auditor.

Both internal and external audit are the subject of the CIMA definition[13] of audit: 'A systematic examination of the activities and status of an entity based primarily on investigation and analysis of its systems controls and records'. The reliability of records and adequacy of the reporting and accounting systems are interests shared by both types of auditor.

Co-ordination and difficulties

However, although the best use of resources should ensure that the work of internal and external auditors should be co-ordinated to avoid unnecessary duplication, this is not without its disadvantages. Internal audit must not, as a consequence, be seen merely as a service to the external audit. As set out in the previous section, the internal auditors in the Kimco case performed a number of tasks that would not be within the scope of an external auditor. The programming of internal audit work should not be so distorted in order to fit with external audit needs that its own function is materially reduced. It should not be assumed that internal audit is always a cheaper way of carrying out an external audit function. The special position of the external auditor may make them the more effective and appropriate at times and in certain situations.

Differences between internal and external audit

The resolution of these matters is facilitated by an awareness of the major differences between internal and external audit. The principal differences are:

- *Appointment and independence.* Internal auditors are usually employees (although in some cases the management of organizations unable to support full-time internal audit may appoint an external agent to fulfil this role); external auditors are independent of the management and, in the case of companies, appointed by the shareholders.
- *Responsibility.* The external auditors are principally responsible to the owners of the entity; internal auditors are responsible to management.
- *Duties.* The duties of external auditors are determined by statute; those of the internal auditor are not subject to legal restriction but can be extended as determined by management.
- *Principal concern.* The external auditors of companies are principally concerned with the presentation of results and position in the financial reports of the company; the internal auditor should be concerned with the operation of the entity and its internal control.

These differences will have an impact on the working methods of each auditor and on the relationship with management. External auditors can be expected to have a more formally defined relationship with senior management than their internal counterparts.

Principles of internal audit

In carrying out their functions internal auditors must pay attention to the key principles, which are paramount in determining the quality of the work undertaken. These principles are independence, accountability, materiality, evidence, and objectivity.

Independence

The CIMA definition of internal audit used earlier in this chapter began with the words 'An independent appraisal activity . . .'. Independence appears in other pronouncements from CIPFA,[14] the Treasury and the Institute of Internal Auditors.[15] Although the internal auditors are part of an organization and report to senior managers, they must be independent of the management they audit and independent of the decision-making functions. Only in this way can they be objective in their critical appraisal of both the work carried out by other people and of the decisions made. Critical comment of their own decisions or of managers on which they depend is likely to be inhibited. Many other influences which would reduce independence must be guarded against. For example, they must ignore undue pressure on their judgement, personal relationships, and conflicting interests.

Accountability

The principle of accountability is that those with the authority over resources and those taking decisions should account for the actions for which they are responsible. This is the basic objective of many of the internal controls which aim to identify responsibility, ensure these are consistent with regulations, job specifications and policies and record and report the actions taken. Management is charged with the stewardship of funds through accounting for the resources it is trusted to control.

Materiality

This principle is important throughout all stages of audit, including planning, testing and review. It may be regarded in simple terms as identifying what is important. In describing this principle the APC stated: 'In an accounting sense a matter is material if its nondisclosure, misstatement or omission would make possible a distortion of the view given by the accounts or other financial information'.[16] It must be recognized that the principle is always applied *relative* to a particular set of circumstances. As a result, no absolute measures can be given as standards for general application. The determination of materiality always depends on the judgement of the auditor.

In carrying out auditing work it is necessary for the auditor to establish what levels of error are tolerable. He or she must set the critical level which determines whether or not those errors are significant. In addition, levels of accuracy must be set, and decisions must be made to identify when nondisclosure becomes significant and when it is sufficient to present information in aggregate form.

The assessment of materiality must be carried out in terms of users who may themselves be unknown at the time, and the manner in which they are to use the information provided may depend on future conditions which themselves are unknown. Rarely is there any opportunity to test to see if correction of error in some cases or inclusion or changed presentation of information in others is significant to any of the many potential users.

The application of the auditor's judgement to the determination of materiality should give consideration to the following properties of an item:

(a)   Amount or value.
(b)   Nature.
(c)   Form or means of disclosure and presentation.

Amount or value

The design of sampling techniques in audit tests depends critically on the determination of the levels of materiality of errors. Setting materiality at lower levels will increase the amount of testing but provide more detailed control. The determination of levels should take into account both relative and absolute size. An error of £100,000 may be critical in a report on a small company but insignificant in a financial report of a major corporation or nationalized industry. If, however, this error related to a cash balance, the possibility of fraud or misappropriation would make such an error potentially significant in an organization of any size.

In addition to error size, materiality considerations are relevant to the rounding and aggregation of reported data. In reporting the results of a company with a turnover of £1,000m or more, it *may* be entirely appropriate to round figures disclosed to the nearest £1m, even though this is large in absolute terms. In the context of such a large company, giving separate disclosure of an activity responsible for a £5m turnover *may* add so little information that it would be preferable to combine the data with that for other activities. The use of the word 'may' reinforces the point that particular cases demand different treatment; no definitive rule is being proposed and judgement still has its place. In exercising this judgement the auditor can turn to a number of sources of guidance. The pronouncements of the APC and the accounting professions must be applied in the light of the auditor's experience and that of other auditors.

In setting materiality in terms of relative size in the context of commercial organizations, reference is very commonly made to one or more of the organization's turnover, total assets or profit levels. A further source of indication of scale is given by values for previous years.

Nature

Just as amounts may be significant in either relative or absolute terms, the nature of an item may be important in determining its materiality, due to the group of items to which it belongs or due to its own special properties. The earlier example in which an error concerning cash was considered material in absolute terms was itself dependent upon the nature of the item.

Errors and levels of accuracy of an arithmetical or recording kind are not the only factors an audit is concerned with, so in turn materiality is a principle which must extend beyond sheer arithmetical accuracy. In relation to accounting, classification of items as capital or revenue has such impact on reported profits and balance sheet values that the methods of achieving classification can be considered of a critical nature to accruals accounting systems. One particular aspect of nature that has an impact on materiality is derived from legal or other requirements. Where disclosure of a particular item of information is mandatory, this requirement ensures an item is material. An example of this is the inclusion of directors' salary information in published accounts.

Form of disclosure

The form in which information is disclosed also brings in considerations of materiality. The auditor must determine which information should be included in reports from the masses of potential data, with the object of enabling users to be able to interpret the resulting reports in a meaningful manner. Disaggregation of total turnover into elements arising from activities of substantially different types may be essential to give a proper understanding of the results of an organization engaged in a range of markets or products. In this connection the materiality of an item may be critically dependent on who is to use the information. What may be vital information to one user may be of no significance or even misleading to another. An example is realizable values of the assets of a going concern. To a banker looking for security this may be of prime interest, but to employees of the same company, providing this information as a supplement to financial accounts may be considered of limited significance.

Timing of materiality decisions

It has been suggested that materiality is relevant at all stages of internal audit. Not least is its relevance to audit planning. Of course levels of materiality will determine the extent of internal audit activities, and, hence, the resources and time to be made available. In addition, the inclusion of materiality determination as part of audit planning will have an impact on the quality of the work. If determination of materiality is postponed until an error is discovered, it will be much more difficult to make such a decision than if the auditor has a predetermined level of significance. If a material difference would cause the auditor extensive further work, he or she might be tempted to classify an error as immaterial, when a prior view might have set levels to give the opposite result.

Evidence

The major properties of the evidence the auditor obtains in arriving at his or her opinions are identified in the Auditing Standard,[16] which states 'the auditor should obtain relevant and reliable audit evidence sufficient to enable him to draw reasonable conclusions thereon'.

Attention is directed in this definition to relevance, reliability and sufficiency. Reference may also be usefully made to objectivity.

Relevance

The relevance of an item can only be assessed in relation to the particular audit objective. It is closely related to materiality but is concerned with ensuring that information used in internal audit has a bearing on the opinions, recommendations and controls.

Reliability

Again this is dependent upon circumstances. It will have an impact on the confidence the auditor can place on particular sources of evidence. Some guidance may be offered:

(a) Documentary evidence is presumed to be more reliable than oral evidence.
(b) Evidence obtained from independent sources is likely to be more reliable than internal evidence.
(c) Evidence originated by the auditor would be expected to be more reliable than that obtained from others.

When evidence from one source conflicts with that from another, it casts doubt on both sources. When evidence from different sources is mutually consistent, a cumulative degree of assurance is provided.

Sufficiency

The amount and type of evidence required for the auditor to have enough to enable the formation of an opinion will vary, depending upon prior knowledge and the inherent risk of the situation and upon the persuasiveness of the evidence. The risks will in turn depend upon the nature and materiality of the matter being investigated, as well as the reliability of the personnel and record system providing the relevant information. The properties of relevance and reliability are brought together in establishing sufficiency.

Objectivity

It is important that evidence is not unnecessarily biased by the individual obtaining it. The need for subjective judgement can never be completely avoided in internal auditing but evidence can be collected in a manner that is independent of the collector of the evidence or other individuals. In this way the elimination of individual bias improves the quality of the information. However, all four properties considered here (relevance, reliability, sufficiency and objectivity) are important, and objectivity should not dominate the others. Generally a trade-off must be made between these properties in selecting the form(s) of evidence to be obtained.

Sources of evidence

Audit tests are carried out to provide and check evidence. Two major types of test can be identified. These are compliance and substantive testing. Compliance testing is defined[17] as 'those tests which seek to provide evidence that internal control procedures are being applied as prescribed'. The same source contains the following definition of substantive testing as those tests 'which seek to provide audit evidence as to the completeness, accuracy and validity of the information'. The greater the extent to which compliance testing indicates problems with internal control, the greater the need to extend the substantive testing.

The approaches to collecting test information include inspection of records and of the reality the records represent, as well as observation of the operation of procedures by computational checks and by enquiry. The last approach seeks explanations and information from individuals. The APC considers the reliability of enquiry to be dependent upon 'the competence, experience, independence and integrity of the respondent'.[18]

A preliminary stage in compliance testing is provided by 'walk-through' tests. These tests consist of tracing a small number of transactions right through the system, and so they are sometimes referred to as 'cradle-to-the-grave' testing. Not only do walk-through tests provide guidance for recording and understanding the system and associated internal controls in operation, they give an initial indication of any flaw in that control. It may also be useful at this stage to consider the extension of substantive testing into analytical review. This calls for the study of resulting data to assess how reasonable they are in relation to each other, to past experience and to an understanding of the business, including knowledge of events which should have been reflected in results. The unusual, unexpected or infeasible require further investigation. Ratios, trends and other statistics are particular sources of information utilized in analytical review procedures.

Management of internal audit

Just as any other activity within an organization requires to be managed, the work of an internal audit department must be managed if it is to be effective and efficient. Planning and follow-up are major elements of this. The nature of internal auditing, relying on the efforts of audit staff and being dependent on evidence, give special importance to supervision and to recording.

Planning

The four major functions of audit planning identified by the APC are that it

'(a)   establishes the intended means of achieving the objective of the audit
(b)   assists in the direction and control of the work
(c)   helps to ensure that attention is devoted to critical aspects of the audit; and
(d)   helps to ensure that the work is completed expeditiously'.[19]

It is widely recommended that internal audit planning can be considered in terms of three stages distinguished by the time-scale to which they apply on a basis comparable to other planning, as discussed in Chapter 3: strategic, tactical and operational planning.

Strategic planning

This focuses on the determination of objectives and an assessment of the environment to establish policy. Discussion with senior management will be necessary, for it is ultimately responsible for audit policy and the provision of policy statements. The internal audit function itself is in a good position to suggest and advise on policy development through the generation of proposals. In carrying out strategic planning it is necessary to identify the fields to be covered and the nature of coverage in terms of the two dimensions frequency and depth. The form of coverage should reflect the policy objectives, consideration being given to the following six forms:

1   Financial transactions: considering volume of transactions, values of assets, levels of income and expenditure and the associated accounting recording systems.
2   Internal control: evaluation of the system.
3   Regularity and probity: adherence to company policy, rules and regulations; incidence of misappropriation and fraud.
4   Business impact: threats to business survival, use of opportunities, direct and indirect effects across the organization.
5   Operational and management audit: value for money, effectiveness, economy and efficiency.
6   Special investigations: assignments from management, including fraud, major change, contracts.

In providing guidance on the basis of audit planning, the APC[20] point to the need 'to understand the nature of the business of the enterprise [or other entity]; its organization; its method of operating and the industry [or other environments] in which it is involved'. An element of this is the creation and maintenance of permanent fields holding records of the organizational structure, including the positions of individuals within the structure and their authority and responsibilities, identification of locations, operating rules, records and reporting procedures.

Assessment of the purposes, fields and forms of audit in the context of the particular entity is a prerequisite to resource planning. The aim of this assessment is to identify resource needs and resource availability, and to take action to reconcile any difference between need and availability by adjusting purpose and resource provision. Recognition that the major resource requirement is for staff with particular skills and qualities indicates the potential for difficulties in adjusting resource availability. It is a task to be considered over a strategic horizon, even if this time-scale does not permit fine precision.

Tactical planning

This is directed at identifying the programme of audits to be carried out and their objective, specifying staffing needs and probably detailed staff allocations, and dates of commencement and anticipated completion. Tactical plans need to retain a degree of flexibility in order to be able to respond to unidentified needs and problems but must be sufficiently specific to show how the strategic plans are to be implemented.

Operational planning

This provides the details of the operation of each individual audit. Detail is needed to show the stages to be reached and the timetable for each stage. It is in this aspect of planning that the procedures to be adopted must be set out. The selection and design of procedures requires particular skill to ensure they are appropriate to the task. Since the operational plan identifies the work to be carried out, specified procedures provide a valuable check against which the completion of the audit can be determined.

Supervision and staff

It would be all too easy for internal auditing to become so concerned with its assessment of the performance of other managers and members of the organization that it failed to give sufficient attention to performance in its own department. The Institute of Internal Auditors recognizes that 'the Chief Internal Auditor should establish and maintain a quality assurance programme to evaluate the operations of the internal auditing department'.[21] The management and supervision of the internal audit staff are especially important because their functioning is so dependent upon the quality of the work the staff carries out. Supervision extends beyond monitoring the progress of work carried out, although this cannot be ignored, attention needing to be given to identifying the current status of audit work, evaluating progress and adjusting work programmes and tests as required, and finally ensuring all procedures have been completed and properly performed. Supervisory action embraces all that goes into ensuring due professional care has been exercised. This depends upon starting with the right individuals. The management of internal audit begins with assigning, to particular work, staff that has the required:

1   competence and is in possession of the skills and knowledge that are needed;
2   experience of the industry or other key environmental context;
3   experience of the special problems of the particular operations or area to be examined; and
4   integrity so that the judgements they might be expected to make can be trusted.

Supervision can take many forms. Some situations require very close personal observations, others permit more extensive delegation. The closeness of supervision will be a function of the complexity and sensitivity of the particular assignment as well as the attributes of the staff assigned to it. The critical attributes here are the same as those which bear on the selection of staff for particular work – their proficiency, experience and integrity.

Demands for competent staff must be supported by education and training. These can be provided in many ways, but should include professional qualifications, audit manuals, communication of technical developments, access to relevant books and journals, and job experience through working alongside experienced colleagues. Allocating work to staff of appropriate quality must be followed up by ensuring that what is required of them is clearly specified. In achieving this there must be good communication of the following:

(a)   Responsibilities.
(b)   The objectives of the assignment.
(c)   The procedures to be followed.
(d)   The relevant background through the provision, as appropriate, of well maintained files showing the history of the particular job and other related knowledge.

Item (d) draws attention to a further aspect of control. Work records must be well maintained. Generally this requires the maintenance of working papers that may be reviewed as part of the supervisory process by staff other than those who prepared the papers. Further review of the results and reports must take place before an assignment can be considered complete.

Recording and review

Working papers and internal audit records have many uses. The information provides:

1   Indications of the work that has been done and of its proper execution and discharge.

2   Details of problems encountered.
3   The audit evidence itself and conclusions drawn from that evidence.

It should be remembered that the principles of sufficiency, relevance, objectivity and reliability must apply. 'Audit working papers should always be sufficiently complete and detailed to enable an experienced auditor with no previous connections with the audit, subsequently to ascertain from them what work was performed and to support the conclusions.' APC *op. cit.* section 2.1.[22]

Having put forward this statement, drawing attention to the future reference which may be made to audit records, the APC guideline continues by setting down another important principle, i.e. that 'audit working papers should be prepared as the audit proceeds so that details and problems are not omitted'.[23]

Particular requirements within the records of work carried out are indications of errors or exceptions identified and how these are followed up. It should also be clear who did what work, and evidence that the work has been reviewed should show by whom the review was carried out. Significant matters should be summarized, making clear where judgement has been exercised. The adoption of procedures leading to good working papers should encourage a methodical approach, which may be made more efficient through the use of standardized working papers. Standard forms setting out, for example, space for the reviewer to comment and sign should reduce the likelihood of this stage being omitted by oversight. What must not be overlooked is the security of records. The appropriate action must be taken to ensure that working papers are kept safe and that due confidentiality is maintained.

Quality control

Emphasis has been placed on quality considerations in all aspects of audit management. Just as the APC provides focus by issuing a guideline devoted to quality control, this section brings together the matters relevant to quality.

- Appropriate procedures should be established and communicated to all relevant staff – in all but the smallest audit functions this would necessitate setting down the procedures to be followed, normally in writing. Manuals and standardized programmes must be regularly updated and staff kept informed of their content.
- Procedures should be designed to achieve adherence to ethical requirements. The statement issued by the accountancy bodies sets out principles relating to independence, objectivity, integrity and confidentiality. Special attention may be necessary to provide guidance on these matters to staff members who are not professional members of accountancy bodies.
- Staff should have attained the skills and competence required – this begins with personnel recruitment and calls for planning the staff resource requirements not only in terms of numbers but in terms of ability to perform the required work. Experience, qualifications and reliability must all be considered.

Attention must be given to staff training to maintain staff quality, with technical updating through courses and access to publications, including those issued by professional bodies, relevant legislation, books and journals. In addition, on the job training and professional development are required.

- There should be procedures for consultation, and a structured approach to audit file review, including review of working papers, is necessary. The means must be made available for technical problems to be dealt with by reference to specialists and for the resolution of matters involving judgement.
- The effectiveness of quality control procedures should be monitored – an element is the independent review of samples of audit files. This differs from the regular review of working papers, as part of day-to-day supervision and monitoring. By contrast, it is intended to assess standards, and procedures should be established so that it is not regarded as ad hoc or casual. The procedures should set out selection for review and frequency, timing, nature and extent of reviews.
- Recommendations for improvement should be followed up, for quality control is not a static matter. It is important to identify weaknesses but insufficient unless recommended responses are implemented.

Performance audits

Operational audit

The appraisal of the performance of organizations is a valuable audit service. Although the classification is not entirely precise, a distinction is sometimes made between management audit, concerned with senior management performance of a particular organizational unit, and operational or operation's audit, concerned at levels subordinate to senior management. At other times operational audit is used as a more general term concerned with the range of audit approaches used to appraise the effectiveness of organizational performance. The terms performance audit, effectiveness audit, efficiency audit and value for money audit are also in use and some attention has been given to these in Chapter 11. Concentration, in this chapter, is given to management audit. The principles and methods of this form of audit are applicable to the various forms of performance audit.

Management audit

This has been defined as 'An objective and independent appraisal of the effectiveness of managers and the effectiveness of the corporate structure in the achievement of company objectives and policies. Its aim is to identify existing and potential weaknesses within an organization and to recommend ways to rectify these weaknesses'.[24] The definition may be taken to indicate that management audit extends the traditional audit scope to examine total organization. By focusing, as it does, on management and organizational performance, it goes beyond those considerations capable of being expressed in financial terms. Mere compliance and propriety may no longer satisfy the demands of audit when extended in this way, so that achievement becomes an object of attention.

The appraisal of effectiveness requires examination of value for money encompassing the '3Es': economy, efficiency and effectiveness. Value for money audit was required by statute in local authorities under the Local Government Finance Act 1982. The Code of Local Government Audit Practice for England and Wales, approved by Parliament in 1983, expanded on this requirement, providing definitions of each of the 3Es. This built upon an earlier non-statutory Code of Practice 1973, which had directed audit to be concerned with 'the possibility of loss due to . . . extravagance, inefficient financial administration, poor value for money. . .'. The added element of 1983 was to ensure that management had made 'proper arrangements to secure economy, efficiency and effectiveness'. Not only the ends but the means come under scrutiny.

During the period 1973–83, a decade in which the concern for value for money developed into a legally backed audit requirement for local authorities, there was considerable attention to management audit in the literature (see, for example, Sayle,[25] Banham and Tristrum[26] and Santocki[27]). Many examples of practical application have also been observed (see Inlogov's *Register of Local Authority Research Projects*,[28] which identifies in excess of 1,000 value for money projects).

Although there are numerous differences between various authors, Jan Santocki provides a definition which includes many of the salient properties: 'Management Audit is an objective, independent, informed and constructive appraisal of the effectiveness of managers / teams of managers . . . It must be seen as a managerial function and as such must assist management'.[29]

The need for independence is worth stressing if impartial audit judgement is to be maintained. In achieving this the internal auditor must restrict his activities to monitoring, reconsidering and reporting. Responsibility for implementing might affect the auditor's view of performance. Independence is supported when the authority for audit comes from senior management. Management audit may be carried out on a regular programmed basis or may be introduced ad hoc, as required by particular circumstances. It is not, however, a routine process but an in-depth investigation. Whether programmed or ad hoc, it should start with identification of its objective. The area and problems to be investigated must be defined, and managers to be brought into the scope of the investigation specified. Central to management audit is examination of value for money by considering economy, efficiency and effectiveness. This must be carried out both in terms of evaluating outcome and in terms of establishing the existence of arrangements made by management itself to secure value for money. Any weaknesses in these arrangements must be brought to light and recommendations made for dealing with them.

Implementing management audit

As with other forms of internal audit, the success of management audit is founded upon good planning. For each area to be given attention it is valuable to consider the scale of resources to be devoted to the task at an early stage. An important consideration is value of, and scope for, financial savings through avoiding waste and other improvements in the particular area. If the cost of resources put into the investigation exceeds the potential for any savings, the net impact of the audit must be realized as a loss, and this, itself, cannot give value for money.

In evaluating its potential, we find management audit may be used to fulfil a number of purposes. Through the attention it gives and by taking the perspective of the organization as a whole, it can contribute to motivation of management, control, performance improvement, career development and organization succession, and change. As a catalyst for change, management audit can provide the channel for crossing responsibility barriers to identify and convey the requirements for resolving problems and for taking advantage of new opportunities. Given that adequate planning should precede implementation, the subsequent steps are:

(a)   Examination of the function's objectives.
(b)   Identifying weaknesses in management performance.
(c)   Evaluation of arrangements to ensure value for money in achievement of objectives.
(d)   Reporting the audit findings together with any resulting recommendations.

Throughout the investigation the procedures of internal audit must be maintained. Evidence must be collected, recorded and reviewed. Use should be made, when appropriate, of standing files, providing the accumulated background knowledge and formal structure.

To turn to the four steps identified above, the examination of objectives must start with ascertaining the targets, limits and requirements of the function. The means by which they are set and communicated to particular managers is a further consideration. The broad perspective which management audit is able to take is put to good use when these objectives are appraised from the point of view of compatibility with total organizational goals. Similar consideration should be given in relation to the other steps. Specific organizational goals include financial performance in terms of cash flow and return on capital for example. Closely linked are capital development and asset position. Less susceptible to financial measurement are development of technology and relevant knowledge. Business organizations, in particular, will be concerned with product development and maintenance of competitive position through securing opportunities and developing relative advantage.

Comparison of targets with achievement gives an initial indication of the scope for further investigation. If results are failing to meet targets, the cause must be sought. The problem may lie with the target itself, either because it is being inadequately communicated to managers or because it is unrealistic in relation to the function, its resources and its environment. When the fault is attributable to management, its potential cost and other effects on the organization will be a pointer to the scale of the problem. Financial performance measures provide an important element in assessing achievement. These may include variance reporting, profit contribution and return on capital measures. Management audit does not have to be confined to these, and in a case of material problems would want to investigate in more depth, extending to areas not readily assessable in financial terms.

The approach to the identification of weaknesses may be guided, in part, by indications drawn from failure of a function to achieve its objectives or failure of those objectives to be compatible with organizational goals. Although it may not be possible to provide an exhaustive list, a number of areas of potential weakness may be particularly important, owing either to their incidence or effect on the organization. A failure to comply with the law or company rules could have significant implications. Although maintenance of professional or company norms may not always be as conclusively established, management audit extends to such considerations. Since weaknesses represent risks for the organization, the exposure to risks must be investigated. This includes risks through loss of security or confidentiality, and commercial risks.

Managers' responsibility for establishing organizational structure and for planning for the future come under scrutiny in management audit. Planning weaknesses may be identified by a poor information base, caused either by inaccuracies or limited scope. The latter may well reflect inadequacy of management's perception of factors relevant to their planning. Given the inherent uncertainty of the future, good planning can only be fully evaluated in the light of events, and examination of past success is pertinent. Both planning and organizational structure require attention to be given to recruitment, training, promotion, management development and organizational succession. A vital element of planning is the provision of finance, and management audit extends to this consideration.

Although management may not be directly responsible for all sources of waste or inefficiency, it must provide the means to ensure sources are pinpointed. Indeed efficiency may require delegation. The system of monitoring and control is a subject for enquiry in the context of the procedures to be followed; it may be necessary to study the manuals which set out the procedures and the extent to which they are being followed in practice. Monitoring creates accountability in those in authority. The quality of the management information will impact on the quality of monitoring and of decision making. It follows that management audit needs to give careful attention to the adequacy of the information systems in supporting the arrangements set up to achieve value for money.

Summary

The principles of internal control and audit which have been the subject of this chapter apply equally to performance audits. The work of internal audit has been examined and attention paid to the principles which govern this work. The principles of materiality and evidence are the subject of extensive consideration in the practice of internal audit. Detailed attention has not been given to the procedures which are likely to be the subject of external auditing; attention has been drawn to the potential control functions that can be carried out utilizing internal audit. It is worth repeating that these should be seen as complementary to other control mechanisms and need to consider the control objectives of the organization as a whole.

References

1. CIMA, *Management Accounting Official Terminology*, 1986.
2. Auditing Practices Committee, *Auditing Standards and Guidelines* section 2.4.
3. *Ibid.*, section 4.8.
4. APC, *op. cit.*
5. *Ibid.*
6. *Ibid.*
7. CIMA, *op. cit.*
8. APC, *op. cit.*
9. *Accounts and Audit Regulations*, 1983, HMSO.
10. CIMA, *op. cit.*
11. See Coates, J.B., Rickwood, C.P. and Stacey, R.J., *Management Accounting in Practice*, CIMA, 1995.
12. APC, *op. cit.*
13. CIMA, *op. cit.*
14. CIPFA, *Statements of Internal Audit Practice – Public Sector.*
15. Institute of Internal Auditors (IIA), *Standards for the Professional Practice of Internal Auditing.*
16. APC, *op. cit.*
17. *Ibid.*, section 2.3.
18. *Ibid.*
19. *Ibid.*, section 2.1.
20. APC, *op. cit.*
21. IIA, *op. cit.*
22. APC, *op. cit.*, section 2.1.
23. *Ibid.*
24. CIMA, *op. cit.*
25. Sayle, A.J., *Management Audits – the assessment of quality management systems*, McGraw-Hill, 1981.
26. Banham, J. and Tristrum, R. Getting the facts for Local Authorities, *Public Finance and Accounting*, November 1983; RIPA, Value for Money Audits, 1982.
27. Santocki, J., Meaning and Scope of Management Audit, *Accounting and Business Research*, Winter 1976.
28. Inlogov, *Register of Local Authority Research Projects*, Institute of Local Government Studies, University of Birmingham.
29. Santocki, *op. cit.*

Further reading

Boys, P.G., Management Audits, Touche Ross Technical Digest No. 17, 1985.
Chambers, A. *et al.*, *Internal Auditing.* Pitman, 1987.
Venables, J.S.R. and Impey, K.W., *Internal Audit*, Butterworths, 1985.
Woolf, E., *Auditing Today*, Prentice Hall, 3rd ed., 1986.

Questions

1 The concept of 'materiality' is very important in the work of an auditor. However, its interpretation and application in practice rely to a large extent on the exercise of judgement and opinion on the part of the individual auditor, so that the treatment of identical circumstances may differ between auditors. You are required to provide an explanation of the concept of materiality and an assessment of the validity of the above statement, illustrating your answer with examples.

2 (a) You are required to
   (i) explain the basic principles on which value for money audits in local authorities are conducted;
   (ii) give three specific examples of methods of analysis which may be employed in practice.
   (b) Discuss the problems experienced with programme planning and budgeting systems and the major differences between PPBS and VFM.

14

Auditing techniques and procedures

Introduction

As described in the previous chapter, the practice of auditing is divided into internal and external, with the latter responsible for the 'true and fair view' of published company accounts. We are primarily concerned with the operation of internal auditing. However, the two activities are of a parallel nature to a considerable degree, as evidenced by the willingness of external auditors to accept relevant internal audit reports as fulfilling certain of the requirements of the external audit, without the external auditor duplicating the examination procedures and tests carried out internally. Naturally, before such a situation is reached, external auditors must assure themselves of the competence, procedures and standards of their internal counterparts. Not all organizations as yet boast an internal audit department, though it is now a widely recognized function.

Where it exists, it is likely to carry an extensive range of responsibilities, from what might be termed the 'checking' activities of traditional auditing through to what is really an internal consultancy service. Originally concerned with financial records, the investigative techniques developed are now applied to the analysis of the effectiveness of all parts of an entity's operations and management.

The second part of the CIMA terminology description of internal audit is the key to appreciating the comprehensive nature of today's internal audit practice. The position of the function in the hierarchy of organizations varies, but is frequently observed as reporting directly to the managing director and board of directors. At this level the function head reports on the success or otherwise of sectors of a business, as well as on how efficiently and effectively managers within the company have developed and operated its systems and procedures. The operation of internal audit thereby provides an important channel of information and advice not just to departments but also to top management, which is otherwise unlikely to have the time to collect and assimilate the necessary detail. Internal audit's central investigative role, contacts with departments and level of reporting led to a wry self-assessment in one company as the 'accounting Mafia'.

In the present chapter we consider further the audit of systems and procedures from the general viewpoint of the types of testing and some of the main tools of the trade which may be employed to assist the process. Elsewhere, Chapter 5, Budgets and control, briefly discusses the performance evaluation role. In view of the immensity of the subject and the limited space available here readers are referred to others[2,3,4] for a wider, more detailed exposition.

System documentation

For a start any systems audit needs a clear, precise, accurate and up-to-date documentation of the system itself. Depending on the diligence of the proprietor department(s), this may range from being rather less than coherent or complete paperwork to properly produced and maintained manuals. In the former situation the auditor must first of all work out how the system is actually operated. Once this task is completed, subsequent audits will have the more complete documentation to work on.

Testing internal systems

Systems are used to capture and process information, which in turn is used as the basis for the preparation of accounts. The parallel interests of the internal and external auditors are apparent here: both need to know that the internal systems and control procedures are being operated as planned and that the information they produce is reliable. The two traditional system tests are (i) compliance, and (ii) substantive.

Compliance tests

These tests are defined by the Auditing Practices Committee as, 'tests which seek to provide evidence that internal control procedures are being applied as prescribed'.

Although readily defined, they are not all observed or conducted to the same level by all auditors in all circumstances. Basic of course is testing the systems, which is done by examining in detail the reports, records and documents, authorizations and so on, to see they have been used, applied and operated as they were designed to be. This procedure could be carried out through or accompanied by walk-through ('cradle to grave') tests, where the auditor follows through a set of transactions as recorded by systems operators to see that proper entries and systems checks have been made.

An 'error' detected by a compliance test is of course non-compliance, which says nothing by itself about its size, significance or seriousness, but nevertheless requires initial recording. Ultimately an assessment has to be made as to how to proceed where non-compliance has been discovered.

Following through records is not the sole type of compliance test. For example, it may be necessary to actually observe how certain systems checks are carried out, say with respect to access to stores and parts of buildings where computer systems are housed.

Compliance tests are concerned with evaluation of the way systems and their controls are operated and implemented. Eight principal categories of internal control were introduced in the previous chapter as:

- Organization
- Segregation of duties
- Physical
- Authorization and approval
- Arithmetic and accounting
- Personnel
- Supervision
- Management

The nature of compliance tests and their emphasis on systems controls leaves an auditor with many qualitative and judgemental assessments to make, e.g. the number (level) of tests to carry out. There is also the possibility that, because of the interrelated character of systems, proper functioning of a control examined at one point may mean it can be inferred that another must also be functioning properly, i.e. it is not necessary to examine all control points, or at least not to the same extent.

A further consideration is whether a single failure of a control requires investigation or whether a number of failures are tolerable before such a step is taken. Judgement may be guided by anticipating the consequences of a breakdown, e.g. failure in an estimation procedure can affect prices, orders, or the stage in the system at which the failure occurs.

The usual sampling problem of bias has to be covered. However, some difficulties in sample selection, such as it being representative of the type or value of transactions, are not of particular importance here, since it is the operation of the control (by a particular person) which is under test. Even after completion of tests, the only clear situation is where no compliance failures are revealed, in which case one could conclude that reliance can be placed on the system and its controls. Otherwise a view has to be taken as to whether the degree of compliance/non-compliance recorded is tolerable or not, e.g. if it is not expected to occur other than infrequently. Conversely, if regular occurrence is suspected, further testing may have to be done, which may lead to a review and amendment or redrafting of the control in question.

This point also influences the need and extent to which substantive testing is conducted following the compliance test stage. Venables and Impey[5] illustrate the situation as shown in Figure 14.1.

Substantive tests

These follow on from and complement compliance tests as indicated by Figure 14.1. Where compliance tests suggest that reliance on system controls is soundly based, the need for substantive tests is reduced, and vice versa. In themselves substantive tests are comprised of a number of features, principally (i) the verification of transactions and account balances, and (ii) the verification of the existence of assets and liabilities and their valuations.

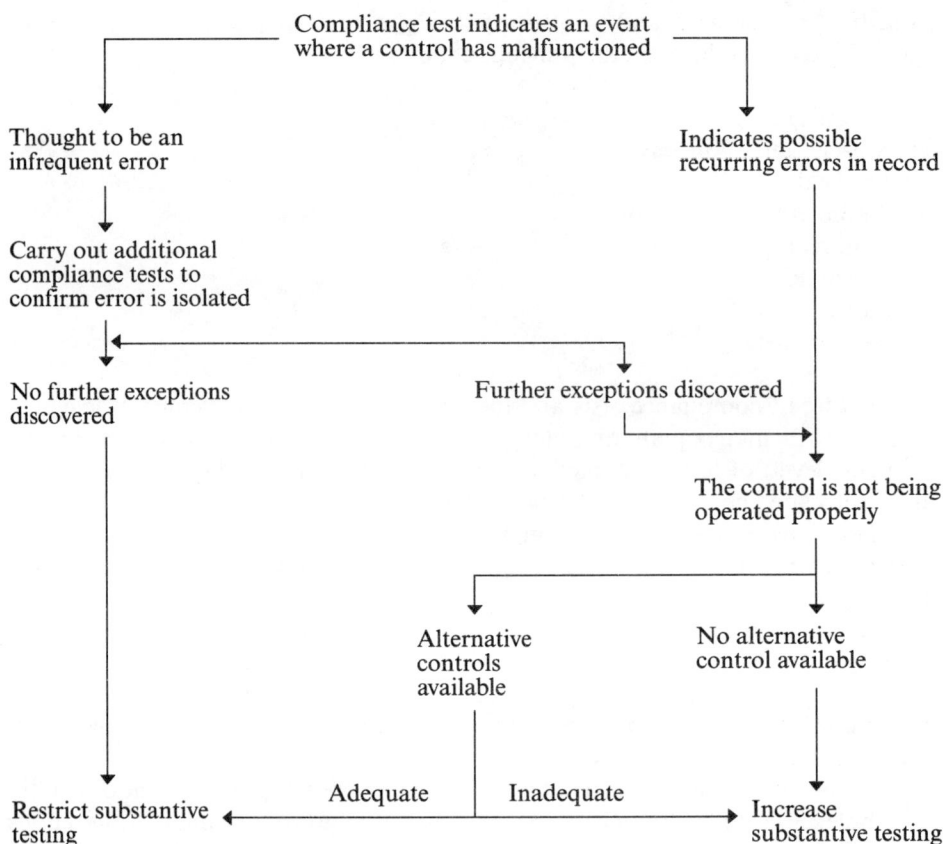

Figure 14.1   *Testing*

The definition given by the APC indicates the extensive nature of substantive tests: 'those tests of transactions and balances, and other procedures such as analytical review, which seek to provide evidence as to the *completeness*, *accuracy* and *validity* of information'[6] in the accounting records or in the financial statements.

As part of the substantive test procedures, analytical reviews enable an auditor to gain a perspective on the accounts, and to see they are coherent and consistent, i.e. 'add-up' to a sensible picture. Analytical reviews follow the substantive tests of accounts to a degree which is likely to be dependent on the auditor's judgement of the reliability of the detail contained in the accounting records: the greater this is, the less the need to conduct these reviews, at least in detail. The reviews are composed of:

1   Analysis of fluctuation in accounts' statements, e.g. debtor to sales ratios. A change here may lead to examination of credit controls and provisions for bad and doubtful debts. Other examples are in the changes in proportions of cost to total cost and turnover.

2   Comparisons of actual and budget in the management accounts.
3   Examination of explanations for noted changes in these items given in accounts' reports.

Analysis of trends where appropriate is an important part of the study. Clearly these reviews could be very extensive and take auditors (internal and external alike) into very wide ranging comparisons, not just within company records but also making use of relevant outside comparator information, say reports and statistics produced in the *Financial Times*, inter-firm comparisons, government statistics, and company reports to insurance companies. The auditor's aim is to find out whether the portrayal of the company's affairs as represented by the accounts is one in which confidence can be placed. Throughout the exercise many general factors condition the auditor's interpretation of the information acquired, e.g. changes in the rate of inflation, government legislation, and such changes in the macro economy as expansion or contraction in trade, competition and technological change. They are factors which supply some of the more obvious explanations for variations in accounts, period-to-period; but the collection of analytical evidence can be seen in principle to be almost limitless, and once again a judgemental approach is likely to determine just how far to go.

Whereas analytical reviews contribute to the understanding and acceptability of accounts records, the fundamental activity within substantive testing is the test of detail. Aimed at the verification of account balances the objective is to guard against the risk of their misstatement and the further possibility of fraudulent activity. The extent to which these checks are carried out is conditioned, as already noted, by the results of the compliance tests (in the case of external auditor, the degree of reliance it is felt possible to place on the internal control procedures). Beyond this lies the application of the principle of *materiality* of the item under scrutiny. This relates to its significance and hence the benefit likely to be gained from putting resources into detailed investigations.

The principal substantive tests carried out may be summarized as:

1   Computation – a check on the calculations performed in arriving at an account balance.
2   Inspection/observation – actual counts or observations of counts (associated procedures underlying how they have been carried out), e.g. of stocks, petty cash.
3   Enquiry of third parties to verify the fact of an account balance, e.g. a purchase order or the existence of assets (title deeds held in solicitors' offices, banks, etc.).

It should be noted that names given to these tests vary and the list is not exhaustive.

The determination of materiality is essentially a matter of judgement by the auditor, and is generally to be interpreted as relative to a particular set of company circumstances. Precise rules by which to judge materiality cannot be given, but some guidance can be found in the following considerations:

(a) The absolute value of an error.
(b) The percentage value of an error.
(c) The impact of the item in question on a group of items to which it belongs, and the ultimate effect on a company's final report.

By way of examples for (a) and (b), £0.5m could be seen as quite a large error in the recording of turnover totalling say £10m, but relatively small in the case of £50m turnover, yet in either case £0.5m could be regarded as a significant absolute error; then, with respect to the size of a firm, £0.5m would be of crucial importance in a small/medium-sized firm, but much less important in a large one. These are very similar considerations to those pertaining to the investigation of budget and standard cost variances.

Errors of an arithmetical or recording kind are not of course the only factors an audit is concerned with. For instance, absolute stock of either goods or plant or equipment maintained in the accounts instead of being written off affects both the balance sheet values of the business and the level of reported profit; this situation further affects the assessment of a company's liquidity, its security as judged by suppliers of finance, and its general financial standing. Materiality is thus a concept dealing with situations which go well beyond sheer arithmetical accuracy, relative or absolute, and which have far-reaching consequences for a business.

So some further requirements of the above guidance on deciding materiality may be:

1 Establish a level of materiality, such that smaller size errors are not regarded as material. Since investigations, following a judgement that an error is material cost time and money to carry out, some assistance in determining the level might be gained via cost-benefit studies of the situations.
2 Considering the cumulative total of errors, i.e. the individual errors themselves tested against a particular item, may not amount to much, but when the set is aggregated, it may amount to a significant absolute total.
3 The nature of an item, i.e. its influence on materiality, may arise through changes in accounting, for example of depreciation, stock valuation, expensing or capitalization of items, or the way in which items may (or may not) be reported in relation, for example, to statutory requirements.

The level of substantive testing

Materiality is a concept with many facets. As part of substantive testing it also features in the determination of the level of these tests, in particular the degree of statistical sampling which may be employed.

The level of substantive tests is again a matter of choice among several possible approaches, ranging from 100 per cent examination of all items comprising an account balance, through mixtures of 100 per cent examination of all items above a certain amount with a sampling of the remainder, to sampling the entire account balance. Information leading to a judgement here will come from confidence in the internal controls, evidence from analytical reviews and evaluation of materiality.

A full examination of all items obviates any problem concerning sampling, but at the same time can be very costly to pursue. On the other hand sampling schemes based on strict observance of the requirements of statistical theory can also be expensive to set up and maintain and there is the additional problem of having personnel who understand them.

Materiality can play its part in reducing the amount of sampling that needs to be done, e.g. by assessing its level at say £500, all items below this sum being left out of the sampling frame. It could help to cut out the examination of many low value items, which would probably, though not necessarily, produce little benefit in return. It is not essential that sampling should be based on statistical methodology, but to do otherwise prejudices the representative nature of the sample through the possible introduction of bias, even though all the features of a statistical sample size – acceptable error limits, stratification and so on – could otherwise appear to be recognized. Equally, pure reliance on statistical approaches may miss the valuable input of an auditor's experience in detecting the signs, themselves apparently not significant, which lead into a related and significant series of events and results.

Computer assistance can greatly relieve the problems in this area, since a great deal of computation work can be completed very rapidly. Nonetheless, auditors' experience and judgement will always be a major constituent in deciding the best among the options open.

Recording and appraising the system

Before the start of a systems audit, it is obviously necessary to have clear documentation of the system, stating how it should operate. Many companies will probably possess systems manuals for this purpose, but auditors will need to check them out. In other cases they may have to find out how a system works themselves. Reliance by external auditors on the examination of systems carried out by internal auditors obviously depends on evidence that systems are properly recorded and that checks on controls have been completed by the internal staff.

The following are the most widely used techniques for understanding and appraising systems operation:

(a) Flow-charting.
(b) Use of Internal Control Questionnaires (ICQs).
(c) Use of Internal Control Evaluation Questionnaires (ICEQs).

Flow-charting

This technique produces a diagrammatic representation of the system. Completed properly, it provides a comprehensive visual map of how the system operates,

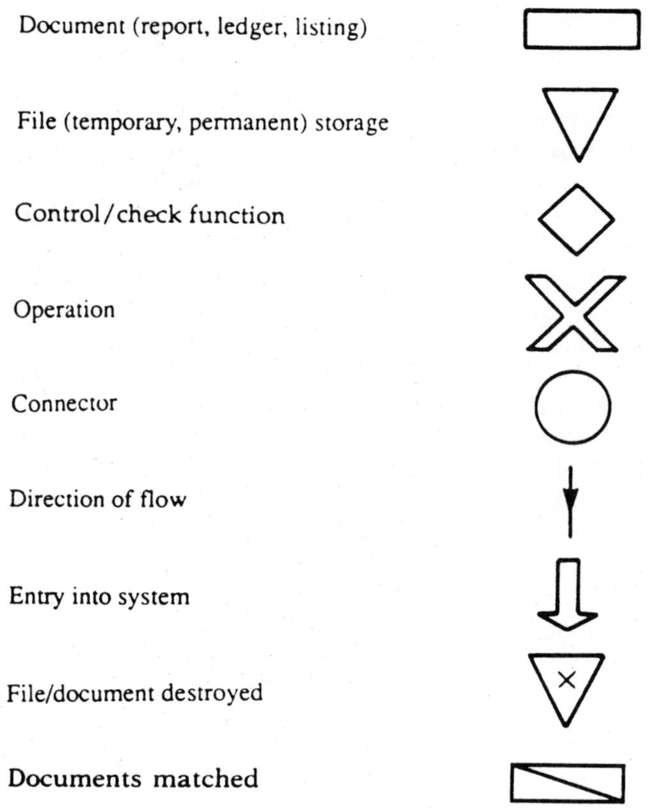

Document (report, ledger, listing)	▭
File (temporary, permanent) storage	▽
Control/check function	◇
Operation	✕
Connector	◯
Direction of flow	↓
Entry into system	⇓
File/document destroyed	▽ˣ
Documents matched	▱

Figure 14.2 *Flow-chart symbols*

how sections/departments interrelate and where internal checks are or should be carried out. The use of symbols may reduce the need for narrative description to provide back-up explanation of the chart, though they may not eliminate it entirely. In any event the language of the symbols has to be learnt.

There are various types of flow-chart, but for present purposes it is the flow of documentation which is usually the main interest. Files and reports should be identified in the sequence in which they are processed, so that there is a complete picture of a system's operation from beginning to end. Activities will generally be grouped by transaction, a separate chart being required for each one, e.g. 'sales' as a generic transaction could be broken down, for instance, into sales of original equipment and sales of spares.

The symbols themselves differ to some extent among individual users, but there is a substantial measure of comparability. Basic ones, not specifically computer application symbols, are shown in Figure 14.2.

The chart is usually joined by horizontal or vertical lines, and flows from top left to bottom right of the chart as the sequence unfolds. A small example follows (Figure 14.3), but the art and detail of flow-charting is quite considerable and readers are referred to other works[7,8,9,10] for further discussion and examples.

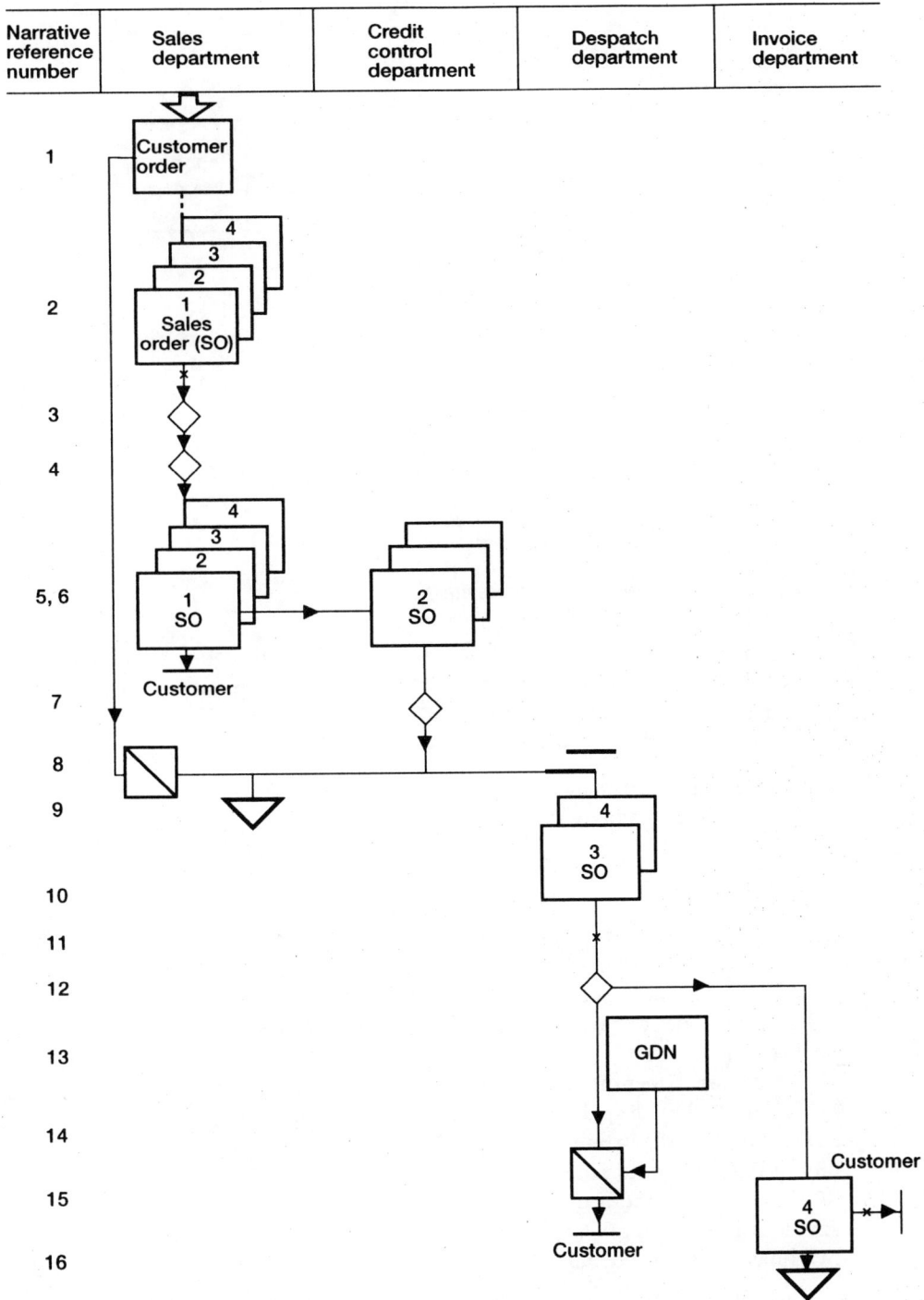

Figure 14.3   *Flow-chart examples: recording credit card sales orders*

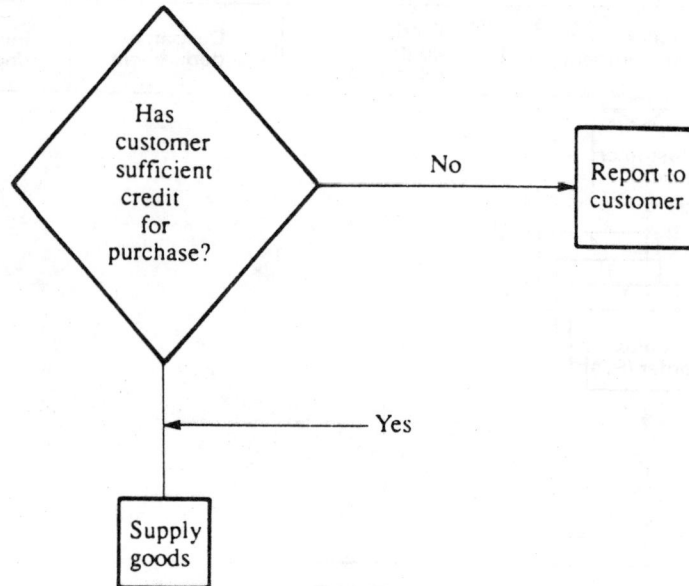

Figure 14.4 *Logical sequence convention*

An alternative presentation of systems is to use the logical sequence convention, where yes/no answers are given to questions, indicating a course of action. A very limited example is shown in Figure 14.4.

Key to Figure 14.3:
 1 Customer order received
 2 Sales order (SO) (4 copies) raised
 3 SD clerical check
 4 SP supervisor check
 5 SO 1 to customer
 6 SO copies 2, 3 and 4 to credit control and despatch departments
 7 Check by credit controller and report issued
 8 Customer order matched to SO 2 in sales department
 9 SO 2 filed in sales department and SO 3 and SO 4 sent to despatch department
10 Despatch department make up order form SO 3
11 Order checked by despatch department manager/supervisor
12 SO 4 to invoice department
13 Goods despatch note raised (GDN)
14 SO 3 matched to goods dispatch note (GDN) and sent to customer
15 Invoice raised from SO 4 and sent to customer
16 SO 4 filed in invoice department

Note: In addition to raising the GDN and invoice, there would be further check functions in the despatch and invoicing departments. The invoice routine is not complete.

Internal Control Questionnaires (ICQs)

The use of these may be linked to the flow-chart. Their objective is to provide an auditor with an indication of strengths and weaknesses in internal control of systems' operation. These should give comprehensive coverage of a company's systems of processing and control. Questions incorporated in the questionnaire are formulated in a way that a 'no' answer indicates a weakness. ICQs are not standard documents between firms, and they require a regular check themselves to be kept up to date; in addition, they are frequently very detailed and lengthy documents. A brief example is given in Figure 14.5. A 'no' answer to question 2 would be an obvious weakness. The flow-chart reference number ties the ICQ to the flow-chart. Provision also has to be made to record the detail of answers requiring a fuller statement than just Yes, No or N/A.

Internal Control Evaluation Questionnaires (ICEQs)

These are prepared principally for senior audit management. They concentrate on key control points, being considerably less detailed than the ICQs. Senior staff are thereby enabled to achieve an overview of the most significant points, but can still find back-up detail where necessary. A further major difference to an ICQ is that ICEQ answers are formulated so that a 'yes' answer indicates a weakness. A brief example from the sales function is shown in Figure 14.6.

Once again, though, there is variety in the way these questionnaires are designed, particularly in their detailed content. However condensed or abbreviated they are, they all seek to highlight the affirmation of weaknesses which exist in key areas and which spell serious problems in the way system controls have been designed (or omitted) and operated.

Statistical sampling

The purpose of using statistical sampling in internal (and external) auditing is to verify the reliability of accounting records within specified limits of accuracy without examining every transaction. It is most applicable where the sheer volume of transactions makes it unrealistic to contemplate the examination of every single item and is mostly used in conjunction with compliance and substantive testing. Although founded on rigorous statistical/mathematical theory, a statistical sampling scheme calls for important judgements to be made with respect to the materiality aspect of errors and the precision limits of the sample. There are many trade-offs between the accuracy of the sample results and the economies of carrying out a sampling procedure, but at least the parameters of the sample can be stated explicitly and accepted or rejected and ultimately interpreted on a common basis.

Not all circumstances lend themselves to statistical sampling: clearly where there are only a few transactions, each one could be material and hence require

Reviewer ....

Auditee ....

Date

Question	Response			
	Yes	No	Not applicable	Flowchart note ref.
1 How are sales orders recorded?				
2 Is customer credit standing checked before an order is accepted?				
3 Is customer credit checked by a department separate from sales?				
4 Are sales invoices compared with (i) sales orders, and (ii) GDNs?				
5 Is the person responsible for (4) separate from personnel who (i) prepare invoices, and (ii) record dispatches?				

Figure 14.5   *Internal control questionnaire*

examination; and other features, such as the degree of under-valuation of items, may render particular types of sampling inappropriate. The volume of literature

Sales dept Key question	Answer (Yes or No)	Comment/explanation
1 Can goods be supplied to customers without being invoiced? 2 Can goods be supplied to customers with an unsatisfactory credit rating? 3 Can accounts become overdue without immediate detection?		

Figure 14.6 *Internal control evaluation questionnaire*

on the subject is very large and it is only possible to present the fundamental elements of such schemes here, while referring readers to more advanced texts in the references.

Selecting a sample

Random sampling is the basis of statistical sampling schemes. In a random sample each member of a population has an equal chance of inclusion in the sample. There are a number of variants in the approach to collecting sample data which may be adopted in conjunction with random sampling, from simple random sampling itself through to systematic, stratified, and multi-stage samples, with 'variable' or 'attribute' characteristics. 'Variable' relates to measurable parameters such as heights, weights, values, whereas 'attribute' refers to inherent characteristics such as 'heads' or 'tails', 'black' or 'white'. Whatever the nature or detail of the scheme, the aim is to be able to draw inferences about the condition of the underlying total population (which in practice may be either finite or infinite) from the information provided by the sample. The size of the population is not a key factor in determining the validity of sample information; it is the size of the sample itself and the fact that random sampling has been used to select it.

The principal alternative to this approach is the use of judgemental sampling, where, as the name suggests, the auditor uses their experience to decide on how much sampling to do and of what items. The principal danger of proceeding in this way is that it may bias the contents of the sample in such a way that they do not fairly reflect population values; it is also not readily possible for others to judge the adequacy of the sample. However, the contrast between statistical and judgemental sampling is not quite so stark as the foregoing may seem to imply, since, as has already been indicated, various judgements must also be exercised in deciding on a statistical sampling scheme, though they are more overt than in the purely judgemental case.

There are also risks to be recognized in sampling, that a sample may incorrectly indicate that a population is not of acceptable quality when in fact it is and vice versa. Thus a number of conditions need to be determined before a statistical sampling scheme comes into operation, to make sure it is accurate and economic. The main considerations are:

(a) Identify the sampling frame, the population from which the sample is to be drawn.
(b) Define the 'error' which the sample is seeking to identify and which is the objective of the audit.
(c) Ensure as far as possible that the system which generates the information eventually to be sampled is sound.
(d) Determine the *precision limit* judged to be acceptable. (Other terms for precision limit are precision, precision range, and monetary precision (in monetary unit sampling).)
(e) Determine the *reliability* that is acceptable. This will normally be expressed as the confidence level required. A commonly chosen level is 95 per cent, which would be interpreted to mean that on 95 occasions out of 100 the sample should reflect the true condition of the population and 5 occasions out of 100 it may not. The latter is the risk of the sample producing inaccurate results.

Both (d) and (e) are related with each other and the sample size. Other factors to be considered will be introduced, along with examples.

Attributes sampling

In auditing, the principal objective is to assess the level of error in population from the number identified by a sample. 'Errors' are attributes, i.e. the item concerned is either correct or incorrect, an inherent characteristic. Attributes sampling and a form of attributes sampling, monetary unit sampling, are therefore most appropriate and commonly employed in auditing, compared to variables sampling. Monetary unit sampling (MUS) is of special interest, since it provides a result in money values, which can be readily understood and their significance appreciated.

Foundation of attributes sampling

The statistical basis of this type of scheme, apart from the application of random selection, rests on the use of the hypergeometric, binomial and Poisson probability distributions. For most purposes the Poisson distribution is selected because it is easy to apply and approximates (in the way it is generally applied) the binomial, which in turn approximates the hypergeometric distribution. In the latter case the chance of selecting an error or non-error from a finite population varies as the selection process proceeds. Thus if a population of 1,000 items is known to contain 5 per cent errors, i.e. 50 items, then the chance of successive selections of a sample which would contain no errors varies as each item is selected and the chance of no errors in, say, a sample of 100 would be:

$$\frac{950}{1000} \times \frac{949}{999} \times \frac{948}{998} \ldots \times \frac{851}{901} = 0.004475$$

This is referred to as sampling without replacement.

In the Poisson distribution, two values are used:

n = sample size
p = expected error rate

'p' is a constant percentage and in terms of the previous example would mean that on average (np) the sample should contain 5 errors.

The Poisson formula is

$$\frac{e^{-np}(np)^x}{x!}$$

and gives the *exact* probability of a sample showing x errors when the average number expected is np (np is often abbreviated to 'm' in statistical texts). There are tables for the calculation of these and cumulative values. The tacit assumption of the Poisson distribution is that an item once sampled is deemed to be returned to the population and may be reselected, thus the error rate in the population always remains constant. For this example, the chance of finding 1 error in a sample of 100 is 0.0437, compared to the corresponding value for the hypergeometric distribution of 0.0263.

In practice of course the true error rate in the population will not be known. Given that random sampling is used to select a (representative) sample, which in turn produces a number of errors, the latter rate will be assumed to be the most likely rate for the population as a whole. If 1 error was found in the sample of 100, i.e. 1 per cent, it would be interpreted as meaning the population rate would also be 1 per cent; 10 errors would be likely to be present in a population of 1,000, which is referred as the most likely error rate (or projection), MLE. However, as noted, samples do not necessarily correctly represent the true population error level. It could be either overstated or understated by the sample.

The risk which is used to establish most sampling schemes is the maximum rate in the population which could be considered tolerable, in turn meaning one considered to be a material influence on the auditor's conclusions. This will be referred to as the upper error limit rate (or frequency), UEL.

Examples: Given a UEL of 3 per cent, a 95 per cent confidence level and a sample of 100 items in which no errors are found. A result like this would be interpreted to mean that the population error rate is no higher than 3 per cent. The UEL of 3 per cent and a sample size of 100 can be shown to meet the desired 95 per cent confidence level as follows:

The risk of drawing a sample of 100 containing no errors from a population which really contains 3 per cent errors is:

$$= \frac{e^{-100 \times 3\%}(np)^0}{0!}$$

$$= e^{-100 \times 3\%}$$

$$= e^{-3}$$

$$= 5\%$$

i.e. there is only a 5 per cent chance that a sample of 100 from a population which contains 3 per cent errors could contain no errors. The 5 per cent is the counterpart of the 95 per cent confidence level.

A series of UEL values can be constructed from cumulative Poisson probability tables for different sample sizes, number of sample errors and confidence levels. Thus, for example, if one error were found in the sample of 100, then at 95 per cent confidence the UEL rate becomes 4.75 per cent. At 80 per cent, everything else remaining as before, the rate is 1.61 per cent. These variables are linked:

$$\text{UEL rate} \times \text{sample size} = \text{cumulative values}$$

$$\text{or} \quad \text{UEL rate} \quad = \frac{\text{cumulative values}}{\text{sample size}}$$

Using the earlier example figures

$$\text{UEL rate} = 3 \div 100 = 3\%$$

determined for a 95 per cent confidence level.

Monetary unit sampling (MUS) – a simple example

Let us assume we have a set of stock balances totalling £75,000 to verify. MUS regards these are 75,000 £1 units, each of which, using simple random sampling, would have an equal chance of selection in a sample. Of course it is not the individual £1 units which are to be verified, but the account balances from which they derive, i.e. selection of a particular £1 unit automatically and simultaneously identifies the account balance to which it belongs.

The account balances are listed sequentially, e.g. as taken from the records. Five-figure random numbers would be used, i.e. in effect numbering the £1 units from 00001 to 75000. The account balance sequence may appear as in Table 14.1.

No attempt is made here to stratify the balances or deal with any other difficulties, such as accounts which may be partly right or wrong. For a more advanced treatment of the subject readers are referred to Leslie *et al.*

With the listing prepared in this way, it is an easy matter to identify the sample

Table 14.1

Balance number	Value (£)	Cumulative value (£)
1	250	250
2	763	1013
3	1029	2142
.	.	.
.	.	.
.	.	.
350	897	75000

Table 14.2

Balance number	Cumulative value (£)	Random numbers assigned
1	250	00001–000250
2	1013	00251–01013
3	2142	01014–02142
.	.	.
.	.	.
.	.	.
350	75000	74104–75000

required. It is worth noting that this procedure will tend to give a greater representation to higher value balances than would be the case if each balance were given an equal chance of selection. This is because there are, for example, four times as many £1 units in a balance of £400 as in one of £100.

To illustrate the use of random numbers, let us refer to Table 14.2. From a random number table, the following sequence was derived:

06270, 62400, 00984, 50641.

The first value is regarded as the 6,270th £1 unit, the second the 62,400th £1 unit and the third, which is within the example, the 948th £1 unit and so on. The third item is within the range of numbers allocated to balance number 2, and hence this balance is selected for examination.

Direct selection of account balances

The principal alternative to MUS would be to make a direct selection of balances. Each one would be numbered and, again, a random number stream used to identify the particular balances for examination.

Thus, in the preceding example, the random number block is 001 to 350, i.e. three-figure numbers. The principal difference to MUS now is that *each balance* has an equal chance of selection and there is no in-built weighting in a simple

Table 14.3

Sample errors	UEL value (sample size = 100)	Precision limit (£)	Precision gap (£)
0	4.61	3,457.5	3,457.5 − 0 = 3,457.5
1	6.64	4,980.0	4,980.0 − 750 = 4,230.0

random sampling scheme towards the larger value balances, as there is in MUS. This difference essentially underlies other important distinctions in the way the two approaches to sample selection operate, distinctions which go beyond the scope of the present book to deal with. Readers are again referred to Leslie *et al.*[11] for further explanation.

To create a MUS now requires an understanding of the links between the elements of sample size, reliability and precision. Assume a sample size of 100 is drawn from the 75,000 £1 units and it is found to contain no errors. The UEL value is known to be 3 for a sample of that size at a 95 per cent confidence level and the UEL rate is 3 per cent. In monetary terms this gives a precision gap of 3 per cent × £75,000 = £2,250; the most likely error rate in the population is projected to be 0 per cent.

Imagine now a sample of 100 has been drawn and a single error has been found, i.e. a 1 per cent error rate, which is again projected to be the most likely population error rate. The UEL value is 4.75 and the rate 4.75 per cent, which produces a monetary value of £3,562.5; the precision gap is £3,562.5 − £750 = £2,812.5. The corresponding values if a 99 per cent confidence level were to be chosen are shown in Table 14.3.

Consider now the effect of having a sample size of 200, maintaining the 95 per cent and 99 per cent confidence levels. Taking the 95 per cent case first, to record a 1 per cent sample error rate two sample errors must be found; the UEL value is 6.3 and 6.3 ÷ 200 = 3.15 per cent, which is the UEL rate. Multiplying £75,000 by 3.15 per cent gives £2,362.5, compared to £3,562.5 for the sample of 100. At the 99 per cent confidence level the corresponding value would be £3,153.75, compared to £4,980.0 for the sample of 100.

It can be seen that changes to any of the values of the components of the sampling scheme have consequential effects on the values of others. Viewed in an alternative way, the value of a certain element could be specified and a scheme developed to meet it. In the above example the value of the error may be judged with respect to its materiality; and once the latter is determined, size of sample, confidence level, and sample error rates may all be manipulated to produce a scheme which would keep within the bounds of this material error figure. By way of a summary of the example, see Table 14.4.

An assessment of materiality requiring a finer precision limit can be met by increasing the sample size, all other things being equal.

A final point concerns the interpretation of the UEL rate. For the population this is an unknown value; the only actual information about the errors is the number recorded in the sample. Using the example data again, with a result of

Table 14.4

Changed variable	Constant variables		Resultant changed variables
Sample size	Sample error rate (%)	Confidence level (%)	Precision limit (£)
100	1	95	3,562.5
200	1	95	2,362.5

zero errors, at the 95 per cent confidence level, it could be stated that if the population error rate had been 3 per cent, then we could be 95 per cent confident that this would be discovered as a result of the sample containing more than zero errors.

Procedures for applications

An internal auditor's prime duty is to ensure that controls over systems operations are in place and effective. This assessment should be made while bearing in mind an organization's objectives and the broad requirements of economy, efficiency and effectiveness in the utilization of resources. The primary duty requires the auditor to investigate:

(a) The existence of the officially recognized control systems (using documentation etc.).
(b) The way these systems are being operated, compared to how they were intended to operate.
(c) Whether the control systems in place achieve their objectives.
(d) To review and report recommendations.

As indicated earlier, ICQs will be used to prepare the ground for this activity, the professional standard of the internally adopted procedures greatly affecting their acceptability or otherwise to the external auditor.

The regard for the organization's objectives was referred to above, but this entails consideration of many other factors, such as:

1 The management structure of the organization.
2 Controls specified as required by senior management.
3 The effect of legislation on the organization.
4 The degree of bureaucracy in operating the system.

The controls themselves will not be of uniform significance, some obviously being more important than others. Levels of importance should be clearly designated. In the following we illustrate the application of basic principles of effective internal control, the types of control and their implementation, to some of the main accounting procedures. These illustrations are intended as such and not as fully comprehensive descriptions.

Purchases

(a)   *Aims*, to ensure:
- Purchases are properly authorized and recorded with reference to customer requirements.
- Goods received are properly recorded as such, and are to required specifications.
- Goods failing to be acceptable are properly identified, with controls to ensure appropriate credit is claimed.
- Supplier invoices are properly recorded, checked and approved before payment is authorized.
- Suppliers' accounts are properly maintained.

(b)   *Controls*

Purchase authorization
- Through responsible officials in the buying department.
- Order forms properly completed and authorized.
- Use of pre-numbered order forms for purchases of goods and services.
- Commitments-outstanding record maintained.

Goods received
- Proper recording of goods inwards at point and time of receipt, using sequentially numbered goods received notes.
- Proper inspection of goods received at time of receipt for quality and quantity.

Credit notes
- Goods returned to suppliers are immediately recorded in a goods-returned book, covered by sequentially numbered documentation to suppliers.
- Records of reasons for return are made.
- Shortfalls in supply are similarly documented.
- Supplier credit notes should be matched to original claims showing those still outstanding.

Supplier invoices
- For accuracy: as to terms to agreement, pricing, totals, etc.
- No outstanding credit notes exist.
- Evidence that checks have been carried out by requiring signature on documents of responsible personnel.

All the above transactions give rise to accounting record entries which must be checked as to ledger postings, credit control and individual creditor accounts, totals reconciliations and so on. These checks will incorporate the features listed under Types of control in Chapter 13 and can be carried out against a formal compliance test procedure. It is necessary:

- That there is a proper separation of duties, for instance, in that checking of invoices and credit notes is completed by persons other than those who prepare purchase orders or GRNs.
- That there is supervision of these checks, evidenced by signature.

Sales

(a) *Aims*, to ensure:
   - Customer orders are properly recorded, with full sale conditions.
   - Goods delivered/services rendered are properly recorded as to date and customer, to trigger invoicing routine.
   - Goods returned/credit notes issued are properly recorded, to assess liability.
   - Accounting transactions and entries into accounts are properly made and therefore valid.
   - Payments and outstanding payments are monitored, and doubtful debts assessed.

(b) *Controls*

Customer orders
   - Records of completion of customer orders maintained, using sequential numbering; regular examination of orders not yet completed.

Goods delivered
   - Delivery notes raised or otherwise properly recorded.
   - Delivery notes should be sequentially numbered, and matched with invoices.
   - Invoices properly raised following delivery note issue.

Goods returned and credit notes issued
   - Match with delivery notes/invoices, using sequentially numbered records.
   - Monitor outstanding claims.

Accounting entries
   - Invoices and credit notes should be sequentially numbered.
   - Regular reconciliation of control account with total of customer account balances.
   - Procedures for entering details into accounts and ledgers.

Payments routines
   - Means exist to determine creditworthiness for both new and existing customers.
   - Procedure for identifying and handling overdue accounts.

Income (receipts)

(a) *Aims*, to ensure:
   - Cash owing is collected.
   - Cash receipts are entered immediately and accurately into the books of account.

- Proper arrangements for cash to be deposited in a secure place such as a bank as soon as possible.

(b)   *Controls*
- Cash sales should be recorded on numbered sales notes, completed when sales are made. This applies to all situations: cash registers, tills, and individual hand-completed sales notes.
- There should be a reconciliation of the total of cash and cheques received at frequent intervals, e.g. at least once a day in retailing.
- In the case of credit sales, etc., the receipt should be matched to sales invoices, and again proper procedures should exist to ensure collection is made.
- Receipts of cash and cheques are to be entered into records as soon as mail is opened.
- Persons checking cash and cheque receipts should not be those dealing with initial sales, and proper supervision is required to see checks are made.

That these requirements are complied with can be tested by checking through sales note documents, to examine the evidence of entries into proper records and that supervisory duties have been carried out as required.

Inventory

(a)   *Aims*, to ensure:
- Records of all types of inventory – materials, work in progress, finished goods – are accurately maintained. For example, that issues (and returns) of stock from and to stores are properly controlled and recorded; similarly from production into finished goods stock.
- Physical stocks are matched with ledger totals.
- Stock is properly costed/valued.

(b)   *Controls*
- The existence of supporting records for all transfers of stock from suppliers, through the various stock categories and to customers, e.g. sequentially numbered documents backed up by matched recording of transfers in accounting records.
- Cost accounting routines are examined to ensure that cost standards are maintained, variances calculated and investigated overheads properly attributed to centres, and issues from stock priced accordingly to accepted policy.
- Again there should be division of duty between those responsible for physical stock verification and those dealing with entry and completion of records. Supervision must also be present in the form of personnel with authority and responsibility to see that checks have been made, routines are complied with and so on.

Verification of compliance must be carried out. It is a matter which will vary between firms, depending on the exact nature of their procedures which of course must be assured to be adequate in themselves. For example, a full annual physical stock count or perpetual inventory procedures are both methods to underpin verification of balance sheet stock values.

The procedures an auditor may use to judge the validity of these records are once more the following:

- Examine the systems procedures and documentation.
- Ascertain the division of responsibility between record-keeping and actual physical stocktaking.
- Following through records.

Trade debtors

(a)   *Aims*, to ensure:
  - Amounts recorded as owing by customers are accurate.
  - Proper provision is made for bad and doubtful debts.
(b)   *Controls*
  - See 'Sales' above.

Fixed assets

(a)   *Aims*, to ensure:
  - The physical existence of assets is recorded as on site and that acquisitions and disposals are properly authorized.
  - Proper records of purchase cost and depreciation of fixed assets are maintained.
(b)   *Controls*
  - The existence of proper authorization for the purchases and disposals of fixed assets.
  - Enhancements and modifications are similarly authorized.
  - Proper records detailing each item acquired are kept.
  - A physical check routine at reasonable intervals is specified.
  - Actual expenditure is matched with estimates given at the time of authorization.
  - In appropriate cases proper title exists to the ownership of assets such as land.

The principal means to ensure the above controls are properly executed is to have a separation of the physical check responsibility from that of recording, and that responsible staff are charged with the task of seeing procedures are duly completed.

The internal auditor will again have to inspect documentation and the existence of proper approval for account entries. Following through records will be an important feature, e.g. the auditor should check the actual existence of assets, and ask for and inspect copies of titles to property and land.

Summary of applications' procedure

There are a number of other areas where procedures of a similar nature will be required, e.g. for wages and salaries, bank reconciliations, petty cash. The obvious essential ingredients are sound and clearly documented systems for recording and verification, the separation of duties as appropriate for checking physical existence (of assets) against recorded amounts and proper supervision. Observance of the demands of relevant statements of standard accounting practice will be needed.

Compliance tests are the ones which have been predominantly referred to, but in a full audit these will be followed up by the application of substantive tests. In the main these latter tests are directed towards balance sheet items, on the argument that if these are correct, then the general set of accounts for the period will also be correct. Substantive tests are directed at the verification of the account balances: in a sense they are not mutually exclusive of compliance tests since they provide additional evidence that control procedures have been observed. It may also be remembered that other tests, such as 'analytical review procedures', form a part of general substantive testing and in turn provide information which helps to bear out the validity of the information given by the accounts.

References

1. Coopers and Lybrand, *Student's Manual of Auditing*, Gee, 1985.
2. Woolf, E., *Auditing Today*, Prentice Hall International, 1986.
3. Venables, J.S.R. and Impey, K.W., *Internal Audit*, Butterworths, 1985.
4. Chambers, A.D., Selim, G.M. and Vintner, G., *Internal Auditing,* Pitman, 2nd ed., 1987.
5. Venables and Impey, *op. cit.*
6. Auditing Practices Committee, PO Box 433, Moorgate Place, London EC2P 2BJ.
7. Chambers, A.D. and Court, J.M., *Computer Auditing*, Pitman, 2nd ed., 1986, Ch. 22 and Appendices.
8. Coopers and Lybrand, *op. cit.*
9. Woolf, *op. cit.*
10. Venables and Impey, *op. cit.*
11. Leslie, D.A., Teitlebaum, A.D. and Anderson, R.J., *Dollar Unit Sampling: A Practical Guide for Auditors*, Copp Clark and Pitman, Toronto, 1979.
12. *Ibid.*

Questions

1 (a)   Statistical sampling techniques may be applied in a number of auditing situations. You are required to discuss the nature of those situations and

the objectives, advantages and disadvantages of applying statistical sampling techniques to them.

(b) You are given the following information in respect of a particular sampling scheme:

Population size   2 million
Confidence level   95 per cent
Monetary precision   £10,000

Reliability (R) factor at selected confidence levels:

Confidence level %	63	78	86	92	95	97
R factor	1.0	1.5	2.0	2.5	3.0	3.5

R factors are based on UEL (upper error limit) rates in the population at the given confidence levels.

You are required to (i) explain the basis of a scheme of monetary unit sampling (MUS), (ii) indicate how it would be utilized in the situation given above; and (iii) state how you would interpret the result of obtaining no errors in a simple random sample derived in the manner you have indicated.

(CIMA, May 1988)

2 (a) You are required to explain the function of analytical reviews with particular reference to the conduct of an internal audit.

(b) As internal auditor of AB plc you are conducting an investigation of the company's trading results. Your directors believe a further issue of debenture stock is needed to fund both the repayment of the 10 per cent stock due for repayment in 1989 and for investment in new plant and machinery. The industry in which AB plc operates is, and is likely to remain, highly competitive. The following financial information has been provided.

Balance Sheets at 31 December

	1987	1986	1985	1984	1983
	£m	£m	£m	£m	£m
Net fixed assets					
Land and buildings	3.0	2.5	2.4	1.6	1.5
Plant and machinery	3.2	2.0	1.2	0.8	0.6
Current assets					
Stocks	5.0	4.7	3.0	2.4	1.9
Debtors	2.6	2.0	1.9	1.5	1.4
	13.8	11.2	8.5	6.3	5.4
Total assets					
Creditors: Amounts falling due within one year	4.3	4.0	3.5	2.2	2.0
Total assets *less* current liabilities*	9.5	7.2	5.0	4.1	3.4

Creditors: Amounts falling due
after more than one year:

10% Debenture Stock 1989	1.5	1.5	1.5	1.5	1.5
12% Debenture Stock 1995	2.0	2.0	—	—	—
Net capital employed	6.0	3.7	3.5	2.6	1.9

Capital and reserves:
Authorized and issued £1 shares

fully paid	1.5	1.5	1.5	1.5	1.0
Retained profit	4.5	2.2	2.0	1.1	0.9
Shareholders' interest	6.0	3.7	3.5	2.6	1.9
* Includes bank overdraft	1.9	1.3	0.6	0.8	0.9

Extracts from profit and loss account

Net sales	16.4	13.5	10.0	8.5	7.3
Cost of sales	8.9	7.1	6.1	5.5	4.8
Net profit before tax	3.0	1.5	1.4	0.8	0.5

Some average statistics for the industry as a whole in 1987 are given as:

Net profit before tax: Sales	14%
Net profit before tax: Sales	14%
Net profit before tax: Total assets less current liabilities	18%
Working capital (current) ratio	2.2:1
Liquidity ratio	0.75:1
Sales: Fixed assets	3.0
Turnover of stock	2.8
Debtors collection period (based on average debtors)	45 days
Age of stock	120 days

You are required to
 (i)   present a schedule of data derived from the financial information provided for AB plc which would be used as the basis for an Analytic Review;
 (ii) use the data to (1) analyse the financing proposals (2) assess the reasonableness of the figures in the statement of results.

(CIMA November 1988)

3   The interpretation of the concept of materiality and its application in practice rest to a great extent on the judgement of individual auditors.
   Explain the concept of materiality and assess how far the statement may be true even where statistics are employed to assist in making an auditor's decision on whether errors found in accounts records are material or not.

4   (a)   What factors should an auditor take into account when deciding on the level of materiality to be taken into account in an audit.

(b)   Discuss the view that lack of precision in the concept of materiality seriously undermines the benefits thought to be gained by the employment of statistical sampling techniques in auditing.

15

Ethics

Introduction

Many of those first coming to the study of management accounting consider that mathematical algorithms exist which can be used to identify the solution to business problems. Earlier chapters have drawn attention to the significance of uncertainty and aspects of human behaviour which ensure that management is not simply a matter of arithmetic. Most business decisions involve considerable judgement and many entail some degree of ethical judgement. Difficulties were identified in Chapter 11 in the measurement of performance in the public sector. It would be all to easy to ignore the situations in which moral values play an important role in the management of businesses and to concentrate solely upon the more measurable profit objectives. Although ethics have been given attention in a number of other professions, its relevance to accounting, specifically, and business in general have received explicit recognition only recently and even then this has been limited.

The nature of ethical problems is identified with situations where decisions are guided by moral principles. The large majority of these include dilemmas in which each possible alternative is expected to produce outcomes which have social benefits and social costs. The accountant faces a range of pressures as an individual, as a manager and as a professional which test the sense of responsibility. The importance of both confidentiality and full disclosure creates an obvious source of conflict. This is emphasized by recognizing the more derogatory expressions 'economical with the truth' and 'indiscreet'. The accountant is likely to come into possession of information which puts him or her in a position of substantial responsibility as a potential insider. Disclosure may benefit many others while commitment to a client would suggest that a duty to be discreet existed.

Ethical actions need not necessarily be identical to self-sacrifice. Indeed, one of the underlying reasons for the professions' concern to achieve good ethical standards in its members is that a major attribute which professional membership can confer on its members is public approval of their standards. Recognizable trust and high moral standards contribute positively to the value society places on the services of professionals and this is reflected not only in social status but in financial rewards as well.

In practice it is often suggested that moral judgement is entirely dependent on an individual's sense of moral values. However, it is relevant to ask the question of what sources of guidance on ethical issues are available. In attempting to address this question, reference can be made to three sources: theoretical concepts; the law; professional and other guides which do not have formal legal status.[1]

Theories of ethics

Since two distinct theories of ethics can be discerned and these do not give mutually consistent guidance on action, theory is not a panacea for ethical problems. The theories can be set out in the following manner:

Type of theory	Teleological	Deontological
Example	Utilitarianism	Kantian ethics
Summary	Consequences of acts	Rightness of acts regardless of consequences

Teleological theories

Utilitarian theories present little problem to accountants. Having studied economics, and its extension into the use of marginal costs for decision making, they are familiar with the concepts of utility, and maximizing utility. Utilitarian theories look at the consequences of acts adopting principles which may be expressed as achieving the greatest balance of good consequences in the form the greatest good for the greatest number. Utilitarian philosophical writings include those of David Hume (1711–1776) and Jeremy Bentham (1748–1832).

Two forms of utilitarianism can be presented:

1 *Act utilitarianism*, considering only the consequences the balance of utility, from the act in question.
2 *Rule utilitarianism*, which gives consideration to the rules under which life should be lived, and rules chosen to give the maximum good consequences.

The main problem of utilitarian approaches is one which accountants find familiar; the problem of quantifying and evaluating other than the most direct short term consequences of actions. The greatest good for the greatest number is not an operational phrase unless there can be some form of calculation. Chapter 11 drew attention to the measurement problems that arise in the public sector. These are all present here. Any accountant who has grappled with the application of cost-benefit analysis in the evaluation of social projects will again be aware of the difficulties. Utilitarian evaluation would require not only indications of benefits but would have to apply weightings of the benefits received to the various groups involved. This is a very subjective process and ethical decisions remain firmly rooted in the area of judgement. Another problem of utilitarian logic is that it can lead to injustice for minorities. The usual example for this is slavery, which can lead to a more comfortable life for those who are not slaves and be good for a large majority of the population. More modern examples of excluded minorities can be identified.

Deontological theories

While utilitarianism concentrated on the ends (consequences) rather than the means, the alternative philosophical approach, exemplified by Immanuel Kant (1734–1804) focuses on the act (the means) rather than the consequences. Again two forms can be identified, concentrating either on the individual act or rules which, as with utilitarianism, are intended to lead to acts which are consistent with the philosophy. To this end, Kantian ethics sets out a range of imperatives. Broad guidance is offered by Kant's statement 'Act in such a way that the action taken could be a universal rule of behaviour for everyone'. More specific rules would be 'You should always tell the truth' and 'You should honour your contracts'.[2]

Deontological ethics (the word derives from the Greek *Deos*, duty) emphasize motive, conscience, consistency and duty. This contrasts sharply with the irrelevance of motive to utilitarian thinking, of which an extreme example can be Adam Smith's argument in *The Wealth of Nations* that an invisible hand can lead the self-interested acts of businessmen to produce the greatest good.

Most people's ethical beliefs, if analysed, are a mixture of utilitarianism and concepts of duty. The same holds for most formal codes. Conflicts will arise where a given act can be seen to be a clear duty with unfortunate consequences. The obvious example for the accountant is the clear duty to report accurately, to take a true and fair view, reporting to shareholders, bankers and tax authorities even when the consequences can be predicted as not the consequences desired by the directors and managers and possibly a large number of the employees of the organization.

Two other closely related conceptual bases can be mentioned which are less clearly based on theoretical foundations. These are prudence and populist[3] ethics. The former is dependent upon a view of the value of democracy. It suggests that actions of social leaders should be governed by virtue and will become examples of good behaviour. To the extent that democratic forces, fuelled particularly by the media, will drive leaders to act in ways which earn public support, it is democratically expressed ethical values that will emerge. Market forces will drive business leaders to consider public opinion in a similar manner. However, criticism of this approach to ethics argues that it becomes no more than a public relations approach. The populist approach places less emphasis on the mechanics of achieving ethical behaviour and more on the formation of ethical values. These are attributed to current views that can be attributed to the public at large. Views on the importance of the environment, sexual equality, capital punishment and political correctness may not be consistent over time but a perception of general acceptability at any one time may be assessed.

The law as ethics

The prudence and populist approaches might lead to the view that the law should provide a code of ethics. It is endorsed by the legislature of the day and provides a set of rules which that governing body identifies as appropriate for maintaining society and social behaviour. In a democracy, there is an expectation that the law reflects public opinion. However, such codes are unlikely to be complete. Ethical problems will arise which would not have been anticipated by the lawmakers or are regarded as not the subject of law perhaps because they are unenforceable, private matters or too trivial. One might hope to receive what is regarded as decent treatment and behaviour but not all exceptions can be expected to lead to legal action.

There has to be a range of situations where possible legal actions are not acceptable to the creators of ethical guidelines. This is not a static situation; the law changes making actions which were unethical illegal under changing legislation, e.g. insider trading, or the USA Foreign Corrupt Practices Act. Equally public opinion changes and actions which were regarded as acceptable are no longer so regarded. An obvious example of this is whistleblowing – taking objections to an organization's actions beyond internal procedures and debate, breaching duties of confidentiality, and attempting to get public and/or official action to change the organization's actions. Like most similar codes, the *CIMA Ethical Guidelines,*[4] which are discussed in more detail later, do not support whistleblowing, and regard the duty of confidentiality, which is included in the law of agency, as paramount in all but quite exceptional cases. After such well publicized problems as BCCI, Maxwell and Barings Bank, public ideas of what constitute exceptional cases and what actions are appropriate could well change even if the legal and regulatory framework does not change.

Professional guidelines and codes of conduct

Guidelines for independent professionals

Professional ethical guidelines have existed for a long time. Their logic is seen most clearly by looking at the professional form assumed by the structure of old professions such as medicine. This is an association of independent practitioners working separately for different clients. Their regulation is carried out by their association, not by the state, and the regulation is expected to cover ethical matters as well as technical competence. It will also tend to cover routine matters such as professional etiquette in such matters as a client moving from one adviser to another. Here an ethical code and its enforcement by the association can be seen as part of the price of independence and the privilege of self-regulation rather than state regulation. It can also be seen in the case of a developing profession as part of the process of demonstrating to the world at large that the group concerned are not just sharers of common technical knowledge and skills, but are a profession. The code of ethics is part of the demonstration of professionalism. Thus Lynch[5] (Institute of Management Consultants) can write:

> The Institute is examining the feasibility of establishing a code of ethics for management consultants to supplement the professional code of conduct. This is in line with the Institute's mission to promote high standards for our members. Other professions have ethical guidelines, and there is no good reason for management consultancies not to as well. This is seen as a practical service to members aimed at enhancing their (and the profession's) image and standing in the community.

The basic problem of an ethical code for a self-regulating profession is that of enforcement. Beets and Killough[6] discuss possible methods of enforcement including government regulation, self-regulation, the use of the legal and judicial system by enabling injured parties to claim damages for unethical behaviour, and the complaints based enforcement system that most professions employ. Under a complaints based system the witness or victim of an unethical act which contravenes a published code can complain to an authoritative body which can discipline the offending party. This may dissuade unethical behaviour if the practitioner believes the risks of detection, being reported, and sanctions to be unacceptable. The American research on which this article was based suggests that the violations may not be recognized as violations in about one quarter of cases, that less than half would be reported, and that sanctions would only be applied in one third of cases.

This complaints based enforcement model is used by the vast majority of professional bodies, including CIMA. To quote from the Preface to the CIMA *Ethical Guidelines*:[7]

> In the event of a complaint being made against a member, failure to comply with the appropriate guideline, or with advice given by the Institute, will be taken into consideration in deciding whether their action constitutes a *prima facie* case of professional misconduct requiring further investigation by the Institute.

There is evidence to suggest that this sort of procedure will lead to formal sanction only after major incidents which have lead to court action (civil or criminal), but that in lesser cases little is likely to happen, not least because of the reluctance of professionals to report other professionals.

The model of independent professionals controlled by their independent association persists as the basis of thinking about the regulation of professionals, even when significant numbers of members are in reality employees of organizations.

The effective controls over accountants in practice are the more direct controls of the partnerships in which they are employed – in effect corporate codes of conduct.

Guidelines for employed professionals

Employed professional accountants are normally regulated by two codes: their institute/association and their employer. This applies whether the employing organization has a formal written code or an informal set of values and rules. The codes and guidelines may and almost certainly will say many of the same things, but the member's position is significantly different from that of the independent professional. Hence separate advice is offered by accounting bodies to members in practice and members in industry.

The Institute of Chartered Accountants in England and Wales has a separate Industry Members Advisory Committee on Ethics (IMACE), and provides a confidential advisory service. Its Director, Julian Osborne, writes frequently in *Accountancy Age* discussing ethical problems. The IMACE analysis of cases arising shows a wide range of problems, part ethical, part legal. Problems arising in significant numbers include misleading accounts, insolvent or near insolvent or fraudulent trading, tax evasion, directors' expenses, issues of confidentiality and relationships with directors and auditors. Some of these problems, baldly analysed, seem to be simple legal issues where the appropriate action is clear. In practice, for instance in the case of a small building firm with large contracts in progress, difficult technical managerial and financial judgements may be required of the stage reached on contracts and the time and money required to complete the contracts. Optimism will show a legally sound situation; caution could suggest insolvency.

This selection of issues faced by accountants consulting IMACE may well reflect the service mainly being used by accountants who are the sole accountant employed by a small- or medium-sized firm. Accountants in large organizations could face different issues, but have other routes to resolve the problems – senior colleagues to help, procedures for problem resolution defined by the organization, an audit committee.

Another example of separate guidance for non-practising accountants is that of the Chartered Association of Certified Accountants who, in 1990, published *Ethics and Accountants in Industry and Commerce: Potential problems and existing guidance* (A. Likierman and A. Taylor).[8]

The difference between the position of the accountant in industry and that of the accountant in practice is easily evident from comparing the *CIMA Guidelines* with the new *Chartered Accountants Guide to Professional Ethics*.[9] CIMA emphasize integrity and objectivity; the chartered accountants emphasize (for members in practice) integrity, objectivity and independence. The difference is independence, and this independence is obviously not possible for an employee. But if the interpretation of integrity and objectivity are read carefully they amount to behaving in the same way in reporting and advising management as an independent advisor would. This may be difficult, but it is in effect what is required by fundamental principles.

The underlying issues are discussed by Westra[10] who questions whether the accountant owes 'loyal agency' to the client or employer to use professional skills to their best advantage within the law, or whether the principal target of the accountant's resolute professionalism and unswerving loyalty is some definition of the public sector or public interest. There are obvious difficulties here in defining public or stakeholder interest. There are also difficulties in seeing any benefit to employer or to accountant in some actions which the accountant feels obliged to undertake. Westra describes the dilemma:

And if we leave aside completely the question of agency, the accountant's position appears to be equally unclear, as the only professional whose duty within a professional relationship appears to be to an ideal (truth, perhaps) which may or may not be to his 'patient's' advantage.

This would place the accountant as one governed by concepts of duty and the rightness of the act, regardless of the consequences. The logical consequence of this approach would be to argue that the solution to the dilemma of whether the accountant serves two masters (employer/client and public interest) or just one (the public interest) would be to argue the case for all accountants to be employed by independent, possibly government funded, agencies.

To try to suggest a practical solution to this dilemma it is worth considering why an accountant is employed. The employer, or client, engaging an accountant, is not just buying technical skills, though these are essential; the honest idiot will not become a professional. The employer is also buying objective judgement and integrity. The easiest example to consider is when a new business is persuaded by bankers or venture capitalists to hire a financial director. This may be partly in the employer's best interest to acquire good reporting and financial management, and the financier's best interest in monitoring progress. It is also a way of ensuring an objective assessment of the developing situation, whether it is in the employer's interest or the financier's short-term interest, or the accountant's personal interest, to recognize an honest assessment of possible failure of the venture.

Corporate codes of conduct

Consideration of the use of corporate codes of conduct for an individual business organization fits with coverage of the range of control mechanisms, formal and informal which is the subject of much of this volume. Corporate codes of conduct can be seen as a form of control mechanism, ensuring that all members of an organization behave in an acceptable way, and do not commit acts that the organization would disown, if it were aware of them. Within the largest organizations, and certainly in most large American organizations, formal written codes have largely superseded the informal rules on conduct that have always existed in all organizations. Formal codes can be seen as inevitable given increasing organization size and geographical dispersion of employees. Informal influence towards the achievement of common standards of conduct, like any other form of influencing organizational culture, depends on direct personal contact, which becomes harder to achieve as organization size increases.

Formal codes can also be seen as part of a manifestation of a socially responsible organization, along with fair employment policies, environmental policies, and community involvement, ranging from support for the arts, sports, and charities to participation in urban regeneration projects. They are in this sense part of the price that large organizations have to pay for their position in society. They can in this sense be seen as emphasizing the need for managers to consider corporate reputation as a major long-term aim in all decision making.

There have been many criticisms of management accounting and of business decision making in general as too short-term, typically Jacobs[11] arguing that the American problem is mutual mistrust between managers, bankers and shareholders leading to a total emphasis on short-term earnings. This is linked to ethical issues by articles such as Wolfe[12] which argues that most ethics teaching only discusses surface problems, and does not look at the underlying cause:

> The misplaced emphasis on efficiency and profit ... the game approach to business activity *is* now so prevalent that it has produced a whole generation of thoughtlessly taught yuppies whose world view and major purpose *is* to win the game of life.

This issue can be seen in market terms, as by Dobson.[13] This article starts from the general acceptance of the importance of corporate reputation, even if this is difficult or impossible to define. It argues that reputation is built by showing a consistent pattern of behaviour to its stakeholders, in the expectation of increased long-term revenue. The first difficulty of this theoretical approach is the need for compliance with the consistent pattern of behaviour to be observable by the stakeholders as well as within the firm. This increases the requirement for written and published ethical codes. The second difficulty is the need for corporate decision makers to assume that they will in the long term be dealing with the same stakeholders, or stakeholders with access to the experience of past stakeholders. Finally there must be a belief that past good behaviour is a valid predictor of future good behaviour. The assumptions made here differ quite sharply from the assumption in the usual analysis of marginal costs for decision making that all decisions are separate and unrelated.

It is worth noting that the change from informal to formal codes can have significant effects. It is possible to have a recognized informal situation where certain actions seem permissible, but are not referred to in reports or discussed at meetings and minuted. A written code, if it deals with the area in question has to say whether the actions are or are not permissible, and it is very difficult to say they are permissible. This problem can be illustrated by the guidance on corporate bribery given by The Chartered Association of Certified Accountants:[14]

> The position is less easy in countries where bribery (often disguised as commission payments) is a way of life. The organization for which a member works may do business in such countries as a matter of course. If so, the member must exercise the greatest care to be aware of any potential compromise of professional ethical values. This means taking whatever steps are necessary to see that the issue is discussed at an early enough stage for the member to be able to withdraw, if necessary, before a compromising decision has to be taken.

The preference for a written code can be an example of what Cyert and March[15] describe as uncertainty avoidance, for which Hofstede[16] developed specific measures showing significant differences between national cultures. Thus, to give one example, uncertainty avoidance appears much higher in Germany than in Britain. Attitudes to ethical codes can be equivocal and can vary from country to country. Thus Langlois and Schlegelmilch[17] assessed attitudes to codes of ethics in Britain, France and Germany. For example, 'various UK companies regard (them) as the latest import from Wall Street and therefore of little relevance to British industry'.

National differences in cultural values are reasonably accepted, chiefly from the work of Hofstede.[18] There is a developing literature on national differences in ethical values. To date there have been a limited number of small scale studies, limited in validity by the small sample sizes, that compare Western values with values in the Far East. There is no shortage of anecdotal evidence of differences in attitudes. A useful example of an academic study is Karnes, Sterner, Welker *et al.*[19] which compares accountants' perceptions of unethical business practices in Taiwan and the USA. The choice of countries was obviously partly convenience of study access, but justifiable in terms of Hofstede's prior finding of significant differences between the societies, especially on an individualism/collectivism dimension. This is defined as the tendency of individuals to take care of themselves to the extent of sacrificing, or at the expense of, the group interest. Taiwanese public accountants appeared to perceive a smaller degree of risk with beneficial unethical practices, and a higher degree of risk with harmful unethical practices. Also there appeared to be greater Taiwanese concern for confidentiality.

National differences should not be overemphasized given all the pressures that exist towards international standardization. The accounting requirement is consistent financial information for international users, a world-wide financial market or a world-wide corporation.

Corporate codes of culture have become multinational codes. Getzt[20] reviews and emphasizes how these have been influenced not just by home country values but also by code development by such organizations as the International Chamber of Commerce, the Organization for Economic Co-operation and Development, the International Labour Organization, and the United Nations Commission on Transnational Corporations. These codes are not dissimilar and develop normative principles for multinational behaviour towards host governments and other stakeholders. Frederick[21] argues that these codes show the emergence of a transcultural corporate ethic, based on the primacy of human rights as the fundamental moral authority of these transnational compacts. Dobson[22] discusses the same convergence of global corporate culture, and the difficulties in enforcing the intricate web of implied contracts between stakeholders on an international scale. The problem is that it is easy to see the internal control systems of line management, accounting and internal audit. Within one country the external controls of the legal system, a generally accepted moral code, and the long-term interests of the stakeholders are easily understandable, even if their efficiency may be doubted. But internationally the external controls are much weaker.

Corporate codes of conduct can have obvious weaknesses as control systems. Only too often they are best seen as unexceptionable statements of good intent for internal or external consumption. Assessing codes of conduct as control mechanisms one has to ask if:

- The aims, stated or implied, are achievable.
- The aims are compatible with other aims, and if not how conflicts are resolved.
- A monitoring system exists that will detect an acceptable proportion of code breaches. (No monitoring system is ever 100 per cent effective.)
- There is a system for taking corrective action on breaches of the code.
- There is a system for motivating managers to conform with the code.

It is easy to think that professional ethical codes are as ineffectual as corporate codes of conduct. Clear definitions are elusive, enforcement is weak. In practice they are probably significantly more effective:

- Corporate codes of conduct are generally more recent and less accepted as normal and inevitable.
- All corporations have genuine problems of reconciling long-term objectives with the need for short-term profit. Too many managers in difficulty will see codes of conduct as contributing to long-term aims, possibly at the expense of short-term profits.
- There is a clearer public acceptance of professional codes of conduct. This is very often a belief that professional status implies an (undefined) ethical conduct. It may well be an extrapolation of standards from old professions such as medicine to newer professions such as accounting and to professions still formulating ethical codes such as management consultancy. A new profession will, by claiming professional status, adopt substantially the ethical stance of older professions.

The CIMA *Ethical Guidelines* 1992

In the context of management control and ethics, the ethical guidelines by CIMA represents an important publication in the accounting arena. These guidelines supersede earlier Institute[23] guidance and are in line with the International Federation of Accountants' development of harmonized world-wide standards for the profession.

The introduction sets out clearly the need for professional accountants to act ethically, emphasizing objectivity and integrity. The assumption is made that a profession is distinguished by responsibility to the public as well as to employers and clients. The public, as defined, is not dissimilar to the stakeholders interested in the corporate report. The key public interest is the reliability of accounting numbers, true and fair as well as technically correct, for all who need to use them for a wide variety of purposes, leading to efficient and effective use of resources and sound decision making. The introduction continues to set out the fundamental principles:

- Integrity.
- Objectivity.

- Professional competence and due care.
- Confidentiality.
- Professional behaviour.
- Technical standards.

Many of these fundamental principles are explained in more detail in Part A of the Guidelines, which also includes a most important section on the resolution of ethical conflicts. Given the infinite variety of circumstances and problems that exist, it is impracticable to devise ethical guidelines which give simple unequivocal answers to all problems. The fundamental principles give a framework for reasoning about the best action. The treatment of resolution of ethical conflicts addresses the possible solutions when organizational (or client) pressures conflict with ethical principles (usually objectivity). It does not pretend that there is always a solution. What is stressed is the need for due, deliberate procedure, going through all possible steps to ensure that the ethical viewpoint is heard and considered. In a large organization this means going through all laid down procedures to ventilate one's point of view up to the board, or more appropriately the audit committee if such exists. It also recognizes that professional status and an ethical stance, which cannot be separated, may ultimately lead to a need to disassociate from any proposed action and resign. Resignation should be accompanied by explanation. But there is no support for whistleblowing – taking the issue beyond the employing organization or the client to a wider audience of stakeholders. This is regarded as in breach of the fundamental principle of confidentiality.

Analysis of ethical problems

Considering ethical aspects of business problems is not dissimilar to all other business problems. There are the same requirements for analysis of facts, consideration of alternative actions, consideration of consequences of actions, and presentation of conclusions and persuading management of the correctness of the conclusions.

Analysing the relevant facts is never easy. Determining what is relevant is in practice a way of determining the conclusion. The obvious danger is discarding critical items as irrelevant.

Listing alternatives is critical. The list will probably include actions which will be eliminated at an early stage. The most common failing is not to look at a wide enough list at this stage – and then finish up with no possible alternatives.

The evaluation of consequences of action is always difficult when not all factors are conveniently quantifiable; many consequences are long term rather than short term, probabilities are not known. But these problems are identical with all other business problems.

The difficulties with problems with an ethical dimension that are additional to the normal problems are:

- Managers, and often accountants, are unfamiliar with ethical reasoning and with reference to codes of conduct. They are accustomed to accepting arguments that action x is illegal, and cannot be considered, but uncertain of the argument that action y contravenes the organization's code of conduct, or the accountant's ethical guidelines.
- Attempting to look at ethical issues in purely economic terms, which may instinctively be easier for many managers to grasp, is almost impossible:
  - consequences are normally long term, and decision making systems handle short-term consequences better than long-term consequences.
  - consequences are difficult to value in cash terms.
- Even where the problem can be agreed to be strictly an ethical problem there can be differences in ethical attitudes which may be traceable to different national, religious or political viewpoints. These may be resolved by reference to an agreed organizational or professional code, but such codes do not cover all eventualities.
- Many managers find it difficult to discuss quietly and rationally problems involving ethical issues. This may not have bad consequences if the attitude instinctively adopted is highly moral. It can be difficult or impossible to argue effectively with a manager who regards business life as a jungle in which everything is permissible.

There are some possible tests for appropriate ethical action:

- That the manager or managers are prepared to have actions, reasons and responsibility minuted.
- That actions can be documented and available for inspection by higher management.
- That any payments can be fully and correctly described and documented.
- That it is possible to explain actions truthfully to customers, suppliers employees, local community leaders and all other stakeholders.

Written guidelines are helpful but, just as with the law are unlikely to be comprehensive or static. There are inherent problems in any system of guidelines which can be seen in the context of accounting:

- It is relatively easy to propound a set of principles which gain ready acceptance but if all the contents of guidelines were self-evident and universally accepted, and actioned, the guidelines would be redundant. Ethical codes and guidelines tend to be very similar, reflecting a broad societal consensus on principles, and no doubt also the tendency of those drawing up such codes to look at parallel work in other professions, and for other organizations. Accounting codes are even more similar in that the International Federation of Accountants (IFAC) promotes harmonization.
- It is not always easy to see how to apply these principles in practice. On the occasions when it is easy to apply principles few are conscious that they are applying ethical principles – action is instinctive. But when there is no obvious instinctive course of action it is difficult to reason from ethical principles to

the appropriate action in a world where shades of grey are far more common than pure black and white.
- It is easy to think of situations where these principles do not seem to apply; or the principles seem to contradict each other.

Written guidance alone is inadequate and resort to the significance of individual moral judgement guided by theory is essential.

References

1. The contributions to this discussion by John Williams are gratefully acknowledged.
2. Kant, I., *Grounding for the Metaphysics of Morals*, 1981 (originally 1785).
3. Further explanation is found in Cashmore C, Some Preliminary Considerations on Ethics in Management Accountancy, Occasional Paper, London Guildhall, 1994.
4. *Chartered Institute of Management Accountants Ethical Guidelines*, CIMA, 1992.
5. Lynch, P., Code of ethics would project better image, *Management Consultancy*, April, 1992.
6. Beets, S.D. and Killough, L.N., The effectiveness of a complaint based ethics enforcement system: evidence from the accounting profession, *Journal of Business Ethics*, Vol. 9, No. 1, 1990.
7. CIMA, 1992, *op. cit.*
8. Likierman, A. and Taylor, A., *Ethics and Accountants in Industry and Commerce: Potential Problems and Existing Guidelines*, Chartered Association of Certified Accountants, 1990.
9. Chartered Accountants Joint Ethics Committee, Guide to professional ethics, *Accountancy*, March, 1992.
10. Westra L.S., Whose 'loyal agent'? Toward an ethic of accounting, *Journal of Business Ethics*, Vol. 5, No. 1, 1986.
11. Jacobs, M.T., *Short-term America*, Harvard Business School Press.
12. Wolfe, A., The corporate apology, *Business Horizons*, Vol. 33, No. 12, 1990.
13. Dobson, J., Corporate Reputation: a free-market solution to unethical behaviour, *Business and Society*, Vol. 28, No. 1, 1989.
14. Likierman, A. and Taylor, A., 1990, *op. cit.*
15. Cyert, R.M. and March, J.G., *A Behavioural Theory of the Firm*, Prentice Hall, 1963.
16. Hofstede, H.G., *Cultures and Organizations: Software of the mind*, McGraw-Hill, 1991.
17. Langlois, C.C. and Schlegelmilch, B.B. Do corporate codes of ethics reflect national character?, *Journal of International Business Studies (USA)*, Vol. 21, No. 4, 1990.
18. Hofstede, G., *Culture's Consequences: International Differences in Work Related Values*, Sage, 1980.

19. Karnes, A., Sterner, J., Welker, R. *et al.*, A bi-cultural comparison of accountants' perceptions of unethical business practices, *Accounting, Auditing and Accountability Journal*, Vol. 3, No. 3, 1990.
20. Getz, K.A., International codes of conduct: an analysis of ethical reasoning, *Journal of Business Ethics*, Vol. 9, No. 7, 1990.
21. Frederick, W.C., The moral authority of transnational corporate codes, *Journal of Business Ethics*, Vol. 10, No. 3, 1991.
22. Dobson, J., The role of ethics in global corporate culture, *Journal of Business Ethics*, Vol. 9, No. 6, 1990.
23. Chartered Institute of Management Accountants, *Statement on standards of professional conduct and competence*, 1987; *Institute of Cost and Management Accountants Ethical Guide for Members*, 1979.

Further reading

Albrecht, S.W. (ed.), *Ethical Issues in the Practice of Accounting*, SouthWestern Publishing, 1992.

Andrews, K.R. (ed.), *Ethics in Practice: Managing the Moral Corporation*, Harvard Business School Press, 1989.

Cottell, P.G. and Perlin, T.M., *Accounting Ethics: A practical guide for professionals*, Quorum Books, 1990.

Landekich, S., *Corporate Codes of Conduct*, National Association of Accountants (USA), 1989.

Likierman, J.A. and Taylor, B.A., *Ethics and Accountants in Industry and Commerce: Potential problems and existing guidance*, Chartered Association of Certified Accountants, 1990.

Mackie, J.L., *Ethics: Inventing Right and Wrong*, Penguin, 1977.

Mintz, S.M., *Cases in Accounting Ethics and Professionalism*, McGraw-Hill, 2nd ed., 1992.

Windal, F.W., *Ethics and the Accountant: Text and Cases*, Prentice Hall, 1991.

16

Conclusion

It is well recognized that the business environment of many organizations today is increasingly uncertain, changing both substantially and rapidly. In order to contribute efficiently and effectively to an organization's survival and success under such conditions, management accounting must adopt a proactive role in operational decision making and strategy development. The generation of relevant information for management and the way that information is utilized within organizations, is more important today than at any time in the past. The continuous introduction of new ideas, requirements, methods and techniques for the development and processing of information currently taking place puts in question the passive acceptance and perpetuation of long established routines even in companies experiencing only limited change in their business circumstances. The foregoing chapters have explained some of the more important areas of management accounting expertise. It is the task of management accountants however, to *adapt and innovate* in order to provide appropriate information to management to address the uncertainties and change facing their enterprise in operational and strategic planning control and decision making.

Studies carried out within companies by the authors[1,2,3,4] reflect, as might be expected, a very wide range of actual practice and views about the future within management accounting and among accountants. A particular feature was the need for accountants to be active in the capture of information, so that the control of an organization – using the term in its broadest sense – was placed in the position of anticipating events rather than merely reacting to them.

Readers interested in practical applications of the substance of this text may be interested in reading *Management Accounting in Practice.*[4] This text consists of 12 in-depth case studies of situations in practice which illustrate many of the points made in the foregoing chapters. In particular, the cases illustrate the use of management accounting information to influence decision making and the differences between standard textbook theory and actual management accounting practices. Examples of the insights these cases can give are given in the following paragraphs.

The Stapylton company[2,4] provides a good example of a company accountant taking a positive lead in the creation of information necessary to enable it to meet the challenge of competition both by securing external intelligence and by the quantification of responses needed from within the organization. Lynnfield, the competitor company to Stapylton, was the subject of a detailed examination by

Stapylton's accountant as to every aspect of its business, from its technology through its cost structure to its pricing policy. The intelligence used for this purpose came from a variety of external sources, such as customers, suppliers and company reports, as well as members of Stapylton's staff, using their own knowledge and experience to piece together a picture of their competitor's business:

> ... an estimate of Lynnfield's prime costs could be made, which, although not based on actual information about the Lynnfield operations was considered sufficiently accurate as a starting point. The cost structure identified by this process of what may be termed simulating the activities of the competitor was checked out in the first instance by an analysis of Lynnfield's company accounts.

As part of the response to the competitive threat, Stapylton itself had to formulate its own marketing strategy. Here the accountant made the following observation:

> My problem as the accountant was to pin down the marketing man to having to quantify the various options. Accounting played the right part and made them quantify. I would ask 'if you want £1 million for advertising what will you give us in sales volume? What would be the effect of a price cut of 2%, 4%, zero?' These questions I made them answer so it was capable of quantification, but it was up to me to work them out.

In neither of the above illustrations did routine, readily available internal accounting information play a significant role. There is no implied diminution of the value of such information by this, merely that on its own it only constitutes a part of what management accountants should be aiming to secure in their role of prime suppliers of information to top management in their running of the business.

As an example of the more intelligent analysis of information than would be gained by slavish adherence to simple cost classification, the same study contains the cases of the 'Quadratic', 'Waterloo' and 'Midlands Metals'. In the former, how cost and volume of activity are related was the subject of the investigation.

Simple linear relation models abound in the accounting literature, suggesting there is perhaps some automatic mechanism whereby a certain volume of activity naturally produces a predictable amount of expenditure: the accountant can only sit back and let it happen, apart from quantifying the relationship in the first place. As many would at least intuitively recognize this cannot be the case; even in the very short run the exigencies of the state of the business, however caused, need expenditure to be managed. The fact that much financial thinking is perhaps distorted by trying to fit information and effects into precise time periods may well contribute to rather inflexible and stereotyped responses to issues such as the way costs behave and how they may be managed. The time horizon over which an objective has to be achieved is a continuous variable, and this removes many problems from the arena of simply utilizing budget data, produced for a specific and different purpose, for a decision problem.

In the case of Waterloo the budget information itself was generated on the principle that 'costs are matched to the underlying level of business rather than, in part at least, being expected to change more or less immediately and in direct proportion to changes in business activity'. There is a substantial difference between these two approaches in the context of cost management.

A degree of psychology was also observed in the practice of the accountant at Midlands Metals. In what might be taken for a fairly standard budget report format, with expenses classified as to whether they were regarded as fixed or variable costs (though even this is an advance on the commonly observed budget-actual-variance presentation) the subtlety lay in keeping the fixed cost elements as few as possible, on the grounds that calling a cost 'fixed' tended to produce the reaction on the part of managers that they could do little to manage it effectively.

In a further study, entitled 'Kimco',[4] the question of the real independence of divisions in a situation where they were regarded as autonomous, conducting 'arms length' trading with each other, was addressed. In this case the role of the internal auditor became critical in ensuring that the benefits of autonomy were not completely lost through the individual divisions producing potentially damaging goals of their own in conflict with those of the group. The internal auditor was able to utilize his own information system to provide top management with the checks and balances needed to keep group and divisions working towards the same goals without the former seeming to interfere too obtrusively into the latter's affairs.

These and other cases cited[2,4] are mainly aimed at illustrating the need for management accounting to provide a positive lead in the generation of information and its application in facilitating the processes of business decision making and control. The common feature is not to rely on existing records alone, but to be constantly aware of emerging needs as business demands change.

There is of course, a well documented body of literature in management accounting, generally referred to as contingency theory,[5] which has pointed out, largely in a non-specific way, how various factors may influence the design and development of accounting information systems (AIS). Four major factors are cited as having the greatest impacts, namely: environment, technology, organization and decision-making style. A contingency theory is also applied to organizations.

The objective of contingency theory, put rather superficially, may be thought of as being to project the information needs of an accounting information system at all stages of its design or redesign. For instance, as regards the environment, there are varying degrees to which it is dynamic and therefore demanding of information beyond the normal requirements of a stable market. Each factor in turn exerts varying degrees of influence on the design of the AIS. As a matter of logic, it may appear possible to synthesize a range of situations and draw up an AIS to match at least the basic requirements of each. Even this relatively limited objective for the production of tailor-made systems appears unattainable; there is little evidence so far to suggest that the theory can be turned into practice in this way.

It is possible that the best which can be expected of contingency theory is that it heightens awareness of the variables which should be addressed in the design of a system (or its revision). Beyond this, it has to be recognized that management accounting information systems, like many other internal systems, depend for their actual configuration on what the company management perceives as being needed. Its collective opinion would carry at least as much weight as its accountant's clearly diagnosed appraisal of a business's information needs.

It is not suggested there is a need to categorize everything into neat AIS packages. The main point of the argument is that systems should not be allowed to atrophy to the stage of becoming an irrelevance to the circumstances of the business whose interests they are supposed to serve. The danger of continuous perpetuation of outdated systems, for whatever reason, is well illustrated by the study of Crossways, where information output had reached the point of being largely ignored within the plant.

Kaplan[6] debates the issue, while in a recent study carried out for CIMA,[3] and referred to early in Chapter 5, the whole purpose of the investigation was to look at the question of how firms were responding to changes brought about by being in new and high technology industry. The study used detail with respect to the traditional features of a management accounting system, such as its budgeting/ standard costing system, performance measures, and capital expenditure appraisal measures, principally as a touchstone against which to contrast change. Of major interest was the impact of information technology in improving the information collection and processing capability, and the views of company accountants as to how they saw change affecting their responsibilities in the provision of information. As such, much of the work deals in effect with the technology and environmental variables of contingency theory.

The range of industry covered by the investigation was substantial, taking in what would be recognized as many of the most important of the new technologies, such as the production of silicon chips, printed circuits, office automation systems and so on; it also incorporated the change to high technology manufacture now being extensively experienced in many long established industrial firms. It was felt that the substantial diversity of influences on the development of management accounting was well represented by the study. The following repeats most of the main findings of the enquiry in order to illustrate the breadth of issues which must be faced proactively rather than reactively.

1   The general requirement of the AIS in new and high technology industry was for the provision of 'higher quality' information: its scope, content and availability must be aimed at the anticipation of events rather than forcing the firm into the relatively passive stance of reacting to them as events unfold and their effects become known.

2   A central requirement for the achievement of 1 was seen to be in most cases the deployment of information technology systems which facilitated the necessary capture, storage and analysis of information, if the proactive vision is to materialize.

3   Co-ordinated evolution of company strategies for product and process development was emphasized as a factor needing significant support from within management accounting.

4   The implementation of strategy almost invariably commits a company to significant investment expenditures. Apart from underlining once more the importance of 1, this commitment is frequently very specific to the extent that a company's options as to its operation either in volume terms or product variety are narrowed down. Together with the level of finance invested, this throws emphasis on to the control activity in particular: the investment, once made, has to succeed. Short-term cost analysis is relatively downgraded in significance.

5   Absorption costing remains the principal accounting routine for providing information on department and product cost. This is of course a very 'traditional' process, and, paradoxical as it may seem, reference to it was generally accompanied by statements on the need to improve the 'accuracy' of product cost. This is perceived as very important in respect of product profitability and the ability to react effectively to change in the competitive environment – all this in spite of the well documented problems arising in respect of cost allocation and apportionment. However, it is a challenge to the ingenuity of accountants, under conditions where a high proportion of cost is at least short-term fixed and jointly determined over several lines of business, to attempt to produce cost analyses in such a way as to disaggregate them effectively to individual product groups. One observed approach was to analyse separate elements of the businesses to determine what its requirements for resources would be in order to operate independently, but recognizing the effects of economies of scale.

6   The comments in respect of 5 may give the impression that contribution analysis was rarely encountered. In the sense of being by product it rarely was in detail, but was part of the build-up to identifying and directly attributing cost to business sectors.

7   A variety of developments in the modern manufacturing scene impact on management accounting: material requirements planning, just-in-time supplier systems, and total quality (which incorporated in large measure, the previous two concepts). However, it is interesting in respect of 'quality' on its own that this did not necessarily emerge as a factor which should be 'accounted for' in the normal sense; it was rather an attitude of mind to be generated throughout an organization. It was observed to be rather illogical to design a product to certain specifications and then to make it almost an issue for congratulation if the standard were achieved; achievement should be the expectation without a need for an expensive panoply of cost measurements to record how far off target actual results were. Accounting would still play a role in helping to determine where quality problems might lie, though much reliance is now placed on quality groups established throughout a plant.

8   As regards the question of whether management accounting needs a new array of methods and techniques in the sense of acquiring new algorithms for data manipulation in order to meet new industrial environments and technologies, the answer appeared to be that it did not. What was required was a more

active and intelligent use of what is available, coupled with a willingness to change.

The points made above may read as though they represent a widely accepted statement of general tendency. This was not the case: reactions to questions posed were frequently very different for all kinds of reasons but they added up to the fact that uniformity in the detail of management accounting practice is unlikely to be realized.

The best that probably can be hoped for is that accountants are alert to the information requirements of a business and are willing to implement change in so far as they are permitted to do. In this context perhaps the ultimate observation came from one or two companies where accountants themselves were reporting to management on the value to the company of their own activities – no more daunting a problem than the same type of measurement applied to other activities, but seldom contemplated.

References

1. Coates, J.B., Rickwood, C.P. and Stacey, R.J., Examination of the Differences Between Academic Concepts and Actual Management Accounting Practices, Report to ESRC, British Library Document Supply Centre, August 1987. Many of these cases are now published in:
2. Rickwood, C.P., Coates, J.B. and Stacey, R.J., Managed Costs and the Capture of Information, Accounting and Business Research, Vol. 17, No. 68, Autumn 1987.
3. Coates, J.B. and Longden, S.G., Management Accounting in New and High Technology Growth Companies. Report to the Chartered Institute of Management Accountants, November 1987.
4. Coates, J.B., Rickwood, C.P. and Stacey, R.J., *Management Accounting in Practice*, CIMA, 1995.
5. Emmanuel, C. and Otley D.T., *Accounting for Management Control*, Van Nostrand Reinhold, 1986.
6. Kaplan, R.S., Measuring Manufacturing Performance: A New Challenge for Managerial Accounting Research. *The Accounting Review*, Vol. LVIII, No. 4, October 1983.

Author index

Subject index